Rawhide Ranger, Ira Aten

Enforcing Law on the Texas Frontier

Bob Alexander

Number 8 in the Frances B. Vick Series

University of North Texas Press
Denton, Texas

10 9 8 7 6 5 4 3 2 1

Permissions:
University of North Texas Press
1155 Union Circle #311336
Denton, Texas 76203-5017

The paper used in this book meets the minimum requirements
of the American National Standard for Permanence of Paper for
Printed Library Materials, z39.48.1984. Binding materials have
been chosen for durability.

Library of Congress Cataloging-in-Publication Data

Alexander, Bob (James R.)
  Rawhide ranger, Ira Aten : enforcing law on the Texas frontier /
Bob Alexander. -- 1st ed.
      p. cm. -- (Number 8 in the Frances B. Vick series)
  Includes bibliographical references and index.
  ISBN 978-1-57441-315-1 (cloth : alk. paper) 1. Aten, Ira,
1862-1953. 2. Peace officers--Texas--Biography. 3. Texas
Rangers--Biography. 4. Texas Rangers--History. 5. Law
enforcement--Texas--History. 6. Frontier and pioneer life--Texas--
History.
7. Texas--History--1846-1950. I. Title. II. Series: Frances B. Vick
series ; no. 8.
  F391.A83A44 2011
  363.2092--dc22
  [B]
                              2011013576

Rawhide Ranger, Ira Aten: Enforcing Law on the Texas Frontier is Number 8 in the Frances B. Vick Series

Contents

Preface

Ira Aten was not a braggadocio fellow. Had he chosen to, Ira could have unleashed bragging rights with legitimacy. He owned not just a few. Unlike some of his better known counterparts Mr. Aten apparently found discomfort in speciously puffing about his Old West law enforcing days. While recounting thrilling experiences for inquiring journalists or even writing an occasional piece himself, Ira Aten did so matter-of-factly, with pride—not for hope of financial reward. Accurately preserving the historical record—for posterity and his family—was weighty business for Ira. And if anybody of the frontier era policing fraternity had a gritty tale worth telling, it surely was Mr. Austin Ira Aten.

What makes his biography worthy while other bona fide Wild West lawmen lie buried in obscurity? The answer is not elusive. Perhaps it is an oversimplification, but the cards just fell Ira's way. Dissimilar to the majority of old-time Texas lawmen who could proudly bank enviable and honorable years of public service, many of Aten's adventures transcended mere local recognition. As a courageously competent lawman Ira Aten was favorably known statewide. Through no fault of his, or as product of any self-aggrandizement, simply said, Ira Aten was a high-profile Ranger. Though it may have been the result of pure chance, Mr. Aten was directly linked to several episodes of Texas' colorful past that scholars and grass-root historians have penned thousands—maybe millions—of words about. We now know a number of these epic developments were momentous to the Lone Star State's overall history—sociological and socioeconomic upheavals—and Ira Aten was right in the middle of more than a few. Peeking in on Ira's exhilarating saga is much more than looking at another Old West lawman in a vacuum. Makings of the state's history swirled around Mr. Aten in a panoply of installments. Objectively peering at Ira Aten's life story does, assuredly, expose much more than narrative of but one man.

Before he had even reached the age of majority Ira Aten signed on as a Texas Ranger, assigned to Company D, one of the most noteworthy companies during the Frontier Battalion epic. As with any rookie there was a learning curve, and Ira was given ample opportunity to incorporate the good and discard the not so good into his law enforcing psyche. He did so proficiently. While yet at the journeyman level Ira Aten caught the approving eye of Texas Ranger management and, in turn, the state's chief executives. Hardly any individual Rangers from the working ranks could speak of personal audiences with governors of Texas, but Ira could. He had earned their trust.

Few, if any, institutional histories of nineteenth-century Texas Rangers—those serving as professional lawmen—fail to make mention of Ira Aten. Conversely, though, despite cursory recognition, the real Ira Aten does not emerge from these fleeting inclusions. In the broadest angle the unintended slight is understandable and, thankfully, fixable. During his law enforcing years Ira Aten walked across the stage of Texas history in the making. In the earliest days, although the backdrop was significant, Ira's part was small, though never that of a bit player. Over time, as he matured and incorporated updated policing techniques into his repertoire, Ira Aten assumed the lead when the curtain was jerked back revealing high-drama in the theater of Texas doings. It was then and is now a spellbinding performance.

Ira Aten rode horseback along the Rio Grande when the international line was simply known as the Bloody Border. He witnessed and participated as a "Winchester Warrior" providing security while suspicious delegates from both sides of the river met on a tiny island, reaching an accord that lasted—for a little while. While scouting in that same region of catclaw and sotol and greasewood the young Ranger witnessed death of a comrade and underwent his baptismal gunfire. He learned a lesson or two about Texas politics as well.

Ranger Aten hunted fugitives throughout the Texas Hill Country, successfully most of the time. Several of those owlhoots were notorious all over the state; many were dangerous adversaries, *mal hombres* who would unsmilingly kill at the drop of a hat. In fact, Ira's skill and tenacity during manhunts was so well honed, special missions straight out of the governor's office were laid in his lap. One of those secret assignments from the state's hierarchy was to bring in a murderous fugitive "dead or alive." Texas Ranger Ira Aten complied.

Perhaps no other Texas Ranger's name is more closely associated with the acts of violence generated by fellows stringing barbwire—the Fence Cutting Wars—than that of Ira Aten. On at least three occasions in three separate counties, Ira Aten assumed an undercover identity—when he didn't have to—in efforts designed to ferret out nighttime nippers of the wire. One case netted two cutters, another two more—although they died in a gunplay resisting arrest. The last of Ranger Aten's field assignments in this regard revealed an ingenious exit strategy, one that has been massaged to legendary proportion and is now cemented in Texas Ranger folklore—deservedly so.

When four bodies—a quadruple homicide—were found floating in the *Rio Bravo*, Ira Aten was tasked with the criminal investigation which by its very nature was drawing national attention. Ira Aten, by now Company D's 1ˢᵗ Sergeant, exhaustively built an airtight criminal case based largely on circumstantial evidence. Interestingly, for the time and place, Sergeant Aten employed a forensic technique, the first time it was used in Texas—*possibly* in the United States. As a result of tying his investigative leads together Ira Aten opened a defendant's cell door—so the condemned could climb a scaffold's stairway to eternity.

And when warring political factions southwest of Houston suspended spewing hot air and began spitting hot lead, where would Ranger Ira Aten be? Well, not surprisingly, right in the middle—literally. As a newsmaker the episode was a humdinger. Shamefully it exposed an entrenched vestige of racism. Theatrically, however, it was great—Texas history at its best—or worst. Discharges from Winchesters and six-shooters echoed across city streets in a supposed civilized community, now engulfed in a bloodletting, feudist mentality. There were dead bodies, and bodies yet standing upright but punctured by bullets and leaking blood. An innocent child had been killed, too. Texas Rangers, the state militia and, even the governor tried to straighten out the horrific and embarrassing mess. Once the blood had been mopped from the streets and after a funeral or three, the aftermath was as sad as the beginnings. There were filing of criminal charges—some quite outlandish—half a hundred arrests, counter charges, civil lawsuits, an out-of-court settlement, and in trust with doing it right, Texas style—an extra murder: That killing occurred in a county courthouse, no less. Eager newsmen were awash with good copy, a feeding frenzy that would shame even the Gulf Coast's predatory sharks. Ira Aten was swimming in the thick of it—typically.

As a Texas Ranger Ira Aten witnessed Texas history—and Texas Ranger Ira Aten made Texas history. But there is more.

Although it was near routine for an ex-Texas Ranger to some-times become a county sheriff after separating from the Frontier Battalion, Mr. Ira Aten—characteristically doing his bang up job—did it not once, but twice: He was the sheriff of plantation disposed Fort Bend County and, later, hundreds of miles away, Castro County in the lonesome Texas Panhandle. Ira Aten's two tenures as a plucky county sheriff were each marked with high drama—rich episodes putting the "Western" into a Western.

It didn't end there. Afterwards, for near a full decade, Ira Aten was a division manager on the largest fenced ranch in the world, the XIT Ranch. He landed that job not because of his cow sense, but his common sense and six-shooter sense. The subdivision he com-manded was the toughest of the tough, meanest of the mean. On one side of the fiefdom an honest man had to worry about getting shot by cow thieving strangers, or poisoned by supposed friends, or toasted to death in a raging inferno—one purposely set. There was some real bad company to keep—if one was not watchful. Ira's orders were straightforward: There was a problem—fix it. Diplomacy would be okay if it worked, Winchesters would do if not. For sure, he would steer clear of gratuitous sentimentality. Protect the ranch? He did.

Ira Aten's biography—though the study of but one man—is unique for it plays out in front of a backdrop of larger events, as mentioned earlier. That said, it also provides opportunity for critical analysis of the personal profits and pitfalls of choosing a law enforc-ing career in nineteenth-century Texas. It is perhaps all too com-mon in reconstructing the lives of lawmen of that era to focus on the spectacular, the shoot-outs, the blood and thunder. From his very childhood—due in large part to his upbringing—Ira Aten's moral compass had been set, the course straight and true. He would not and did not deviate when it came to religiously instilled core principles. Was he then, for his chosen profession, somewhat naïve? Not hardly. Although many of the fellows he worked with drank and gambled and whored, it was not in Ira Aten's blueprint to succumb to such temptations. He knew—and commented—that much of the trouble he was forced to deal with could be traced backwards to the doorways of barrooms and bordellos. If Ira Aten sometimes fell short, which he did, booze and bimbos and blackjack were not factors.

The overriding doctrine of Ira Aten's life was a solid commitment to family. Ira wanted above all else to see in the mirror's reflection a good husband and good father and good provider. In the end he succeeded on all fronts, admirably so. By zeroing in on Ira Aten's story there is an inside look at a lawman's life outside the framework of scooping up badmen and testifying in courtrooms. Particularly intriguing for Ira's biography is enlightenment about how Mrs. Aten felt about her husband's calling to the six-shooter and badge. Sneaking a quick look at those delicate family matters puts a human face on Ira—and by extrapolation, many of those he "Rangered" with. They were but people, with people's problems and dreams. Then does examining Ira Aten's life's story in the round relegate the reader to the humdrum of daily reality? Not by a long shot.

For if the reader turning these pages is in want of gunshots, Ira Aten's biography—the law enforcing part—is loudly jam-packed. The breathtaking episodes offer more than a thrill, but also an additional insight into Mr. Aten's overall law enforcing makeup. Talented novelists, nonfiction writers with pens too liberal, screenwriters, along with Hollywood movie and television producers, have sometimes etched illusory portraits of Old West lawmen. For the most part their fanciful creations were a twentieth-century merchandising phenomenon. If factual evidence got in the way of a good story, it could be damned and often was. Some of those literarily exaggerated fellows have unarguably—and undeservedly it may be averred—attained wide-spread name recognition. Outside the tight circle of reasonably serious historians—grass roots or academicians—and a cadre of Texas Ranger enthusiasts, a niche market to be sure, the name of Ira Aten is wholly meaningless. But a slight comparison begs hearing.

Wyatt Earp, thought by many to be America's foremost gunfighter, cannot be unequivocally credited with killing anyone. Truthfully it is a somewhat anemic record for the supposed iconic gunman of the Wild West. Mr. Earp never stood *alone* during a shoot-out or murder. The likelihood Wyatt *might* have actually made a telling shot is reasonably high, but with his dubious pals or relatives always shooting too, absent modern day ballistics technology, no unyielding conclusiveness attaches despite the unsurpassed and unrelenting labors of mythmakers. In contrast, based on explicit primary evidence accounts—written and eyewitness—it is more than abundantly clear Aten had the nerve to stand *alone* during gunfights, once even taking on a pair of adversaries at the same time. One a so-called two-gun man, blasted away at Ira with shooters in each hand. Ira walked away unscathed; his opponents did not. On another occasion when things waxed hot, Aten again stood *by himself*, killing the murderous desperado. At other times—and there were several—Ira Aten was but one of several lawmen participating in a gunplay. No matter, alone or with teammates, Ira owned what it took to, well, "stay hitched." The identifiably sharp contrast between Mr. Earp and Mr. Aten is noteworthy; a sociological commentary on how the entertainment media can and has warped history. One man rode a crest of posthumously touted and overblown melodrama; the other went about his daily business, everyday, pocketing public acclaim and contributing to the community's betterment. Ira Aten needed not a third party to prop up his profile: He was tough as rawhide—for real.

Such fortitude was a family trait it would seem. Although admittedly less well known than Ira, two of his younger brothers carved their notch in the annals of Texas Ranger lore. Calvin Grant Aten and Edwin Dunlap Aten each saw service with Company D. And, just like their brother Ira, both Cal and Eddie while Texas Rangers survived gunfights with desperadoes of the deepest dye. Both would lead—in the final analysis—adventuresome but commendable lives.

Aficionados bent toward Texas Ranger history generally categorize a quartet of men as being the four great Ranger Captains: William Jesse McDonald, John Harris Rogers, James Abijah Brooks, and John Reynolds Hughes. No argument will be herein proffered. They may stand at the top of the list, unchallenged. It is, however, germane and more than a little important to note that it was Aten who recruited Hughes into Texas Ranger ranks, and it was under Ira's tutelage that John learned much of his law enforcing craft. Aten mentoring Hughes not only put a young Ranger on the pathway to a first-rate captaincy, but led to a lifelong bond as well. Death would be the only impediment to their mutual admiration and friendship.

Although Ira Aten would for years lead a productive and commendable life outside the law enforcement community, which will be covered in the final chapter, the focus of this narrative—as the subtitle suggests—is on his law enforcing life. For the armchair adventurer that is where the excitement is, in addition to a sampling of authentic Texas history. Ira's societal contributions may well have been as great in business and altruistic work, but it is the Wild West platform that supports this endeavor, a fresh and detached examination.

More than fifty years ago a practiced journalist Harold Preece offered his short biography, *Lone Star Man, Ira Aten: Last of the Old Texas Rangers*. He portrayed Ira Aten wearing a pristine white hat and never faltering. Perhaps in vogue at the time, the little tome is bloated with dialogue—which even the author attributes, in part, to fashioning words "from the recollections of people who heard him speak." Troubling, too, is the fact a few real characters were bestowed with "another name from that which he bore in life." The core strength and weakness of Harold Preece's work is that it is partly true. Factually, however, it often suffers deficiency and inaccuracy and omission. Likewise, noticeable by their absence are citations to source materials. This too, at the time it was written, was good enough—even customary. Today it is not. Hopefully mentions of these shortcomings will not be interpreted as undue or mean-spirited censure. They are not. Nonfiction writers owe much to those that forged the way a half-century ago. To a large extent their work kept the Old West genre alive. The twenty-first century reader is more demanding, though. With that in mind this text was developed with careful attention to source citation and truthfulness and a conscientious effort aimed at fair play. Mr. Austin Ira Aten would not have asked for more than that.

Acknowledgments

The obligation of mentioning names of those lending a helping hand is pleasurable. Such a process brings to the forefront of one's memory congenial visits and conversations during the research phase of gathering data. On the one hand skilled novelists may be envied for their colorful imaginations and talent, but nonfiction writing is above all else, as it should be, people business. An author trying to tell a true story—and tell it right—is wholly dependant on a wide array of helpmates, be they fellow nonfiction writers and warm friends, or archivists, librarians, museum directors, antiquarian book dealers, periodical editors, county and district clerks, and, with good luck, persons genealogically linked to the biographic project underway. *Rawhide Ranger, Ira Aten* is no exception. The list is long. The tributes so well deserved.

Before there can be a book there must be a publisher. The collective expertise at University of North Texas Press is mindboggling. When they adopt a manuscript for publication, putting their all into it, the finished product is guaranteed first-rate. Specifically for *Rawhide Ranger, Ira Aten*, an overflowing bucketful of thanks is due Ron Chrisman, Director; Karen DeVinney, Assistant Director/Managing Editor; Paula Oates, Director of Marketing; and Mary Young, Administrative Assistant. Consistently rolling out top quality nonfiction books simply means one thing—UNT Press is a well-oiled machine with a workforce bent toward maintaining efficiency and expanding our awareness of bona fide Texas history.

Donald M. Yena is a good friend. Thankfully, he's an artist too. His genre is the Old West. There are none better when in comes to telling a story—with a brush—on a single piece of canvas. One does not simply amble by a Don Yena painting. As if caught in Pecos River quicksand a spellbound viewer is drawn in. Standing in front of Don's work is an experience, a memorable experience, a sensory experience. For if it is a chuck-wagon scene you'll smell Arbuckles boiling, feel heat from the smoldering ash-white coals, and give near anything for a peek under that Dutch Oven lid—deftly not burning your fingers, of course—trying to catch a glimpse of fluffy cathead biscuits with their tantalizing golden crowns. If a horse is pitching you'll involuntarily, scarily, grab for the apple (saddlehorn) trying to stay atop, screwed tight, so as not to bust a collarbone—or something. And don't dare stare into the merciless maneater eyes of Don Yena's despicable badman. Gazing into those compassionless deadpan orbs will haunt your slumbering dreams—nightmares. You'll want to sleep with a Colt's six-shooter under the pillow. Don graciously allowed his captivating painting *Rustler's Camp, Running Iron and Rangers* to be used as the book cover for *Winchester Warriors: Texas Rangers of Company D, 1874–1901.* Accolades were unanimous. Now, for *Rawhide Ranger, Ira Aten,* Don has courteously stepped up once more, gracing this volume's cover with *Rough Country and Rangers on the Lookout.* This mesmerizing piece of Western art dovetails seamlessly with one of Texas Ranger Ira Aten's real life Winchester adventures along the Texas/Mexico border: Eerily so.

Underpinnings of Austin Ira Aten's rousing biography from the document perspective were for-the-most-part amiably ferreted from archival institutions. At the Texas State Library and Archives Commission, Austin, Texas, Donaly E. Brice—as he always does—dug deep locating archived Texas Ranger reports and pertinent Adjutant General correspondence files which were essential to forwarding Ira Aten's story. Jim Bradshaw, Archivist, at the Nita Stewart Haley Memorial Library and History Center, Midland, Texas, unfailingly answered every inquiry and request promptly, not only with professionalism but with enthusiasm. Closer to home at the Research Center, Texas Ranger Hall of Fame and Museum, Waco, Texas, Christina Stopka, Director, and Research Librarian Christina Smith characteristically—with smiles—willingly delved into the archives, locating part of the paper treasures and photographs that make Mr. Aten's life story whole. Words of heartfelt thanks seem wholly insufficient for folks who simply ask: "How else may I help you?" These four devoted historians are genuine Aces. A nonfiction writer can't beat a hand like that. Thank you, my friends.

Also deserving a carved out mention of appreciation is Warren Stricker, Director, Research Center, Panhandle-Plains Historical Museum, Canyon, Texas. Diligently and admirably Warren mined the museum's archives, ultimately excavating some real treasures for furthering Ira Aten's life's story. Indisputably, old ranch records and interviews with cowmen and cowboys who actually knew Ira are valued supplements to the biography, but Mr. Stricker really hit paydirt. He uncovered a series of 1936 letters written by Ira to his wife. While on an extended return trip to Texas for the Centennial celebration, the aging lawmen visited and reminisced with many of his old-time law enforcing and ranching colleagues. Thankfully, from the historical perspective, Ira would then pen his beloved wife the details of visits, oftentimes reaching back in time, recalling particulars about thrilling episodes of bygone days. The letters are rich sources. Acclamation is due Warren Stricker from this writer and the readers of *Rawhide Ranger: Ira Aten.*

Although all are most capable researchers in their own right, four more stalwarts, each a published author with numerous books stacked to their credit, also made their selfless contribution to the biography at hand. Knowing *Rawhide Ranger, Ira Aten* was well underway, as these guys accomplished their own research they were always on the lookout for material making mention of Mr. Aten and/or his brothers, who were also Texas Rangers. Their familiarity with the field of Outlaw/Lawman history is as matchless as their help was invaluable. Chuck Parsons, researching for his *Captain John R. Hughes, Lone Star Ranger* routinely forwarded relevant primary source material as it was uncovered. While preparing the groundwork for *The Horrell Wars: War to the Knife*, nonfiction writer Dave Johnson discovered a wealth of data about Mr. Aten and collateral events, especially through contemporary newspaper articles, which he persistently copied and dropped in the mail to Maypearl. Rick Miller, who also just happens to have a Texas Ranger work in progress, *Texas Ranger: John B. Jones and the Frontier Battalion, 1874–1881*, was continually helpful, particularly regarding the Brown County fence cutting cases transferred to Bell County and their ultimate dispositions. And last, but certainly not least, was the exceptional support given by Robert W. Stephens, an author who began his Texas Ranger research in the 1960s and is still at it, turning out book after book—some now quite rare.

Fortunately for this writer while trying to flesh out the real story, the real truths, about the life and policing adventures of the Aten brothers, was the fact that genealogical linkage could be happily traced to kinship's doorsteps. During the course of wide-ranging personal interviews and telephone conversations these generous folks kindly and wholeheartedly opened the shoeboxes and photo albums, affording opportunity for the reader to historically profit from the old letters, documents, and never before published photographic images. Simply reeling off their names seems inadequate, but rest assured each and every one willingly shared their family treasures. Particularly helpful and enthusiastic were Ira's one and only grandchild, Gary Boyce Radder, and his tireless wife Jeri, Alamo, California. Hearty thanks must also be extended to Betty Aten, Austin, Texas; Doug Turner, Lindale, Texas; Bruce Archer, Dallas, Texas; Shirley Aten Roberts, Amarillo, Texas; Mark Lane, Amarillo, Texas; Sally Walker, Hereford, Texas; Leta Rutter Hawks, Commerce City, Colorado; Juanda Hawks Herse, Henderson, Colorado, and Jenifer Susan Hawks, Snowmass, Colorado.

Nonfiction Old West writers are frequently up against the box canyon wall, needing to, but unable to locate a particular book or magazine article. Hard riding to the rescue for *Rawhide Ranger* were two gentlemen who can always be counted on for digging up that often out-of-print resource. For periodicals one only has to contact the ever affable workhorse Larry J. Walker, Owner, Magazine House, La Pine, Oregon. For books and/or pamphlets the go-to guy is rare book specialist and connoisseur of Southwestern nonfiction literature, a widely recognized authority in the field, Bob Pugh, Proprietor, Trail to Yesterday Books, Tucson, Arizona. Their friendship is valued, their expertise is priceless.

Making his contribution is another of those fellows a nonfiction writer turns to on matters of a mechanical nature—when in a bind for technical accuracy. Writing that a *mal hombre* jerked out his Colt's Peacemaker and punched a .45 caliber hole in someone—years before the particular six-shooter was even patented—in certain quarters might near lead to a lynching. It is smart to ask. If nineteenth-century firearms expert Stan Nelson of Harris, Minnesota, does not already own the answer, he knows where and how to get it. Most importantly, the published author, a well-read authority on Western Americana and the firearms carried by pioneers, Indian fighters, soldiers, outlaws, sheriffs, town marshals, Texas Rangers, cowboys, Pinkerton detectives, *demimonde* vixens, a bushwhacking Billy the Kid, sodbusters—and Mark Twain—stands ready to share that tremendous wealth of knowledge. Stan's the real deal.

Genuine thanks must also be extended to two New Mexico professors emeritus, Charles H. Harris III and Louis R. Sadler. Exhaustive research has netted them more than one volume dealing with well-known Texas Rangers of the Mexican Revolution timeframe, two particular works having won the highly prestigious Spur Award from the Western Writers of America. Beside the fact both are first-rate gentlemen and *bueno amigos* their groundbreaking biographical rounding up of Texas Rangers, Special Rangers, and Loyalty Rangers plays right into the Aten family's long and historic association with the Lone Star State's best known law enforcing outfit. Charles' and Ray's wise and willing counsel is never undervalued and is always appreciated.

Two other nonfiction writers consistently earn their spurs when it comes to pitching in, imparting combined years of knowledge about lawmen and outlaws of the Southwest. Turning to emeritus history professor John D. Tanner, Jr., Fallbrook, California, and/or corresponding with the renowned Jeff Burton, England, is necessary business for anyone poking about for solidly researched data about Texas yahoos run off to New Mexico and Arizona during the woolly territorial years. Tapping into their edifying books and articles is a wellspring. More importantly, though, is their unflagging devotion to preserving history and unselfishly sharing every tidbit they hold dominion over. If they have it, it is to be shared. Inquiries addressed their way are answered forthrightly, upfront and honestly. John and Jeff, both dear friends, market not myths—they're historians.

Although it is late, and they'll not hear the adulation, the author and readers of this volume will be pleasantly in debt to J. Evetts Haley, Hervey Chesley, and Earl Vandale. Their foresight is to be admired. Many talked about getting an old-timer's remembrances before Father Time closed the gate. These okay fellows put their money and time where their mouths were—no idle boasting. Two interviews with Mr. Aten, one in 1928, the other in 1941, fill the biographic hopper to the brim. Combining the two nets a 275-page typescript. The end product is seldom cited, sometimes overlooked, assuredly underused, but it is a treasure-trove of absorbing historical data—straight from the horse's mouth, so to speak. Supplementing this is the plethora of interviews conducted in the early twentieth-century. There were personal visits with other old-time cowmen, cowboys, and Texas Rangers who personally knew and worked for or with Ira Aten. Clichéd words "gonna do" were not in this trio of historians' vocabularies. We reap the reward.

Following, too, is a listing of other folks who played integral parts in recapturing Ira Aten's real story. Many are longtime friends, some are newly found acquaintances, but one and all stepped commendably to the mark. Michael L. Toon, Associate Professor and Librarian, The Texas Collection, Baylor University, Waco, Texas; David S. Turk, Historian, U.S. Marshals Service, Washington, DC; Harold J. Weiss, Jr., Emeritus Professor of History, Leander, Texas; Paul N. Spellman, Professor of History and Division Chair, Wharton Junior College, Wharton, Texas; Dr. Robert Tidwell, Curator of Historic Collections, National Ranching Heritage Center, Texas Tech University, Lubbock, Texas; Linda Briscoe Myers, Harry Ransom Humanities Research Center, University of Texas, Austin, Texas; Clarissa Chavira, Library Assistant, Texana/Genealogy, San Antonio Public Library, San Antonio, Texas; Karen Ellis, Director, Taylor Public Library, Taylor, Texas; Jane Hoerster, Mason County Historical Commission, Mason, Texas; Nicky Olson, Director, XIT Museum, Dalhart, Texas; Dr. John T. Baker, Dallas, Texas; Jim Ryan, Sabinal, Texas; Chris Wright, The Wright Collection, Waxahachie, Texas; Mavis Meadows, Assistant Librarian, John Mosser Public Library District, Abingdon, Illinois; Marie Howell, Librarian, Rhoads Memorial Library, Dimmitt, Texas; Clara Vick, Castro County Historical Society, Dimmitt, Texas; Carlene Long, Deputy District Clerk of Castro County, Dimmitt, Texas; Sal Rivera, Sheriff, Castro County, Dimmitt, Texas; Roger Malone, Mayor, Dimmitt, Texas; Claire Rogers, Education Coordinator, and Chris Godbold, Archivist, Fort Bend Museum, Richmond, Texas; Carol Beauchamp and Bettegene Coyle, George Memorial Library, Richmond, Texas; Anita Tufts, Archivist/Librarian, Texas Heritage Museum, Hill College, Hillsboro, Texas; Sheriff Leslie "Les" Cotten, Navarro County Sheriff's Office, Corsicana, Texas; Sheriff W. T. Smith and Dona Fritsch, Administrative Assistant, Burnet County Sheriff's Office, Burnet, Texas; David L. Meyer, Board Director, Zane Grey's West Society, Kennewick, Washington; Bobby Santiestaban, Research Specialist, Texas General Land Office, Austin, Texas; Ronald G. DeLord, Executive Director, Combined Law Enforcement Associations of Texas, Austin, Texas; Evelyn McDonald, Director, Dimmit County Public Library, Carrizo Springs, Texas; Bert Bell, Carrizo Springs, Texas; Paula Edwards, Director, and Pearl Salinas, Staff Assistant, Deaf Smith County Historical Museum, Hereford, Texas; Martha Russell, Librarian, Hereford Public Library, Hereford, Texas; Sheriff Emmett Benavidez and Miriam Valdez, Swisher County Sheriff's Office, Tulia, Texas; Brenda Hudson, County/District Clerk, Swisher County, Tulia, Texas; Terresa Collins, Deputy District Clerk, Armstrong County, Claude, Texas; Becky Groneman, County/

District Clerk Oldham County, Vega, Texas; Carolyn Richardson, Oldham County Library, Vega, Texas; Robin Crow, Reference Librarian, Amarillo Public Library, Amarillo, Texas; Terry Humble, Bayard, New Mexico; Linda Moore, Director, Tucumcari Historical Museum, Tucumcari, New Mexico; Deen Underwood, El Paso, Texas; Shannon Simpson, Curator, Ellis County Museum, Waxahachie, Texas; Ed Walker and Clay Riley, Brownwood Public Library—Genealogy Branch, Brownwood, Texas; Gerald and Patsy Johnson, Early, Texas; Vonda Williamson, Early, Texas; Bill and Jessica McInnis, May, Texas; Elna Clark, Brownwood, Texas; James Franklin "Jim" Dempsey, Wills Point, Texas; Herbie Belvin, San Antonio, Texas; Ted Weaver, Weaver Ranch, Wortham, Texas; Lynn Blankenship, San Saba County Historical Commission, San Saba, Texas; Alan J. Lamb, Santa Fe, New Mexico; Amy Parker, Waxahachie, Texas; Robert Ernst, Ponca City, Oklahoma; Jim Dillard, Georgetown, Texas; Bill Neal, Abilene, Texas; Mallory Honea, Leslie Bell, and Barbie Arevalo, Design Shop, Office Depot, Waxahachie, Texas; John McWilliams, Three Rivers, California; Roy B. Young, Editor, *Wild West History Association Journal*, Apache, Oklahoma; and Byron A. Johnson, Managing Editor of the *Texas Ranger Dispatch*, and Executive Director of the Texas Ranger Hall of Fame and Museum, Waco, Texas. Lastly, but certainly not least goes a heartfelt thanks—she knows why—to award-winning nonfiction writer Jan Devereaux, Maypearl, Texas.

Chapter 1

"When he got a little older"

Ten-year-old David "Dock" Davis fidgeted. He was idly kicking Texas dirt, shifting weight from one scuffed brogan to another as he held the team's reins. Dock's instructions had been short and simple: stand by with the family's wagon in front of a hardware store on Georgetown Avenue. Whatever he did, he wasn't to let those mules stray. Perhaps he waved to a fellow ten-year-old, James Warden, who likewise was in Round Rock with his father, sitting beside him while their wagon's wheels churned July's powdery dust. For sure, Dock knew when his papa returned to their wagon he'd be the proud owner of a spanking new pocket knife. Daddy had promised. William F. Davis' word was good, always. Twelve-year-old Jefferson Dillingham was not anticipating presents—from anybody—he just wanted to finish unloading that wagonload of feed at Henry Highsmith's livery stable. After all, the hour hand was nearing four o'clock and it was a Friday afternoon. Near Brushy Creek on the worn road passing through Old Round Rock, the initial town site, for-the-most-part now unoccupied due to the railroad passing it by, thirteen-year-old Clara playfully sat in the fork of a giant live oak shading the Fahners' front yard, casually swinging her legs and daydreaming. Lonesome? She was a carefree teenage girl and the 1878 subscription school-year was out—shut down for the summer. Lazily, so it seemed to the outside world, the evening of the nineteenth was peacefully closing in on Williamson County. Tomorrow, the weekend, and after a few Saturday chores the afternoon fishing and fun would take over. Then church on Sunday, followed almost routinely by a grand picnic with the red and white checkered tablecloths spread for wicker baskets overflowing with fresh sourdough bread and fried chicken—maybe even a chocolate cake.[1]

Dock seemed not to notice the mules in his charge perk their ears, but at the sound of gunshots he felt the volcanic tug on the leathers as his team quaked in its traces, the wagon rocking forward for a split-second before it and the frightened animals were again parked,

stock-still. He, too, heard the shrieking cry—a desperate plea for
mercy—"Don't, boys!" Then deputy sheriff Ahijah W. "Caige" Grimes,
a man chasing after him, gun in hand and shooting, fell flat on his
face, dead, right in front of Henry Koppel's corner store.[2] Inside the
German merchant's emporium the crescendo of gunfire did not abate,
but rhythmically echoed. Again! Again! The roar was deafening. Pun-
gent wisps of blue smoke—burnt gunpowder—billowed from merchant Koppel's doorway. First one man emerged, leaking blood and
wobbling, steadying himself by leaning against a nearby post, a cocked
Colt's six-shooter dangling at the end of a quivering hand. Two more
fellows, one with the ring and middle finger shot off his right hand
and, mad as hornets it seemed, burst from the tiny store racing for
safety and sanctuary—somewhere. Weak and losing consciousness
the man already outside, the one needing support, with considerable
difficulty raised his arm and let go with another round—the last in
his six-shooter. Then he crumpled to the street gasping for breath.
Such goings-on were heady doings for a boy of but ten years. The
show, however, was far from over, not by a long shot. Dock's mules
could stand it no more, nor could a startled boy hold back the team's
temperamental lurching. They pulled loose from Dock's grip, try as
he might. Alas, at the first sound of gunfire Dock's father had rushed
outside to protect his son. Just in the nick of time. He leaped into
the wagon, fighting to control the spooked team: Dock leaped too,
straight into a store. From within, the curious ten-year-old peeked
out. It was irresistible high drama: Too good to miss.[3]

Regaining his feet, with trembling fingers trying to stuff cartridges through his Colt's loading-gate, the lung-shot man was clearly
chasing after the other fellows—three in number. All of them, the
shooter and the runners were foreigners to young Dock. None were
from Round Rock. At that instant a fellow dashed out of Henry Bur-
khardt's barber shop. His was a new face in town, too, but plainly
he was a lawman, a Texas Ranger if Dock were to hazard a guess.
He soon began taking potshots at the fleeing trio with a long-bar-
reled Colt's six-shooter. Quickly he was joined by another man with a
smokin' pistol, a newfangled Colt's self-cocker.[4] He must have been a
fellow Texas Ranger also, Dock would sure bet the new pocket knife
on that. Unbeknownst to little Dock Davis, normally sedate Round
Rock was brimming with Rangers.[5] They had slipped into town on
police business, and they meant business. More were on the way at
the gallop—and by train.[6]

On Georgetown Avenue the gun battle was raging, a ghastly street-fight. Even citizens, faces well-known to Dock, were lending a helping hand—popping caps as three obviously bad men were racing to regain their saddles. Assuredly young Dock didn't have a hint about what the Texas Rangers knew, or thought they had known— that part about Mr. shameful Sam Bass and his gang planning to rob the Williamson County Bank, the old Miller's Exchange Bank on Georgetown Avenue. Dock was not alone in being clueless. The would-be robbers also didn't have an inkling about two items of the utmost importance: For a time now they had been carelessly conspiring with a shrewd snitch in their midst and, more germane for the blistering moment, Texas Rangers were already pre-positioning themselves in the alley behind the bank where they had tied their horses. Uncompromisingly pushed by the crowd of lawmen and citizens on the street, and wholly unawares their mounts were now under surveillance, there was every reason to proffer the hot little game would soon be over. Such was not to be, not just yet. The badmen had made it to the alley, trying to climb atop gyrating horses high-stepping to the tempo of pinging Colt's and zinging Winchesters. The bandit newly missing two fingers caught a spiraling bullet left of his spine, one that ranged upward into the kidney region, exiting three inches left of his bellybutton. Shaken horribly he screamed, pitiably, "Oh, Lord!" He did, though, manage to mount and ride out of town, thanks in large part to the gutsy aid of an unscathed companion in crime—much to the amazement of excited Texas Rangers. The third owlhoot, well, he was not near so lucky: He too managed—with difficulty—to gain stirrups, for an instant. A lawman's bullet fiercely plowed into his head just behind the left ear, channeling toward exposure through his right eye, smooth knocking him out of the slick-forked saddle: The ill-fated outlaw was a dead man falling, lifeless even before his body slammed into the narrow alley's bloody grime.[7]

Clara Fahner, the stonemason's daughter, perched in her tree, could hear the fast pounding of eight hooves. Suddenly they were in sight, two very scary-looking strangers racing by the yard-gate fronting the Old Round Rock Road. Plainly one was reeling in the saddle, barely able to hang on as the horse charged beneath him. The man was hurt, badly, to be sure. He did, however, muster from within a warning: She should get in the house, right now! Presumably the injured man was thinking a gun-happy posse would be but a hoof-beat and a heart-beat behind. Clara in a single bound dismounted the limb, and hurriedly ran for home seeking comfort and reassurance from her mom and dad, Barbara and Paul. During the madcap dash she inadvertently stepped right out of her shoes, but she kept running, ruining "a good pair of stockings."[8] She would have a good story to tell, though. Her girlfriends would want to hear all about such an adventure, such a close call.

In town the imminent danger had passed, but the excitement had not ebbed. Men were scrambling, securing whinnying saddle-horses and searching for wheel-guns, Winchesters, and double-barreled shotguns. Pursuit was mandatory, at least for the Texas Rangers. Dock Davis, awestruck, took it all in. He, like the rest of his childhood pals in town that day, would have a whopping good story to tell playmates—those not there—and it would all be true. It was exciting. He had been right there when Hell popped at New Round Rock. Listening to the big folks Dock picked up a few details.

The two that got away, he soon learned, were none other than the disreputable and heretofore wily Sam Bass, now severely wounded, and his coconspirator Frank Jackson. The fellow lying dead in the alleyway, well, that was Seaborn Barnes, an outlaw deluxe. Of course Dock knew the dead deputy Caige Grimes, or at least knew who he was, but that other guy, the wounded one, was an unfamiliar face. He wanted to know more. Especially about that fellow, one who suffered a bullet hole in his chest yet kept coming, shooting and shooting and shooting some more—then reloading as spurting blood painted his blouse. Dock was brought up to speed. That guy was an ex-Texas Ranger by the name of Maurice B. Moore, now working as a Travis County Deputy Sheriff at Austin. He had come to town, on the quiet, with the Texas Ranger's headman, Major John B. Jones. And it was Jones, with plenty of pluck, who had joined that Ranger surreptitiously stationed in the barber shop, Richard Clayton "Dick" Ware, a cool customer, a man as brave as courage itself. Ware was afterward credited with firing the shot that killed Seab Barnes. Texas Rangers in the alley, who were they? The Ranger shooting the reckless Sam Bass was George Herold, a career lawman and border country veteran, and although illiterate, he was widely known as a Spanish-speaking terror to thieves. Herold's salty partner during the heat of battle had been twenty-eight-year-old Christopher Reyzor "Chris" Connor, a stand-up Texas Ranger whose nerve was never doubted.[9]

Whether he wanted to go with the posse or not was immaterial; his youth capped any such notion. Without a doubt Dock was spellbound with the commotion uncorking before him—and the cast of colorful, if not hard-looking, characters suddenly appearing in town that Friday. Rangers seemingly came out from under the woodpile, from nowhere, but they were everywhere. Texas Ranger Captain Lee Hall was there from the get-go, although he missed the actual fireworks. After a punishing ride from San Saba County, Lieutenant N. O. "Mage" Reynolds and his boys made their presence known, but were two hours too late for the grand ball. Then, that evening, Lieutenant John Barkley Armstrong and several other Texas Rangers arrived. For a boy, any boy, it was a fantastic program. The Texas Rangers were wearing wide cartridge belts stuffed full, and all had at least one Colt's six-shooter—some had two—and most everyone of them were toting a Winchester carbine. They were a dashing set, iconic molds for men or boys wanting to jump from following the plow or quit chewing dust while trailing the "festive cow." Wherever they went, in a cluster, the Texas Rangers caught notice—favorably most of the time. Others were in town, too. One thousand folks were calling Round Rock home. They were all on the jam-packed streets, men, women, and children—inquiring, gawking, gossiping, and guessing. This was no humdrum day, it was newsy. Many of the grownup townsmen, like the Texas Rangers, were sporting long guns.[10] Maybe, a few just had them for show.

Though an initial posse had left town in the late afternoon, sundown forced its return to Round Rock. Chasing after bad guys at night, those that were not in the least reluctant to shoot, did not make for good common sense, not even for a toughened Texas Ranger. The hunt could wait till daybreak.[11]

Hot news broke on Saturday morning, further setting Round Rock's folks agog. Texas Rangers and two Williamson County deputy sheriffs, without too much exertion, had found Sam Bass under a big tree, alive, but bloodied and suffering terribly. Quickly Texas Ranger Sergeant Charles L. Nevill, at gunpoint, had disarmed Bass, making him a prisoner. After calling for an "ambulance" (light wagon), and an exploratory examination by Doctor C. P. Cochran, the severely injured but lucid Sam Bass had been started for town. In Old Round Rock, another physician, Dr. Alexander McDonald, physically examined Bass, offering a second opinion—the prognosis was not good. Before restarting the prisoner for Round Rock, the exasperated doctor shooed his sons Alec and Robert off the wagon's rear wheel. They had climbed aboard for a disapproved peek along with Livingston M.

May's children.[12] Everyone—young and old—was anxious to catch a glimpse of America's most wanted badman.

Adamantly refused admittance to the Hart Hotel, Texas Rangers prevailed on August Gloeber to allow a cot be placed in his Round Rock tin shop next door, a makeshift hospital of sorts, with bedding furnished by the Harts. Dr. Cochran and a colleague, Dr. A. F. Morris, confirmed the worst, but the obvious: Bass was on his deathbed. Fearing Sam might die too quick, taking all the secrets with him, Major Jones quizzed him about past crimes and accomplices, hoping to clear cases, nabbing others involved in the gang's Texas crime spree. Sam Bass, in this regard stood pat: "It is agin my profession to blow on my pals. If a man knows anything he ought to die with it in him."[13] Astutely after hiring a black man, Jim Chatman, to serve as a private nurse, Major Jones stationed a Texas Ranger in the room with pencil and paper—take down his every word was the unambiguous order.[14] During a fit of delirium might he spill the beans?

Round Rock was buzzing. Crowds of spectators were milling. "No other Saturday in the history of Round Rock had seen such excitement.... The news of the capture had traveled throughout the countryside and the streets were filled with horses, buggies and wagons."[15] Newsmen were in town jotting in their notebooks. At least one reporter representing the *Galveston Daily News* was allowed a brief bedside visit with the dying outlaw.[16] It was page one news, even back East: *The New York Times* headlined, "Capture of a Texas Desperado."[17] Steely-eyed Texas Rangers, armed to the teeth, paraded the Round Rock streets in high-top boots, jingling spurs musically announcing their presence. Certain Texas Rangers were laughing and joking, no doubt glad that such a nasty desperado as Sam Bass was low-sick, about to die. Other Rangers were somber, stomping their feet in feigned disgust and whining because they'd been too late for the finale.[18] By any man's measure though, these Texas Rangers were a remarkable and admirable lot. Winchester Warriors, if you will.[19] They had nailed Sam Bass' hide to the wall, even though he wasn't dead—yet. Seaborn Barnes had paid the price too, a terminal toll for his day of Round Rock badness. A good number of men romanticized action, and the state's Texas Rangers were men of action. Williamson County's boys, too, were more-than-a-little captivated, their eyes and minds spinning with expectancy of additional episodes of six-gun excitement. Immature and starry-eyed imaginations ran wild.

Other eyes were tearing-up. Should not a touch of sympathy be in order now that the real threat had been annulled? Was not that severely injured boy—yet in his twenties—going to have a chance to make things right, a time to repent? Could not Texas Rangers grant him a moment to talk with the Lord?[20] Or, a man of the cloth? Even though Bass had spurned prayerful overtures earlier in the day, a few citizens religiously bent had concocted a spiritual plan. Persuasiveness they owned. A preacher they knew.

Forty-six-year-old Minister of the Gospel Austin Cunningham Aten, pastor of the Round Rock Christian Church, had made a Saturday trip to Round Rock from his farm a few miles outside town. Enthusiastically accompanying him were two sons, Frank, seventeen years old, and fifteen-year-old Ira. The two youngest boys, Cal and Eddie, had been left at home doing odd jobs with their industrious mother Kate. Though fortuitous, that twentieth of July excursion to Round Rock would appreciably impact the life of Ira, and with a domino effect, his younger brothers, too.[21]

Almost from the moment he arrived in town Reverend Aten was updated about the big doings: the gunfight, the capture, and about the less than stellar medical forecast for the notorious outlaw. And, too, from the outset of his arrival he had been besieged to visit the tin shop: To carry the word of God, to comfortingly pray with and/or for the witty, yet unapologetic little gangster, to sit with him or kneel at his bedside, just for a moment or two. Preacher Aten demurred. He did not believe, not for one iota, in any deathbed confessionals.[22] There was black and there was white. Conveniently contrived last-minute pleas to God, after willingly frittering away one's earthly life in an orgy of sinfulness and unashamed unlawfulness, was sacrilegious. A substantial congregation of Round Rock's devout denizens—church goers—were not to be so easily denied. They appealed to Reverend Aten's compassionate temperament. Would he please reconsider? The zealous entreaties were powerful and persuasive. Purportedly Preacher Aten cleverly mused: "If there was mercy for a thief who died on the Cross, there may be some for a thief found dying in a cow pasture."[23] Reverend Aten acquiesced. He would see the boy.

Sam Bass, as immobile as he was, was nevertheless a prisoner. Sound judgment demanded he be treated with consideration, but with watchfulness and caution. Major Jones was smartly attuned to reality. He must guard against any asinine escape attempt. Bass could not run fast or far, but he could yet pull a trigger. Too, Frank Jackson was still on the dodge, whereabouts unknown. Might he venture a try at rescuing his pal Sam? Then, there was that other side of a law enforcer's coin. Fidelity to a solemn oath required he protect Sam Bass from the outside world, from mob justice, or, perhaps even personal revenge. Nineteenth-century Texas was widely known for its unremitting blood feuds. Deputy Sheriff Caige Grimes had brothers. One was allegedly—and convincingly—threatening: "This boy must not leave this house alive."[24] Texas Rangers casually ambling about Round Rock may have seemed unoccupied, idly wandering around town, wasting time, but they were on the alert. Their presence was a touch of preventive enforcement, a deterrent. Other Rangers, when not catching a quick nap on down time, were standing watch. They were pulling assigned shifts at the tin shop, ensuring Sam Bass didn't get out, and guaranteeing curious onlookers and souvenir hunters didn't get in.[25]

There was a protocol for gaining the ringside seat at Sam's cot: an okay from the Ranger stationed at the doorway. As Reverend Aten, walking abreast with his boys, approached the tin shop's door—the checkpoint—a leathery-faced Ranger looked them over from hat to toe. Most likely Ranger John R. Banister or his brother William Lawrence "Will" Banister was the gatekeeper on duty.[26] After the nominal pleasantries Reverend Aten and son Frank were granted permission to enter.[27] Crestfallen, Ira was denied—he was just too young—so said the grizzled Ranger. No argument. No admittance.[28]

There is no reason to doubt Ira and an inquisitive pal peeked through a window while Parson Aten said a prayer for the hurting outlaw reposed before him, as has been written.[29] Nor would it be an overreach to think an adolescent Ira talked with more young friends that day in Round Rock. Perhaps he even gabbed awhile with young Dock Davis. Now that boy, he had a good story to tell. It is no outlandish stretch to believe Ira Aten, at some point about then, became infatuated with the Texas Rangers—what Lone Star lad wouldn't? Most boys like the outdoors, guns, and horses. Texas Rangers carried guns and rode horses, and most nights of the year slept under moonlight and stars.[30] If the account be true, Ira even told one of those stalwarts, that very day, "when he got a little older" he would enlist and become a heroic Texas Ranger himself. The Ranger patronizingly replying, "I'll be looking for you, son."[31] Whether or not he was vicariously fantasizing while in Round Rock about gunfights with the badmen from Bitter Creek and rounding up scurrilous cow thieves in the cedar breaks of western Williamson County is unclear. He did however, in a boyish sort of way, begin altering his plans for the future: "The Rangers were there in town with six-shooters on, swaggering around there. I thought it would be nice to carry a six-shooter and thought I would just stop the cowboy business and join the Rangers."[32] Preacher Austin Aten had his prayers with Sam Bass, made the weekly purchase of necessities, then ushered his sons back to the family farm. Teenagers Frank and Ira had Saturday chores prior to any leisure time—he had a sermon to prepare. The Sabbath was next day.

Sunday, July 21, 1878, was a big day for Mr. Samuel Bass; it was his birthday, the twenty-seventh year of his life. It, too, was his last day. During the afternoon, five minutes in front of four o'clock, Bass incoherently mumbled about the "world bobbing up and down" or something to the effect that "the world was but a bubble, trouble wherever you go." Then he died.[33] Sam Bass, whatever the reason, had taken the wrong fork, the dead end road. Round Rock had been end of the line. Austin Ira Aten would take the right fork in the road. It began at Round Rock. The preacher would be proud.

* * *

Austin Ira Aten was not a native Texan. In fact, he was a Mid-westerner. Originally the family's last name had been VanAuten, but when the first branch of Ira's ancestors chose an emigration passageway to North America from the Netherlands the surname was shortened for simplicity's sake. Ira's grandfather, Peter Aten from Kentucky, a veteran of the War of 1812, and his beloved grandmother Margaret Quinn from Wrightsborough, Georgia, who celebrated the twenty-sixth day of October 1797 as her birthday, had migrated to the rich farm country of Preble County, Ohio. And it was there, not far from the Ohio/Indiana borderline at the settlement of Eaton, some twenty-odd miles west of Dayton, that Ira's father Austin Cunningham had been born on August 4, 1832, the oldest of four brothers.[34] The following year, on the nineteenth day of March, also in Ohio, the pleasantly disposed Katherine (Katheine) Eveline Dunlap's mother lovingly welcomed her into the world. Twenty years later, on May 19, 1853, Kate Dunlap and Austin C. Aten, a devoutly religious man, were married.[35]

Austin Ira Aten's grandmother, Margaret Quinn
Aten. *Courtesy Gordon D. Turner.*

Precisely pinpointing an exact time Austin and Kate Aten decided
on removing from the Buckeye State is elusive from a genealogical standpoint, but for easing the biography forward it is relatively
inconsequential. Preceding outbreak of the North/South hostilities
the Atens had settled in what is now the Land of Lincoln, Illinois.
It was there on May 12, 1854, that the couple's first baby was born,
a cherished daughter, Margaret Angelina "Angie" Elizabeth. This
beloved child was followed by three more prior to the cannonading
of Fort Sumter. The first two were Thomas Quinn during 1856 on
the sixteenth day of February, and Clara Isabell [Belle] on June 8,
1858. Stirring emotions all through the United States and the like-

lihood of a possible Civil War prompted Austin, it is presumed, to name his next son, who arrived on August 26, 1860, Frank Lincoln. At that time the Austin C. Aten family was living at the small township of Millbrook, Peoria County, picking up mail at the Elmore Post Office. Whether or not at this juncture twenty-eight-year-old Austin Aten was a part-time preacher is uncharted. A census enumerator was silent about him being a minister, enumerating him as a Peoria County farmer.[36]

Maintaining Illinois residences throughout the Civil War it seems Austin Aten had carved out the family's geographical niche. Not being privy to dinner table discussions and/or debates, if Austin Aten had any sympathy for the Southern cause due to his mother's origins, it was at best lukewarm.[37] Where his support lay is chiseled by harsh reality: He did not rush headlong to carry a musket for the Confederacy, though Austin did not stand by idly. The rallying call had gone out for area volunteers. On August 18, 1862, Austin Cunningham Aten willingly—enthusiastically—enlisted in the Union Army's 77th Illinois Volunteer Infantry, Company I, the Federal unit being locally recruited at Peoria.[38] The entire regiment was provisionally stationed at Camp Peoria. Therefore it is quite probable that Austin, ministering to the spiritual needs of the company, might have been allowed a short leave of absence to be at home when Kate gave birth to Austin Ira, the central figure in this vignette, on the third day of September 1862.[39] Surely Austin Cunningham Aten didn't miss the coincidental irony. On that very same day the 77th Illinois Infantry was formally mustered into Federal service.[40] Company I's martial movements may be meticulously tracked, but such is not necessary for this undertaking. Advancing to the rank of corporal, Austin C. Aten saw service throughout the deep South, primarily in swampy and sweltering Louisiana.[41] After just under a three-year-stint Austin Cunningham Aten was honorably discharged on July 10, 1865. For his gallant and committed performance, Austin C. Aten was, on paper, commissioned a 2nd Lieutenant on the twenty-fourth day of July 1865, but was not mustered back into the U.S. Army, the need having past.

Apparently with at least a tinge of wanderlust, Austin Aten moved his family again. This time it was to Indian Point Township, still in the state of Illinois but just west of Peoria County in Knox County. He continued farming, providing for his growing family, but at least for awhile Austin was also engaged in the hardware business,

Austin Ira Aten's parents, Katherine Eveline (Dunlap) and Reverend Austin Cunningham Aten. *Courtesy Research Center, Texas Ranger Hall of Fame and Museum.*

so said the census man for 1870, backed up later by Ira: "In Illinois my father got tired of farming, as most people did, and went in the hardware business with a good friend that had the experience, and in a few years his good friend had all the money and my father had the experience."[42] Sometime around Ira's fifth birthday the family moved to a locale near Abingdon, Illinois.[43] Ira's two younger brothers were

From an Aten relative's fascinating antique photo album. Front row L to R: Austin Ira Aten, Thomas Quinn Aten, and Franklin Lincoln Aten. Back row L to R: Edwin Dunlap "Eddie" Aten (still clothed in a toddler's dress), Clara Isabell "Belle" Aten, Calvin Grant "Cal" Aten, and Margaret Angelina "Angie" Elizabeth Aten. *Courtesy Gordon D. Turner.*

born there: Calvin Grant on December 7, 1868, and Edwin Dunlap on the fifth of September 1870.[44]

The relocation was advantageous because of educational opportunities for his children—which speaks authoritatively to Austin Cunningham Aten's foresight: providing a good foundation and "higher education" for his brood.[45] Abingdon was home to Abingdon College, a long established institution with a heavy emphasis on religious training and Christian principles. Interestingly for Ira's biography, his uncle Aaron P. Aten was a distinguished member of the faculty.[46] Though the seeds for Austin Ira's Christian upbringing were sowed at Abingdon, the continual nurturing and fertilization of his moral fiber would long outlast any formalized education—Austin C. Aten would see to that.

Paradoxically and interestingly for an Old West lawman's biographical sketch, Abingdon is only a short distance southeast of Monmouth, Illinois, Wyatt Earp's birthplace. Although it is unlikely Ira Aten knew Wyatt or knew anything about him, since Earp was his senior by fourteen years and was already treading the crooked road of criminality, such an irony cannot be brushed aside categorically. Austin Cunningham Aten had not yet taken to preaching full-time, but there is not a shred of doubt his brand of ardent fire and brimstone religion had been parentally instilled at an early age; he was no born-again Christian.[47] Forgiveness in the eternal sense was okay with Austin C. Aten, but only after a derelict sinner had swallowed a bitter spoonful of comeuppance. That said, it is not at all unreasonable—though undeniably not provable—to wonder if Austin was subconsciously thrilled after reading Peoria's *Daily National Democrat* and the *Peoria Daily Transcript*? It really was quite a sensational story: Journalistic pieces about Peoria peace officers raiding an anchored boat on the Illinois River, a floating whorehouse. They had arrested a hotbed of local police characters, one of whom, not surprisingly, now knowing his authenticated criminal history, was the aforementioned Wyatt Berry Stapp Earp, whom an incisive hometown newspaperman was caustically tagging "the Peoria bummer." He was so nicknamed because it most certainly wasn't Wyatt's very first arrest in Peoria's second-rate brothels. Pleased with their success at sneaking undetected to the water's edge and gaining entry to the movable Palace of Pleasure, jubilant gendarmes were truthfully bragging they had scooped up, according to the newspaper reporter, "the quietest set of bawds and pimps they ever handled, they felt so cheap at their unexpected capture."[48] Exposing him as "an old offender" was a print correspondent's oblique suggestion that Mr. Wyatt was more than a horny customer paying for play, but was instead, perhaps not really a first-class pimp, but nevertheless a leechlike pimp. Characterization as a pimp wasn't solely limited to Wyatt B. S. Earp's mysteriously lost year in Peoria; it was a black mark following him relentlessly as he narcissistically and vainly chased after stature and dollars throughout the American West.[49] Ira would have been but nine years old when Earp was stringing a shameless record of Peoria pimping arrests, so in all probability any comments of damnation made by Austin C. Aten about profiteering procurers and whorehouse hangers-on were shushed from the tender ears of his children. Or, on the other hand, maybe it is possible young Austin Ira did hear a laudatory comment from his dad, a remark praising policemen for their work—keeping society's sinners and riffraff in check. Could it have been the spark that lit a fuse burning toward a young man's career choice?

Surely Ira and his brothers played cops and robbers, cowboys and Indians, hide and seek, tag, and occasionally toppled a king off the

Two of Abingdon's foremost early-day business establishments. Top: The Abingdon brickyard. Bottom: The Animal Trap Company incorporated by W. C. Hooker, Knox M. Marks, and John E. Cox. Mr. Hooker, among other talents, was the inventor of a nifty contraption—the mouse trap.   *Courtesy Abingdon Historical Society.*

mountain—most boys did. Since Abingdon was in a rural setting, a farming community, with an abundance of rabbits and squirrels, turkey and deer, the Aten boys must have begged for rifles or shotguns, for their very own. Such speculation would not be out of place. For little guys—and some girls—growing up in farm and ranch country

The Aten children—those of school age—attended this school at Abingdon, Illinois. *Courtesy Abingdon Historical Society.*

it was tradition: Boys ached for the hunt, it pushed them to big boy status. A father giving his son a gun was a rite of passage, the obliging deed nudging a boy down the road toward manhood.[50] A boy capable of putting meat on the table, well, it was big doings—for the boy. It signified the march to maturity was underway.

Ira's oldest brother Tommy was near a grown man. Certainly his oldest sister Angie had blossomed into womanhood, with fundamental adult responsibilities. At age nineteen she had married Americus Jerome Kimmons, three years her senior and a tinner by trade. The next year Angie gave birth to daughter Virginia May on May 26, 1874. For this branch of the Aten family tree, the precious baby girl would always be known as "Virgie." Sadly, Angie's next child, Frank Clyde, died before celebration of his first birthday.[51]

Although we can't know when Austin C. Aten actually began turning his eyes toward Texas, there is no doubt about when push finally came to shove. Ira was fourteen years old, geared up to move west. Details of the grueling day-by-day trip during the autumn of 1876 are nonexistent—thus far. What is not unclear is their destination. Austin C. Aten had set his sights on the northeastern edge of the Texas Hill Country. With five younger children in tow, the Atens departed Abingdon leaving fond memories on an abandoned

Yours always,

Aaron Prince Aten

One of Austin Cunningham Aten's brothers, a professional college level educator, Aaron Prince Aten. *Courtesy Bruce Archer.*

doorstep. Their oldest boy Tommy came too, as did Angie and her husband, and toddler Virgie. Also making the trip were Ira's grand-mothers—both of them widows.[52] Their new life had begun. After an arduous trip they settled and set up housekeeping in the Lone Star State on the twenty-ninth day of October.[53]

Technically Austin Cunningham and Kate's newfound home was situated in Travis County, near present day Pflugerville, but

burgeoning Round Rock just north across the boundary line in Williamson County was the nearest commercial center for shopping,
or marketing agricultural commodities, or socializing on a grander
scale than the recently occupied homeplace afforded.[54] The Texas
state capitol was not far to the south. Austin C. Aten would farm on
the shares for his family and circuit ride for the Lord.[55] There would
be ample time to convince a congregation and build a church: he was
yet a young man, still in his mid-forties—in the prime of life. The
attractive Hill Country, along the Travis/Williamson County line was
an ideal choice for forging a future.

The survey lopping off approximately 1200 square miles from
Milam County had taken place during March 1848. The new county
was named after wooden-leg wearing Major Robert M. "Three-Legged
Willie" Williamson, an early day Texas pioneer and an expert on Mexican land laws. Roughly six months after the formalized mapping, on
the seventh day of August, Williamson County was organized, newly
installed county officials happily assuming posts at the county seat,
Georgetown, eighteen miles north of Round Rock.[56]

With a rich Texas heritage and gently rolling acres of farm and
ranch land drained by the San Gabriel River and its tributaries, the
Williamson County area was just the right spot to raise a quartet of
adventurous boys. Winters were ordinarily mild, excepting when
Blue Northers blew in dealing a spate of mercury plunging misery.
Summertime was always a scorcher, but bearable. Hunting, especially for Whitetail deer along the creek bottoms, was fantastic. Of
course there were skunks, wildcats, wolves, rattlesnakes, and sometimes a black bear, but that only added to the fun. Fishing was good,
too. Beehives were plentiful, tempting targets for robbery. Pecans—
during a good year—littered the ground. There were delicious wild
grapes and plums for the taking. Arrowheads by the thousands, if
one were inclined to look.[57] Old-timers, fellows that were actually
there, could spit and whittle spinning yarns about skirmishing with
Comanches and Kiowas during days when "thair was Indions nearly
evry light moon."[58] Boys and young men took it in, with relish.

That was then, the old days. Now, the 1870s, cattlemen and cowboys were an omnipresent feature attraction in Williamson County.
Sometimes, after an overnight stay in Austin, wealthy cattle barons,
comfortably seated in their buggies for an early morning jaunt, trot-
ted to the outskirts of Round Rock bidding adieu to trail bosses herding up the Chisholm Trail, or a little later drovers angling northwest

for the Western Trail, then on to Dodge or Ogallala or colder temperatures beyond.[59] There was also a healthy sampling of big ranches in Williamson County: Cattle operations where boys so prone could learn the art of deftly tattooing a loop around the horns of some stubborn cow brute, then tripping it to the ground for doctoring or branding or marking an ear. Topping off cold-backed horses was exhilarating too, and sometimes entertaining to those with boots yet on the ground. The cow country classroom was a school of hard knocks, not a place for sniveling crybabies. Not in cow camps or on the ranches. Not in a crowd where some men in a split-second moment of dumb carelessness lost a finger or thumb, simply by catching it between a tightly stretched rope and a rawhide-covered saddle horn. And, there were even stories about men getting caught on the ground between their horse and a belligerent Longhorn steer—somehow entangled—a lariat rope accidentally draping around their sunburned neck, then bingo—their head cut smooth off.[60] Less serious mishaps earned laughs and/or teasing all around, even if someone was wincing with pain. Too, a real man had to stand a joke—bugs in a bedroll—or run for mama's apron strings. The colorful cadre of horseback cavaliers caught Ira Aten's attention: "I wanted to ramble around, wanted to be a cowboy. The big herds passing there every year in the Spring."[61]

Besides gutting a deer, running a trot-line, riding and roping and roundups, there were more things a Texas boy had to know if he were to make a man—a good man: like, minding his manners; when to keep quiet; tending to his own affairs. Personal business was guarded with the same passion as personal property. The tenet prohibiting carrying of six-shooters was on Texas' legal books, but selectively ignored—enforced at the law enforcer's pleasure. Instantaneous six-gun redressing of perceived insults was commonplace, if an affront demanded a quick settlement.[62] Theoretically and practically 1870s Texas, especially away from town, was a place where it was fine to welcome a stranger with open arms—but always be armed. Closer in, such a supposed need significantly diminished. Within confines of town the Wild West really was not that wild, apart from anomalies, like when Sam Bass and gang had stopped to case the local bank. Mama's trite admonishments, "You're judged by the company you keep," and "mind your own business," were spot-on pieces of sound advice. An act of violence taking place inside city limits, more often than not, was aftermath of pigheaded revelry spawned by whiskey or wagering or whoring—or all three. Letting the hammer drop on

Will Brown, left, and Ira. After the Atens' move to Texas, Will
was an especially close "chum" of Ira's. This pair, marching to
maturity, along with their older brothers, would spend many
days—and protracted overnight trips—hunting and fishing
in Travis and Williamson Counties. Ira's and Will's friendship
would endure into old age.   *Courtesy Jeri and Gary Boyce Radder.*

truth, though it may well diminish a preconceived notion about the
Old West, an 1877 penman writing for the *Galveston Daily News* is
emphatically opinionated: "A great deal has been said about shooting men in Texas, but my observation teaches me that it is 'diamond
cut diamond.' Good men, who mind their own business are rarely
molested, considering the unavoidable dangers of all new coun-
tries."[63] The really big name sporting men—the truly professional
gamblers—rarely were any headache for frontier communities. Their
demeanor and gold-plated reputations for a square deal were static.
There was no profit in downright piracy. Repeat customers, giving
a fellow another chance to recoup losses, was the bona fide gamblers' lifeblood. Unprincipled tinhorns were the nuisance. The lower
tier sporting crowd—pirating pimps, cheating cardsharps, slippery
swindlers, and seductive *demimonde* gals—could always be counted

on to overturn the formula of a town's peacefulness. The bottom-of-the-bucket saloon crowd was normally catalyst for all the murder, mayhem, and madness. More often than not, that nest was the transits; leeches sucking blood from a community, then moving on to the next boom town or railroad terminus or hellhole.[64] Contributions they made were to their own pockets or purses, nothing for a budding township's betterment. They were scavengers, hyenas of humankind. Reverend Austin Aten's message to his boys was firm—and well heeded—stay away from taprooms and faro layouts and fancy ladies.

Propriety of the times forbade Clara from riding horseback astride, but make no mistake, the Williamson County section was a good spot for raising daughters as well as boys, although by time of the family's relocation Austin and Kate's girls were already young ladies, Angie with a family of her own.

Absent confirmation to the contrary it would appear that Ira and his brothers were living the typical life of farm boys: knocking off a list of everyday chores, feeding and caring for the hogs, horses, and milk cows, working the fields, and incessantly fantasizing about being somewhere else, doing something else. And attending school.

Close to home there may not have been—in fact there were not—any business houses, and would not be until 1890. But, as the Aten boys' luck would have it, there was a school located on Henry Lisso's farm, and had been since 1872.[65] Extrapolated from his later writings it would seem that Ira made an above average student if attending school, really becoming quite articulate.[66] Ira was assimilating a wealth of knowledge, but not only in front of the blackboard. From the farm he was formulating a strong work ethic, a genuine sense of responsibility. Roaming the nearby hills and creek bottoms, gun and fishing pole in hand, Ira was gradually honing outdoor skills that would serve him well. At this stage in his life, Ira and his brother Frank were allowed overnight hunting trips by themselves, even lasting a full week or more.[67] Taking cues from cowboys Ira developed practical know-how about horses, ropes, and cantankerous cattle. More importantly, perhaps, from the cattle culture Ira learned about men, when a prickly barb could just be a joke, and when it wasn't. What words, even to a friend, had best be spoken with a smile, and the likelihood of a disastrous dustup if the same were said to a stranger. From his mother Kate, Ira learned humility and a heartfelt sense of family. From papa, Ira and his siblings were given—blessed by some accounts—with a formidable religious upbringing: an adherence to stern discipline and a strictness regarding issues of morality and character. It has been written that Pastor Austin Aten's lively sermons were not just the "fifteen to twenty minute variety." "He believed in giving us enough to last a week. We often brought our dinners."[68] Reverend Austin Aten didn't let the distractions of frontier life knock him off the good Lord's preordained course.[69] The Ten Commandments were just that: commandments with a capitalized C. Preacher Aten knew there was right, and there was wrong—and his children best know the difference, too.

Chapter 2

"We buried him on the side of a road"

The killing of Sam Bass had catapulted young Ira Aten right to the brink of a sensational story. Frank Aten's buttons were no doubt popping off his store-bought shirt: He had been accepted as a grownup, at least adult enough to stand quiet at the bedside of a dying desperado. Owing to worthwhile efforts of a hardworking, productive, and overall munificent population, Williamson County's pioneering folks—in the main—fittingly earned their rightful spot in the Texas history books. But, if truth be told, Round Rock's day in the sun is best remembered due to dogged Texas Rangers interdicting Sam Bass' ill-advised bank robbing scheme and that gruesome gunfight on Georgetown Avenue. Texas Rangers, a year earlier, had also cut short another miscreant's misadventures, and he also owned a tie to Round Rock, albeit a somewhat tenuous link.

John Wesley Hardin, like Ira, was a country preacher's son. Unlike Ira, John didn't pay attention to dad's good advice—most especially that part about turning the other cheek. When it suited him, or when he was drunk, Wes Hardin could be downright mean. Cuts on John Wesley's notch-stick bore witness to his viciousness: A murder warrant spoke to his true social status. For *mal hombres* wanted by Texas Rangers, John Wesley Hardin was ahead, in first place. He, too, could boast of owning an education, a diploma from Headmaster J. C. Landrum's school at Round Rock, the Greenwood Masonic Institute. Ira's niece Virgie had the teacher pegged:

> He was a very likable man and smart, but dreamy and impractical. He said there were only two books in the world— the Bible and Shakespeare. He would read from the latter in that sonorous voice of his and we would sit there fascinated, not in the least understanding what he was reading.... He had a mop of black, curly hair....[1]

An attendance roll would show Wes Hardin present—but just for one day. Wes wanted to graduate with his brother, Joe Hardin, who was one of Professor Landrum's regular students. John Wesley Hardin sat for the graduate's exam, passed it with flying colors, and then hotfooted out of Round Rock before any Texas Rangers put together the ABCs of his whereabouts. That little slipperiness had taken place before the Atens had migrated to Texas.[2]

The next chapter in Wes Hardin's dark little melodrama may have had as much impact on Ira Aten's life as the gunning down of Sam Bass. In a Pullman car parked on Florida's rails at Pensacola, Texas Ranger John B. Armstrong, assisted by Private John Riley "Jack" Duncan, a former Dallas detective, and a gutsy squadron of local authorities, caught Mr. John Wesley Hardin—after some shooting and a head thumping. The long-overdue arrest on August 23, 1877, had not only netted a prisoner, it served as a springboard jumping Texas Rangers to the forefront of national news coverage.[3] Lone Star State newspapermen were gleefully cranking the presses. Young Ira Aten's head had not been inattentively buried in the Hill Country's sand. Texas Rangers were catching accolades about scooping up the near-legendary Hardin, and later, more public praise regarding the zipping up of Sam Bass' nefariously chosen career.

Just short of his sixteenth birthday when the Round Rock business unwound, Ira Aten began toying with plans about his future as most adolescents would. Older brother Frank was too, but he really seemed more fascinated with bumblebees than he did with bullets or badmen.[4] There was nothing sissy about Frank Lincoln Aten. Off-handedly characterizing him as "the quiet stay-at-home type" might be a colossal misnomer if misinterpreted.[5] Frank had an uncanny appreciation of the outdoors, but more in the role of a caretaker than as a wild-eyed adventurer in search of death-defying excitement. Frank, too, along with Ira, shared an undying enthusiasm for history—preserving it for future generations' gift. Ira's two younger brothers, Cal and Eddie, well, their ideas at the time were aimed at the given moment, not where they might end up, or how they would get there. Boys will be boys, and they were boys.

Clearly one youthful idea of Ira's centered around becoming a Texas Ranger, and had been since that day Sam Bass met his Maker and a mortician.[6] While yet in his mid-teens it has been written Ira commenced qualifying himself for enlistment with the Texas Rangers. "Ira began to practice riding and shooting." Finding father's horses

The Austin Cunningham Aten family in Texas. Seated L to R: Calvin Grant Aten, Austin Cunningham Aten, Katherine Eveline Aten, and Edwin Dunlap Aten. Back row L to R: Austin Ira Aten, Clara Isabell Aten, Thomas Quinn Aten, Margaret Angelina Elizabeth Aten, and Franklin Lincoln Aten. *Courtesy Betty Aten.*

too tame, Ira begin topping-off other folks' ponies—for pay. Making a good story better, sometimes he would mount ones with real buck: cinch-binders, twisters, pile-drivers, or a belly-up sunfisher. Ira Aten, it is said, rode the wild ones—the widow makers. Whether thrown skyward or pitched hard to the ground, it made little difference to Ira. He would fast remount, screw himself down tight in the saddle, challenging the bucking beast to another round—at least so goes one colorful story. Austin Ira Aten, though still a kid, was earning his spurs, casually wiping dust from his threadbare britches, morphing into a tophand. Most of the bad broncos, if mythos is peppered with a slight shake of practicality, were more-likely-as-not just a cavvyard of crow-hoppers. An unbending declaration that "even the wildest mustang would acknowledge him as conqueror and master," was hyperbole reserved for a publicist, not words spoken by Ira. He was a dead shot, too. Charitably anointing young Ira Aten as "one of the best marksmen in Williamson County" is indeed high-caliber praise for a boy living in Travis County.[7] After bringing down a scampering whitetail deer, purportedly Ira smirked to a hunting buddy, "I could do the same with a running outlaw."[8] Perhaps he said it.[9] He did want to be a Texas Ranger.

The Texas Rangers, just like young Ira Aten, were on an inescapable march through formative years. Of course there had been hardened Texas volunteers tasked with chasing after raiding Indians for half a century or more. These ranging companies, on the whole, had valiantly prosecuted temporary assignments laid at their doorsteps. After a normally punishing pursuit, and occasionally a harrowing battle, these ranging fellows returned to hearths and homes, usually after short enlistments. There they again harnessed the mules and stumbled behind the plow, intent on eking a living from Mother Earth, though Mother Nature in a foul mood could donate her indifference.[10] Next time around, grab a rifle, saddle a horse, and chase after raiding Indians once again. For the politically goaded war with Mexico in the 1840s many volunteer Texans stepped up, toe to the mark, rifle in hand, two heavy pistols in splendidly rigged saddle scabbards—and at least one real big and real sharp Bowie knife. They teethed on a good row. For the U.S. Army's top-brass these hard-riding, fast-shooting, and no-nonsense human tigers were also known as Texas Rangers: For unsuspecting and uninitiated Mexican soldiers or Mexican nationals unwisely treading in their warpath, the gunmen later armed with the whopping knockdown power of .44 caliber Walker Colt's revolvers were simply *Los Diablos Tejanos*—The Texan Devils.[11]

Conclusively awarding Texas Rangers an official birthday in light of their rich heritage under the umbrellas of frontier volunteers and/ or as quasi-militia units, is a wooly undertaking. Although knowledgeable academics and grass-root historians still banter about it, a common consensus is elusive.[12] Early examples of Texans ranging with rifles at the ready, protecting their lately wrestled homeland, simply defy an oversimplified delineation. In point of fact, these fellows were an "irregular" assemblage of fighting Texans. They were of necessity fierce and fearless, and intermittently brutal, but certainly "distinct from the regular army and also from the militia."[13]

The Texas Rangers were institutionally birthed—as law enforcers—during May 1874, only two years before Ira and his family had relocated from Abingdon, Illinois. Subsequent to dissolution of the unpopular State Police, the Texas Legislature, now controlled by Democrats, answered the need to provide a modicum of protection for counties found at the western edge of settlement. America's military arm had not been flexing powerfully enough to suit most Texans. For many folks' way of thinking, though culturally insensitive, there was a remedy.[14] Political maneuvering by representatives in Austin's legislative hallways, could make right what politicians in Washington, D.C., were seemingly loathe to do: make the inept U.S. Army run those Indians out of Texas! The Fourteenth Legislative Session's lawmakers ratified Chapter LXVII, General Laws of the State of Texas, part of which was "An Act to provide for the protection of the Frontier of the State of Texas against the invasion of hostile Indians, Mexicans, or other marauding or thieving parties."[15]

Somewhat ambitiously the new legislation called for creating a sizeable corps of mounted gunmen. Collectively the outfit would be known as the Frontier Battalion, though that was an administrative designation rather than one formally decreed by Texas lawmakers.[16] Patterned after a military model, the command structure was sharply defined: Its composition, on paper, was to be of six 75-man companies, each headed by a hand-picked captain, and the whole force commanded by a battalion major answerable to the Adjutant General of Texas. The six companies, A through F, were to be highly mobile, a light cavalry so to speak. Units were to be strategically deployed in the western counties—on the frontier—forming a fluid north/south line stretching from the Red River to the Rio Grande.[17] Answering to the company captain would be two lieutenants, who in turn held oversight of the non-commissioned officers and enlisted personnel. Likely recruits, in addition to a good attitude and no wife, had to furnish a horse—a sound one. The prospective private reporting for duty was expected to also bring with him an "Army-size" six-shooter, but if he did not personally own one, the state would give him a Colt's .45 and dock his first quarterly pay for the favor. The same would be true if he was in want of a carbine, a Sharps .50 caliber.[18]

Since the companies were expected to be kept "actively employed during their term of service.... living in the field rather than town.... the men were issued an abundant ration of bread, beef, coffee, and sugar & salt" for themselves and feed for their horses.[19] The state would also spring for all the ammunition they could possibly shoot at Indians. That was the hard core of their job description: scout for sign that Indians had made an incursion into the settlements, then chase them and kill them. Recapturing stolen horses and terrified captives, if possible, would be a secondary goal within the broader policy. In addition, the Frontier Battalion was assigned another task, a duty many early day Rangers disdained, but they were legislatively charged and had taken an oath: "Each officer of the battalion and of the companies herein provided for shall have all the powers of a peace officer..."[20] Although the battalion's scouting record is generally commendable with respect to rigorous campaigns against marauding Comanches and Kiowas, it is this latter stipulation that would be of particular interest to young Ira Aten. The Aten family had departed Illinois in 1876, just three months after George Armstrong Custer had given up the ghost, sorrowing the US Army's 7th Cavalry, and distressing a flabbergasted nation. But, by the time fourteen-year-old Ira had arrived at his new Lone Star home, any serious threat of an Indian attack in the Texas Hill Country was for-the-most-part nil. Despite sarcastic mumbling and grumbling of the past, the majority of Texans knew Uncle Sam had flexed his muscles—powerfully and unmercifully in the Panhandle Country. The strategically and successfully prosecuted Red River War of 1874–1875 had broken the Comanches' and their allies' backs, although in far West Texas campaigning against recalcitrant Apaches would yet prove a troublesome chore. Since its inception in May 1874 the Frontier Battalion's front office management staff, field officers, noncoms, and enlisted men had been on a fast track of transition: They were now lawmen.

And too, collectively, they were a bureaucracy—with paperwork. Major John B. Jones, the battalion commander, was a stickler for written reports and accountability.[21] Aside from reams of back and forth correspondence of a general nature, each company captain was duty-bound to submit a "Monthly Return." It was not a new concept. Liberally conceding Texas Rangers the earliest birthday, if that hypothesis is evoked, likewise would reveal a Monthly Return of Lieutenant Moses Morrison, dated June 5, 1823. This Monthly Return identifies by name the ten stalwarts ranging along the Texas Gulf Coast, near the mouth of the Colorado River. It was the province of Karankawas Indians, sometime hostile, sometimes cannibalistic. An inventory of the company's armament is provided in this remarkable document. Nine of the men had long-rifles, one a musket. Should any Karankawas have issued an unwelcome invitation, Lt. Morrison's company, in the aggregate, were in possession of 162 "Charges of Powder" and 162 "Balls."[22] At such an early date geographical intelligence was also vital, and Moses Morrison faithfully recorded: "and I find the water is very shallow not Exceeding 2½ feet water in the deepest part and no fresh water to be found under the distance of 15 miles from the Mouth and no timber to be got Sufficient for building a fortification Sufficient for our protection. I therefore have thought it naught advisable to Establish at the Colorado landing—there has not any vessels arrived here as yet."[23] Fifty-one years later, as would be expected, the Frontier Battalion's Monthly Returns would be much broader in scope, providing not only technically factual data but, as well, an insight into the everyday lives and episodes specific to particular Texas Rangers.

If Ira Aten intended on sculpting himself after a Texas Ranger, the model would have been a lawman, not an Indian fighter. He had come along too late to catch them in the dimness of that light.[24] Those memories were but flickering campfire tales—mostly true. Boys typically find a measure of inconvenience with bridging the generational divide. Ira was no different. Ira may have dreamed day and night about enlisting, but he had to kill a few more rabbits and deer—and years. Ira didn't have to stand still, though.

And he didn't have to be ignorant—bookwise or otherwise. The Austin C. Aten brood attended school, formally and informally—and church—religiously. Parson Aten's whip cracked lessons of tough love. Another fellow, a grown up, was an area personality and he, too, was devout—apart from being a bigwig cowman. Dudley H. Snyder and his younger brother, J. W., had early on come to Texas from Mississippi.[25] Ira Aten, yet an adolescent, was impressed and seems to hint he actually knew the brothers, remarking when he alighted in Texas during October 1876, "the Snyders were in their heyday as trail drivers—big trail drivers."[26] Dudley and J. W., who had profitably trailed herds north during numerous cattle shipping seasons, had whopping caches of good stories to tell, and a storehouse of choice advice. Mr. Dudley Snyder delighted the most, it seems, from passing on a light touch of cow country wisdom, meaningful knowledge well beyond the simplicity of semantics: "A man never makes money in selling a horse—the money is made in buying it."[27]

Something that young Ira Aten wasn't buying was whisky. Williamson County's wives and mothers may not have been the championing out-front voices, but be assured they were heard. A reform movement was underway in 1878. A temperance society was clamoring for prohibiting alcohol consumption in Williamson County. Throughout the county local option elections were slated: the preachers and teachers and teetotalers vs. the tavern owners, bartenders, and spirituous liquor connoisseurs. Prohibitionists were headstrong with beliefs that "carousing, brawling and shooting spawned around open saloons."[28] Not everyone was so bothered— they just wanted to wet their dry whistles. "The war waged on. The Temperance League members were increasing their numbers, and many preachers condemned the sale of liquor in Round Rock."[29] Highlighting which camp Reverend Austin Cunningham Aten belonged to is pointless. And, although there has yet to surface any solid documentary proof, the good minister must have been appalled after learning that the Cocklebur Barn, a tavern, was actually just inside the Travis County line on the road between Pflugerville and Round Rock.[30] Aten's homestead was in Travis County, south of the Williamson County line, near Pflugerville. Sermons and sour-mash do not mix well. A myriad of Williamson County folks, a few on the sly, were making short excursions, bellying-up to the Cocklebur's bar, and skipping church too.[31]

What would have grabbed Ira's notice, more so than some brouhaha about booze, was the scuffling going on to build a suitable jail at Round Rock. Lawmen latching on to Sam Bass had been an eye-opener. If he had not been shot, they would have been forced to chain him to a mulberry tree. There was no dungeon at Round Rock. Of course there was the county jail at Georgetown, an improvement over an upside-down Conestoga wagon that had housed early-day prisoners, but it was at the county seat, not Round Rock.[32] Round Rock folks wanted their own lockup, a city jail. Quickly plans were made, and in the alley between Liberty Hill and Georgetown Avenue—behind the Otto Reinke building—a triple-wall, fourteen by sixteen, single room, wooden jail was hurriedly but stoutly built. It was not a hotel: "The only allowance for a person's convenience was a small hole in the floor, and a single mattress."[33] Austere as it may be, there is something intriguing about a jailhouse, especially to certain boys and grown men, those inclined to keep the peace. Perhaps, and it cannot rise above that caveat, Ira Aten began seeing himself in the role of a lawman, a well mounted Texas Ranger, six-shooter at the hip, Winchester within reach. There would be, Ira Aten may well have mused, an incredible feeling, quite exciting—personally rewarding—about riding into town, a handcuffed badman in tow, bowing to the public's exaltation after depositing a prisoner with the local sheriff.

The stunningly attractive Imogen (sans the typical e) Boyce. She would play a significant role in Ira Aten's personal and professional policing life's story. *Courtesy Jeri and Gary Boyce Radder.*

Another item that seemed pretty neat was that good-looking girl going to school named Imogen Boyce. She was smart, spiffy, a little spunky, and always smelled springtime sweet, even in dead winter, sitting in front of the classroom's pot-bellied stove. Little Miss Boyce was a charmer, a charismatic personality bubbling with allure. That girl might bear watching. Austin Ira Aten was not blind or a dummy; Imogen Boyce was a fair maiden.[34]

What was not fair, however, was hard-driven home that summer of 1880 when Ira was just two months shy of his eighteenth birthday: Texas Rangers were not bulletproof. On the third day of July in faraway Presidio County, a few miles north of the Rio Grande, while on horseback patrol Sergeant Ed Sieker and a troop of Texas Rangers

caught sight of a notorious band of outlaws. It was the gang nominally headed by Jesse Evans, a certifiable ne'er-do-well and killer.
On the steep side of a rocky and jagged Big Bend country mountain
the lawmen locked up with the desperadoes for a desperate gunplay.
Luckily during the blistering exchange of Winchester bullets an outlaw paid the supreme penalty for guys of that ilk; unluckily Texas
Ranger George R. "Red" Bingham did, too. As bad luck would have it,
foul weather prevented Sergeant Sieker and his inconsolable Texas
Ranger comrades from removing Red Bingham's body to town for a
suitable burial—not after the downpour had stopped, not beneath
July's sweltering sun: "Bingham's body wouldn't admit of moving far,
so we buried him on the side of the road, and our little squad showed
him all the respect we could, we formed and fired three volleys over
his grave, and with saddened hearts we wound through mountain
passes to [Fort] Davis, arriving safely with our prisoners."[35]

The year 1880 had not been a good year for Texas peace officers.
Texas Ranger Bingham's death had been preceded by two others. At
Sherman just below the Red River, city policeman Samuel D. Ball had
been fatally shot down inside the Red Light Saloon. In the coastal
county of South Texas near Sinton, the sheriff of San Patricio County,
Hugh Timon, had suffered mortal gunshot wounds at the hand of
Andrew Hart, a local troublemaker he was attempting to arrest.[36] For
certain folks, the possibility of action, a flashing dalliance with danger, has an inexplicable magnetic pull, irresistibly drawing them in.
Austin Ira Aten was on the march. He was a young man teetering at
the precipice of a career: A yet wet-behind-the-ears fellow bent on
becoming a Texas Ranger.

By most accounts the Reverend Aten was hoping Ira would follow in his agricultural footsteps, not by becoming a circuit-riding
preacher, but by tilling the soil as a farmer and/or becoming a bona
fide livestock man—a cowman.[37] Not a cowboy. Cowboys did not
own any cattle. Cowboys drew monthly wages from those that held
title to the herds, the astute fellows with brands registered at the
courthouses, the cowmen.[38] Parson Aten's thoughts are not indistinct: "My father didn't oppose me to join the Rangers so much. He
knew I was going some place. He knew there would be some restric-
tions, some discipline. He was afraid for me to be with the cowboys.
There was no discipline with them at all, you know."[39] Still, Preacher
Aten was not blind to the wants of young men, especially Ira—at
least on one occasion.

Christmas for the Aten clan was usually celebrated at church. That was where the Christmas tree stood, mysteriously wrapped presents strewn beneath. Impatient children, raring to go, would be sitting on pins and needles waiting for their name to be called. Then, with anticipation immeasurable they would briskly walk down the aisle, rescue their gift from obscurity, and take it back to their seat for an unwrapping.[40] Christmas of 1880 would notably standout in Ira's mind. The present was unique, as well as practical. Reverend Aten had made an extra effort for eighteen-year-old Ira. His gift was a Bowie knife, handmade by J. Rodgers & Sons, an extraordinarily nice gift in and of itself. This knife was even more special. On the leather sheath's brass coupling was an engraved inscription: *"To: Ira from Daddy, Christmas 1880."*[41] It was the perfect gift for a boy bent toward becoming a lawman. Ira Aten was apparently dead-set on wearing a badge and carrying a six-shooter. He would not be dissuaded. Even if he had to wait two years Ira would give that Texas Ranger business a try. That is, if somebody could pull a string.

Emmett White, lawman and future Travis County Sheriff, personally knew the Austin C. Aten family, and favorably so. He would be more than pleased to write a formal letter of recommendation to the Texas Adjutant General, Wilburn Hill King. Mr. White had stroke

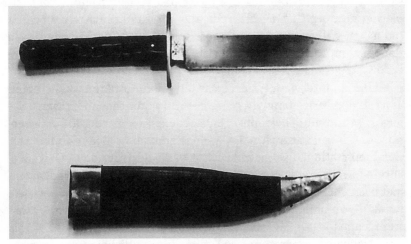

A first-rate and serial numbered J. Rodgers & Sons Bowie knife and sheath given by Reverend Austin Cunningham Aten to son Ira. Hand-engraved inscription on the leather sheath's metal coupling reads: "To Ira from Daddy, Christmas 1880." *Courtesy Robert W. Stephens.*

enough to get him to the threshold. After that, well, twenty-year-old Austin Ira Aten would simply have to sell himself if he really wanted to fill any vacancy on the Texas Ranger's muster rolls.[42] Trying to shed a somewhat baby-faced appearance, Aten "let his sideburns down....to look a little older."[43]

Making a good impression on the Adjutant General would not be any heartburn for Mr. Austin Ira Aten. The blue-eyed young man stood five-feet, seven and one-half inches tall, having a somewhat ruddy complexion, but was overall considered quite handsome. He was clean-cut and well groomed, articulate and polite. And, too, he owned a clean slate as far as any arrest record was concerned. Not all of the Old West's celebrated lawmen could make that chaste claim. In fact, some high-profile peace officers of the era had a not insignificant chain of shameless and inexcusable brushes with the law. Some had even been run out of towns and territories. While not necessarily obdurately puritanical, Ira's upbringing had been strait-laced and stiff-necked, notably in regards to being a "saloon rounder" or a "gambling den habitué." He was no innocent "Sunday school boy," by any stretch, but he was unable to "see any good in such actions" as carousing and consorting with hard drinking dregs. In Ira's mind the downfall of many a man, criminals in particular, could "be traced to the saloon."[44] Perhaps on these matters of character, Ira's rating would be practical but wholesome. For a youthful fellow contemplating a career chasing brigands and bandits he may have been a tad naive. Wilburn King would not hold that against anyone. Texas Ranger companies were loaded with "rookies." Everyone, even Rangers, started somewhere at sometime.

After an interview, twenty-year-old Austin Ira Aten was accepted as a salaried Texas Ranger, a private—$30 a month with kitchen privileges—a communal campfire. Subsequent to swearing in by Governor John Ireland at Austin, Ira was assigned to Company D. The unit was then stationed seven miles west of Uvalde, Uvalde County, seventy-odd miles west of San Antonio. The Company D headquarters had been christened Camp King, and Ira was to report at once. Ira's family—parents, brothers and sisters—did not think he'd stay away from home too terribly long, chiding "he will be back before the year is out." Ira would have rather "died" than quit, mulishly intent on making a good show. He was welded to the notion of being a Ranger.[45]

Many folks knew that rawhide "once hardened was almost as tough as iron." That piece of dried cow hide could handily be used

Ira's youngest sister, Clara "Belle" Aten, married George Bachman, the couple eventually settling in Goodletsville, Tennessee, just north of Nashville. *Courtesy Betty Aten.*

to mend a broken wheel, tie corral posts together, repair a gun-stock, sole a boot, fashion a whip, or make hinges for doors and gates. Everyone knew—some by necessity—that rawhide was durable and tough. Those same folks, especially those outside the Lone Star, often characterized "Texans as tough as rawhide."[46] Although transplanted, Austin Ira Aten was a Texan. He would prove himself tough—tough as rawhide. Over time, working as a seasoned Texas lawman, and making it through some "real tight places" Mr. Ira Aten would harden—toughen—molding himself into a Rawhide Ranger.

Though it may somewhat depreciate a good story, Ira had not been singled out or recruited due to alone having talents Texas Rangers were in need of. Also reporting for duty with Ira on April 26, 1883, were newly sworn-in privates John Case, George W. Forbes, who owned an interval of prior Ranger service, and J. A. Puckett.[47] Company D's captain, thirty-eight-year-old Lamartine Pemberton "Lam" Sieker, had not sought out the new recruits; he merely welcomed personnel sent to him by the Texas Rangers' front office. AG King had hand-picked and forwarded this quartet of rookies.[48]

When the Frontier Battalion came into existence, its authorized manpower strength had been 75 Rangers for each of the six companies. Such a legislative proposal sounded great—on paper. Financially it was unworkable: the state of Texas owned land, lots of it, but had no overflowing strongbox of hard cash. Consequently, in order to meet regularly reccurring payrolls, reductions in force had been adopted as the solution. When Ira Aten made his appearance at Camp King during the spring of 1883, Company D was authorized but twenty positions in the aggregate, officers and enlisted men.[49]

Logically it may be assumed, the four new Ranger privates had to undergo and deferentially endure an indoctrination session. Perhaps more so than any Texas Ranger captain of the Frontier Battalion era, Captain Sieker personally believed and infused in his men a way of thinking; they were a breed apart. Fellows camping with him were not just lawmen, they were special. For the men of Company D, the *esprit de corps*—the camaraderie—the gloriously instilled idea of upholding or trying to uphold an honorable tradition flowered at his insistence. He left not an iota of doubt, there was "a sense of duty" a true Ranger should have.[50] Lam Sieker saw no merit in keeping a man in state service just because he was bound by an enlistment agreement. If a fellow wanted out, so be it: "He ceases to be a good Ranger, for the reason he lacks interest and does only what he is compelled to do, and does not do his duty from a sense of duty as a good Ranger should."[51] Ira Aten and his newly hired friends could be good Rangers, or they could be ex-Rangers. Captain Sieker was sure about that—and so were they.

A good Texas Ranger needed a good gun—or guns. Apparently Ira and his new pals had reported for duty sans any armament whatsoever. On April 26 they were each issued "1 Win Carbine & Colt's Pistol, 1 Win Scabbard & Pistol belt & Holster."[52] The Colt's .45 revolver was the previously mentioned Single Action Army model. Forward thinking and continually improving firearms technology had allowed Texas Rangers to discard the single shot Sharps in favor of the improved Winchester model 1873, a multi-shot lever-action carbine.[53] The four rookie Texas Rangers could gladly reimburse the state for their issued arsenal over time, deductions made from their quarterly pay.[54] There would be absolutely no charge for the 150 rounds of ammunition divvied up between them.[55] Company D had plenty of Winchester cartridges on hand, 1,860 rds. to be exact.[56]

What may be said of the other three young men's previous living arrangements is nebulous, but Austin Ira Aten had been living in a house, for the times, a reasonably nice house. Camp King was an out-door camp. Company D's personnel were living in tents, and they were in need of replacement. A citizens' inspection committee had con-demned all but two of Company D's nine wall tents as "unserviceable and worthless."[57] Captain Sieker was near pleading with the Frontier Battalion's quartermaster at Austin: "As per request I enclose a state-ment of two citizens of Uvalde Co. as to the condition of the property I wish condemned. And I would respectfully ask that the tents be for-warded at once as the men are without shelter in case of rain...."[58] In this particular instance headquarters was on the ball. By the middle of May 1883, Company D Rangers could lay their blankets beneath a canvas canopy—four to the tent.[59] By the time Ira began kicking around a Texas Ranger camp, many of the mundane everyday chores had been passed off to a non-Ranger: Each Frontier Battalion com-pany had a teamster on the roster and, in addition to caring for the unit's mules (Company D had seven), the hired laborer was to "also make himself generally useful in such other work as may be required of him...."[60] So, with a not inconsiderable amount of leisure time on their hands, Ira and his fellow Company D Rangers could enjoy a few of the pleasures provided by a camp squarely planted in the gorgeous Texas Hill Country. Fishing, hunting, swimming in the Nueces River, racing horses, shooting guns, and playing practical jokes were but all in a day's work. There was, too, another niggling side of the coin—police work. Ira Aten had enlisted, perhaps, if anyone had asked, to benevolently serve the great state of Texas, selflessly protecting her people and property. That was a stock answer then, and a good one now. Misleading? Legitimate career lawmen are inescapably drawn to the dodgy game like fireflies to the darkest night, bloodhounds to the scent, or kids to peppermint sticks—it is instinctive. Yes, Ira was now a Texas Ranger, but he was raw meat.

Chapter 3

"We'll do the shooting"

Upon becoming a Texas Ranger, Ira had bitten from a hard plug; now it would be Captain Sieker's turn to see if he could chew. There would be no manual to study. There would be no end-of-semester test to take. The training program was straightforward: Ride with more experienced Texas Rangers, young as they were, learning the job from their tutelage. They were also full of advice, of a personal nature. Private Forbes, "who drank and smoked and everything else that went with the Frontier," proffered his opinion: "Now, Aten, you haven't got any bad habits and I am going to give you a little advice. Now, don't drink, whatever you do, don't drink. Look at me. Smoking is a useless habit. Don't bother anybody much. Just one of those useless habits. You don't smoke and I would advise you not to do it." Even one of the experienced noncoms cautioned: "Aten, don't take up the habits that we have, that can't do you any good. I see where it has been my downfall all my life. I might have been Governor of Texas if I hadn't gambled and drank."[1]

Ira's apprenticeship would take place in the saddle. Texas Ranger peers would be his harshest critics. He would pass or fail with their verdict. Living with them twenty-four and seven, riding through hardships absent a complaint, and sometimes charging through horror's doorway would furnish *compadres* with ample truths for an evaluation. Fooling them would be near hopeless; fooling the big boss next to impossible. Captain Lam Sieker had eyes and ears, and tough standards. He would not allow acrimony or incompetence or cowardliness in his Company D camp. A good Ranger could stay; a bad Ranger could decamp for parts wherever.

Before having been at Camp King even a month, Ira Aten personally witnessed Captain Sieker's down-to-earth management style: "Private W. T. McCown's condition being such that he thinks his life depends on his going immediately to Hot Springs, I have this day given him a discharge from the service...."[2] On April 28, 1883, a physician at Eagle Pass, Maverick County, Doctor G. M. Devereaux, had

Ira Aten at age 20, about the time he became a Company D
Texas Ranger reporting to an outdoor camp in Uvalde County,
west of San Antonio. *Courtesy Jeri and Gary Boyce Radder.*

handwritten AG King that Texas Ranger J. D. Coopwood's syphilitic
condition had "been treated and cured," but that he had not been
paid the $25 fee for rendering medical services and medicine.[3] Not
surprisingly, less than a month later Captain Sieker updated Texas
Ranger headquarters. He had discharged Private Coopwood, "he no
longer being fit for the service...."[4]

Directly south of Uvalde County lay under-populated Zavala
County. Although painstakingly surveyed and formally named,
Zavala County had not been officially organized at the time Ira Aten
swore an oath with the Texas Rangers.[5] There was, then, no county
government—no sheriff, no law. Zavala County's line did not actually touch the Rio Grande, but practically speaking it was on the

Mexican border, close enough to cause heartburn for Company D. Zavala County was cow country. Off the beaten path as she was, the county was well suited to mask bad work of badmen—a cow thieving mob.

One fellow in particular, John Bowles, had "been making a wholesale steal." He and his crew of "Mexican hands" had honest folks in Zavala County scared out of their boots, afraid to act, afraid to even "go on his range."[6] Local citizens, few as there were, could do nothing. They requested Texas Rangers be sent to deliver them from evil.[7]

Mr. Bowles may have been big and bad, but the Texas Rangers of Company D sallied forth onto his sprawling ranch lands, gathered thirty-two head of cattle with "blotched" brands and returned them to citizens who after inspection swore to rightful ownership. Carefully intent on walking legality's line—an illustration of changing times—Captain Sieker sent one of the owners with a Texas Ranger escort to Eagle Pass (Maverick County for judicial jurisdiction) where the victim signed an official Complaint: A warrant issued for the arrest of John Bowles. While waiting for the warrant, other unsmiling Company D men captured twenty head of "Wet" stock supposed to be from about Piedras Negras, on the Mexican side, arresting Tobe Sproull who, caught red-handed, readily admitted guilt. Finally with legal papers in hand the Texas Rangers searched for, located, and arrested Bowles. Then they rode the backtrack to Eagle Pass with their prisoners, turning them over to an appreciative sheriff. During another Zavala County sweep the Texas Rangers of Company D swooped down on W. W. Burton and Joe Cornet, arresting both for Theft of Cattle. The Maverick County jail's census count was increased by two. Before they were through on this "general roundup" the ten men of Company D, assisted by eight men from Captain Joe Shely's Company F and approximately forty local citizens, would seize 131 head of stolen and blotched cattle.[8]

Captain Lam Sieker continually kept scouts (patrols) in the field, particularly concentrating efforts in Zavala County, rounding up burnt cattle and returning them to their rightful owners. At this stage in Ira Aten's newfound career as a Texas Ranger his name is absent in scouting reports and the Monthly Returns. Not finding Aten's name yet in print does not mean he was not a participant. Normally only one Texas Ranger was specifically named, even though more than a handful rode alongside. For illustrative purposes one such entry

Although snapped prior to Ira Aten actually becoming a Texas Ranger, this is an image of Company D Rangers, the unit Ira was assigned to after enlisting in the Frontier Battalion. These doughty lawmen are geared up for a horseback chase and war—or a traveling photographer. *Courtesy Research Center, Texas Ranger Hall of Fame and Museum.*

is herein cited: "June 2: Captain Sieker and ten men made scout to Bowles pasture in Zavalla [*sic*] County to assist stockmen in recovering stolen cattle. Found and returned to owners 42 head. Out 8 days and marched 300 miles."[9]

Undoubtedly at this point, still classed a rookie, Ira's name may have been nonexistent in recoverable administrative documents, but it is reasonable to presume he was doing his part. Riding hard and learning the mechanics of making an arrest—safely: How to professionally manage self-control and not impetuously give in to fight-on-the-brain issues. On the continuum of necessary and reasonable force, gunplay was the last resort. Killing someone was not too difficult, but often an overreach, a usurpation of legal authority. Competently making an arrest absent injury—or headlines—was the challenge. Newsmen or historians hardly write of a good arrest, but always key on one turned sour. Ira was taught another cold hard fact of sound police work: He represented the rule of law, but was not the law, only a cog in its slowly grinding wheel. There were magistrates, grand juries, district attorneys and district judges—even Supreme Courts—each with their own parts to play if the criminal justice system was to work at all—for all. After he matriculates into a journeyman Texas Ranger, finding Ira Aten's name in correspondence of an official nature will become commonplace. Likewise, although it falls outside the realm of absoluteness, it would be safe to bet Ira Aten was there—or heard about the captain's next issuance of discipline, that zero tolerance for whining: "Hammer made the following statement, upon which I discharged him, viz That he was dissatisfied and did not think he could faithfully discharge his duty and a whole string of complaints about his mistreatment."[10] There can also be little doubt Ira Aten willingly pitched in after the pronouncement that Company D's camp was to be relocated. Captain Sieker had made the command decision to move camp five miles southeast of Uvalde, advantaging himself of a better quality and quantity of fresh water in the Leona River. Company D's new headquarters was publicly dubbed Camp Leona.[11]

Still, even with a base camp, Texas Rangers from Company D were working a wide-spread swath of real estate. In the broadest historical context the raging hostility between cattlemen and sheepmen has been much overblown.[12] Nevertheless there were horrid instances of violence. For a short time a hot little war was breaking forth in Hamilton County, quite a distance northeast of Camp Leona. A hundred sheep had been mercilessly clubbed to death while the blindfolded caretaker was being held hostage. Nearby at the Carlton community, a sheepman was physically assaulted and his flock reduced in number by club-wielding thugs. Another incident erupted when a sheep raiser refused to move his flock off of a water hole during the severe drought of 1883. Gunfire exploded when sheep owner J. H. Langston from Dublin in Erath County tried to shield his flock: He fell to the ground nastily wounded.[13]

Whether or not Ira Aten was part of the detachment goes unrecorded, but on the fourth day of September 1883, twenty-seven-year-old Corporal Benjamin Dennis "B. D." Lindsey and five Texas Ranger privates from Company D were dispatched to Hamilton County "to keep the peace between cattle and sheep men."[14] Straight as a ramrod, the six-foot four-inch Lindsey was not a man to foolishly monkey with: Quiet and soft spoken most of the time, but when Hell popped B. D. was a fighting machine, nerveless, and unquestionably very courageous.[15] Captain Sieker had confidence Corporal Lindsey could settle the hash of would-be troublemakers, and he did. Making Texas Ranger presence known throughout the section, he capably interviewed warring parties, friendly but firm. None questioned his no-nonsense demeanor. None were desirous of testing his grit. Ranger Lindesy was no shoot-'em-up lawman. His job was to keep the peace, not disrupt it. After not being on the ground too long, Corporal Lindsey updated Captain Sieker, posting a second letter from Hamilton, Texas.

> I have just returned from Carlton & Hico, investigating the late troubles in that section.... I sent to Bosque Co. and escorted the man Reilly spoken of in my first letter, to this place. He made complaint against two men who he claims to have recognized the night he was assaulted, these men are said to be of the very best Citizens of the Co., one a deacon in the church, they have been arrested and put under bond.... To the best of my judgment there is nothing here to warrant our continuance....[16]

The reason for mentioning the Hamilton County troubles is uncomplicated. Although it is not categorically provable Private Ira Aten was along on this assignment, it clearly demonstrates that small detachments of Texas Rangers—often led by a noncom—were being utilized for investigative and/or peace keeping missions. Except in extraordinary circumstances, the operational model for manpower deployment had altered drastically after cessation of Indian raids. It was no longer the norm for Texas Rangers to operate at full company strength. The myth of one riot, one Ranger, can be dispelled, but practically speaking in most instances a few Rangers could handle most situations.

Private Phillip Cuney "P. C." Baird wanted to go it alone, however, at least long enough to sweeten his nest egg. Twenty-two-year-old Ranger Baird (a future Mason County Sheriff) had developed, so he figured, some hot news. Someone had told him where Frank Jackson, the Sam Bass gang member eluding capture at Round Rock, was hiding. The fugitive was not in the state of Texas, and Ranger Baird was asking for leave long enough to reel him in. By the way, he wanted to know, was there an outstanding reward and who was offering it? If AG King would also see that he was deputized as a federal marshal it would be helpful, too. Allegedly, Jackson was hanging out with two more outlaws, one of whom had earlier killed a man in Williamson County. Ranger Baird could not remember that guy's name, though. If King could hurriedly respond to his letter, he could continue with his plan: "sending a man to him [Jackson] so as to have all things ready before I start after him which it will take some time to arrange, before I shall want to start."[17] It seems AG King was not as anxious as Private Baird. Scribbled across the top of the request was King's reply: "Answer him that I Know nothing of any reward. That the matter is too uncertain & difficult for his request to be granted at this time."[18]

Ira Aten, with three quarters of a year behind him as a Ranger, was not purposing he be granted any holiday leave that Christmas season of '83. He was no longer a rookie. Ira had toed the mark, watching, listening, and learning. Subsequent to a grand New Year's celebration, Ranger Private Austin Ira Aten could expect independent assignments—he had proved himself worthy. Sadly, perhaps, a fellow law enforcing comrade had not. Private W. H. Elliot, a Ranger of but three months' standing was not making the boss a happy camper: Captain Lam Sieker discharged him for "worthlessness."[19]

On the eleventh day of January 1884, Private Ira Aten, traveling solo, left Company D's Camp Leona intending to nab a suspected thief. Tom Rickerson was reportedly riding a valuable hot-blooded horse stolen in Llano County. Whether suspect Rickerson was hard to trail, tricky, or a totally bungling rascal is irrelevant for an overview of Texas Ranger history. For Ranger Ira Aten's story, nevertheless, it is meaningful. Ira finally tracked his man down at Taylor, northeast of Round Rock in Williamson County—not too far from Pflugerville. It was Ira Aten's very first single-handed arrest. With prisoner in tow Ira began the trip back, via a sojourn through Travis County—and likely a fast stopover at home. The unforeseen break would have been too good to waste: a homegrown Texas Ranger, six-shooter stuffed into a fancy Mexican-loop scabbard, and a securely manacled crook in custody: A knight in shining armor, dashing and debonair. Ira was no exception; he had signed on with the Texas Rangers for a life of "adventure" and "romance" and to impress girls, hopefully someday rescuing a damsel in distress.[20] Which twenty-one-year-old Texas Ranger could not massage that ego-bumping scenario? Maybe for safekeeping and an overnight visit, he even ensconced Tom Rickerson in the Round Rock jail before moving back over to Llano County. At any rate, Private Ira Aten soon turned his prisoner over to Sheriff George W. Shaw, returning to Camp Leona following an absence of nine days, after doggedly traveling 450 miles.[21]

Hardly had Ira returned to camp before it was time to move Company D—again. Owing to incessant fence cuttings and brand blotching, Ira's team was ordered north of Uvalde, 130 miles or so, to Menardville, Menard County. There near Peg Leg Crossing on the

Taylor, Williamson County, Texas. Ira Aten made his first unassisted Texas Ranger arrest at Taylor, not too far from home. *Courtesy Taylor Public Library.*

San Saba River, Captain Sieker established Company D's new nerve center, Camp Johnson.[22]

There was plenty of work. Captain Sieker reported to AG King that he found "considerable excitement here over the cattle burning in McCollouch county, and the citizens here are very glad we have come in. I will attend a big stock meeting at Brady City on the 5th of March as trouble is anticipated. There is said to be 2000 head of blotched cattle on the range here, or rather in McCollouch Co."[23] After making the meeting, Captain Sieker reported that most of the area's honest stockmen wanted action. They passed a resolution condemning thievery in general, brand blotching in particular, furthermore pledging that "they would try the law, but cattle burning must stop."[24] By month's end Captain Sieker was expecting a temporary lull in the cowmen's hollering for blood, as his boys had arrested Tom Page and Tom Anderson, charging them with Theft of Cattle. Not content, the Company D Rangers had put Sherman Dorris and Bud Moore, suspected cow thieves, on the run. They were hiding, not stealing.[25] Yet, Captain Sieker was somewhat worried. Concerned that once the April roundup had started, "and the cattlemen see the extent of the burning and blotching business," the smoldering bitterness would ignite without warning, followed by bloodshed—and extralegal justice below stout overhanging limbs.[26]

On one roundup occasion, according to Ira, Captain Sieker and his Texas Rangers had to intervene between warring factions lining up to do battle, about twenty men to the side. The banter escalated to some downright mean taunting, profusely punctuated with profanity. Hair-triggers and hot tempers were at full cock. Impervious to personal danger, and while Ira and other Texas Rangers looked on, Captain Lam Sieker positioned himself between the arguing cowmen and cowboys. His message was clear: "If there is any shooting to be done, men, we will do it." The roundup continued, no one daring to trade profit for peril. Cowmen, through a negotiated agreement with Captain Sieker and his men's rulings, complied with turning over burnt cattle or those not plainly marked to the Texas Rangers of Company D. Rightful ownership of calves, mavericks, and blotch-branded cows could be decided later.[27]

Although there were no doubt strays unaccounted for, at conclusion of the general roundup Texas Rangers were vigilantly herding between five and six hundred head of cattle, those that could not be positively or satisfactorily identified. Sometimes irate cowmen questioned the correctness of a Ranger's cut, but with twenty state-paid *pistoleros* covering his back, decisions were not overruled—not by a cowman. After advertising in the newspaper that the sequestered cattle would be auctioned, a sale took place, the proceeds deposited in the county's bank account. "Through this action many rustlers lost a whole winter's work and whined mightily."[28]

Private Ira Aten would not have to, at this point, worry himself with burnt cattle. He caught a relatively dangerous assignment. Not only that, for this work he would take the lead, showing J. L. Bargsley, a Texas Ranger with two months' service, the ropes. On April 12, 1884, Aten and Bargsley left Camp Johnson, destination the Devil's River country of Crockett County.[29] They were leading a mule, thirty days' rations, cast iron cookware, and extra ammunition carefully lashed onto its cross-buck pack saddle. Traveling slowly, leisurely marveling at the countryside, the pair of exploratory Rangers worked their way southwest, 100 miles or so. Geography had progressively changed before their eyes, until they found themselves in the broken Devil's River country marked by many "rough, ugly draws."[30]

Today the section would be in Sutton County (Sonora), but then it was Crockett County with judicial attachment to Kinney County, all courthouse business taking place at the county seat, Brackettville.[31] Then or now it is still rough country. Privates Aten and Bargsley were to meet up with a Kinney County deputy sheriff, and protect him while he probed the hidden canyons and far-flung ranches for would-be tax dodgers. A few, it was near rightly supposed, would have no qualm about standing toe to toe, shotgun in hand, saying "Hell-No" to a tax man. Of the few residents, most were squatting on public land, but the value of their livestock was taxable. Generally they were "dead set against paying taxes of any kind," and a dead taxman would hardly be missed in their out-of-the-way neighborhood. During 1883, they had boldly run the tax collector out of the Devil's River country, empty sack in hand, but glad to be alive.[32]

Lam Sieker's selecting Ira for the task, from a personnel management perspective, might suggest four favorable dynamics the captain measured: Private Ira Aten did not require day by day supervision; Private Ira Aten was gutsy; Private Ira Aten was honest, trustworthy enough to handle and guard tax-payers' monies; and Private Ira Aten would set a fine example, making a first-rate training officer for Private Bargsley. Captain Lam Sieker was not wishy-washy; in his mind it was cut and dried: a man was either "a good Ranger" or he wasn't. Ira Aten was "a good Ranger."

After meeting with the deputy sheriff who had donned his hat as a tax-collector, Privates Aten and Bargsley made the rounds, providing six-shooter security. For a rancher the choice although not palatable, was very simple. Pay up, or forfeit cattle to the county. Rangers Aten and Bargsley had no dog in the hunt. Their only stake in the game was to put the kibosh on any thoughts of a killing. Though grudgingly, after gauging the strength of mind in the two Rangers' unsmiling faces and eyeing Winchesters resting across pommels of their saddles, the heretofore tax dodgers protested no more. They forked over their ten- and twenty-dollar gold pieces to the buckboard-driving deputy. Then it was on to the next ranch. For nearly a month the two Rangers meandered through the region doing what they were paid to do, providing protection for the deputy and his bag full of coins—between four and five thousand dollars.[33]

Now riding jaded horses, Ira and his trainee started for the Company D camp, still in the interior, still on the San Saba. Taking their time, the boys finally reined in on the eleventh day of May 1884. They had been gone thirty-one days and had ridden about 616 miles.[34]

Ira may have been given a day or two to relax and rest his horse. For a short time his name does not appear on scouting reports. So, either Ira stayed in camp awhile, or he was working in the nondescript role as one of "the four men" going with Corporal Baird to the Little Saline, looking to arrest Steve Boyce and Ben Johnson. Or, maybe he was one of the "three men" accompanying Corporal B. D. Lindsey who was chasing after a reported herd of pilfered cattle.[35] Ira's invisibility will be shortlived.

As would be expected the promotion of Frank Jones to lieutenant created a vacuum, prompting personnel readjustments. On the last day of May, Captain Sieker updated his boss, AG King: "I have promoted first Corpl. B. D. Lindsey to First Sergt. Second Corpl. P. C. Baird to First Corpl., and appointed J. W. [Wood] Saunders as second Corpl., these have all been in the service sometime and are worthy men."[36]

During the first week of June a detachment from Company D was detailed to stand by at Llano in Llano County; District Court was in session. Private Ira Aten, under the command of Lieutenant Frank Jones, was a member of the squad.[37] Evidence of Ira's maturing—

as a lawman—is buttressed by this peace keeping duty at Llano. Ira, acting in conjunction with Texas Ranger W. W. Collier, arrested the more often than not drunk and disorderly man-killer Ruben Hornsby "Rube" Boyce for creating a scene. They turned him over to a Llano County Justice of the Peace. Later in the day, he and Ranger Private J. A. Puckett served a Grand Jury's warrant on Tom Moore, turning him over to Llano County's sheriff. Later in the month, while yet detailed to Llano, Ira made a one-man apprehension, going after Jim House for Bond Forfeiture.[38]

Leaving a Texas Ranger presence in Llano County, Captain Sieker, under orders from the adjutant general's office, began making the necessary arrangements to vacate Camp Johnson and reopen Camp Leona. It was, again, a logistical nightmare. But relocating near Uvalde advantaged Company D's leadership with proximity to mail, telegraph, and railroad facilities, important communications assets if they were to "get information from the surrounding counties."[39] One piece of data they received demanded hurried attention. C. C. Davis was wanted by Llano County authorities for Murder and he was on the loose. A snippet of criminal intelligence indicated he might be headed for Mexico. Immediately Captain Sieker rallied some Texas Rangers already at Camp Leona, and they raced for the border, making scouts looking for Davis at Eagle Pass and upriver at Del Rio. Three days later they returned to Uvalde, frazzled and empty-handed.[40]

Meanwhile, the Company D detachment temporarily stationed at Llano had been busy, particularly Private Ira Aten. Acting alone, which is indicative of his pluck, Ira had scouted southeast to Johnson City in Blanco County trying to find fugitive Davis. Not finding him where he thought he might be, Ira followed his trail, not necessarily looking down at horseshoe dints, but by skillfully interrogating folks along the roadway. Aten's astute sleuthing led to Brady City. The details are shadowy, but there Private Ira Aten made a prisoner out of the flesh and bones of badman Davis, most likely at the point of a cocked Colt's six-shooter. Texas Ranger Ira Aten knew full well, typically there were not second-place winners in a gunfight. While in Brady City, one Mr. Will Paschal was raising hell, disturbing the peace. Ira arrested the disorderly Mr. Paschal, finding him a vacant bunk in the McCulloch County Jail. That done, guardedly, but professionally, Ranger Aten transported suspect Davis back to Llano County, handing him over to an appreciative sheriff.[41]

Sadly, news broke from Williamson County. The report's short-term impact on Ira Aten's day by day law enforcing business would be but minimal. On the other hand, the long-term bearing would be measurably distinct, and even historically significant. On the night of July 14, 1884, the city marshal at Taylor, John G. Morgan, was fatally shot down by S. E. Stiles, proprietor of an "ice cream saloon." In a *dying declaration* the wounded lawman asserted that he had been gunned down absent any provocation or personal squabble. Newspapermen described the six-shooting act as but "cold-blooded murder." Stiles turned himself in to deputy sheriffs, claiming he had shot in self-defense. Four days later the Williamson County Grand Jury indicted Stiles for Murder, but for this treatment, that is another story. For Ira the violent death of Officer Morgan held a twofold dimension. Taylor was really close to home, accenting the inflexible fact that professional lawmen, indeed, sometimes skated across dangerously thin ice. In the second instance, John Morgan's replacement, Thomas Calton Smith, a thirty-eight-year-old native of Williamson County, would along the timeline play a determinative role in Ira Aten's life.[42] In the interim, Private Ira Aten worked—and worked hard.

Maneuvering his way throughout the territory assigned to Company D's Llano detachment Ira was not just lazily ambling along, asleep in the saddle. By any standard he was an assiduous Texas Ranger. Passing through San Saba County he came across one J. R. Hightower, smartly established the fellow was wanted for forgery, and turned him over to a San Saba County constable.[43] Ira Aten's fine police work was not going unnoticed, not by Captain Sieker, nor by the Texas Rangers' headquarters command staff. When it was learned that C. C. Davis' bond had been forfeited (or he had escaped), Captain Sieker summoned young Ira. Private Aten departed Llano on the twenty-fourth day of July, riding hard for Camp Leona and a hurried conference with the boss. Captain Sieker had a special assignment for Ira, one of many to be handed his way.

Private Aten was to take up a post at Eagle Pass, keeping a close eye on the sector between Piedras Negras, on the south end, and Ciudad Acuna, the Mexican town across the Rio Grande from Del Rio, Val Verde County, Texas, on the north end. Private Aten was to work closely with Thomas L. "Tom" Oglesby, a former Texas Ranger captain, but at the time sheriff of Maverick County. Most of Ira's spare time, if he had any, was to be spent on the lookout for C. C. Davis.

Unbeknownst to Ranger Aten, a fellow was on the lookout for him—
or any other nosy lawmen. Scouting the country east of Eagle Pass
the plucky Ranger attempted to arrest a fugitive wanted by the sheriff—albeit for a misdemeanor violation. Undaunted by the fact he
was working alone, Ira located the man's camp and rode in. Invited
to step down he dismounted, taking his place at the table beneath
a shady arbor. Ranger Aten didn't spill his coffee, but he did wind
up with egg on his face. Ira told the fellow there was a "little charge
against him at Eagle Pass" and that he would have to accompany
him to town and "straighten things out." At first the man seemed
resigned to his fate, but then Ira let his guard down, losing the upper
hand: Ranger Aten found himself scarily peering into the depths of
a Winchester's muzzle. A quick *adios* on the owlhoot's part left Ira
cooling his coffee and souring his appetite for breakfast. The joke
was on Ira, but he didn't think it funny. On the other hand, when
his fellow Rangers learned of the audacious trickery, they thought it
hilarious. Condolences among *macho* Rangers—unless one was dead
or near it—were a commodity in short supply. Their even learning
of the foul up speaks volumes about Ira. When Mr. Aten ripped his
britches he owned up to it.[44]

While Ira Aten was deployed along the border in Eagle Pass, not
too far north in Edwards County several of his fellow Company D
Rangers experienced their very own dalliance with danger. Corporal P. C. Baird, along with privates W. A. Mitchell, Oscar D. and W.
W. Baker had set up surveillance at Green B. Greer's sheep rancho.
Secreted in a cedar break the Texas Rangers were watching a watering hole formed by drainage from the South Llano River. Locally it
was known as Green Lake. The summer drought had been severe,
and Greer had strung wire preventing cattlemen access to water. The
fence had been cut, rebuilt, and was expected to be cut again—thus
the Texas Rangers had been sent, by Governor John Ireland no less.
On July 29, 1884, with Rangers as eyewitnesses the fence was cut.
When intrepid lawmen jumped from the brush the shooting started.
Green B. Greer had stationed himself on a nearby hill to observe
any fireworks, later remarking that the exchange of about 150 shots
produced a "rather hot-little fight." He was dead right, and so was a
fence cutter named Mason, a bullet in his chest, another in his brain.
Unluckily Private W. W. Baker had caught a ball in the left side, very
painful, but not mortal. The other cutters fled, making good their
getaway—for awhile.[45]

Something that did not go away, though, was less than keen feedback for the Texas Rangers' doings at Green Lake. Lieutenant Frank Jones, after an inspection tour, posted Captain Sieker: "I find the people up in the section of Green Lake very bitter against Rangers and say that they had no right to come into the country in the night."[46] There was talk of legal action. A relative of one fence cutter was bragging that he had "sixty thousand dollars to spend in the prosecution of the Rangers who participated in the fight...."[47] Threat of prosecution was not idle. Captain Sieker appraised AG King:

> Burton's son who was one of the Green Lake fence cutters has made complaint against Corpl. Baird & squad for attempt to murder. I instructed them to go by Bull Head and waive examination and give bond to appear before the Edwards Co. Grand Jury—we will make it interesting for them before they get through with it. Please see the Gov. about counsel.[48]

Money talks. The very next day Captain Lam Seiker fired off an update: "He [Lieutenant Jones] is attending Justice court there [Bull Head], where Corpl. Baird & squad are being tried before the Justice for assault with intent to killing young Burton at Green Lake"[49] There is a oft repeated saying in law enforcer's parlance: "You might beat the rap, but you can't beat the ride." Translation is straightforward. An arrest may prove inconvenient, expensive, and humiliating, even though in the end filing of criminal charges may not be sustained. In this instance Rangers beat the rap.

Aside from antipathy *sometimes* exhibited between sheepmen and cowmen, the Green Lake affair did highlight a problematic irritant for Texas Rangers, those go-getting lawmen who, at the time, wore no uniforms and sported no badges. The Texas Rangers knew they were Texas Rangers. For men behind the wall (at Green Lake), four scruffy-looking strangers running toward them from the cedar breaks with Winchesters and/or Colt's six-shooters already in hand was not plain sign that the doughty fellows were lawmen... There were no mind readers in Edwards County. The cowmen knew nobody could prove or disprove what they thought or did not think—a pretext of self-defense sounded pretty good from a legal perspective.[50] Possibility of an innocent misidentification, not too far down the timeline, will make a noteworthy contribution to Private Ira Aten's story.

When Private Aten learned of the Green Lake fracas is not now known. Word does travel fast, but Ira Aten was busy at Eagle Pass. Though for the most part details are sketchy, the end results are not. Ira arrested Robert Dow for Murder, Pedro Padaz for Theft of Money, Pedro Rodriquez for Theft of a Horse, and Clemencia Garza for Aggravated Assault.[51]

Ira's next string of arrests leaves room for haziness on one hand, but not the other. Whether or not there was a near one riot situation, with just one Ranger, is lost. Perhaps the arrests took place during a multi-day period. Nevertheless it seems Private Ira Aten was a one-man holy-terror for disturbers of the peace. Texas Ranger Aten arrested John Huch, Julia Ludington, Antonio Bernetis, Clemencia Garza (again), Carrie Murray, J. Porter, Francisco Neueic, R. Lumbard, T. Flores, Cecilia Ragal, Antonio Gonzales, and George Rader. These mouthy miscreants were all charged with Disturbing the Peace, turned over for safekeeping to a Maverick County JP—until they paid their fines.[52]

Not content to sit still, not for a minute, Private Aten learned that John Shoemake was wanted for Theft of a Horse. He made a scout to Presidio and arrested him. Then he hauled him to San Antonio, making sure defendant Shoemake had a room for the night at Bexar County Sheriff Thomas P. McCall's hotel.[53] Not only was Ira Aten making a good Ranger, he had the makings of a hell-of-a-good Ranger. Captain Sieker called him home to Camp Leona. On September 22, 1884, Private Ira returned to camp and unpacked his gear— ready for more action.[54]

While Ira had been keeping the peace and scooping up *mal hombres* in a border town, a nasty crime closer in had taken place: an act of criminality that would ultimately impact Aten's life drastically. On September 3, 1884, in the heart of the Texas Hill Country at Fredericksburg, Gillespie County, highjackers cooked up an evil brew. Over time, fifty-five-year-old John Wolfgang Braeutigam's Beer Hall and entertainment layout, one with a large grapevine arbor, dance pavilion, and race track, had become just the spot for the "town's most gala celebrations," be it weddings or birthdays or family reunions. Finding Braeutigam alone, the would-be robbers boldly marched in, mischief on their minds. By most accounts it was simply a robbery gone awry, knocked sideways when the plucky proprietor made a play for his old musket standing against the wall. The owner's try was most commendable, but foolish. Deafening reports of Colt's six-

shooters reverberated throughout "Braeutigams Garten" (Braeutigam's Garden), shattering all peacefulness and killing the owner.
Not surprisingly the desperadoes hightailed it. Mr. Braeutigam's ten-
year-old son, Henry, found the bleeding but lifeless form of his father.
The grief-stricken widow, Christine, mother of eleven children, and
but two days short of her thirty-fourth wedding anniversary, was
a Fredericksburg favorite.[55] To most folks it was clear cut, a brutal
and heartless murder just for the sake of bulging one's pockets at the
expense of another person's labor.[56] The whole of Gillespie County
was in a stupendous uproar—wanting satisfaction—revenge. Texas
Rangers were summoned. Local officers went on the hunt.

The outlaws' trail went down the Colorado River, to the vicinity
of Travis Peak in the northwestern section of Travis County, not too
far from the Burnet County line. There the Texas Rangers began getting a handle on just who they were looking for, a set Ira tagged as
"just bad country boys, starting out being bad."[57] The badness didn't
deter the Texas Rangers. A scout led by Corporal P. C. Baird latched
on to three of the prime suspects: Jackson "Jack" Beam, C. W. "Wesley" Collier, and William "Bill" Allison. Ira Aten remarked with simplicity: "We rounded up their houses at night at two different places
and caught them in bed." The suspects were taken to Fredericksburg
on the 5th day of October 1884, to stand for a Preliminary Hearing
and bond setting.[58] Quickly the defendants were bound over—no
bail—pending action of the grand jury. Not satisfied with the security of the Gillespie County Jail, the Texas Rangers—with no opposition from Sheriff John Walter—opted to temporarily house their
prisoners in the newer and much more secure Bexar County Jail at
San Antonio, an "escape proof facility." Most Gillespie County citizens were ecstatic. There was a big party at Fredericksburg before the
prisoners were shackled and removed to San Antonio.[59] The detachment returned to Company D's camp.

Captain Lam Sieker kept men in the field, constantly scouting
after alleged cow thieves and cow killers, such as Jim Murphy and
George Phillips. Texas Rangers arrested both. Lieutenant Jones and
his detachment, which Ira had *probably* rejoined, kept the peace in
Edwards County, camped at Green Lake. Near there, they even took
into custody one of the suspected fence cutters, Henry Burton, relin-
quishing custody to Edwards County's judiciary. Lieutenant Jones
"and one man" were making a cattle theft investigation near Fort
McKavett in Menard County.[60]

The following month, on November 18, Privates Ira Aten and James V. Latham, a Missouri-born twenty-four-year-old, while on a purposeful horseback scout through Kimble County (Junction) apprehended another suspect wanted in connection with Braeutigam's murder in Gillespie County. The methodical lawmen watchfully—and safely—removed the prisoner, Ede (sometimes written, Ed) Janes, a few miles southeast to Fredericksburg, where Sheriff Walter relieved them of further responsibility.[61] Although they came up short, Private Baker and "2 men" scouted the Hudson's Bend vicinity of Travis County looking for James "Jim" Fannon (or Fannin) also thought to have participated in the senseless murder of the Braeutigam Beer Garden's owner in Gillespie County.[62]

At the end of November 1884, Corporal P. C. Baird tendered his resignation. He had accepted the law enforcing job as chief deputy at Mason County, working for Sheriff John Calvin Butler.[63] Ranger Baird's leaving created a vacancy for a corporal. Private Ira Aten was promoted.[64]

It seems that Corporal Aten's promotion, this time, was rather shortlived. Certainly for December of 1884 Ira is referred to as Corporal Aten, but such will not be the case in subsequent Monthly Returns for a lengthy spate of time, wherein he is clearly identified as Private Aten.[65] Certainly a disciplinary action could have been initiated, but does not seem likely. Ira Aten, in Lam Sieker's eyes, was a "good Ranger." Most likely the temporary loss of rank was due to parsimonious distribution of funds by the legislature, a recurrent nightmare for the Frontier Battalion's management staff. Subsequently lawmakers slashed funding for the Frontier Battalion and a whole company was done away with and others suffered a trimming of allocated slots. "The battalion still had five companies, but each had fewer men. In reality, the strength of the Ranger force seldom had anything to do with workload, always the budget."[66]

Not taking any time off for the upcoming holiday, Ira was hard on the job. Two days before Christmas 1884, Ira Aten, still a corporal, "and one man" scouted to the Nueces River. They were full of cheer, carrying a present for Isaac Baker, an arrest warrant for Incest.[67] Unfortunately suspect Baker was not at home, or nearby, and these Texas Rangers returned to Camp Leona empty-handed.

What blew in with 1885's New Year's Day was a biting Blue Norther, plunging the mercury south. Such was infrequent for Uvalde County, but it turned very cold. Captain Sieker acknowledged: "As

will be seen I have done but little on account of the bad weather..."
and "Everything quiet here and we have had some very cold weather
but it has turned off warm here now and grass is beginning to
show."[68] Something else was also beginning to show—difficulties on
the Texas/Mexican border.

Chapter 4

"But few honest men in this town"

Sheriff Tom Oglesby had sent an urgent dispatch to Captain Sieker stating that trouble was anticipated at Carrizo Springs, Dimmit County, the province adjoining his bailiwick's southeastern border-line.[1] Apparently, Ranger Ira Aten was at Company D's headquarters the evening of February 6, 1885: "About sundown one evening, a man rode into our camp on the Leona river below Uvalde. He was wild-eyed and his horse was well spent. He gave us a wild story about Mexican bandits who crossed the Rio Grande, driving off cattle after killing their herdsman."[2] Immediately Captain Lam Sieker ordered Lieutenant Jones and seven Texas Rangers to saddle, Ira Aten among them. Taking rations for ten days and well supplied with ammunition, the detachment set off at a gallop. That done, Captain Sieker, complying with orders from Austin, hopped a train that very night, rushing to San Antonio for a high-level confab with officialdom.[3]

The distraught Maverick County Sheriff had simply been overwhelmed. Bandits and *bandidos* were shamelessly jumping back and forth across the meandering *Rio Bravo*, with not even the slightest fear of apprehension.[4] Earlier in neighboring Dimmit County, the sheriff, Joe Tumlinson, had grown tired of bureaucratic inaction. In the words of Adolphus Petree :

> It started out this way, you see, that whole thing started with stealing.... That used to be all open country in there clear up to the Eagle Pass road. Three or four of our boys would go out there and camp and the damn Mexicans would run them clean to town. They would just round up what they wanted and drive them through. Our sheriff was old Joe Tumlinson. He wrote the governor. He said, "I can't get any reply from the governor. I guess we had better break this thing up ourselves."[5]

Sheriff Tumlinson "riding a big white horse" was daringly in command of an armed bunch of leathery-faced cowmen and cowboys.

They started in pursuit of a band of suspected Mexican stock thieves. After splashing across the Rio Grande trying hard to recover eighteen stolen horses, the Texans were in for a surprise. Once on Mexico's ground, the roles had reversed. Two dozen Mexicans (400 in other accounts) opened fire on Tumlinson's posse, killing a horse. The sheriff and his boys scampered in reverse, making tracks for the Rio Grande. One of those fellows, Adolph Petree, remembered a partner giving him some advice during the flight: "When you come up this hill you kind of zigzag." "I said, 'Zigzag, hell', if I ever get up that hill I will be lucky."[6]

Fortunately the hard-riding but anxious Texans made it back across the river, barely escaping annihilation.[7] Another pal of Petree's, once the boys were safely planted on American soil, registered a new-found appreciation: "Adolph, I didn't know I thought as much of my wife and children as I do!"[8] Along that section of the border country vitriolic talk had become ubiquitous and incendiary. Beseeching letters to Austin were flying off the ink-pads. Stockmen were disgustingly outraged—and scared. The South Texas border country was aflame with reports of violence—and unfounded rumors galore. The bodies of three Mexicans were found, "riddled with balls." They were suspected of being gang members fond of slipping across the border for plunder.[9] An official inquiry was buried. Nobody wanted to 'fess up.

Ranger Ira Aten punches in with a forthright and unmasked personal assessment: "Before this at Carrizo Springs people had got into some trouble with the Mexicans across the Rio Grande. Mexicans were coming across, stealing cattle and horses, and there was a lot of feeling up. It got so bad that white men were killing every Mexican they caught over the line, and Mexicans were killing some of the white men."[10]

Silas "Si" Hay, a well respected Dimmit County pioneer, riding as head of a contingent of no-nonsense volunteers, rounded up five Mexicans who they alleged were thieves. There was no summary justice—this time—though such was not infrequent for possemen populating either bank of the river. In this instance the prisoners were placed behind bars in the county jail in Carrizo Springs, a recently constructed stone fortress.[11] Other fellows from south of the border fared not as well. Local lawmen, on a scout looking for stolen cattle, bumped into their quarry. During an ensuing exchange of gunfire, besides a deputy sheriff being wounded, two suspected outlaw brothers, sons of Rafael Reyes, were killed outright. Captain Sieker, unusually well-informed, noted: "there is an uneasiness among the Ranchmen who fear the Mexicans will Kill some Americans to avenge the Reyes boys death."[12] Many believed, even though gossip, that Dimmit County would soon be invaded by Mexicans, jailed prisoners would be liberated, and Americans killed at a ratio of fifty to one.[13] Panicky talk was skyrocketing. Hot news was not regionally confined; it was breaking nationally. At Petersburg, Virginia, the *Daily Index Appeal,* picking up a story from the *New York Herald,* howled its headlines: "Rows on the Rio Grande: Trouble Between Texans and Mexicans That May Lead to Serious Complications":

> That some serious collision is apprehended there is not the slightest doubt, and perhaps the outbreak may have even now occurred, for aught we know to the contrary. Carrizzo [*sic*] Springs is located in Dimmit county, Texas, on the border of the Rio Grande, but the nearest Telegraph office is some fifty miles distant, and therefore the news is slow in coming in. The Mexicans vow vengeance against the Americans because two of their number, caught in the act of stealing cattle, were killed on Sunday.[14]

Governor John Ireland was being barraged with urgent appeals. To be sure he was alarmed. He, too, was a politician. Texas' chief executive was not geared to dilly-dally. Along the river, sovereignty had meaning to diplomats and military attachés; but it was a meaningless notion to thugs lying low in the sweltering tangle of willows, canebrakes, and cattails. The governor directed Adjutant General King and Texas Rangers to tidy up the mess:[15]

> I wish you to proceed at once to Dimmit Co. and restore order. If it is necessary to use a larger force than that of the state troops you are directed to call to your assistance any military organization on the frontier either to repel any force from Mexico or other unlawful force presenting itself. Make no unnecessary inroad into Mexico but punish unlawful organizations if you can do so. You will remove the Company of Captain Sieker now at Uvalde to or near the Mexican border...."[16]

Adjutant General King blistered into action. Arms and ammunition were shipped from San Antonio, presumably aboard the same train he and Captain Sieker and other Texas Rangers were riding. Their ultimate destination was William Votaw's ranch, "about nine miles from the Rio Grande."[17] Other Texas Rangers, Private James Abijah Brooks and Sergeant George W. Farrow, from Joe Shely's Company F, were accompanying the ten-man posse headed by the La Salle County (Cotulla) Sheriff, Charles Brown "C. B." McKinney.[18] The US Army was to make their presence, if not felt, at least known. Fast

Charles Brown "C. B." McKinney, left, sheriff of La Salle County (Cotulla) and a former Ranger, and George W. Farrow, Company F Texas Ranger. *Courtesy Chuck Parsons.*

as possible all were to converge at the prearranged meeting spot. By mid-morning February 9, 1885, the assorted outfits, finally, had merged into one.

At last making contact with Lieutenant Jones and his detachment, Captain Sieker was posted: Along the Rio Grande, Jones reported, everything was in "a violent state of excitement with the citizens of Dimmitt [sic] Co. in arms expecting an invasion from Mexico."[19] Ira Aten's remembrances are far less dramatic, but he did recall that when Lieutenant Frank Jones and the squad had made their nighttime arrival in Carrizo Springs, the little town seemed completely deserted, "not a light could be seen nor a man found." Waiting for good light, Jones' detachment had taken charge of the county courthouse and then turned in for the night.[20] Rubbing sleep from his eyes Ira greeted the dawn: "When we woke up in the courthouse the next morning, we could see men walking around with Winchesters. They did not know but that we were the Mexicans who had come during the night and captured the courthouse."[21]

Now, with the whole command in a cohesive wad, they stood poised to act—or react. Adjutant General King carried the big stick. Texas Ranger Captains Sieker and Shely, assisted by Sheriff McKinney and ex-Ranger Captain Lee Hall, were AG Kings' on-the-ground eyes and ears.[22] Though there are some inconsistencies in stories penned by Rangers during twilight years, the meat and potatoes are basic, and blend into the historic pot rather nicely. Eyewitnesses seldom see the same thing, exactly the same way.

On each bank of the Rio Grande stood gun-toting partisans, lawmen and cattlemen, and maybe a few bandits on the American side, Mexican *jefes* and *vaqueros* and perhaps a few *bandidos* on the other. Each lineup held complaints, touchy issues demanding redress. Ira Aten, in part, remembered: "After much parleying we [the leadership makeup] agreed to exchange notes on the situation. This was done by having a man from each side of the river ride into the middle of the stream carrying a white flag, a handkerchief, tied to the muzzle of his carbine. The rifle was held high above his head. Meeting in the middle of the stream, each rider would exchange notes and return."[23] From Ira Aten's writings it seems the young Texas Ranger was one of the high-water messengers, as he remarked: "The water ran high up on our horse's sides, filling our boots with water."[24] Meanwhile heavily armed companions looked on: "the Americans were ready to fight on signal—the drop of a handkerchief."[25] Beneath Winchesters'

front-sights aimed from both camps and mutually divided fortitude, an accord was finally reached: There would be formalized talks
between persons empowered to speak. Of course, the meeting would
take place on neutral ground, a sandbar in the middle of the Rio
Grande known locally as *Las Isles*.[26]

Captains Lam Sieker, Joe Shely, and Company F's lieutenant,
William Scott, constituted the Texas Ranger delegation. They were
accompanied by Sheriff McKinney and Lee Hall.[27] By agreement the
envoys would cross over to *Las Isles* unarmed. From the Mexican side
came a Doctor Pope and two yet-unidentified Mexican *compadres*.
Before starting for *Las Isles*, and the reason is somewhat inexplicable
considering the Frontier Battalion's chain-of-command structure,
Captain Lam Sieker personally invited Private Brooks to "go along
with them," which in retrospect turned out to be "one of the proud-
est moments of his life."[28]

After wide-ranging wrangling, with everyone trying to stifle
any angry outbursts, an agreement—not a treaty—was managed.
The settlement had gravitated well past hot air. The Americans
were to guarantee that the prisoners, at least four of them, held in
the Dimmit County Jail were turned out and repatriated to Mexico.
There was to be no more indiscriminate shooting at Mexicans in
Dimmit and Maverick Counties, at least until after an investigation
and a determination was made that warrants would issue, and they
were resisting arrest. Persons should not be fired on solely due to
their nationality, no matter which side of the river they were on.
Stock thieves caught on the American side with cattle or horses or
sheep—or even a goat—stolen in Mexico must be given up. The
tidy pact was not wholly one dimensional. In return: "The Mexicans
were to use all efforts to prevent robbery and pillage of Americans;
to deliver up thieves now protected by them, and to break up the
camp of bandits now [then] near the Rio Grande, opposite Dimmit
county, with numerous stock in their possession belonging to Texans, which is [was] to be restored."[29] "For the short term a truce—of
sorts—held, though it was still called the 'Bloody Border'"[30] Texas
Ranger Austin Ira Aten, all too soon and all too personally, would
learn why.

Once he had been issued an order, Captain Sieker was not the
type to tarry. He and the main element of Company D had taken up a
short-term position in Dimmit County southwest of Carrizo Springs.
Captain Sieker wanted to see for himself how the peace was holding,

and on the thirteenth day of February 1885 he gathered around him a squadron of Rangers, determined to make a scout along the river, one of "several days" duration.[31]

For those several days Captain Sieker explored the area, upriver and down river, taking the pulse of area ranchers—few as there were. He even spearheaded a scout south of the border, using his utmost effort to "allay excitement." The captain's assessment was guarded, but seemed optimistic for the interim: "I scouted up the river and found the Ranchmen considerably excited, but I apprehend no trouble at present as the Mexicans will be afraid to come over the river in any force for sometime."[32] Lam Sieker's instructions had been explicit: not only was he visiting with folks, he was also taking the lay of the land. Choosing the most advantageous camping site was not a task to be taken lightly. Many factors demanded practical consideration. Captain Sieker finally selected a spot:

> I have established a camp 4 miles from the Rio Grande on San Ambrosia Creek within a mile of the corner of Maverick, Webb & Dimmit counties. The selection was made with regard to outlet in all directions [and] is outside of all pastures and near the several prominent crossings where wet stock are supposed to be crossed back and forth. The water is permanent and the grass good.... Eagle Pass would be the best P. O. for the following reasons. They have a daily mail, telegraph & telephone & my men going & coming for the mail would scout 45 miles of river and notice any trail making for or from the river....[33]

And noticing a trail was in the cards for Company F's Captain Joe Shely. Riding from his La Salle County base camp at Cotulla, sometimes tagged the "rustler capital of the world," Shely and Sheriff C. B. McKinney, accompanied by a few citizens were hot on the tracks of fellows suspected of committing two murders in nearby Dimmit County. One of the deceased was Jesus Sanches, the other Simon Perez, both were *vasierros,* sheepherders working for wages. Suspects, three of them riding gray horses, the other a bay, had apparently gone on a crime spree, restricting their wickedness to indiscriminately gunning down Mexicans. Sanches had been shot at such close range his clothes had caught fire. His body had been horribly burned, toasted. At a separate spot, Perez, after being toyed with, finally realized the quartet's evil intent. He broke and ran, trying to hide in the *brasada*, the thick brush. Winchesters sounded and sledgehammered Simon to the ground, several bullets in his torso, at least one in the back of his head, tearing through brain matter, exiting by way of the forehead. Both killings, even to experienced lawmen, seemed especially gruesome. After some nifty sleuthing the tireless possemen finally overhauled and physically took custody of John Laxon, the alleged ringleader, Simp DeSpain, and Felix Taylor. Wisely separating the suspects to cross-check their alibis, Captain Shely successfully employed progressive interrogation techniques. Taylor, the youngest gangster, once the idea had been planted and was fermenting in his psyche, fearfully thought the only way to get out of trouble was to roll over on his pals. Felix "let his milk down" (police lingo for confessing), tearfully admitting to his participation in the foul murders. Then, keeping his end of the turning state's evidence bargain, Taylor somberly snitched Laxon and DeSpain into the depraved equation. Furthermore, since he was already at it, he aptly fingered William M. "Billy" Brummitt as the fourth triggerman. The motive, according to the whining Felix, was "that they wanted the sheepmen out of the country, as they wanted the range for their cattle." Other testimony, later, would indicate it all had started with an impetuously mean query: "Suppose we kill a Mexican today, the first one we strike this morning?" And they did, and did again. Ranger Captain Joe Shely characterized the crime as "one of the most bold, high-handed murders ever perpetrated in this section."[34]

Even though satisfied he had solid evidence, Captain Shely was worried that the killers would walk scot-free. John Laxon was the son of Jesse Laxon, a particularly good friend of state Senator Edward F. Hall, a politician responsible for "instigating all petitions and charges conferred against rangers in this county."[35]

The friction between Captain Shely and the senator from Laredo was not a secret. In faraway North Texas it was noted in the *Dallas Daily Herald* that Senator Hall had been trying to have the entire Frontier Battalion, and Joe Shely's Company F in particular, disbanded; "and his conduct, [is] alleged to have been governed by motives of personal dislike to Capt. Sheely [*sic*], commanding, is most bitterly condemned."[36] Just the year before Senator Hall had publicly decried: "It is a shame upon the people to have such an armed mob in their midst, and is a disgrace to the state of Texas to have her citizens over ridden by a set of men who occupy the position of state rangers."[37] The political discord was waxing hot. An attorney

Captain Joe Shely's Company F Texas Rangers. A political squabble between Captain Shely and Senator Hall, the state senator from Laredo, may have contributed to an embarrassing legal entanglement for Texas Ranger Private Ira Aten and his companions. The Texas Rangers, standing L to R: J. W. Buck, Pete Edwards, Captain Shely, George Farrow, Brack Morris, and Charlie Norris. Seated L to R: Washington "Wash" Shely, Tom Mabry, Bob Crowder, and Cecilio Charo. *Courtesy Research Center, Texas Ranger Hall of Fame and Museum.*

from Cotulla chimed in: "I am informed that the opposition to the ranger force commanded by Capt. Shely is directed mainly by Senator E. F. Hall, of this District, and that the grounds of opposition are personal. I do not know what these grounds are but it seems to me that no personal opposition to Shely should be permitted to destroy the entire service. So far as we are personally concerned we believe Capt. Shely to be a brave and efficient officer. He may not admire Senator E. F. Hall, and he is by no means singular in that respect if he does not...."[38]

Captain Joe Shely was not ingratiating himself with Senator Hall or some of the other local officials, to be sure. Worrying that the supposed murderers would be turned out, Captain Shely cast a wide loop of censure to AG King:

> I have but little hopes and confidence of the result of any trial in Dimmit County on account of the relationship existing between the alleged murderers and the officials of that county.... after the murders had been committed.... at once sent a runner, who informed Sheriff Tumlinson the same night. Strange to say the gallant Shff. Did not put in his appearance at all but instead sent a Justice of the Peace and a crowd similar to the one that was with our men at Las Ysles during the "International Interview." They came down with 2 wagons & team making about the same time as U. S. Infantry.[39]

Although the rift between a Texas Ranger captain and a state senator would not directly gobble up Ranger Ira Aten, in the near future a collateral offshoot may well have been the catapult launching him into a month's worth of misery. Meanwhile, he and his fellow Company D Rangers were busy trying to uphold commitments made at *Las Isles*. During the last eight days of March 1885, Lieutenant Jones, and presumably Ira Aten, along with two other Rangers, provided a protective escort for the aforementioned Rafael Reyes, while he and his saddle-weary *vaqueros* gathered drifting cattle along the Rio Grande.[40] Adolph Petree, in his mid-twenties, knew many of the players along both banks of the river, and while he condemned Reyes' sons, he was thoroughly impressed with the father, in his own ethnocentric way: "....Reyes was a white man. He was as true as steel, that old Mexican was.... This Reyes boy was one of the ring leaders. The old man was all right, the old man was true as steel. Never was a finer man in the Mexican world...."[41] Seemingly the Texas Rangers had no beef with the old man either, watching him and his men wring wild cattle out of the *brasada*.

Then disturbing news broke from the interior. The "escape proof" Bexar County Jail at San Antonio was porous. The heartless killers of John Braeutigam, the murdered Fredericksburg Beer Garden owner, had dug "out through the floor, under the foundation, and to the outside."[42] The Texas Rangers were again called into service.

Bill Allison's bid for freedom was shortlived. He was arrested near Austin at Oatmanville and, this time, ultimately put in the county lockup at Fredericksburg. The German community was mad. They would keep custody of a monster alleged to have killed the beloved Braeutigam, not ship him off to ineptness. According to Ira, "It was not a week until they burned the jail, with its spiked roof down on him."[43] Recounting the same incident to different persons Ira Aten reiterated: "took the road in there after Allison, met him right there close to Austin and brought him back and put him in jail at Fredericksburg. That night the jail was burned down on him. Was rock, with wooden insides. It killed him."[44] For an alternative account, perhaps softening any accusations of extralegal justice, the inferno was thus recapped: "Another [Allison] was delivered to the local jail and met with death when the jail was destroyed by fire."[45] And, even a more benign notion suggests the prisoner died as a result of his own misguided hand, setting fire to the jail in a bungled try at an escape.[46] Whether by intentional arson or inadvertent accident, the wild-eyed murder suspect Bill Allison had melted into nothingness.

Captain Sieker was finding out not everyone along the border might be "good." Even some of the folks supposed to be enforcing the state's laws and working for laudable purposes, it was alleged, were suspect in borderlands where the *mordida*—the bite—the bribe—was as common as chili peppers.[47] The captain's updated findings to the adjutant general are corroborating, not only in the fact rumors were running rampant, but enlightening as well:

> Sir: In accordance with instructions promulgated by your letter of February 27th 1885, I will say that I have exhausted every avenue of information Known to myself and suggested by the best citizens on this, and the other side of the Rio Grande river, without getting any tangible proof of the "crookedness" referred to regarding the Dimmit Co. officials. As you state

there are various rumors and intimations connecting the parties referred to with dealing in "wet stock" but the parties who know positively, are the very ones who would shield them from exposure. After talking with Mr. Votow a wealthy stockman on this side, and he being of the opinion that should any evidence exist in writing, it would be found at Presidio Rio Grande [Mexican village]. I therefore called on the collector of customs at Piedras Negras and he wrote a letter to the best citizens of Presidio, requesting them to give me all the information they could regarding thieves on this side. He had the river guard escort me to the town and I met some ten or twelve of their best men, and explained to them my mission. They through fear or complicity would tell me nothing. Dr. Pope, an American, who has resided some nine years in Presidio said, "there are but few honest men in this town, and if they had the information and evidence you desire they could ill afford to give one of their gang away." Notwithstanding I have been baffled so far. I will continue my inquiry and should I obtain any evidence I can verify—will report to your office. The excitement and uneasiness existing here for a while is fast subsiding and everything now seems to be running smoothly.[48]

Also running smoothly was the wool gathering on Kellor's ranch. Private Aten, the lead Ranger for a two-man detail, spent twelve days at the shearing camp. There were not disputes of note, nothing significant to report—other than tedium.[49] Such was not the case farther inland, near Montell, Uvalde County. The stealing of horses, sheep, goats, and cows, was taking place at a wholesale level. Certain thieves that had two years before been run out of the area by Texas Rangers and into New Mexico Territory had returned and were back in business. One rancher in nearby Edwards County stocked his range with 1000 goats. Six months later he owned but half-a-dozen bucks and "100 nannies out of the 1000." In another incident, owl-hoots drove off "a bunch of goats." "The herder (an Englishman) and a Mexican followed on foot and owing to the toughness of the county overtook them and fired on the thieves who abandoned their horses and dropped a coat & hat. In the coat was a letter disclosing the name of the parties." Another rancher's house was burned to the ground, his livestock driven away. It wasn't just the stockmen who suffered depredations in the border counties and those that adjoined. The cry

Ira Aten's personally designed and handcrafted Texas Ranger badge. This may be the very first Texas Ranger badge fashioned from a Mexican coin. If not—it was definitely among the first.   *Courtesy Jeri and Gary Boyce Radder.*

for Texas Ranger help was deafening if words from the page could have spoken. One salty old fellow, a former Texas Ranger, rather dryly noted: "The state is [in] too [much] poverty to afford protection to those who live on the frontier and in fact the only powers it Seems to have is to impose and collect taxes. I write this to, knowing that if you can, you will help us."[50]

Adjutant General Wilburn King wasn't deaf, or unsympathetic. There is no need to read between the lines; the orders were plain. Company D's Lieutenant Frank Jones was to—and did—lead a five-man detachment into Edwards County "to look into general lawlessness there."[51] Texas Ranger Private Ira Aten was elsewhere.

He and another Ranger private, Oscar D. Baker, were caught up in a supposed murder investigation. A "Mexican" was missing from the Negleys' rancho, and presumed dead. There were even suspects in jail at Eagle Pass, though the evidence was flimsy. Private Aten and his colleague made inquiry and a search at the ranch, but came up empty. Then, they traveled to the Maverick County Jail where they took charge of the less than talkative alleged murderers on a "down and out" (physically out of jail, but yet in custody). With their shackled prisoners riding horseback, the Texas Rangers returned to the scene of the alleged crime. Their intention was, of course, straightforward: "for the purpose of inducing them to make a confession...." Unfortunately for the wheels of justice, neither of the suspects squeaked. The disenchanted Texas Rangers "failed to obtain any valuable Evidence," and the prisoners were returned to jail at Eagle Pass.[52] Good guys don't win all the time, not in the law enforcing game.

Private Jim Latham was not, at least for awhile, unduly concerned with border country affairs. He had participated in the initial capture of the gang suspected of killing Mr. Braeutigam, Allison, Beam, and Collier. Bill Allison had been crisply laid to rest after burning up in the Gillespie County jailhouse fire. Wes Collier, Jim Fannin, and Ede Janes were on the dodge, nowhere to be found, probably out of the country; but, Jack Beam might be nearing his day in court. Purportedly he was in the neighborhood. He no doubt, sooner or later, would be run to ground. Private Latham was worried, worried that if a Texas Ranger were not there for the legal battle, and that if Beam were to actually be found guilty, that the boys from Baird's squad, the ones making the initial arrests, "might be defrauded out of the reward in case of conviction."[53]

Spring was giving way to summer. Good rains had the Rio Grande cresting. On the whole, along the Texas/Mexican border, at least that section patrolled by Company D, there was an aura of tranquility. After a three-day scout, Sergeant B. D. Lindsey and his two-man unit reported "all was quiet." Corporal Wood Saunders and his two-man team had made a scout to Carrizo Springs, reporting "everything quiet."[54] Their reports seem to square with Captain Lam Sieker's overall assessment, one he posted the adjutant general with from Camp San Ambrosia: "No news here, everything very quiet, and the Rio Grande being up gives us a chance to recruit up our horses."[55]

No doubt, probably as a child or young man, Ira Aten had waded into a cool and calm river for ceremonial services of a religious nature. Ranger Ira Aten was fixing to get baptized, again.

Chapter 5

"We opened fire and they returned it"

Accurately focusing the lens of objectivity in an Old West context is often tricky. Sometimes, troublesome as it may be, the exercise is steeped in ambiguity. Conclusive findings are customarily thwarted—or at the minimum skewed by perspective. Unwinding absolute truths regarding nineteenth-century episodes taking place in the Texas/Mexican borderlands is particularly niggling. Texas Ranger Private Ira Aten would soon find himself at the epicenter of such an installment.

Governor John Ireland's dander was up. Escaped convicts were on the loose, and Texas Rangers were on the hunt. Particularly the search was zeroing in on South Texas, the section of ground standing between the fugitives and their supposed freedom if they could but splash across the Rio Grande, gaining entry into Old Mexico.[1] Supplementing investigative work expected of the short-staffed Texas Rangers, the governor had also hired and put special detectives on the case. Company D's Captain Sieker was likewise responsive, advising his boss, Adjutant General Wilburn King, "I arrived here [Uvalde] this morning having recd. a telegram from the Gov. to be on the alert for the men who turned the convicts loose. I have ordered Lt. Jones to be on the lookout for them on the head of the Nueces river & Sergt. Lindsey is scouting the country from Carrizo Springs to the Hardin crossing on the Rio Grande. I am here with the two men employed by the Gov. and after talking the matter over we are inclined to the opinion that they will try & cross the river about 18 miles above Eagle Pass. We have every point guarded and I think if they come this way they will be caught."[2]

Private Ira Aten was riding with Sergeant B. D. Lindsey's detail, as were Privates Ben C. Riley, C. W. Griffin, Oscar D. Baker, C. D. Grant, and Captain Sieker's youngest brother, Frank, who measured his Texas Ranger service in months, not years.[3] By the best reckoning, Sergeant Lindsey supposed their quarry would be headed west for the river from Cotulla, more-or-less a straight line to their

Willburn Hill King, Texas Adjutant General. King would be favorably impressed with Ira Aten's work ethic, courage, and tenacity. *Courtesy Texas State Library and Archives Commission.*

camp on San Ambrosia Creek.[4] The boys in Sergeant Lindsey's command outfitted a pack mule with provisions and set out to intercept the "two bad men."[5] During midmorning of May 31, 1885, ten or twelve miles southeast of camp, the Texas Rangers on pack detail could see dust being stirred in the distance. Pitching the pack animal's lead rope to ground, a quick dismount, and hurried squat with elbows resting on knees to steady the field glasses, revealed two "Mexicans" forking saddles, leading a bareback horse, "way over a mile away."[6] The other Rangers, through hand gestures it is presumed, were alerted.

"How could Anglo lawman tell the difference between good Mexicans and bad? Because of cultural biases, an Anglo lawman distrusted any Mexicans he did not know personally, especially if their behavior appeared suspicious."[7] This was not the day or place of cultural sensitivities. The border country was volatile, a powder keg for rows with racial overtones. Moral judgments made now are fine, but on that thirty-first day of May 1885, Rangers of Sergeant Lindsey's seven-man detachment were riding in real time. Those two "Mexicans"—rightly or wrongly—owed Texas Rangers an explanation as to their business in the section. They would have an answer one way or another.

Encumbered with the pack mule, Privates Aten and Riley had been lazily and nonchalantly ambling along, lagging behind their cohorts, a signal fact not denied, but confirmed by Ira: "Riley and I had been talking that morning and unintentionally let our pack mule drop some distance behind, which was strictly against the rules."[8]

What wasn't against the rules was for the Texas Rangers to take action. That was par business, protocol. What happened next will have a final ending, but disentangling the competing versions is perplexing, especially when the same voice offers contradictory renderings. There is, however, an initial agreement among all sides. Geography was an obstacle prohibiting a smoothly executed law enforcement maneuver. By dawdling along in the rough and broken country Privates Aten and Riley had unintentionally set a course angling that of their comrades, not following directly behind. Due to recent rains the watercourses were up, the Rio Grande was running with spirit, the ancillary creeks with vigor. The other Texas Ranger boys had already crossed over an arroyo choking with water and mud, and now to make a beeline after the two unknown riders, they would have to dash back across. Ira Aten and Ben Riley riding the oblique trail had a clear pathway, even though they were farther removed.

Unfortunately the reader is also removed, by time not distance, and unable to stand as an eyewitness to the unfolding high-drama. So, we are stuck with what we have. Whether myths are shattered or preconceptions cemented will be the hard choice at hand. Or, as a third alternative, simply admit we do not know and will not know—for sure?

Ira Aten's remarks about the affair for an extended 1928 interview are germane. Thirteen years later in another and lengthy interview, Ira's remembrances will have undergone a slight, but telling recalibration, one that will later square with the 1945 publication of his memoirs, an unarguable gemstone of Texas Ranger history. Ira Aten, in part, first recalled:

> I was on pack drive that day and behind the others. B. C. Riley was with me. There were six [besides Aten] of us in all. These two men were cutting across the country, and Sergeant Lindsey, who was a considerable distance ahead of us, started across a slough with his men and their horses bogged. Riley and I saw this and avoided the slough and took right in behind the two men. When about a hundred yards from them, we opened fire and they returned it, all of us shooting with Winchesters....[9]

Just who, in point of fact, fired off the first rounds may be a persnickety academic question, except to the persons shot at. Ira Aten's comment, "took right in behind the two men," does suggest the good guys were on the chase, and by implication, the other guys—good or bad—were on the run. Along about this point in the story, winding down phase one of the pursuit, is where divergent accounts typically meld into a timeworn version penned for popularized Texas Ranger histories. And, here, too, is the spot where indisputable truths began to emerge.

For whatever reason, the two supposed *mal hombres* decided it was in their best interest to hightail it. A tether to the lead animal was dropped, and they put iron to their horses. The race was on. Unluckily when the Texas Rangers made their madcap dash back across the "slough" at breakneck speed there was a wreck. Private Griffin's gelding bogged down, and in panicky efforts to undo itself from the muck threw his rider, breaking the Texas Ranger's collarbone. Sergeant Lindsey, along with Privates Baker and Grant, too, were mired as their struggling horses—spiders in their minds—fought for footing and traction and liberation. These Texas Rangers hadn't toppled from the saddles, but trying to retain balance their wildly flailing contortions were well underway. Had the dicey circumstances been different the show may have even been comical, for a cowboy. As it were, the "Mexicans" were getting away—and that was not funny. Somehow, perhaps because Lady Luck gave him a teasing wink, Frank Sieker dashed through or over the quagmire and topped out, ready for action.

Then there were three Texas Rangers with clear ground before them. If those "Mexicans" were to be overhauled and questioned and arrested or killed it would be left to Privates Aten and Riley, with Sieker trying to overtake them as backup. Quitting was not an option. The three Rangers leaned forward in the saddles, furiously raking rowels, spurring forward movement—at the gallop, burning the wind.

Their horses blowing, nostrils flaring and sides heaving, Apolonio Gonzales and his thirteen-year-old son (21 in another account) Pedro looked back over their shoulders watching three men speedily trying to close with them. For what purpose, they knew not. The fellows were approaching fast, riding with abandon as aggressors, not smiling allies or good neighbors. They were scared. Whipping their quirts with fervor the pair set in motion again, breaking for the river at a dead run. After racing two miles Privates Ira Aten and Ben Riley began overtaking them, shouting for their quarry to stop right now—*Alto ahorrita*, and they did.[10] But stop and wait for who knew what, they did not. Apolonio and Pedro slid rifles from saddle scabbards and either answered the Texas Rangers' bullet pinging serenade, or they themselves struck the first note.[11] In any event, one of their first shots knocked Ben Riley from the saddle, a nasty hole in his thigh. Another bullet stung Ranger Riley's left shoulder. Yes, it was pretty good shooting for a hundred yards out.[12] Ira Aten explains what happened after Private Riley was shot, involuntarily dismounted: "And they commenced shooting at me. I was about one hundred yards when I commenced shooting. One was a young man and one was an old man."[13]

Stepping backward was not in Ira Aten's makeup. This may have been his baptismal exchange of gunfire, but it would not be the last. Time and again in a gunplay Ira Aten would step to the mark. He was nervy. That was irrefutable. Though Ben Riley was down, and Frank Sieker was yet behind, Ira Aten feverishly began working, levering round after .44 round into his Winchester's chamber and triggering his teed-off response: "I kept on coming, not crowding them too fast, and shooting at them...."[14] All the while Aten's horse waltzed underneath him, Ira's high-top boots glued in the stirrups for dear life. With Colt's six-shooter in hand, Private Frank Sieker finally caught up, for a split-second. A bullet fired by either Apolonio or Pedro punched into Frank's heart, killing him while yet sitting upright in the saddle.[15] Before falling motionless to the desert

floor Frank had managed to scream, "Oh, my God!" That caught Ira
Aten's attention, but just for an instant. He made note that Frank
was down, still clutching his cocked sixgun, but knew in a heartbeat
what he must do: "I turned back and kept shooting, and saw one of
the men drop his gun and fall low on his horse. I knew that I had hit
him.... I saw the second fellow fall low on his horse just as they got to
the top of a hill."[16] Taking into consideration his predicament, atop
a wildly gyrating gelding, with bullets flying all around, Ira Aten's
handiwork with the Winchester was rather nifty. Even from atop a
horse he had managed to inflict wounds on both of his adversaries,
though not mortally. Patrolling the vast and isolated borderlands—
riding Lucifer's Line—is now and was then chancy and dangerous
business. Who fired the mortal shot that killed Private Frank Sieker?
Man or boy? It matters not a whit. In the tough border country boys
morphed into men quick. Teenagers carrying guns was nothing new.
From a border country lawman's viewpoint a thirteen-year-old with
a Winchester was fair game—his bullets would know not any more
remorse than an old man's. Survival counted, sentiment didn't.

After cautiously riding forward, cresting the hill, Private Aten
could see through tinges of fading blue gunsmoke the spot Apolonio
and Pedro Gonzales were making tracks for—the Loyas' Ranch on
the American side of the Rio Grande, where familiar faces would
eagerly cover their play.[17] Or, from another of their perspectives,
protect them from the scruffy looking madmen intent on shooting
them first and asking questions later. Private Ira Aten hesitated, not
unwisely, for a sobering reality check: "On the other side of the hill
where the Mexicans had gone I could see some 'dobe' houses and
many men running about. I well knew that I had no business going
down there alone and decided to wait for the rest."[18]

Catching his breath, letting his horse blow, and cogitating about
the scary mess that had just uncorked, Ira waited for Texas Ranger
reinforcements, who he could see were making their way toward him,
trotting up the hill with grim faces and unlimbered Winchesters. Sergeant Lindsey reined in first, understandably seeking an explanation
as to what-the-hell had happened, and where were the killers. He had
one dead Ranger, another wounded. Someone had to pay. Ira Aten
pointed downhill: "Down among the jacals, Mexicans were running
around with their guns. I told Lindsey they were down there where
the Mexicans were and they had guns, and we would have trouble if
we went down there."[19] An ever gutsy and proud Louisiana-born Ben

Company D Texas Ranger Sergeant Benjamin Dennis "Ben" Lindsey, a fighting machine, future Mounted Customs Inspector, entrepreneur and salty Bexar County Sheriff who couldn't abide any whining "sissies." *From Texas Ranger Sketches, courtesy the author, Robert W. Stephens.*

Lindsey (future Bexar County Sheriff), who could not and never did abide any "sissies," had but four short words to gruffly cough up: "We will go down."[20]

Making doubly sure there was a fresh round in the Winchester's chamber—one under the hammer—Sergeant Lindsey, followed by Privates Aten, Baker, and Grant, did what Texas Rangers were expected to do—something. Determined, they marched off the hill and straight into the Loyas' stronghold, where they were not cordially greeted by about fifteen "Mexicans," all armed.[21]

One in the crowd of unfriendly faces was Pendincia Herrera, a part-time deputy for the Webb County Sheriff, Dario Gonzales. If there was any parlaying to be done, it would be through the auspices of Deputy Herrera. At the isolated rancho, eighty miles from Laredo the county seat, he and he alone, held dominion over the armed *vaqueros*. If the Texas Rangers—who now had been adequately identified—wanted war they could have it, but negotiations did seem more appropriate—no need for additional bloodshed. Sergeant Lindsey, who had met Pendincia Herrera on a previous scout, inquired:

> I asked him who were those men that had just ran into the house. He said their names were Gonzales, Father and Son, and lived near Laredo. I asked him what they were doing there. He said that they had come over to Loyas after a horse and had been out to a sheep camp after said horse. I told him that they had made a bad break by running from us, that we supposed them to be thieves & pursued them & when we come up with them they opened fire on us wounding two of our men. He said the Mexicans were wounded two [*sic*]. I then demanded them & went into the house & saw them. I found them both slightly wounded, one in the shoulder the other through the hand. I told Herrera that these men would have to go to Carrizo Springs.... [22]

At that point the situation became touchy. Pendincia Herrera refused to turn over the father and his adolescent son, unless there was an assurance the pair would be taken straight to Laredo, not Carrizo Springs. There was quite a heated back and forth, Herrera protesting and insisting "that they should go to Laredo." If the Texas Ranger sergeant would but bend a little, Pendincia pledged with his word of honor that he would personally deliver the prisoners to the Webb County Jail. Sergeant Lindsey was brave, but practical. "Our force was too small to take them to Carrizo Springs so I then told him we would go to Laredo with them. It was agreed that three Mexicans & three rangers should carry them."[23]

The Texas Rangers now knew, no matter who they held in provisional custody, it was not the intended targets of their hurried scout.[24] Therein lay the harbinger for a snag, a signal fact pointed out by and seemingly worrying Private Ira Aten: "They were not the convicts we were after."[25] Rubbing like a cocklebur under the saddle blanket was that irritating little question: Were Apolonio and Pedro Gonzales even crooks in the first place? Shortly to be mentioned in the *El Paso Times* was a characterization that Apolonio Gonzales "had been noted as the best guide and Indian trailer in this country, and owns a large ranch."[26] Later, the *Dallas Daily Herald* would also carry the story. Its newsman was aware of the prospect for an emerging reality: "Gonzales bears a high character here and his statements are received with implicit credence, he has always been honest, and he and his boy acted in self-preservation."[27] Absent any conclusive evidence, Ranger Private Ira Aten was nudged into proffering a somewhat anemic generalization: "As to whether they were criminals, I guess they were all criminals in there."[28]

Although in particular twentieth-century writings Apolonio and Pedro Gonzales would be melodramatically labeled as "bandits" and "desperadoes" and "murdering horse thieves," during 1885 those appellations were, perhaps unfortunately for Texas Rangers, wholly lacking. Upriver and down, along the *Rio Bravo*, in many camps and in many *Mexicanos'* minds, it was the *Americanos* who had ridden hell-bent, shooting at unsuspecting peons looking for a strayed sway-backed nag. Even the American press was theorizing that Apolonio and Pedro might have justifiably fought and fled "believing they were being pursued by a band of robbers."[29]

Such a lame-sounding excuse was not necessarily preposterous. The state's law enforcers were not decked out in uniforms, nor were they wearing distinctive badges. As with the shooting affair at Green Lake, the Texas Rangers knew they were lawmen, but did the other guys? Bank and train robbers and cow stealers and *bandidos* ran in packs, riding horses, carrying rifles and wearing six-shooters. Horse-back Texas Rangers carried Colt's six-shooters and Winchesters and, too, worked in small sets: Friends or foes? In the wild and woolly brush country along the border, and at a distance, differentiating between the good guys and the bad guys could understandably be a challenge, especially difficult during those times when hot words were being exchanged—in two different languages. Again, listening to borderland cowman Adolph Petree, although about a different instance, is enlightening: "We went to Juan Reyes' house, and Mr. Tumlinson and I saw a Mexican leave there. We went and overtaken him and he reached down to get his gun. And that damn boss man, old Bill Thornton, like to have shot him in to. I said, 'Don't pull your trigger. He hasn't drawn his gun yet!' The damn Mexican didn't want to give his gun up but finally dropped it. Showing he didn't want any fight. We told him to take the goddamn gun and go on. He couldn't talk a word of English and we couldn't talk a word of Mexican. That is hell, you know, when you get in that shape."[30]

Making a mistake, sometimes, was not fixable. Foolishly allowing strangers to close the gap too quick could prove suicidal—for Texas Rangers or owlhoots or innocent travelers. Even a feted nineteenth-century Texas Ranger captain was ruefully compelled to acknowledge: "Men have been known to resist Rangers claiming that they thought they were citizens banded together for the purpose of a lynching." Astoundingly, and somewhat implausibly, he thought folks should *just* be able to recognize the Texas Rangers as upright and honest lawmen because of their "general appearance" and because they "rode big shod horses, and had pack mules."[31] The onus of identification seems misplaced: Backwards, if you will.

What was not misplaced was the wounded Private Ben Riley sprawled on the side of a hill, and the badly bruised Private C. W. Griffin painfully lying in a muddy gully with a fractured collarbone. Both needed medical attention badly. It was time to move. Sergeant Lindsey was no dithering Ranger noncom; he could drop the hammer on decision making. Without delay he assigned Privates Aten, Baker, and Grant the duty of helping escort the prisoners to Laredo. He, after commandeering an ambulance, rickety as it was, would get the wounded and injured Rangers and Frank Sieker's dead body to William Votows' ranch.[32] Then, after medical attention was assured, he would overtake them somewhere along the eighty-mile road to Laredo.[33] Sergeant Lindsey was confident he could catch up; the trip to Laredo would necessitate an overnight stop for Deputy Herrera's squadron and the Texas Rangers.[34]

Pendencia Herrera quickly secured a buggy, placed the unshackled prisoners inside, slapped leathers over the mules' rumps, and initiated the grueling trip. Beside him rode three heavily armed *vaqueros*. They were along not to prevent an escape, but to keep the Rangers from avenging Sieker's death. The Rangers, on the other hand, were there to assure the prisoners were actually jailed at the county seat. Both parties, hands never far from triggers, apprehensively watched each other.

During daylight hours the Rangers rode behind the buggy, not wishing to turn their backs on Pendencia Herrera and his men. When the veil of night wrapped around them, Privates Aten, Baker, and Grant judiciously took additional precautions, according to Ira: "We camped one night before we got there. We thought we were going to be massacred by the Mexicans. We slept on our arms all night."[35] After night's passing without any six-shooter mishaps the trip was resumed.

In the interim, after being assured Private Griffin could withstand a wagon trip to Eagle Pass for broken bone repair, Sergeant Lindsey could report he had managed phase one of his mission: "After arriving at Mr. Votows, and making necessary arrangements to have the corpse cared for, and Riley's comfort prepared, I followed after the Laredo scout, and overtook them next day near Laredo. We arrived there on the 1st of June...."[36] The Texas Rangers were soon to be in for a rude awakening, not heralded as heroes.

To be sure, Apolonio and Pedro Gonzales were locked away in Webb County's jailhouse, a four-year-old two-story brick structure at 1100 Farragut Street. Father and son were woeful prisoners for awhile, a little while—thirty minutes' worth, just long enough for them to officially execute a criminal Complaint. The tables had turned upside down. Warrants issued. Sheriff Dario Gonzales, a powerful local politician and a kinsman of the arrested persons, was not hesitant, nor was he the least bit cowed by Texas Ranger reputations. The sheriff and "a bunch of Mexican deputy sheriffs" arrested the Rangers, charging them with Assault with Intent to Murder. Sergeant Lindsey, along with Privates Aten, Baker, and Grant were jailed.[37]

Could or should the outcome have been different? Ira Aten pondered: "I always blamed myself that I did not shoot those two men off their horses first, but it is rather difficult to hit a man who is riding up a hill from you along a winding trail and shooting back at you."[38] Pedro Gonzales' and his father's flight up and over a knoll may not have been exactly trouble or pain free, considering the gunshot wounds, but their wading across the Rio Grande's shallowness after their release was. Formalized extradition or a good trick, that is what it would now take to sucker them back onto American soil. Meanwhile, while bureaucratic wheels were spinning, four Texas Rangers languished in jail—day after day.

Surely as Ira was daydreaming he could almost smell the aroma wafting to his second-floor jail cell of Grandma Kate Aten's (Ira's mother) freshly baked treats, and mentally picture that crockery cookie jar that was never empty—and never off-limits. He knew Cal and Eddie would be indulging themselves, as would his niece Virgie and her little brothers, his nephews Samuel Austin, Elmer Clarence, and Albert Floyd. That wild bunch partook of those tasty tidbits every afternoon, for they knew Grandma Aten "never scolded and we [they] were free to do as we [they] pleased. Surely, she was an angel."[39] No doubt he chuckled to himself, thinking of that day Cal and Eddie and Virgie and cousin Elmer had all armed themselves with clubs, and marched to the granary to kill rats as they "were running and jumping everywhere," trying to escape, which Virgie hoped they would. But, she could ill afford to show weakness—as a girl—playing a boys' game. Nor could she chicken out when challenged to walk the "high and narrow beam" in the barn, even though she really thought doing so was utterly pointless. Unquestionably as he sat in that dingy dungeon, Ira recalled days when all the boys and girls went swimming, seeing "snakes raise their heads, look at them, and disappear." Everyone said they were water moccasins but the snakes never bothered the kids, nor vice versa.[40] Ira knew, too, that if daddy was there he would tell him to hang on, persevere, have faith. The Lord Almighty would look after him: Pray for forgiveness and salvation, that would have been Reverend Austin Cunningham Aten's message.

Papa Aten probably wouldn't have been harmoniously attuned to some of Ira's innermost feelings, but Ranger managers and Texas politicos were not tenderfeet, nor were they naive. Once those mad boys got out of jail, if they didn't go to the state penitentiary, they'd have to transfer. San Ambrosia Creek might overflow with blood. The bosses "knew that our feelings was too great after that against Mexicans for them to leave us there, as they knew we would be killing Mexicans whenever we got a chance."[41] One day bled into the next.

Though it cannot rise above the rhetorical, at least without expanded historical sleuthing, could underhanded political intrigues have played a part in a decision to imprison the state's lawmen? Physically incarcerating a whole squad of Texas Rangers was not the norm. More often than not in those situations where a Texas Ranger was compelled to face the legal music, he or they were allowed temporary liberty, a light bail bond or personal recognizance—pending Indictments or until the District Court's docket was called. The bitter brouhaha pitting Senator E. F. Hall against Joe Shely and the Texas Rangers had not abated. The Rangers were locked away at Laredo, Hall's senatorial district. There was no love lost. La Salle County's sheriff, C. B. McKinney, an ex-Ranger, earlier had defended the Texas Rangers by attacking Senator Hall publicly in pages of *The San Antonio Daily Express*. It was not pretty. McKinney pulled no punches:

Hall was not a democrat until he became one for "revenue only." He went to Brownsville, Texas, about the year 1866, as a hospital steward in a negro regiment, and was active in the organization of Brownsville's first Loyal League. What he was before that only Hall himself knows, and he in all probability will never care to impart the information. Whether Hall has ever been naturalized or not, even, is unknown; whether he is a Jew or Gentile, circumcised or uncircumcised; in fact, he landed at Brownsville under the name of Hall. Back of that fact nothing is known.

From that time, however, he has been pretty thoroughly known. He drifted up the Rio Grande to Laredo, and there achieved quite a number of successes. Among other enterprises he became proprietor of a dance house and gambling hall, officiating alternately as "dealer" and "bucker" at the tables of the latter institution, the funds for the gaming tables being the fruits of the division of the spoils of his hired prostitutes. About this time, too, Hall was acting as a lawyer and land agent. In this capacity he received from a gentleman in Corpus Christi four hundred dollars to be invested in town lots in Laredo. Since that date the Corpus Christi investor has never been able to find his city lots, nor has Hall ever returned one dollar of the four hundred sent him.... it would be interesting to let Capt. Shely state what he knows about the senator's unprofessional and dirty work, in defense of criminals on this border.... It goes sorely against the grain to see this unctuous scoundrel, who in his own town could not enter the family of a gentleman, nor even get into the kitchen, unless in the absence of the owner....[42]

These venomous barbs did not touch on the possibility of animosity regarding the earlier Texas Ranger arrests of Felix Taylor, Simp DeSpain, and John Laxson, the son of Jesse Laxson, Senator Hall's good *amigo*. Hard-ball politics were played in Laredo. Senator Hall was a power hitter, swinging a heavy bat. From Senator Hall's dugout, could it have been time for Texas Rangers to suffer a third strike, on the third out, dejectedly retiring from the diamond—and straight into the jailhouse?[43] Did Senator Hall and Sheriff Dario Gonzales put their heads together and fix the game?

Regardless of outside influences, if there were any, Sergeant Lindsey and his platoon were locked in the Webb County Jail. Their situation was dire. The unwelcome vacation, however, did afford an opportunity for collaboration. Sergeant Lindsey would somewhat later report the official version of what happened: "When about twelve miles from camp we saw two Mexicans with a lead horse traveling towards the Rio Grande river. They were about half mile away. I thought it necessary to investigate their proceedings and started towards them. After riding about two hundred yards toward them, they ran. We pursued them. The race continued about two miles. When Aten and Reilly [sic] overtook them, they told the Mexicans to surrender, which they started to do. Reilly reached for their guns, which they had previously drawn. Just as he did so the younger Mexican shot him in the shoulder. He was shot by the older one through the hips. Reilly and Aten returned the fire. About fifteen shots were fired. Frank Sieker was the 3rd man that come up. He was shot as he came up…. "[44] Whether it was in the jailhouse or elsewhere is hazy, but somewhere along the way Captain Sieker interviewed Aten, learning, not surprisingly, that Ira's recollections were "substantially" the same as Sergeant Lindsey's.[45] Everyone, then, was on the same page.

Well, except the newspaper reporters. Writing for the *Corpus Christi Caller*, the editor after praising Frank Sieker with "no more gallant ranger ever drew a breath," lamented the fact that "carelessness and overconfidence will down the best of them." Further, the newsman noted that Mexicans had frequently been killed in the borderlands, especially in Dimmit County, and "arresting them in that section is a perilous business."[46] Reading between the lines is effortless: *Mexicanos* along the border were not unjustly worrying when approached by heavily armed Anglos. Who among them, at first, could distinguish between the lawless and the lawmen, the upright Texas Ranger or the insidious reprobate with cold-hearted desire for killing itching a conscienceless fingertip? Readership in North Texas were not steeped in the perfect distinction between Rangers in white hats and Mexicans in black *sombreros*, as reflected again in pages of the *Dallas Daily Herald*: "The whole affair is regarded as most unfortunate by all concerned. There are not wanting those, however, who unhesitatingly assert that the rangers were to blame. In that portion of Dimmit county where the fight took place many Mexicans of late months have been inhumanly murdered. Gonzales nor his son spoke

Aten family Winchesters and one of Ira's saddle scabbards in possession of Ira's grandson Gary Boyce Radder. As a Ranger Ira may have—or may not have—used this 1873 Winchester during the shoot-out with alleged desperadoes when Texas Ranger Frank Sieker was killed. Below the 1873 Model are rifles of later manufacture, a Winchester Model 1895, .30-40, and a Winchester Model 1894 .30-30. *Courtesy Jeri and Gary Boyce Radder.*

English, and when they saw four Americans armed and in the dress of private citizens closing in on them they naturally deemed it another assassination and fell to working their Winchesters accordingly."[47] In the particular instance at hand, a probing journalist for the *El Paso Daily Times* was convinced and conjecturing that the whole bloody affair was but "a deplorable mistake." He was won over to the idea that the Gonzaleses thought they were being attacked by a nefarious "band of robbers." Self-preservation and self-defense had prompted their shooting and scampering for the protection of the only lawman they knew, Webb County Deputy Pendencia Herrera, and it was then, and only then, that "the fearful error was discovered for the first time."[48] Another newspaperman, too, evidently thought there might have been room for a smidgen of misunderstanding, colossal and tragic as it was: "Some days ago they [Webb County Grand Jury] returned bills of indictment against all the rangers who took part in the recent battle on the Rio Grande, between the rangers and a supposed (?) lot of thieves; but failed to find evidence to indict the Mexicans who were in the same fight."[49]

Ira Aten, especially at the time, did not care. He wanted out of jail. He and his companions had been locked away for twenty-six days. Aten's claim that "we demanded that the sheriff come to see us," does suggests a smidgen of after-the-fact condescension in light of their near-monthlong forced furlough. On the other hand, Ira Aten's assertion that Laredo's then city marshal, Stephen Boyard, "a Louisiana creole from New Orleans," befriended the Texas Ranger prisoners is not outlandish. Ira Aten knew why: He "was a mixture of one-fourth negro, one fourth Mexican, and one-half white. However, he was all white at heart...."[50] Aten's assertion that they "finally" found an "American" to make their bail-bond is somewhat peculiar. At the time, because of the International & Great Northern Railroad entering town from San Antonio, busy Laredo was considered the "Gateway to Mexico." Even though the town was 80 percent folks of "Mexican extraction," there were a considerable number of non-Mexican businessmen: Joseph Christen the Commercial Hotel's proprietor, C. L. Fowzer's undertaking parlor, building contractor Jack Eistetter, H. Schmidt's tailor shop, John O. Buez's lumberyard, A. M. Bruni's dry goods and grocery store, George Woodman's hardware store, Fred Underwood's jewelry store, a saloon run by Charles Moser, and "Uncle" Johnny Thompson's Beer Garden and Ice Cream Parlor. Put into the mix the Laredo Postmaster, H. A. Burbank, Justice of the Peace George Dye, and accredited medical doctors A. W. Wilcox, J. P. Arthur, J. M. McKnight, along with dentist B. G. Atlee, and druggist R. J. Randolph, and the picture becomes clearer.[51] Apparently, not everyone was near as fretful with chipping in, as the Texas Rangers were in chipping out. In the end though, a suitable bondsman came forth. Sergeant Lindsey and boys were at last turned out, free to go—but not too far. A criminal case was still lodged against them, still on Texas' Twelfth Judicial District's books. The blasé interest in the Texas Rangers' plight on the part of Laredo businessmen may very well have spoken to subsurface dynamics: the shooting was a political hot potato. Laredo was a hotbed of local politics.

Privates Oscar Baker and C. D. Grant were hot under their collars. Private Baker while yet in jail had fired off charges to the *San Antonio Express*, repeated here in part:

> The population of this county (Webb) is nearly all Mexicans. They rule the county and are not disposed to give us much show. The county officers are all greasers. The two men who

Private Oscar D. Baker. Although his actions during Winchester fireworks with alleged Mexican bandidos may have been valiant, his after-action remarks caused him and the Texas Ranger's front office a belly full of unwelcome heartburn. *Courtesy Research Center, Texas Ranger Hall of Fame and Museum.*

murdered poor Frank Seiker [*sic*] are relatives of old Darea [*sic*] Gonzales, sheriff of this county, an infernal thief, coward and murderer. He is a villain deep dyed in the wool. In order that these assassins might go free, they have caused the rangers to be arrested, and old Gonzales is the chief villain of the forty thieves that compose the county government of Webb.[52]

Fully a dozen Webb County grand jurors petitioned Governor Ireland to have Captain Sieker's Company D removed from that section of the border: "Harm may occur at any moment, if the company remains. The citizens are excited and much opposed to the company remaining among them." Judiciously the newspaperman picked up on another sagacious detail, lest unwarranted racial overtones are mistakenly blended into the hubbub. "This reporter has only to add that the report was signed by every member of the grand jury, which is composed of the wealthiest and best citizens of Webb county, only two of whom—Juan Ortiz and C. Benavides—are of Mexican birth.... Six of these grand jurymen represent wealth in the aggregate close on to $1,000,000 in value. This reporter can safely say that the above report reflects the sentiments of ninety-nine out of every hundred citizens of Webb county not of Mexican birth."[53]

Someone writing for the *Galveston Daily News*, probably Texas' most widely read newspaper at the time, picked up on the theme of shaking up the Frontier Battalion: "The report of the Webb county grand jury would indicate that a reform of the rangers force is necessary. A reorganization of the force from the adjutant general's office to the bottom might, on the whole, be a public service."[54]

The governor was not happy. That in turn made the adjutant general not happy. The ooze of Texas Ranger negativity was taking its toll: "and you [Captain Sieker] can easily understand how unpleasant it is for the Governor and myself [AG King] to be compelled to scan these reports of constantly recurring and sometimes apparently needless difficulties."[55] Private Baker was undergoing a difficulty. In response to his blistering letter about the sheriff a Webb County Grand Jury indicted him for Criminal Libel.[56] Adding to the steam billowing from beneath Governor Ireland's collar, were the allegations lodged against Private Grant, serious charges. Attorney Charles Pierce was asserting that the Ranger had pointed his loaded pistol at him in a threatening manner, scaring him badly. The accusation was fervidly denied by Private Grant, but the Texas Ranger did admit to a confrontational dustup: "I merely acted as you or any other man would have acted. I attempted, perhaps hastily, to resist an insult."[57] The governor was in a high state of agitation, which in turn, again put Adjutant General King in a stir, in fact, so disgruntled that he forthwith demanded that Captain Sieker discharge both Rangers, no dithering, no excuses. Captain Sieker was a trouper. He forthwith complied with the AG's orders, noting in the Monthly Return: "O. D. Baker, C. D Grant, Dropped from Roll by order from A. G. O."[58]

Texas Ranger Private Ira Aten. Though posed in a photographer's studio with weapons prominently displayed as attention-grabbing props, make no mistake Ranger Ira Aten was a man fearlessly capable of standing alone during a dicey tumult, proving to be one nervy adversary throughout a number of gunfights: A Rawhide Ranger. *Courtesy Jeri and Gary Boyce Radder.*

Ira Aten's comments about closing down this chapter of his Texas Ranger history are laconic. It seems even then he knew that all was not black or white. With schoolboy simplicity Ira owned up: "The Governor ordered us moved from San Ambrosia after we got into our trouble. Our cases were dismissed, you know."[59]

What the governor, the adjutant general, and the Company D captain did know, in reality, was that Private Aten was a stayer. In the heat of battle he had stayed hitched. Ira Aten had sand.

Chapter 6

"If you pull it, Jack, I'll kill you"

In accordance with orders from Austin headquarters, Company D's main camp was shifted from San Ambroisa Creek back to Uvalde County.[1] It would seem Lam Sieker, too, could see the rationale in repositioning Company D Rangers due to hardened feelings. He notified AG King in writing: "All I could do at my present camp [San Ambrosia] would be in a negative way...."[2] Sieker's "negative way" was but gobbledygook: Rangers would brutally settle the score, he feared.

Certainly the captain's assessment may have been on target. Remembering that little law enforcement axiom, "you might beat the rap, but you can't beat the ride," the unforgiving Texas Rangers of Company D acted. On August 1, 1885, in Laredo for court, Sergeant Ben Lindsey and "3 men" arrested Pendencia and Tomas Herrera, "charged in Dimmit Co. with resisting officers." The tables in these Texas Rangers' minds had been turned back upright. The entry in Company D's Monthly Return for August is curt. "Delivered them to Shff. Webb Co.," who would himself soon be ousted from political office. Whether or not Private Ira Aten was one of those "3 men" is indistinct. He was, however, later in the month particularly identified as conveying prisoner Tobe Edwards, charged with Theft of a Horse, to the sheriff of Uvalde County, Henry W. Baylor.[3]

Captain Sieker was also conveying someone, himself. As early as March, upon learning that the Frontier Battalion's Quartermaster, Captain John O. Johnson, was about to accept the lucrative job as Postmaster for the city of Austin, Lam Sieker had been vying to backfill. His career aspirations were honorable, aboveboard—not hush-hush.[4] The Frontier Battalion realignments took place during October. On the twelfth, General Order No. 85 made it official. Captain Lam Sieker was promoted to battalion quartermaster.[5] Leaving Lieutenant Frank Jones in command of Company D and caring for his prized horse, Captain Sieker reported for duty at Austin.[6] Although its impact on Ira Aten's life has been overlooked or underplayed,

Captain Sieker's promotion will factor drastically and dramatically in resetting the young Ranger's law enforcing compass.

For October of 1885, Private Aten was a whirlwind of activity. He and another Ranger made a trip into Edwards County, arresting T. M. Wilmore, wanted in Nolan County (Sweetwater) for Assault with Intent to Murder, covering 160 miles in five days. The prisoner did not take well to confinement in the Uvalde County Jail, so he escaped. Private Aten was put back on his trail. After a grueling trip, Ira finally ran Wilmore to ground on the Burris Ranch in Edwards County and jugged him again. The following week Ira was hunting for cattle stolen in Tom Green County (San Angelo) which were reportedly being driven for clandestine export into Mexico. On the Texas side of the Rio Grande, Privates Ira Aten and W. W. Collier recaptured the stolen beeves in Dimmit County. Realizing they were being pursued by two Rangers, the thieves had abandoned the cattle, racing for asylum at the river. Privates Aten and Collier came in second place, but recovering the cattle was a pretty nifty prize. The owner thought so, anyway.[7]

Though coming to a close, the tail-end of 1885 was anything but quiet for Private Ira Aten. During December on separate scouts he covered more than 500 horseback miles and was away from Camp Leona, which had been reactivated, more than two-thirds of the month. Perhaps his most significant success during these scouts, aside from serving as a deterrent to some would-be cow thieves, was his once again recovering a herd of stolen cattle in Dimmit County.[8] Private Aten aggressively attacking his workday assignment was not going unnoticed, not in the field, nor at battalion headquarters.

One of the most spell-binding chapters in the saga of Ira Aten's law-enforcing days unravels during the front half of 1886. It seems that two of Braeutigam's supposed killers, Jack Beam and Wesley Collier, had been rounded up after their break from the Bexar County Jail, and due to close proximity had been locked away the year before in Mason County's jail—for a little while.[9] There was a second jailbreak, and the bad boys were on the run again.[10] During September of 1885 Private Aten and two men had scouted in Kerr and Bandera Counties but "failed to learn anything of their whereabouts."[11] For several months it seemed as if fugitives Collier and Beam had fallen off the face of the earth. Out of sight does not necessarily equate with out of mind, not for the Texas Rangers—and in this specific case the governor, too. After Father Time had ushered in a new year, news about possible sightings of the wayward fellows picked up. The hunt intensified. Private Aten made one scout trying to locate them, but as far as suspects Collier and Beam were involved Ira met with no success,[12] although he could report while looking for them he had bumbled into Adrian Wilson, wanted for theft, arresting him on January 23, 1886.[13]

Not content to stand idle, Private Aten, teaming up with Sheriff Ira Wheat from Edwards County, on the twenty-fourth of January started looking for Collier and Beam once more. After a four-day search "on the Devil's River in Kimble County [Junction]" that scout was terminated, Sheriff Wheat returning to his home base. Ira Aten remained in the field, this time hunting for John Odle, who was charged with murder in Burnet County. Ira, *alone*, followed Odle's trail deep into the Devil's River country of Crockett County. After the trail played out, Ira returned to Camp Leona via Brackettville, Kinney County. On this one scout he was out twenty-two days, covering some 600 miles. With a quick turnaround, on February 17, 1885, Ranger Aten sashayed over to the Hill Ranch and arrested William Redman for purportedly stealing a horse.[14] Again, Private Ira Aten's persistence did not go unseen.

Particularly friendly to the German enclave in Texas' Hill Country, according to Aten, Governor John Ireland had a mulish plan.[15] The thought that Wes Collier and Jack Beam were time and again outfoxing the Blind Mistress of Justice was wearing thin. There's little doubt the governor had turned to Captain Sieker, validating his scheme and double checking his personnel selection. Ira Aten had caught his eye. On March 6, Private Ira Aten was summoned to Austin on the shadowy pretext of delivering Captain Sieker's horse.[16] Singling out Ranger Aten for an important special assignment is clear indication Ira was maturing as a lawman, earning respect from his bosses. As a man of but twenty-two years, he had satisfactorily reacted under real pressure—galloping hard to join with suspected enemies with Winchester in hand, exchanging scorching gunfire. The good governor had a message for his budding Texas Ranger superstar: arrest Braeutigam's murders using all means at his disposal, overtly or covertly. Time was of not any import; stay after them with the perseverance of a bloodhound—or tiger if they wanted a fight.[17]

On detached service Ira Aten began making an investigation into the whereabouts of fugitive Jack Beam. Ira laid on the pressure, scouting openly and aggressively throughout Williamson, Blanco,

Burnet, and Travis Counties.[18] Figuring, smartly, that the outlaw would be fashioning plans to skip to parts unknown but would probably seek a farewell visit with his sister, Ira too made his move. Beam's brother-in-law's place on Travis County's Pedernales Creek was placed under surveillance. Pressing into service the two Thruman brothers as citizen possemen, the stakeout kicked off. On the second day, from their lair on a brushy hill, with the aid of binoculars, the manhunters espied a lone rider coming in. He was riding a "good" horse and had tied behind the saddle a colorful blanket and an oilcloth slicker, indicators to Ira that the man was traveling, "coming to bid his sister good-bye." When the rider arrived at the homeplace, he didn't put the horse in the nearby barn, but left it saddled and fed grain from a box nailed to a tree. Ira's interpretation was straightforward and reasonable: The fellow was ensuring a fast getaway if need be. Darkness soon enveloped the little ranch. Ira Aten and his helpers moved closer. The Thruman boys actually found a secluded spot inside the barn. Texas Ranger Aten opted to remain outside, explaining: "I took a position between the horse and the tree, squatting down almost under his neck." Around nine o'clock that night the cabin's door opened. Ira could hear the melodic tune of jingling spur rowels as the mysterious form eased toward the saddled horse. When almost eye to eye Ranger Aten jumped up, popping into action, sticking his six-shooter right into Beam's belly, ordering: "Hands up, Jack." Throwing down the saddlebags he had been carrying, Jack went for his Colt's revolver. Ira finishes the story. "I was so close to him that I threw my left hand over on his right wrist and pushed down upon it as hard as I could to keep him from pulling his six-shooter, at the same time saying 'If you pull it, Jack, I'll kill you. I'll kill you if you pull it.'" Thankfully for Ira, once they deciphered what was happening the Thruman boys rushed from the barn and helped physically subdue Jack Beam. After they placed him in handcuffs, the night was passed where they had wrestled him to the ground; it was thirty-five miles to Fredericksburg. The next day (March 24, 1886), at the county seat, Texas Ranger Aten extracted a promise that folks would not "mob" Jack Beam, and then he turned the luckless prisoner over to local authorities.[19]

Two fellows had learned something that day: Texas Ranger Aten confirmed from Beam that another of the suspects in Braeutigam's demise was, indeed, Jim Fannin, a man never to be heard from again. And Wesley Collier, who was supposed to meet Beam that night for a trip out of Texas, knew it was time to make long tracks before he too, landed in the calaboose.[20] Ranger Aten reported success of Jack Beam's capture to Governor Ireland, knowing Wes Collier would show up—sooner or later, here or there. For a manhunter, patience is, indeed, a golden virtue. Now, pleased that he might not lose the German vote, and that justice was at long last being served, an elated governor noted Ira's actual tenacity. Lam Sieker had been spot on right. Aten was a "good Ranger."

Good Ranger that he was, and yet knowing his work was but half done, Ira Aten still managed time to scoop up suspected horse thief C. C. Morrison on March 25, 1886, turning him over to the Travis County Sheriff, Malcom M. Hornsby.[21] Private Aten may or may not have put the San Ambrosia shooting affair and the capture of Jack Beam behind him, but loose ends were hanging, and Governor Ireland was not a forgetful chief executive. Private Ira Aten maintained the hunt for Wes Collier.

During the afternoon hours of the twenty-ninth of April 1886, in Travis County, the young Texas Ranger thought he had—inadvertently—struck paydirt. Working informants and sporadic scraps of criminal intelligence, Ira Aten found himself sitting on the front porch at George Wells' rancho on Long Hollow, about ten miles southeast of Liberty Hill. Ira had unsaddled his horse, put it in Wells' barn, and the two were pleasantly killing time before supper, talking about items of general importance and the possible whereabouts of Wes Collier in particular. Suddenly, George Wells looked up, peered into the distance, exclaiming "I believe that's your man." Ira Aten reacted instantly: "I threw my field glasses on him and saw that he had on a vest with a large red bandanna around his neck and his right hand in it, as if in a sling. He was riding a big sorrel horse." Telling George to sit real tight, Ira quickly slid into the house, trying to maintain clear sight yet hoping to remain unobserved. As the rider drew closer, Ira realized his good fortune: It was Wes. Private Aten checked the loads in his Colt's, his Winchester not handy, still in the saddle scabbard in the barn with his other gear. Fugitive Collier drew yet closer, suspiciously eyeing his surroundings with coyote caution. There was not a clue George had company. When he reined up in front of the porch, Wes Collier inquired of Mr. Wells, wanting to learn the location of the Glasscock Ranch. George raised his hand to gesture directions. Ranger Ira Aten thought that was about the only distraction he would get. From an open doorway the Texas Ranger not bashfully hollered, "Hands up, Wesley Collier" at the same time "throwing my

[his] six-shooter on him."[22] As modern-era lawmen might say, at that point it turned "Western."

Wes Collier's bandanna, the supposed sling, was but a blind. With the quickness of a diamondback's strike, the outlaw's hand was unsheathed and his six-shooter fanged poison in Ira's direction. A bullet struck the doorstep between Ira's boots. Ira can tell it best:

> He was a little excited, I guess, or he would have shot me right in the belly as he was a better shot than I. We almost shot together. I hit his hand hitting the middle finger and his six-shooter, which went a "whirling" in the air, and he spurred his horse and started running downhill toward the creek below the house. I jumped out the door and thought to myself, "I'll just break your back." I took my six-shooter in both hands and shot. Just before I shot he had to go under a live oak which forced him to dodge down under a limb, and I hit the limb center. I would have broken his back otherwise.[23]

Racing on foot toward the big live oak, Mr. Wells and Private Aten found Collier's sweat-stained headgear underneath the tree. Respectfully, but somewhat mockingly and in good fun, George chided Ira: "Oh, you've killed him. Here's his hat with his brains in it." The pair looked around for awhile, hoping to find more clues, but darkness soon put the kibosh on further police work that night.[24]

The next morning George Wells regretfully told Private Ira Aten that pressing business elsewhere, and there is not reason to doubt it, would prevent his participating in that day's hunt for Wes Collier. Aten was advised he might secure help, if he felt he needed it, at the Hughes' Ranch over near Liberty Hill. By then Private Aten had rightly learned for a gunfight an assistant or two was not at all ill-advised and, besides, having a favorable witness might just prove an invaluable asset in front of a judge and/or jury. Aten struck out for Liberty Hill.

There he met thirty-one-year-old John Reynolds Hughes. The two hit it off admirably. Both could trace roots to a birthplace in Illinois. John Hughes unhesitatingly agreed to join in the search. Saddling up, he joined Ranger Aten and the duo mapped a course for the nearest doctor, some thirty-five miles away on the Colorado River. Ira was stuck to the notion that he had shot Collier at least once, maybe twice. The frightened physician, at first denying any treat-

John Reynolds Hughes, as a civilian, aided Ranger Ira Aten during
the pursuit of a much sought Texas desperado. Later, Ira personally
recruited Hughes into the Ranger service, teaching the future Company
D Captain much of his celebrated law enforcing craft. Evermore the two
were especially good friends. *Courtesy Jeri and Gary Boyce Radder.*

ment of outlaw Wes Collier, finally after an interval of aggressive—
but not physical—intimidation, owned up to providing medical
services. Aten and Hughes poked around in the country for a day or
two, but soon realized Collier had flown the coop. They returned to
the Hughes brothers' ranch, and on May 3, 1886, Ira Aten sat down
at a desk or table or board laid across his lap, and in longhand posted
the adjutant general with the latest development—so he could pass
it along to the governor:

On April the 29th I met up with my man Wesley Collier who is wanted in Gillespie county for murder. As soon as he recognized me he drew his six shooter, & I mine. Shooting then commenced on both sides, but I got in the second shot first & hit him in the right hand then he dropped his pistol & run. He was on a fine horse & I was a foot at that time. I tried my best to kill him but it seems I failed to do so. I think I hit twice, once in the hand & a slight wound about the head. I got his hat, six shooter & pocket knife. I have looked the country over & cannot find him. Think he has hid in the mountains some place. Will look for him a few more days. Then report to you officially, say about the 7th [or] 8th. Will give full particulars then. Excuse haste. [signed Ira Aten][25]

Private Ira Aten was not fooling about sitting down with bigwigs in Austin for an official confab. The meeting took place, confirmed by his own voice and in an addendum to Company D's Monthly Return.[26] At the state capital, with arrangements made by Adjutant General King, and in the presence of Captain Sieker no doubt, Private Ira Aten gained another personal audience with the good Governor John Ireland. Deservedly Ira was congratulated in person for successfully and safely rounding up Jack Beam, giving him up to local folks. He could now have a fair trial—of sorts. The governor's striking message about the Wes Collier manhunt was somewhat surprising to Ira Aten, in that a politico would not better cover his rear end, but the words were easily understood and blunt: "Catch him or kill him."[27] Before the month was out, Ira would do just that.

Why Wes Collier had not quickly left the Lone Star State for parts unknown, changing his name, nondescriptly blending in with hundreds—maybe thousands—of other yahoos dodging the law in America's Wild West defies coherent explanation. Murder charges would hold, forever. Were not gunshot wounds and being hounded like a wolf enough? There was, indeed, a common denominator linking the outlaw to the Texas Ranger. Both guys were pigheaded. Wes would not skip and Ira would not quit: Precursors, then, for a showdown.

On or about May 22, news broke Ira's way. Roughly six miles east from Liberty Hill was the Nicholas Dayton household. Although Wes Collier was married, according to Ira, he'd learned that the outlaw was sparking the Daytons' young daughter. On the quiet Ira Aten contacted his civilian helper John Hughes. After securing supplies to sustain them a few days, the pair initiated a stakeout of the Dayton premises. It was a twenty-four-and-seven setup. Ira and John traded off, one sleeping, the other watching. On the third day, May 25, 1886, late in the evening between sundown and dark, Ira could just barely make out the color of an approaching man's horse. It was a sorrel. It was Wes. The hormone-charged outlaw was going to make his gamble, throw the dice, and see the Dayton girl: "He had not been with her for some time."[28]

Putting his horse in the barn, Wes Collier went into the house. Aten and Hughes, their horses tied in a distant thicket, began easing forward under the cover of darkness. Dogs began barking. Aten whispered to Hughes: "John we have got to get to that horse. He suspected something and will leave right now." Actually throwing caution to the wind Aten and Hughes hotfooted to the barn, knowing if they allowed their quarry to regain his saddle they would be utterly helpless—their horses were secreted too far away. As long as Collier's boots were on the ground, it could break even. Somehow, the canine yipping didn't put Wes on the alert—he had something else on his mind. The Ranger and his older apprentice passed the night, waiting to make their move at dawn.[29]

At first light a young boy came to the barn, fed the horses, and returned to the house. Ira Aten and John Hughes had remained undetected nearby. Shortly thereafter, the Daytons' daughter came outside, heading for the barn, presumably to gather a few eggs for breakfast. Ira Aten was flabbergasted: "I thought she was the prettiest girl I ever saw." After a few minutes she returned to the house, entering through the back door. She had not noted the lawmen's presence either. Again, maybe the best voice is Ira's:

> I said, John, you go to the front door and I'll go to the back door. You will likely find the front door locked, but the back door will be unlocked and I can get in. As I went into the kitchen, the girl was preparing breakfast and did not see me. I passed tiptoe towards a door leading out of the kitchen. I saw her skirts turn from the corner of my eye, but I did not dare look as I was already opening the next door with my six-shooter in my hand. Mr. and Mrs. Dayton were in that room. Sound asleep. I did not stop, but went right on through to the next room, as I knew Collier would be in the next room. As I

opened the door, he was sitting on the edge of the bed with one boot on holding the other up in front of him. With his foot starting into it, in the act of pulling it on. He was facing the door that I opened [and] as soon as I touched the knob he was alert, and as I could barely peer through I saw him quickly turn his head slightly and listen and look. I started to say: "Hold Up, Wesley Collier." I never had time to finish. He fell back across the bed towards his pillows as soon as he saw me and jerked his six-shooter with both hands, and as he was bringing it up from the pillows over to line it up on me, I shot him through the heart. He dropped his gun, fell over on his back upon the bed and mumbled something. He was quick as a flash and in another instant would have killed me.[30]

Hearing the gunfire, John R. Hughes, six-shooter in hand, had kicked in the front door rushing to back up Ira. Not finding him in the front room Hughes burst into the second bedroom, frightening Private Aten badly. For a split-second Ira had thought he would be mistakenly gunned down by Mr. John, a lamentable case of friendly fire. Hughes, quickly grasping reality, had cautiously lowered the hammer on his Colt's.[31] Leaving John Hughes with the dead body of Collier, Ira Aten retrieved his horse and rode west to Liberty Hill, where he telegraphed the Williamson County Sheriff, John Taylor Olive, and Adjutant General King at Austin.[32]

Within but a short spate of time—three hours—Sheriff Olive and Deputy (constable) J. F. Hoyle were on the scene, accompanied by Sam Connell, Justice of the Peace, dutifully charged with overseeing an inquest. Editor of the *Liberty Hill Ledger* was along also, as were a gathering crowd of gawkers. Doctor Thorpe conducted a medical examination, suggesting that an autopsy would only satisfy curiosity, not materially adding to scientific results of the death investigation: Wes Collier was dead, a lead bullet somewhere near the heart. Case closed.[33]

The public's general feeling that Wesley Collier was, indeed, a desperado was cemented upon examining his armament: "Under his vest, on each side, was concealed a pistol, and another was found in an inside pocket. The pistols on his sides were arranged in a very ingenious manner, being connected together by a strap which passed over his shoulders, terminating at each end in a scabbard, and in each of these scabbards was a six-shooter, one of them being a Smith &

Williamson County Sheriff John Taylor Olive, a plucky lawman and particularly good friend of Texas Ranger Ira Aten. Sadly he would be fatally gunned down on the depot platform at Echo, Bell County. *Courtesy Jim Dillard.*

Wesson, .45 caliber; the other a Colt's of the same caliber. The smaller pistol which was found in his pocket, was an Invincible, .38 caliber. The whole of them were loaded all around and in prime condition."[34]

Who were not in prime condition were the Daytons. According to their version they had simply been hoodwinked: "The report of the pistol was the first intimation the horrified family had that they were harboring a murderer and a refugee from justice. Their surprise and consternation, when they became apprised of the facts can better be imagined than described. Collier had been stopping there for a week, claiming that his name was Martin...."[35]

At the scene of the shooting a blanket of legal formalities began smothering Private Ira Aten's reassured demeanor. Wes Collier had gone down rather than him; that was the good news. But, would he himself have to withstand any criminal charges? Turning to Sheriff Olive, Private Aten posed the question: "Will you have to arrest me?" Almost indignantly the sheriff replied, no, he would not. He was happy that Wes Collier had been taken off, and so would be the folks of Williamson County. Mistakenly thinking Fifth Amendment protections of the United States' Constitution regarding double jeopardy extended to a grand jury's work, Ira Aten believed that if he were but No Billed the matter could never—ever—be revisited: "I wanted them to indict me and get the matter over so an indictment could not be trumped against me later on. They let me tell my story but would not indict me."[36]

One who did like the story was Adjutant General King. In a complimentary letter to A. L Patton, Esq., Fredericksburg, King praised the Ranger's taking off of Wes Collier, commenting: "Wesley Collier was killed by Aten, at a great expense both to the State & himself and at great risk, for which he certainly deserves a part of the reward offered. Aten is a good & courageous officer, & the killing of Collier has saved infinite trouble to the citizens & authorities of your county."[37]

Institutionally the Texas Rangers may have been dodging a few barbs hurled by Senator Hall. Certain Rangers, it is true, were also running into career-changing snags in South Texas. The harsh criticism and abrasive commentary wasn't affecting Private Aten, not in the Texas Hill Country. He was a hero. One has but to look at the aforementioned *Liberty Hill Ledger* eulogizing the Ranger for embargoing the bad doings of Wes Collier: "Aten has been tracking him with the sagacity and tenacity of a bloodhound for a long, long time.... we feel that the people are under obligations to him for ridding the country of a desperate character and thereby aiding in the triumph of truth and justice and the downfall of heinous crimes and atrocious murders."[38]

Private Ira Aten's immediate supervisor, Frank Jones, who had attained captaincy of Company D following Lam Sieker's promotion to Frontier Battalion Quartermaster, within days added his two cents' worth to the adulation being hastily piled on the private: "Aten is deserving of both credit and reward for his work after those murderers."[39] Post the crime scene cleanup, Private Aten reported to Austin, updating AG King and Captain Sieker. If he met with Governor Ireland again it has escaped historical notice.

Someone that did not manage a getaway was John Glasscock. Although the exactness of what actually happened is murky, while Private Aten was in Travis County he arrested the fellow for resisting arrest and locked him in the county jail. Presumably this is one of the same Glasscock family that Wesley Collier was trying to contact when he had made inquiry at George Wells' rancho, and then spinning his horse in a one-eighty after tasting the hellfire of Ira's Colt's six-shooter.[40]

With instructions from headquarters to keep pressing the hunt for Jim Fannin, the fourth man sought in the Braeutigam murder investigation, Private Aten returned to duty.[41] Though his work had been stellar regarding the capture of Jack Beam and the gunfight with Wes Collier, bolstering his reputation as a manhunter, neither Ira Aten—or anyone else—was ever able to locate the elusive Jim Fannin. That he fled Texas is not unlikely. That Fannin was but an alias is also feasible. The case against Ede Janes would eventually be dismissed. Jack Beam, that was a different story, but it would play out shortly.

Resting on his laurels was not in Private Ira Aten's operational game plan. During July 1886 he was on peace-keeping duty at Del Rio, Val Verde County. After receiving a report from Guadalupe County (Seguin) Sheriff Hugh McGuffin that Appleton Thomas had misappropriated seven oxen, Ira located the wanted man along the Texas/Mexican border. The arrest was quick and uneventful, Ira Aten placing accused thief Thomas in Sheriff W. H. Jones' county lockup at Del Rio. Seemingly with the vigor of a tornado Private Aten was spinning them into the jailhouse, especially after he was dispatched downriver to Eagle Pass to maintain order. There Aten quickly rounded up Susanna Rodriquez for stealing a horse in La Salle County and Pablo Ramirez for a horse theft in Maverick County. Ira Aten then scooted over to Zavala County and arrested Wash Poteet and Ab Love, charging them with smuggling stolen horses and mules into the United States. These prisoners he turned over to Customs House authorities at Eagle Pass. Aside from the successes, he came up short hunting fugitive Bob Finn, who was charged with theft in Gillespie County, but Ira racked up 120 miles and spent three days in the effort. Nor could he locate Bill Ware, wanted for a murder in Reeves County [Pecos].[42]

The month rolled over on Ira Aten still in the field hunting for a fellow named Allen wanted in Edwards County for Resisting an

N. O. "Mage" Reynolds, a former Company D Texas Ranger and future sheriff of Lampasas County, would counsel Ranger Ira Aten about how best to infiltrate a band of fence cutters utilizing an undercover technique. *Courtesy Chuck Parsons.*

Officer. As soon as he returned from this 200-mile scout, empty-handed, Private Ira Aten had new orders waiting for him: Report to Austin and see AG King without delay. He had special assignments for the ever industrious Mr. Aten.[43] One of those delicate jobs was to covertly contact City Marshal N. O. Reynolds in Lampasas County, who was in desperate want of a new face to "ferret out" some very specific "perpetrators."[44]

Chapter 7

"Curling steel tendrils"

Before striking out horseback for Lampasas County under secret orders from AG King, Private Aten had to tend to unfinished business that not even the adjutant general could override. Ira Aten was under subpoena to testify in the Braeutigam murder case in which Jack Beam was the defendant.[1] Par business in court proceedings for lawmen is adjusting to the standby mode—sometimes for hours, sometimes for days. In this instance, *The State of Texas vs. Jack Beam*, Gillespie County Criminal Case No. 418, there was not a long and unnecessarily drawn-out trial. As result of a Plea Bargain, defendant Jackson Beam entered a plea of Guilty to Murder in the Second Degree. The District Court Judge prepared legal clarification for the jury. They would, within the legally prescribed parameters, determine defendant Jack Beam's fate.[2] Shortly, the jury foreman, F. E. Luckenbach, stoically read the panels' unanimous sentencing verdict: "and assess his punishment at confinement in the penitentiary for nine years."[3]

As the convicted Beam was being hustled out of the Fredericksburg courtroom, it is not implausible to believe Private Austin Ira Aten might have done a little soul searching, thoughtful reflection about his career choice. He was twenty-four years old. For the last three and a half years he had carried the Lone Star's flag as a Texas Ranger. Inside one twelve-month period he had been in three gunfights and killed one man. He hadn't taken a hit, not a wound, not a scratch. How long would such odds hold? Adding up the total number of arrests was, of course, calculable but pointless—he had put a lot of men and a woman or two in the jailhouse. Likewise, tallying the number of miles he had traveled by train or days spent in the saddle on horseback scouts would be mindboggling. Yes, Private Ira Aten could say, looking back, he had matured into the role of a first-rate Ranger.

Ranger Aten would do some good work in Lampasas County, too, but only after an investigation. Some undercover work—detective work—was on tap and who better than Private Aten could pull it off? Ira would do: So thought the governor, the adjutant general, and Captain Lam Sieker. In fact, taking special note of Ira's abilities, in a letter to Col. E. D. Linn, Adjutant General King shined: "Aten is the only man in the Battalion who can do what is wanted in this case."[4] Indeed, it was high praise, especially for a young man circulating in the hard world of veteran peace keepers. In a reasonably short time Private Ira Aten had more than amply demonstrated he was rawhide tough—when he had to be—and owned the smarts to gainfully complete most assigned tasks. Ira was no counterfeit lawman.

For the previous three years Texas had been plagued with fellows cutting barbed wire. Although many big stockmen were loathe to capitulate, the freewheeling days of open-range cattle ranching were shortening with each turn of a calendar's page.[5] Joseph Farwell Glidden, Jacob Haish, and Isaac Leonard Ellwood had been issued patents on an innovative and newfangled method of controlling cattle.[6] In the end, their invention would revolutionize the cattle industry, perhaps as much as the formation of stock raisers' associations and refrigerated railroad cars.[7] Whether cows and people were fenced in or fenced out was only a matter of perspective—wholly depending on just who did or did not own the pasture, roadway, or water hole being enclosed.[8] Perhaps one stockman summed up popular opinion for his crowd, wishing that "the man who invented barbed wire had it all wound around him in a ball and the ball rolled into Hell."[9] Although it has received far less historic attention, another nasty tactic sometimes put into the dispute between competing livestock interests was simple arson—malevolently burning another man's pasture could hearken financial devastation for a cow country enemy.[10] As with illegally nipping wire, a purposely dropped match on dry grass—itself consumed in a fire—was a crime absent physical evidence: Tough to prove.

Financially well-fixed cattlemen, realizing progress was upon them, began stringing four-strand wire fences with abandon. Often, they not only fenced land they held courthouse title to, but closed off grazing lands "of which they legally had no control."[11] Sometimes the fences ran as much as fifty or more miles, with not a single gate to pass through.[12] Fences erected across long accepted roadways made otherwise law-abiding people boiling mad.[13] Conversely, a fence bristling with barbs was abhorrent to despicable cow thieves. Not at all surprising to the honest folks was the hard reality that "brand burners, skinners and those who had lived off of the drift cattle often became fence cutters."[14] Adding to the mix were settlers not typed as "free grass men." They were the productive farmers and negligibly invested cattlemen, who were forced to fence their culti- vated fields and smaller pastures in order to keep crops from being destroyed or domesticated livestock from grazing too far from the home range, and/or being swept away as the big boys worked their spring and fall cattle roundups. Complicating the matter, too, were those small-time ranchers who didn't own any land whatsoever, the "ones depending wholly on free grass for their livestock."[15] Fenced off the gratis grasslands, these guys stood to suffer financial ruin. Statewide, blood was being spilled between big ranchers and small, cowmen and sheepmen, and everyday folks sick and tried of having to go the long way round for obligatory trips to the courthouse, all because of barbed wire.[16]

By 1883, the year Ira Aten became a Texas Ranger, more than half of the 171 organized counties in the Lone Star State had reported instances of wire cuttings, some jurisdictions claiming criminal offenses by the carload. The severe drought of 1883 only exacerbated what was already a fast throbbing headache as precious water holes were being fenced in, to keep others' livestock out.[17] The bloodletting and threat of bloodletting had become so widespread that Governor Ireland acted by calling a special session of the leg- islature with one topic on the agenda: Fix the problem—and fix it now. Heeding the no-nonsense message, politicians did what poli- ticians do. They legislated. Taking less than thirty days, the boys behind the little maple desks at Austin upgraded the illicit cutting of fence wire or maliciously burning a pasture to a felony—hard time in the penitentiary; up to five years behind those tall ivy-covered red brick walls at Huntsville. Likewise haggard and hurried lawmak- ers addressed those inordinately long and frequently inconvenient fence lines:

> Be it enacted by the Legislature of the State of Texas; That it shall be unlawful for any person or persons by joining fences, or otherwise to build or maintain more than three miles lineal measure of fence, running in the same general direction, with- out a gateway in same, which gateway must be at least eight feet wide and shall not be locked; provided that all persons who have fences already constructed in violation of this section

shall have six months within which to conform to the provisions hereof.[18]

Murder was against the law, too, as was stealing a horse or having two wives. Most folks are law abiding, but not necessarily all. Despite Governor Ireland's and the elected legislators' best intentions, there was no letup in the fence cuttings. Violators simply went underground. Working beneath the moonlight and stars and in the dark, Knights of the Nippers, as illicit nighttime operatives were now called, carried on their handiwork with gusto.[19] Fences went up. Fences were cut. Fences went up. And so on.

Worsening the already dreadful situation was an abysmal response from not just a few local lawmen. Many of the county sheriffs could lay their lackluster performance to being understaffed and overwhelmed; several others, though, were simply malfeasant.[20] There was, too, a political dynamic. County sheriffs won or lost their jobs at the polls, not by inheritance or by being disowned. Walking that tightrope suspended above townsmen near equally divided was politically risky. Some folks sympathized with a fellow whose fence had been cut: Others empathized with the cutter. Finding twelve honest men—or dishonest men—who would convict a nighttime nipper in the courtroom was well-nigh impossible. Ripping down fences was pandemic in certain sections. Monetary loss, over time, was tallying in the millions: All of that stood square with why Texans needed Rangers in the first place. Governor Ireland, "whose own ranch fence had been cut," hadn't even the slightest qualm about unleashing the state's Texas Rangers; they had no partisan political dogs in the hunt.[21] Nor was the governor opposed to sponsoring the standing reward of $200 for convictions of wire cutters.[22] Private Ira Aten, then, by order of the adjutant general, would sniff out a pack of cutters nipping fences in the Colorado River bottom lands of southwestern Lampasas County.

Catching fence cutters was not easy. There was an inherent monkey wrench thrown into the equation. A contemptible horse thief could be caught riding, leading or selling the evidence—as could the vile cow thief herding beeves with blotched brands or sneakily racing for the Rio Grande. When caught red-handed believable excuses were wasted, almost laughable. Fence cutters, once they had nipped the wire—in the days before forensics—were evidentiary-wise untouchable. The quick nipping cutter simply "rode away from the curling steel tendrils with no evidence upon him."[23] A solid case was best had by catching the cutter in the act.[24] There were, then, three practical avenues for doing just that: random surveillance, an informant's tip, or "detective work."

Distastefully, Private Aten was going to have to dabble in some detective work. Today the terms "detective work" and/or "investigative work" wash out being one and the same. Not so then. Not in Texas.[25] For Ira's time a detective was someone working in the shadows, undercover, akin to a Pinkerton man, slipping around and snooping, one's true identity a tidy little secret. Texas Rangers, now on the road to professionalism as crime fighters, could keep the peace, quell a riot, hunt fugitives, or overtly gather evidence leading to a criminal's undoing. However, for most of those fellows, deviously taking the part of a detective, sneaking and lying and in the end betraying someone's trust—even if the cause be just—was an anathema.[26] According to Ira, for many of those "old-time rangers" it was even "an insult" to be called a detective.[27] In fact, Frontier Battalion management believed they were not legally empowered to force any Texas Ranger into assuming the role of an undercover operative. Such assignments, if accepted at all, were on a strictly volunteer basis.[28] Snitches snitched, selling out their friends: Lawmen policed forthright—up front and aboveboard. Nonetheless, Private Aten had been asked to do a job. Ira wanted to be a good Ranger: "I cannot say that I liked this special duty business, but I was a soldier, and took orders with a smile."[29]

At Lampasas, undercover operative Aten met with ex-Ranger Mage Reynolds, then city marshal and future county sheriff, seeking advice how to best proceed.[30] Taking Reynolds's advice, Ira assumed the role of a down-and-out cowboy looking for room and board in exchange for work. Soon Aten was riding for "some little squatters that owned enough pasture for their horses." Though he astutely never made a point of mentioning it, eventually the subject of cutting a fence came up. Ira was invited to play, and he agreed, remarking that he had "never done any of that but I [he] guessed I [he] could. When I [he] worked for a man, I [he] worked for him." After learning the when and where, undercover man Ira Aten, managing an acceptable excuse, slipped away and notified authorities, advising them that there would be himself and two others in the party.[31]

On the appointed night, and at the appointed place, Ira and the two targets of his investigation began cutting rancher Ben Huling's fence. Although all three had armed themselves with six-shooters, when lawmen jumped from the brush hollering a challenge the three meekly surrendered. Thankfully, there had been no gunplay. The three cutters were arrested and locked in the Lampasas County jail. Ira Aten's arrest being but a sham he was released, while the other two supposed he had posted bond.[32]

This time around the wily detective work had been short and simple and sweet. Really, the job had been child's play, a facet readily acknowledged by Ira: "After some investigation I found that two boys, still in their 'teens, were responsible for the trouble. It was very easy to win their confidence, as they were rather proud that their fence cutting job had created such a stir in the county. They readily accepted me as one of their gang when I told them some wild stories of what a bad man I was."[33] Subsequent to making the necessary inquiries and pocketing a clue or two, Ira had successfully steered the criminal case for docking with a district judge. Aten's true identity surfaced, as did his assessment of reality: "These were young men with me, but the older ones [had] egged them on."[34] The crying culprits, teenage boys, were but vandals. Their costly outbreak of wire cuttings were without motive, other than trying to gain notoriety and be seen as real badmen.[35]

Unfortunately, by its very nature assuming an undercover identity necessitates the telling of untruths, sometimes a big one. Even a lazy lawyer then, is gifted with an unobstructed pathway for cross-examination. Trite as the defense tactic might be, the set-up question for the law-enforcing witness is elementary: "Did you, in the course of your investigation, tell a lie?" There is only one correct answer, if an act of outright perjury is to be avoided: "Yes." The defense lawyer's follow-up query is predictable and stale, but a guaranteed safe bet. In this instance for the Texas Ranger it would be no different: "Ranger Aten, were you lying then—or now? Are you still lying?" Inexperienced as he was at courtroom theatrics Ira responded with bold directness. The insinuation had made him so mad he could barely restrain himself from jumping off the witness stand and administering the red-mouthed lawyer a head-thumping. Shaking his fist in the attorney's direction, Ira scorched, "I want you to understand there is a great deal of difference between swearing to a lie and telling a lie to catch a damn rascal." District Judge William A. Blackburn, an experienced jurist, no doubt saw the hackneyed question coming. Too, he knew Ranger Aten would have to acknowledge telling a few lies while worming his way into the boys' confidence. That was but typical—understandable and pardonable. On the other hand, Ranger Ira Aten's blistering response peppered with a profane word was not acceptable, not in front of his bench. With a stenographer's deftness Ira recaps Judge Blackburn's rejoinder. "He cleared his throat, pulled his glasses down on his nose, and said: 'Mr. Clerk, I fine the witness fifty dollars.' I begged his pardon, but to no avail. He told me that I was an officer of the court, and, therefore, such language could not be overlooked."[36] Plainly, Ira Aten coughed up. The young Texas Ranger did incorporate into his psyche very well just where he was expected to stand in cases of *Campfire chitchat vs. Courtroom courtesies.*

Although successfully arresting and prosecuting the boys from Lampasas County, it had but negligible impact—if even that—on the statewide fence-cutting epidemic then underway. Private Aten's creditable execution of duty, once again, had gained notice at Austin.[37] Soon Texas Ranger headquarters drafted him for another investigative project, more of that disagreeable "detective" work. This time the undercover chore would be much tougher and more dangerous.

Fence cutting in Brown County had mushroomed dreadfully.[38] One sound practical advantage of killing off an open-range philosophy was improvement in livestock breeding programs. Genetically corralling cattle in specified pastures—even if they were huge—was a prudent management technique. Bloodlines could be fine-tuned, breeding seasons regulated, the calving period anticipated, and livestock could be culled and sorted by sex and/or age—tailored to the market's needs. Two of Brown County's earliest pioneering cattlemen, the hard-working Baugh brothers, Washington Morgan "Morg" and Levin Powell "Lev," were carving their niche in the blooded cattle business. Eight to ten miles north of Brownwood, the county seat, in what was known as the Jim Ned Country because of a like-named creek, Morg and Lev Baugh had fenced and crossed-fenced a ranch of some 6,000 acres (later 10,000-plus acres).[39] They and a stalwart brother-in-law, Samuel P. "Sam" McInnis, with his acreage under fence were chiseling a noticeable toehold in the demand for cattle that would grade higher than the usual lean and lanky Longhorns, such as Herefords or Durhams.[40] Not unexpectedly this did not set well with all. First-rate cattlemen they were, but like anyone else, they had steadfast friends and bitter enemies.

In many instances acerbic notes became the scheming fence cutters' calling cards. After cutters visited C. D. Foote's ranch, they also

Brownwood, Brown County, Texas. Looking south from the courthouse. *Courtesy Brownwood Public Library—Local History & Genealogy Branch.*

drove away a valuable imported bull. Though but crudely fashioned the message left behind was readable: "If your bull you hunt for, call at the first ranch this side of hell, and brand him when you get him."[41] That first year Ira Aten was shaking off newness as a rookie Texas Ranger, nighttime visitors had tacked a similar message to one of Lev Baugh's cedar fence posts: "Mr. Baugh, take down this fence. If you don't, we will cut it. If we cut it and a drop of cutter's blood is spilled, your life will pay the forfeit."[42] Lev Baugh had already survived fights with Indians, and was not about to show weakness, not to folks sneakily riding under the canopy of darkness. Scribbling out his own warning, calling the cutters "cowardly curs" and suggesting they best leave his fence alone, Lev brusquely tied his reply to a post, the note fluttering in the Central Texas breeze. Take down the fence or run, he would not. The Baugh brothers, themselves, began patrolling their fence lines. During one dustup with cutters shots were fired, but the scorecard showed zip.[43]

Brown County was a camp divided. Some folks—and the letter of the law—were squarely with the Baughs. Others, with increasing fervor were wedded to a notion that big ranchers were "throwing their weight around unfairly," fencing them off water and roadways.[44] During the early 1880s word was leaked that 200 armed partisans were heading to burn down Brownwood. "Alarm spread in the early morning hours; citizens flocked to the Opera House near the courthouse square, barricading themselves within. About forty stockmen climbed to the roofs of nearby business buildings and kept their guns trained on the streets below."[45] Business at the Indiana-born Joseph Weakley's hardware store was brisk. The forty-four-year-old proprietor sold "every gun in the place and all the stock of ammunition."[46] Without hammering out specific conversations, suffice to say that Brown County Sheriff William Nelson "Uncle Bill" Adams, after the most delicate and diplomatic huddling, provisionally dampened hot tempers. Locally the meeting became known as the "Fence-Cutters Convention," but it led to creation of the "Farmers Alliance," with a secret wing of cutters, some quite prominent citizens.[47] Bloodshed in the near term was averted, but the underlying and smoldering dilemma had not been defused. Months passed. Fence cutters cut. Ranchers rebuilt. The seesaw of turmoil bent across its fulcrum—that damn barbed wire.

Particularly hard-hit, the Baugh brothers resorted to answering their front doors with shotguns poked out first, and never, never,

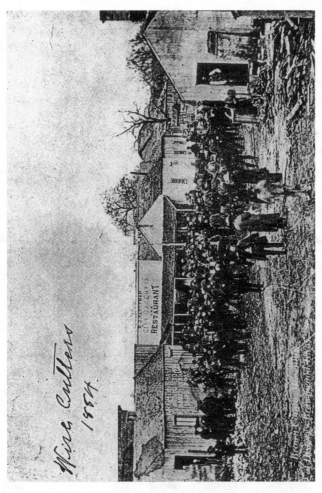

Brown County was a camp divided over the issue of wire cutting. During this 1883 dustup (hand-scribbled date on photo in error) angry farmers and negligibly invested cowmen, fenced off from water holes and roadways, converged threatening to burn the city of Brownwood to the ground unless their grievances were suitably addressed. Diplomatic maneuvering averted bloodshed—in the short term.   *Courtesy Brown County Texas Museum of History.*

going anywhere and returning by the same route.[48] Watchfulness was
their byword; it kept them alive. Through the course of time the brothers did develop evidence sufficient to merit criminal Indictments,
and on March 12, 1885, ten young Brown County men had found
themselves so charged. Not unpredictably the district attorney—no
doubt after application of well-oiled political pressure—forthrightly
asked for a Continuance, then dismissed the cases altogether.[49] The
Baughs went back to work, this time with a two-pronged strategy.
They'd make a double play, stacking odds in their favor. First they
personally hired their own undercover spy, Joe Copeland. Their second tactic was more traditional, but not general public knowledge.
They appealed for Adjutant General King to step up, sending in a
Ranger on the sly. Private Ira Aten got the call.

Apparently the governor was at least mildly suspicious of certain local authorities. When receiving his marching orders to proceed to Brownwood, Ira recalled the governor specifically told him
not to report to the sheriff, "as he had some inside dope on him."[50]
Undisclosed are the reasons, but Private Aten was led to believe that
Sheriff Adams "sympathized with the cutters."[51] Slipping into town
undetected Aten met with the former Brown County Clerk, Henry

Washington Morgan "Morg" Baugh, pioneer Brown County cattleman and frequent
target of Knights of the Nippers. *Courtesy Herbie Belvin.*

Ford, who then introduced him to S. R. and M. J. Coggins, cattlemen heavily invested in the local bank. They, in turn, made sure Ira met with the Baugh brothers on the quiet.[52] That secret conference led to Aten's introduction to their private eye, Joe Copeland. To this point Copeland had been thwarted in his efforts to gain hard evidence, but he was little by little ingratiating himself with the right crowd. "The Brown County bunch was a bad one," so said Ira. They had been so awful that "before this the State had some Pinkerton detectives in there. Being city men, they could not handle the situation, and some of them barely got out alive."[53] Putting their heads together, a plan was hatched, and Private Ira Aten invisibly departed Brownwood— as if he had never made an appearance.

Shortly Private Aten boarded a train, riding it to Coleman, Coleman County, about thirty miles northwest of Brownwood. There he bought "a little pony," and began his ambling southeastern trip into northern Brown County, the "cutters territory." Posing as a poor orphan boy looking for work, Ira meandered throughout the Jim Ned Country, hanging out here and there, sleeping in haystacks—a forlorn

The Ashcraft family. Back row L to R: Robert Lee, Elijah Jefferson, Walter Marion, Tempie Ann, Simon Franklin, and William Henry "Will." Front row L to R: Fannie Belle, Elijah Robert, Amanda Ann (Arnold), and Eva Melvina "Evey." Elijah Robert's not secret membership in the Farmers Alliance and his unexplained nighttime absences from home foster some family members' belief that he—from time to time—was called upon to snip a wire or two. Or, hold the horses. All for a good purpose, of course. *Courtesy Jim Dempsey.*

The Johnson family. Standing L to R. Jefferson "Jeff," Alabama, Frank, Nancy Ann, Charlie," and Etta. Their widowed mother Martha is seated. These three brothers were unashamed wire cutters—rightly or wrongly—fighting for what they solidly believed in. Charlie Johnson would barely escape with his life during the nighttime shoot-out on the Baughs' fence line with Rangers. Two other cutters were not so lucky. *Courtesy Gerald and Patsy Johnson.*

and lonely boy without a home. Knowing human nature, Ira figured someone would soon befriend him, although their motive might be fishy.[54] Bob Parrock (Parrack in other accounts) took the bait. He invited Ira to his place. Aten accepted the offer, noting the stockman said "he could not pay me much as he did not have much work for me to do. He was a little suspicious of me at first, but as I helped his wife at whatever there was to do, he soon changed. I milked the cow, fed the chickens and pigs, chopped wood, and was just a handy boy around the ranch. I never asked questions, but just looked and listened."[55]

Slowly Ira began inching his way ever closer to Brown County's fence cutters. Making no bones about it, Ira himself participated in

Samuel P. "Sam" McInnis and wife, Martha Elizabeth (Baugh). A brother-in-law to the Baugh brothers, Sam was naturally their ally. He was much more though: A seasoned cowboy and later a well-known Brown County cattleman. Sam could withstand frontier hardships with fearlessness, once even killing a puma with his Colt's six-shooter. As a cowman he was the "real McCoy." *Courtesy Jessica McInnis.*

some midnight misappropriation, all for a good cause, of course: "I was invited to go on one of these night beef raids, and when I showed them I was pretty handy with a rope and skinning knife they put more confidence in me."[56] After killing "two or three that belonged to someone else," they divvied up the meat, some choice cuts even going to Joe Copeland, who was not in day by day contact with Ira, but was in cahoots with him. By playing his part with the verve of a Broadway stage actor and telling a string of necessary lies, Ira Aten had at last gained the trust of livestock thieves and fence cutters. So too, had Joe Copeland.[57]

On one devious trip Ira took possession of two horses stolen in Brown County, and during the dead of night quickly rode for the Lampasas/Belton Country intending to sell them. Upon his return—according to the plan—he could keep half the cash, the rest spoken for by the thieves. In the outlaws' eyes Aten, now having proved himself, was one of them, a crook. When Ira looked into his pocket mirror he still saw the reflection of a principled lawman, but now a necessarily deceitful one. After all, he was a "detective." Knowing he'd best not let stolen horses get away, and end up being unaccounted for, Ira had used his noodle: "I made a fifty mile ride that night to a certain ranch in Lampasas county where I was known, and put the horses in a pasture to be left there until I gave an order for them.... I stayed at the ranch a few days so I would not get back to my friends too soon."[58] Yes, his ruse was working. Private Ira Aten was a "good Ranger."

Too, he wanted to be a faithful son and considerate brother. So, although there may not be hard evidence, it is not outlandish to suggest Private Ira Aten finagled a trip home before slipping back to work on that special assignment. By his own voice he had a few days to kill in Lampasas County. Ira's next to oldest brother, Frank Lincoln, the young man who had witnessed outlaw Sam Bass bleeding on a makeshift hospital cot, had plans, big plans. Frank had asked for the hand of eighteen-year-old Josie Jakes McCormick, not a native Texan, but a welcome transplant from Saltville, Smyth County, Virginia.[59] The McCormick family, Texans for half a dozen years now, had settled in Williamson County at Hutto, an early day farming settlement founded by J. E. Hutto and a former slave, Adam Orgain.[60] Frank and Josie were to be married on October 6, 1886, in Travis County—not too far southeast of Lampasas County, close enough for Texas Ranger Private Ira Aten to make a show.

And the curtain for six-shooter high-drama was about to be drawn. Upon his return to Brown County, Ira learned the details of a planned fence cutting. On November 9, 1886, cutters were to quietly gather, and once again cut down one of the pasture fences of cattlemen Morg and Lev Baugh. By at least one report, Joe Copeland had learned of the upcoming nighttime shenanigan and, after sidling up to Morg Baugh in a Brownwood business the day before, "traced on the store counter with his knife, *They are going to cut your fences tomorrow night*."[61] The civilian undercover operative also managed to clue in Ira Aten: "I had been informed by Copeland that the cutters were going to cut the fence."[62]

Forewarned with such valuable criminal intelligence, the wheels of justice were put into motion. Knowing when and where the cutters were to strike funneled lawmen to one pasture, one fence line. William "Bill" Scott had been promoted to captain of Texas Ranger Company F and had been standing by at Belton, Bell County, itching

Frank Lincoln and Josie (McCormick) Aten, a wedding photograph. *Courtesy Betty Aten.*

to strut in a tango with fence cutters.[63] The state lawmen rushed to Brown County, going into camp at a hideaway on the Baughs' fenced ranch. Accompanying Captain Scott to the ball were Texas Rangers J. A. Brooks, Jim Carmichael, Billy Treadwell, and John Rogers.[64] Adding to the stakeout brigade were a few of the Baughs' "supportive neighbors."[65] Behind "brush and rocks" an interdiction squad waited to interdict.

Unlike several nineteenth-century lawmen who now own popularized household names but speciously puffed records, Ira Aten was a man of genuine gunfighting ability. When the fat was in the fire, Ira Aten would step to the mark—alone or with teammates. Likewise, and again dissimilar to several of the journalistically created heroes, Ira Aten was disinclined to inflate his role in a gunplay.

For an article prepared in 1939, and the memoirs serially published during 1945, Austin Ira Aten skimmed across what transpired that night. Fortunately he told the story even a decade earlier with many more details to an all-ears listener, although even then, Ira downplayed his particular popping of a cap or two:

> About ten or eleven o'clock, I think, they came by, all five of them cutting the fence. It was understood with Copeland that he was to be the farthest behind, and when he got to this point to be exceedingly far behind so that there would be no danger of his getting shot. It was understood among us not to shoot at the hindmost man. The moon was shining brightly and we could see them coming up. Then we heard Copeland say: "Boys, you are not cutting this short enough. Let's do this job well while we are at it." And he dropped behind to do a good job of it. As soon as the shooting started, he lay down. When they got even with us Captain Scott demanded their surrender. I think he said: "We are officers, boys. We demand your surrender." Then they opened fire on us. They stopped, of course, as soon as Scott called, jerked their pistols and opened fire. I don't think that they knew the Rangers were there as they had come to Brownwood secretly, and they must have thought us some of Baugh's men. One of their number was killed and one was badly wounded. After the shooting was over two men got away. Three of their horses were killed. They were leading their horses behind them as they cut the wire. Two ran off afoot through the brush and left their horses. The one that was killed was Jim Levitt [Lovell], constable. [Amos] Roberts, who was a brother of the Justice of the Peace of that precinct, died in a little while from his wounds. We built a fire, as it was pretty cold. It must have been October or November of '86, and we carried Roberts up to the fire, and he died there. Bob Herrick [Parrack] and [Ace] Sam Matthews [Mathews] got away.... Both were indicted for fence cutting. They pulled out and were on the dodge....[66]

Characteristically Ira Aten, not glorying in a killing, had bypassed explicitness. Truth of the matter would reveal that when gunfire illuminated that Brown County fence line, the Rangers lying in wait had pre-planned a directed field of fire. Concealed as they were, the Rangers "could hear the wire cutting and posts falling before they could see the fence cutters. One man came ahead leading the horses roped together from the saddle horns."[67] When hell popped it unwound like this, maybe: "Jim Lovell grabbed for his Winchester rifle leaning against a post. Amos Roberts ran for his horse and pulled his rifle from its scabbard. The Rangers stepped out from the bushes, spread ten yards wide on either side of their captain, and opened fire in two rapid volleys. Rogers and Carmichael fired through the darkness first, bright orange flame spitting from the barrels of their guns. Lovell dropped his rifle, grabbed at his chest and fell backwards, mortally wounded. Scott and Aten opened fire. Roberts had taken a step toward the Rangers, but was driven back head over heels when bullets slammed into his torso just under his left shoulder blade."[68] Cutters, denied opportunity, had not fired a shot, at least by one account.[69] Ira recalled it differently, saying the fence cutters "opened fire" and in a later narrative remarked, "this [Scott's verbal challenge] was answered by shots from the fence cutters."[70] Either way it went, and it is most assuredly understandable, that moonlit night in the Baughs' pasture the survival mode kicked into gear. Policing is a hard game. A lawman's top priority is ending each day at home.

Predictably, the news broke big at Brownwood. As with the killing of Sam Bass at Round Rock, townsmen were in a stir the next morning after hearing of the previous night's gunplay. Unlike the Williamson County brouhaha, not everyone in Brownwood was thrilled. Brown County was still divided, still having a vocal camp of cutters and their adherents. Nerves were frayed. Tempers flared. Threats, legitimate or not, reverberated throughout town. It was a mess.

Recognizing the potential for catastrophe, Sheriff Adams circulated through the partisan groups of men, cautioning—reminding—them about the state's legal prohibition about carrying sidearms in public. Brown County deputy sheriffs following orders from the boss were told to disarm violators or kick the pistol packers out of town—with a boot if necessary. Sheriff Adams wanted no hot-headed tragedy on his watch.

Understandably, Joe Copeland, now that the cat was out of the bag, proudly swaggered into town—openly wearing a six-shooter. No longer had he anything to hide. Deputy W. A. Butler knew Copeland to be a Brown County farmer, and only that. Sensibly, since he would be going up against an armed fellow, the deputy drew his six-

Captain Bill Scott's Company of Texas Rangers. The first four Rangers standing L to R, Jim (Frank) Carmichael, John Rogers, Captain Bill Scott, and J. A. Brooks, along with Company D's Ira Aten, were participants in the shoot-out wherein two wire cutters gave up the ghost, while others hotfooted into the dark. Reading L to R standing next to Brooks were Rangers Bob Crowder and Jim Harry. Seated, L to R: Ed Randall, Billy Birdwell, Kid Rogers, Allen Newton, and a Ranger identified only as Hinds. *Courtesy Research Center, Texas Ranger Hall of Fame and Museum.*

shooter, telling Joe Copeland to give up his. Texas Ranger Carmichael, knowing of Copeland's undercover role, pulled his handgun, pointed it at the deputy, admonishing "hands up, hands off Joe." Seeing this, Sheriff Adams jerked out his Colt's six-shooter intending to hold the Texas Ranger at bay while his deputy disarmed Copeland. It didn't end there. Lev Baugh, Joe's real employer, was armed with knowledge not common to everyone: Copeland had been specially deputized by Captain Scott and was therefore legally allowed to carry a six-shooter. The dutiful sheriff had been blindsided, but he could see plainly—right into the twin muzzles of Lev's shotgun. And there you have it, a spicy recipe for comedy—or calamity: A private citizen holding a gun on the county's top lawman, while the sheriff is holding a gun on a Texas Ranger, who is holding his gun on a deputy sheriff, who in turn, is pointing his gun at an undercover man. Luckily a kid's firecracker didn't pop. Thankfully Captain Bill Scott spotted the trouble and came rushing to the rescue, sharply illuminating

Copeland's law enforcing status, and ordering Ranger Carmichael to holster his weapon. Tragedy had been averted, but raw feelings had been ruffled—not soothed.[71]

Private Ira Aten was elsewhere during the morning's misunderstanding. Although it is not known whether he had been ordered to stay away or was on his own hook exhibiting common sense, his absence was prudent. Thus far, the only fence cutters who could have spoken to his true identity, Jim Lovell and Amos Roberts, were dead. With his undercover story still intact, Aten could yet prove to be a valuable Texas Ranger asset for other "detective" work. Although it will not necessarily square with provable facts, an assertion that after the shoot-out with fence cutters Aten hastily left Brownwood so he would not be taking any "chances on possibly becoming a target for snipers," is not altogether sideways.[72] Bushwhackers were conniving.

Driving his buckboard home from town after all the hullabaloo, while crossing Salt Creek seven miles north of Brownwood, Joe Copeland found himself unsteadily fixed in assassins' sights. Fortuitously, at the initial sound of cracking gunfire—the bullets having missed—Joe's mules bolted, the spring-seat coming undone, violently pitching Copeland backwards into the wagon's bed, but saving his life.[73]

Although he had not personally been there during the attempt on Joe Copeland's life, Private Aten did recognize the danger—not only for the Brown County man, but for himself as well, posting Captain Lam Sieker: "Copeland has made enemies as well as myself that will last him a life time. His life is in constant danger from friends of the parties killed upon the fence of Nov. 9/86."[74] And no reading between the lines is necessary to fathom what Texas Rangers had in store for the fellows that made a clean getaway that night. Captain Bill Scott's plans were easily read: "I will leave here today to scout in Concho Co. for some of my Brown Co. Fence Cutters. Will be out 6 or 7 days & should I find them mabe [sic] so, something will 'Pop.' Unless we can make another killing on Fence Cutters very soon the outlook for a Gay Christmas with myself & Boys is rather Gloomy. Brownwood is rather a light night city for the average Ranger."[75]

Illustratively there was a Brown County faction not enamored with Bill Scott's company of Texas Rangers and the displeasure did not wholly rest there. The Bavarian-born Ranger Captain Heinrich Georg "George" Schmitt was known throughout the whole Frontier Battalion for his blustery ego and incessant backbiting.[76] Schmitt couldn't restrain himself from sniping at his law-enforcing colleague, Captain Scott: "Gen. King & yourself [Captain Sieker] thought Capt. Scott's Company done an awful lot of work here, while they actually done nothing. Copeland a Citizen here worked up the fence cutting case, and notified Capt. Scott the night the fence would be cut and where at, and all Capt. Scott had to do to station his men there and Capture or Kill them, and I think the management was very poor[.] He ought to had men enough there to capture all of them and not let them get away...."[77] In every respect consistent with his overall makeup, Captain Schmitt could not let the matter rest there. The following month a tattle-telling Schmitt wrote to Captain Sieker about his displeasure with Captain Scott's handling of the incident: "I seen the acounts [*sic*] of the fight of Capt. Scott and men in the Dallas & Fort Worth Papers, it looks like Capatin Scott & his men got the worse of it, and three of the Criminals got away. It seems to me that Capt. Scott had not near enough with him or else he could have captured the whole gang, this is a very unfortunate affair and I feel very sorry for them...."[78]

Ira Aten, like anyone else, enjoyed a kind word or positive recognition for a job well done, but he was not attuned to stealing credit: "With-out the assistance of this man J. O. Copeland, I would have been powerless to have accomplished any-thing. As it was Capt. Scott, five of his men & a few citizens were notified when & where the parties would cut fence the night of Nov. 9, 1886, by J. O. Copeland & my-self who had been trying to work in with the fence-cutters for sometime past...."[79] Although oblivious at the time those words were spoken, Ranger Aten would all too soon face another round of "detective" work trying to joust with nighttime nippers of the wire.

Notwithstanding the quantifiable measurements of Private Aten's successes and failures, that so-called detective work seems to be manifesting itself in a chasm of Ira's overall makeup. Evenhanded perusal of his written correspondence suggests he was becoming more and more independent, a self-governing type of Texas Ranger, a good Ranger, but a Ranger who would smilingly take orders, then get the job done the best way he saw fit.

After an absence of 144 days and back and forth travel coming in at 2660 miles Private Aten returned to Company D's camp during December 1886. Typically, he didn't sit still. On a quick scout he arrested John Arnold for Swindling, delivering him to the sheriff of Uvalde County. He then scooted over to Leaky, Edwards County, attending a session of District Court. For this holiday season trip, on Christmas Eve, Private Aten and fellow Rangers John Bargsley and twenty-year-old Frank Louis Schmid arrested William Gorman for murder. Atypically and inexplicably, the prisoner was kept in the Texas Rangers' camp over Christmas and escorted straight into the custody of Constable Nelson on December 27.[80]

And it was during that same holiday season that a hard law-enforcing nail was driven home again. On the twenty-sixth down in La Salle County, former Ranger Captain C. B. McKinney, then the sheriff, and deputy Samuel Vaughn Edwards were shot down while making an investigation regarding the rape of an eleven-year-old girl. Sheriff McKinney was killed outright; Deputy Edwards survived.[81] Private Ira Aten's chosen career path was rough. Aten was not blind to reality—someday he could catch a bullet.

Chapter 8

"To make a killing, is why I want Aten"

If Ranger Aten took a brief holiday hiatus it has escaped notice. A rising winter sun on January 1, 1887, shone down on Ira and a fellow Ranger scouting in Edwards County near Bullhead (Vance community). Successfully and safely the duo latched on to a suspected cow thief wanted in Uvalde County.[1] Ira's doggedness and pure grit were not traits solely recognized by the Texas Rangers' headquarters. Others had taken note. The sheriff at Mason County, forty-one-year-old John Calvin Butler, was one. Butler's second in command was P. C. Baird, the ex-Ranger and veteran of the Green Lake shoot-out. On the fourth day of January the chief deputy made his and his boss' wants known to the adjutant general at distant Austin. "If you could favor me with Ira Aten's services a short time I could do the work without any trouble, as he is not Known in this Section.... I have a hard set to deal with and will very probably be compelled to make a Killing, is why I want Aten...."[2]

Whether or not Mr. William Connell was a member in good standing of that Mason County "hard set" is not historically provable. There is a hard fact, however. Nine days after Chief Deputy Baird posted his letter to the AG, Privates Aten and Bargsley arrested Connell for Theft of Cattle and Ira, traveling alone, escorted the prisoner straight into Sheriff Butler's jail.[3] Before the month was out, again working unassisted, Ranger Ira Aten arrested Phil Porter for stealing a number of goats.[4]

Owning earned renown as a relentless manhunter, Private Aten was put in charge of a three-man horseback scout searching for the much-wanted murderer William N. "Bill" Mitchell, aka Baldy Russell, aka John Davis, aka John W. King, aka Henry Russell. Shortly before, the fugitive had shrewdly eluded capture by a squad of Company D Rangers during a dodgy nighttime move on the West Nueces River. Private Ira Aten and his boys, according to the plan, were supposed to slip down into his country from their camp on the Llano River, which would position them "on a side that he does not expect Rang-

Mason County Sheriff John Calvin Butler served from 1881 through 1888. Later he would act as a chief deputy for Sheriff P. C. Baird, his former chief deputy and an ex-Company D Ranger. As sheriff, J. C. Butler was well and favorably posted on Ranger Ira Aten's fearless reputation. *Courtesy Mason County Historical Commission.*

ers from."[5] Alas, the gamy bird had flown the coop—in time, alighting in New Mexico Territory.[6]

Hardly catching his breath, Ira this time accompanied by Ranger Wood Saunders, after hearing that fugitive J. G. Ake was hanging out in the rocky and cacti-studded vicinity of Cedar Springs, made tracks for Crockett County. Following a 110-mile scout, Rangers Aten and Saunders rounded up Ake, who was wanted in Gillespie

Mason, Mason County, Texas. For awhile, partisan disputes at Mason were settled with six-shooters, absent a hint of impartial diplomacy. *Courtesy Mason County Historical Commission.*

Phillip Cuney "P. C." Baird, pictured at left, with a prisoner in tow. Lawman Baird was a former gunfighting Company D Ranger and would be a future multi-term Mason County Sheriff. Fair but firm, he didn't bluff. As chief deputy for Sheriff Butler, Baird requested the gun handling talents of a singular Texas Ranger, a Rawhide Ranger: "To make a killing, is why I want Aten." *Courtesy Mason County Historical Commission.*

County, charged with robbery. The two Rangers then hand-delivered the handcuffed Mr. Ake to Sheriff John Walter at Fredericksburg.[7]

On the first day of March 1887 the eternally busy Private Austin Ira Aten "went to Brownwood under attachment" regarding the Brown County fence-cutting caper. His standby mode in and around the Brown County courthouse was just short of a month's duration, causing no little heartburn at Austin concerning his expense voucher.[8] Outlaw fence cutters were not the least concerned with bureaucracy's penny-pinching. They were yet busy in nineteenth-century Texas. And it was a multicultural game: "The cutting was done by Germans who speak no English and it will be almost an impossibility for an American [a Texas Ranger] to do anything in that case."[9] Along the Rio Grande a gang of Mexican nationals "were raiding from the Mexican side of the river...." Texas Rangers from Company D were sent to keep the peace, fully cognizant of the underlying motive for nipping wire: "that all the water in the pasture was dried up and they were compelled to open the fence so that stock could go to the river for water. This pasture has 32 miles of river front which can now be forded almost anywhere. Just as soon as we have some good rains the pasture will be closed and the necessity for Rangers there will cease."[10] Though Ira would undergo a temporary reprieve from the fence-cutting fuss, those snipped steel tendrils would again, all too soon, knot his time and tangle his mind.

In the meantime, however, Private Aten's gunfighting grit portended his selection for another special assignment. This time he would accompany Captain Frank Jones on a dangerous mission, one wherein a miscue could unwind into six-shooter tragedy. Warily traveling to the upper end of Edwards County, the Rangers figured that they had located their targets, the Odle boys. Ira elaborates:

> ....and located their kinfolks where they would likely be. There was a number of horses there. We got there after night. We judged from the saddles and horses that they were in the house. Captain Jones wanted to make a raid on the house that night. I said, "Cap, let's don't do that. They are very dangerous, you have got a telegram that they are very dangerous men, and have killed a man." I said, "Let's wait until daylight and go in just as they get up. They are off their guard then and the house is unlocked." The Captain said, "Well, maybe you are right. We will just stay here." We were at a spring about 100 yards from the house, where they carried their water from. The next morning about daylight here come a boy down to the spring after a bucket of water. Of course we held him. We got ready and ran around the house and I went in the back door. I said, "Cap, I will go in the back door." I went in the back door, in the kitchen and the Captain was at the front door. Had one of these strings that pulled. Odle was just waking up. There were two of them. I covered them with my six-shooter and arrested them, opened the door, pulled the string, and the Captain came in....[11]

These two lawmen were not swashbucklers; they were professionals. Without fanfare, but with appropriate caution, they had arrested Will and Alvin Odle, along with Henry Cavius, aka Henry Wilson. The surprised fellows were wanted, at this time, for Theft of Horses quite a ways northeast in Burnet County. Evidently the outlaws were guarded at the Company D camp for a few days, giving Ira a chance to make a mid-April scout up the Nueces River into the canyon country, recovering several horses stolen by the trio. Then, on April 18, accompanied by Ranger Wood Saunders, Private Ira Aten handed over the three prisoners to Burnett County Sheriff John Wolf, who after notification of the dicey capture, had met them at Uvalde.[12] Ira's taking part in the arrests of Will and Alvin Odle will in its own way—in due time—play to the paradoxical.

What wasn't fluky was the esteem in which Ira Aten was held within ranks and by the Texas Rangers management team. On the last day of April the tried and true Sergeant Ben Lindsey turned in his resignation; he and another ex-Ranger, W. W. Collier, were going to try their hands at free enterprise. They would become saloon owners. Confidently stepping up to the mark, taking Ben Lindsey's

Perhaps the most well-publicized photograph of Texas Ranger Ira Aten. Often this image is published facing in the opposite direction. The rendition pictured here may be correct. In a handwritten letter Ira mentions that he is right-handed. The rifle was normally carried on the strong-hand side. Additionally, the Colt's revolver, in this instance with butt forward, would be accessed by a "Reverse Draw" with the right hand, a technique common to the U. S. Military. The six-shooter does seem positioned rather far back for a "cross-draw." In either event, Texas Ranger Ira Aten was posing ready and armed "To make a killing." *Courtesy Nita Stewart Haley Library & J. Evetts Haley History Center.*

figurative stripes was Austin Ira Aten, now the brand-new and rookie 1st Sergeant of Company D.[13]

Although he had been promoted, Sergeant Aten was no less busy—not sitting around the campfire poking sticks at dying embers while telling others what to do. Riding alone, he again meandered though the upper Nueces River country searching for one of the remaining horses stolen in Burnet County. After six days and scouting roughly thirty miles a day, Sergeant Aten located the misappropriated horse, ultimately returning the animal to its rightful owner. Claiming his position as Company D's top noncom for but a week, word came that Sergeant Aten's presence was desired at San Antonio. U.S. District Court was in session—livestock smugglers' cases were on the docket.[14] While in the Alamo City big doings uncorked near his hometown.

A reasonably short distance north of Austin—about fourteen miles—sat tiny McNeil Junction, a railroad stopover. On the night of May 17, 1887, a gang led by escaped convict Brackston E. "Brack" Cornett, aka Captain Dick, aka Captain Dick with a Candy Stick, and twenty-three-year-old William Henry "Bill" (sometimes "Will") Whitley, a graduate-level cow and horse stealer, a man devoid of fear who could "look into the muzzle of a double-barreled shotgun in the hands of an enemy and never flinch," did what train robbers were supposed to do. The nasty outfit assaulted the northbound Missouri Pacific (International & Great Northern) and its passengers at the McNeil depot. During the malevolent six-shooter mêlée two innocent folks were shot—luckily, not mortally—by the treacherous thieves. Making good their getaway the foolhardy boys dreamed of divvying their ill-gotten haul, about $4000. Although a hard-riding posse of gritty lawmen was immediately built and launched, it returned to town sans any bloodied badmen left on the field or in tow—or elsewhere. News wise the story was a corker, and an unwelcome embarrassment: "horse-borne robbers within a few miles of the capital of the State.... it was intolerable even to think of such a thing happening so close to Austin! Nevertheless, it did happen."[15]

A month later, on June 18, 1887, the firestorm of interest was fueled again, this time at Flatonia, Fayette County, about the midway point between Houston and San Antonio. Several boys of the same gang, with diabolical ferocity, robbed the Galveston, Harrisburg & San Antonio Railroad's No. 19. Their viciousness is readily perceptible: "When Messenger Frank Folger threw away the keys to his safe, the bandits pistol-whipped him and tortured him by slitting his ears with pocket knives until they recovered the keys. The masked men attacked sleeping travelers in their bunks and beat up a Mexican Army lieutenant and a woman passenger...."[16] The remorseless thieves hightailed it with $7,009.50 plus assorted jewelry stripped from the scared passengers.[17] That's what snooping newspapermen were led to believe. In truth, the correct sum would tally at twice that amount.[18] The scurrilous badmen should have worn screening bandannas over their faces—for the whole time. They did not. Soon their identities were well known.[19] Politically such wickedness was hardly acceptable. Lawrence S. Ross, now the Texas governor, squalled with hurricane force: if he had to, he'd ballast all the trans-Texas trains with Rangers. Furthermore, he was ready to commission an additional 400 Texas Rangers if needed, declaring, "Train robbery is to be a fighting business and attended with almost certainty of failure and destruction. There will be five to ten well-armed fighting men on each train."[20] Such hyper-inflated bombast was hungrily lapped up by both the press and public, but Governor Ross and Texas legislators knew what was in the state's kitty—and what wasn't. Politicos could talk big. Rangers well knew such gibberish as that. Unfortunately, so did train robbers.

Ira, once his court business was officially taken care of, traveled to Jones County (Anson) just north of Abilene, arresting James McDowell, who was wanted for Murder in Kinney County. Then by train Sergeant Aten traveled to San Antonio where he was met by Uvalde County Sheriff Henry Baylor, who took custody of the unhappy but handcuffed McDowell. Transferring the prisoner to a fellow lawman for a merry-go-around delivery to Eagle Pass advantaged the State of Texas. Sergeant Aten was now free to rush off and lend a helping hand to Williamson County Sheriff John T. Olive who was searching diligently for that sadistic train-robbing bunch.[21]

Working the best intelligence available to him, Sergeant Aten learned, no doubt after serious consultation with N. O. Reynolds, who by now had ascended to the position of Lampasas County sheriff, that part of the Cornett/Whitley gang was likely hanging out in their Texas neighborhood, namely, Bill Whitley, and pal John Barber (sometimes spelled Barbour), who most probably would be frequenting the homeplace of outlaw Bill's brother-in-law, Tom Cox. Whitley's wife Cordelia, who was purportedly kept in the dark about her

Company D's Texas Ranger Ira Aten's deputation as a Deputy U. S. Marshal. Many frontier-era law enforcement officers were cross-deputized. Ira Aten also held deputy sheriff's commissions in Travis, Uvalde, and Maverick Counties. *Courtesy Jeri and Gary Boyce Radder.*

Bill's true profession, it is alleged, was staying there. Cordelia naively waited for word from her husband. Sergeant Aten began a hit and miss stakeout. Covertly watching the place when he had time:

> I see her [Cordelia] from the brush very near every morning, <u>when she first gets up</u>. They have never caught me watching the house yet. Sheriff Reynolds send[s] a deputy Sheriff with me when ever I ask for one or goes himself. If Barber & Whit-

ley ever comes back here, they will come to this place beyond a doubt. They have went below now to do some rascality from what we can learn. I have notified the officers in the lower country to be on the look-out for them.... It is only a question of time until we will pick them up if they remain in Texas. They are very badly scared, but determined men....[22]

On the very same day Sergeant Aten penned those words (August 6, 1887) he received a telephone call from part-time Williamson County Deputy Sheriff William Stanley, stationed at Florence in the northwest quadrant of the county. The message was precise: "John Barber & out-fit was making for Lampasas." Ira even speculated that the wanted fellows were, by now, already in the county. The next morning, Sergeant Aten hastily scribbled a note to Captain Sieker that he, Sheriff Reynolds, and an unnamed deputy were heading for Tom Cox's rancho, adding, "We dident go out last night as the Anta Prohibitons had a big time here & trouble was expected. Everything went off quietly. We will certainly search the rough for Barber out-fit. I knew they were below but now they are on their way back. I have no more time for writing. Excuse haste."[23]

Little did Ira know what transpired after Deputy Bill Stanley had telephoned him. After dark, the fifty-four-year-old lawman and father of umpteen kids was advised—by strangers—that one of his pasture fences had been cut or was down. The deputy bid his wife and children adieu. Assassins lay in wait. When Stanley hastened to the scene of the purported break, rifle balls ripped into his torso, ten finding a home. Stanley's widow was now in want of a headstone.[24]

In most folks' minds the murderers were two, Bill Whitley and John Barber.[25] Deputy Stanley had been steadfast in his efforts to run the robbers to ground and was determined to see the job through. Desperadoes Whitley and Barber were stubborn as well—they held a grudge with the best of them and were vicious as rabid dogs. Though charter members of the Cornett/Whitley gang had broken into smaller sets in order to avoid detection—each unit, be they but two or three or four, were viperously mean. They would frantically fight tooth and toenail to stay out of the jailhouse and off the grim-faced hangman's scaffold. Dissimilar to their attitude to some of the Old West's conscienceless and ambushing so-called Robin Hood gangsters, the general public's sentiment was against these murderous thugs, as it had been when a back-shooting Billy the Kid was taken off in New Mexico Territory.[26] Whitley and Barber—and their pals—were riding the short road to Hell, and most folks thought they weren't spurring fast enough. They wanted them caught, right now.

Sergeant Aten was in want of something, too. A working partner—one he could count on, day in and day out, night after night. Sheriff Mage Reynolds and his hard-charging boys were dependable to the core, but their participation in any given case was limited by the demands of other cases and circumstances within Lampasas County. Finding enough time and properly prioritizing are the undying bugaboos for local lawmen. Ira Aten knew where to turn.

Sergeant Aten was thoroughly and favorably impressed with the fellow over on that Long Hollow rancho in the vicinity of Liberty Hill. Like Ira Aten, John Reynolds Hughes, as mentioned previously, was a product of Illinois. Unlike Wyatt B. S. Earp who could also lay claim to an Illinois birthplace, along with sporadic and checkered peace-keeping credentials and more time tending bar than serving as a lawman, John R. Hughes was an esteemed man of unchallenged integrity.[27] His criminal record was naught. Though Hughes had not actually been inside the room when Ira, standing alone, gunned down desperado Wes Collier in self-defense, John R. had rushed headlong to the sound of gunfire, backing up Aten—not waiting outside for the winner to emerge before deciding which way was prudent—press forward or back away. In a six-shooter crisis John R. was standup.

Nudging his saddle horse east, Sergeant Aten rode into Williamson County with a recruiting mission in mind: Make a Texas Ranger out of John R. Hughes. Although Hughes owned seniority in life by five years, Ira Aten held the advantage as a lawman. The age disparity troubled neither man. Sergeant Ira Aten would mentor John Hughes, breaking him in as a Texas Ranger. On the tenth day of August 1887, in Georgetown with Sergeant Aten at his side, John R. Hughes raised his right hand and swore to his oath of office, in a heartbeat becoming a Ranger.[28] Next day the duo, veteran and rookie, left "for up about Lampasas Co." scouting for outlaws.[29] The bond of lifelong friendship had been forged. It would never break.[30]

Thus far, as leaves were beginning to change colors with the approaching fall of '87, Sergeant Aten had been on detached service away from Company D's camp since June 28. Now he and Private Hughes were busily engaged in Lampasas County hunting for newsmakers Whitley and Barber. The Rangers' luck was sour. If truth be told, however, the hunt was but a patchwork of hurried scouts interrupted by Ira Aten's having to answer the court crier's call throughout the region. Leaving Private Hughes to snoop on his own hook, Sergeant Aten whiled away time in Brown County, on standby in the fence-cutting case for twenty straight days. Then it was back to Lampasas County where in light of coming up short on catching outlaws Whitley and Barber, Private John Hughes was ordered on October 1, 1887, to report to Captain Frank Jones at the Company D camp, which was in the process of being moved deep into South Texas.[31]

Shock waves were echoing throughout the law-enforcing community when it was learned that Travis County Deputy Maurice Moore, the lawman wounded during the Sam Bass shoot-out, had been mortally gunned down on November 10, 1887, while serving an arrest warrant with Deputy Sam Platt.[32] Policing was perilous. It was a fact not missed by Sergeant Aten, but he remained in the Lampasas area, still on detached service until November 14, trying to turn up a clue leading to the whereabouts of fugitives Whitley and Barber. But alas, Aten's testimony was again needed in a United States District Court's smuggling case, and it was off to San Antonio for six days, before jumping off to Leakey, Edwards County, to testify at a murder hearing. That took a full week. Then it was off to Belton, Bell County, on November 27. The fence-cutting case had been transferred there, and there Sergeant Ira Aten remained, right through Christmas, until the twenty-eighth day of December, when it had been proven "that the change of venue was wrong and the cases were sent back to Brown County for trial."[33] Worried that his expense report might somehow be questioned, Sergeant Aten commented to Captain Sieker: "Please find enclosed my expenses made out in vouchers from the time I left Camp.... Perhaps they will seem large but they are my actual expenses as named upon the vouchers. If necessary to be sworned [sic] to, I can do it with a clear conscience."[34]

Williamson County Sheriff John Olive received a tip that Whitley and Barber were lying low in the Indian Territory north of the Red River. Ever game to join in a chase, Sergeant Ira Aten, this time in an unauthorized expedition, accompanied the sheriff across Texas' state line, but after scouring around for awhile it was dejectedly learned the outlaws had executed a leapfrog maneuver, jumping back into the Lone Star State.[35] The ever cost-conscious bureaucracy took a bite out of Ira's britches—his billfold:

I never rec'd a cent & never will unless paid through the Adj. Gen'l. Office. My Indian Territory scout with Sheriff Olive, which you & the Gen'l are in full particulars was not order of the Adj. Gen'l but thinking I could do the State of Texas a great deal of service by immediate action I went which you already know & will see in my report. While we done nothing to-wards capturing the criminals it was not because we never tried. It was simply our misfortune as well as many other officers in try-ing to catch Barber & Whitley. I hope to hear of their capture soon but I am afraid I will not....[36]

Hardly had Sergeant Aten had time to turn around before it was time to testify at Georgetown in the *State of Texas vs. Alvin Odle* for Horse Theft. After completing that duty, Sergeant Aten went to Aus-tin and conferred with the adjutant general, where he was at long last ordered to report to Captain Jones' Company D headquarters, Camp Savage, Duval County (San Diego).[37] On February 2, 1888, Sergeant Aten made his appearance at Camp Savage. Company D's end-of-the-month report is clear-cut: "Sergt. Aten returned to camp. Has been on detached service since June 28th. Marched 5,000 miles."[38] Ira Aten was high-spirited and ready to go to work, but his utter frustration in not being able to scoop up outlaws Whitley and Barber is reflected in official correspondence to the Rangers' front office, and he was not mealy-mouthed: "I have not got the cheek to ask the General to work after them longer, being that I have done nothing in a way that it can be seen. The Gen. has given me everything that I could have wished for. I have worked harder than I ever worked before & seem-ingly I have done nothing. Time will tell."[39]

There's little doubt, in the eyes of Frontier Battalion leadership, Sergeant Aten's moral compass had been fixed. He could be trusted to work independently, demanding but the lightest touch of super-vision. Such could not be said for all of the sergeant's fellow Texas Rangers. Ranger J. Walter Durbin had transferred into Company D, having been promoted to corporal due to Sergeant Aten's prolonged assignments away from the rank and file.[40] Durbin, an "old Ranger," didn't pull his punches when jabbing at reality: "I had fifteen men. Some of them was fussy and dangerous when drinking."[41] In particu-lar one, Baz Outlaw, earned the ire of his comrades. Ranger Private Alonzo Van "Lon" Oden pegged it spot on, declaring that Outlaw could not leave liquor alone, and when in his cups Baz morphed into

Winchester repeaters primed and ready, Company D Texas Rangers flank the seated Captain Frank Jones. Standing L to R: Sergeant Austin Ira Aten, Frank Louis Schmid, Charles Henry Van Valkenburg "Charley" Fusselman, James R. "Jim" Robinson, John Woodard "Wood" Saunders, John Reynolds Hughes, Joseph Walter "J. W." Durbin, Bazzel Lamar "Baz" (sometimes written as Bass) Outlaw, James William "Tink" Durbin, Ernest Rogers, and Gerry "Dude" Jones. *Courtesy Chuck Parsons.*

a "maniac, none of us could handle him; none of us could reason with him, we just stayed with him until he sobered up."[42] Another who knew him, a civilian female, characterized Baz as being "heartless" when drunk.[43] Corporal J. Walter Durbin validated their portrayals, noting that when liquored up Baz went out of his way looking for trouble, and of all the badmen he had known, Outlaw "was one of the worst and most dangerous. He never knew what fear was."[44] Texas Rangers were plainly blessed or cursed with the traits of personality. Though in the minority, some few were unpleasantly arrogant and self-centered, belligerent and overbearing, sneaky backbiters and jealously covetous, while several were the wretched prisoners of strong drink. Some were even downright mean.[45] Of course the majority of the Frontier Battalion's men were good guys, possessing courage and valor, sympathy and benevolence, dedication and devotion, loyalty and trustworthiness. Sergeant Aten, because of his religious upbringing and uncanny common sense, steered clear of tipsiness. Ira wasn't a saint, and not much of a sinner. Characterizing another popular nineteenth-century Southwestern law enforcer, an adroit newspaper editor proclaimed that gendarme John Harris Behan was "True blue and will do to tie to."[46] Sergeant Austin Ira Aten could be tied to, too.

Although he carried the 1st Sergeant's commission, Ira Aten would not—perhaps could not—sit still. Even with no specific investigation on tap or a particular fugitive to apprehend, Ira rode at the head of a four-man "prospecting scout" through borderland Starr (Rio Grande City) and Hidalgo (Edinburg) Counties. The boys were out over two weeks, sightseeing over a 325-mile stretch of the Texas Valley's tropical real-estate.[47]

While Sergeant Aten and his boys were prospecting along the lower Rio Grande, further inland Alfred Y. "Alf" Allee struck gold at his South Texas rancho near Pearsall, Frio County, southwest of San Antonio. Captain Dick (Brack Cornett) had been lured to the area by Willliam B. "Will" Jacobs, aka "Speckled Bill" because of a liberal peppering of freckles.[48] Will was trying to worm his way out from under a shaky Murder case. Governor Ross wanted Captain Dick much worse than he did Jacobs, assuring him (if true, no doubt through intermediaries) that his cooperation would be justly recognized with the dismissal of a criminal charge and prompt payment of the state's $1,000 reward for Captain Dick's legs anchored with shackles or for his head in a tightly tied burlap bag. Ranchman Allee owned a

Some photogenic Company D Texas Rangers striking a different—and more relaxed—pose. From L to R: J. Walter Durbin, Ernest Rogers, John Hughes, Dude Jones, Tink Durbin, Charley Fusselman, Wood Saunders, Baz Outlaw, Sergeant Ira Aten, Captain Frank Jones, and unnamed teamster. *Courtesy Nita Stewart Haley Memorial Library & J. Evetts Haley History Center.*

"formidable reputation" and a badge, carrying a part-time deputy's commission from Sheriff W. C. Daughtery. A. Y. Allee wouldn't run backwards and an unsuspected windfall of fresh currency would be handy. In fact Allee was, at least to Texas Rangers, "well known to be a desperate character and is [was] always surrounded by questionable parties."[49] Allee and Jacobs began cooking their plan of deception, though Jacobs would remain afar and aloof—he was yet wanted in several counties for other crimes. Will had earlier dabbled in thieving mischief with Cornett, and had slyly pocketed a degree of the man's trust. That was Mr. Brack's first mistake. The second blunder was showing up at Allee's ranch without smelling the aroma of a baking double-cross—and alone. On the morning of February 12, 1888, Captain Dick lay dead in Alfred Allee's front yard. Warily but forcefully Alf Allee had told him to "Throw up your hands, and consider yourself a prisoner." Physically or mentally Cornett did neither. Instead Brack—no candy stick in his mouth this time—reached for the fully charged Winchester leaning against a tree, a no-take-back error in light of Allee's previously demonstrated skill with a Colt's six-shooter and no-nonsense mindset for dropping its hammer. Four .45 slugs had knocked the life out of badman Brack Cornett, "one of the most desperate and daring lawbreakers that Southwest Texas has ever known," so said an unsympathetic piece in the *Fort Worth Gazette*.[50]

That same February, three days after Brack Cornett had given up the ghost, John Barber and Bill Whitley, now accompanied by "Kep" Queen, pulled a heist in Eastland County, about halfway between Fort Worth and Abilene. The mean boys—not wearing masks—hijacked the First National Bank at Cisco, making off with near $10,000, and a gold watch or two. After feinting to the south, the robbers hightailed it back into the supposed safe haven of Indian Territory, for awhile—again, but a little while. Although the snippet rings anecdotal, purportedly the lieutenant governor—who was from Cisco—wired the governor. Fearing the outlaws' threat that they would return and rob the whole town, the politico posed an intriguing but silly query: "What can be done?" Ostensibly the governor telegraphed his snippet: "If not men enough in town to protect it, burn and evacuate."[51]

What was snipping at Sergeant Aten's heels was that Brown County fence-cutting caper—it would not go away and it was eating time he wanted to spend on other investigations. On March 9, 1888, once again, Sergeant Aten departed Camp Savage, subpoe-

Southwest of San Antonio in Frio County, Pearsall was home turf to not just a few six-shooter men—lawmen and outlaws. The man standing on the ground in front of Hans' Saloon with light hat is thought to be the ever dangerous A. Y. Allee. Farther left, three buildings down, standing in doorway of another saloon, a badge pinned to his vest and in a white shirt, is the tentatively identified lawman, J. Walter Durbin. *Courtesy Louise and Donald M. Yena Collection.*

naed to testify at Brownwood in State District Court. This time his absence would be shorter, just two weeks—the defendants' *motion* for a *continuance* was sustained. For the trip to Brownwood there is little doubt that Ira advantaged himself by traveling by train. Too, it is not unreasonable to assume he worked in a little down time with his family either going up or coming back.

There is a factual basis for the reasoned guesswork. Sergeant Aten's next-to-youngest brother, the gray-eyed Calvin Grant, now nineteen years old, wanted to be a Texas Ranger in the worst way, just like Ira. Whether Ira counseled him to do so, or tried to persuade him otherwise is lost. The bottom line is extant. Sergeant Aten returned to Camp Savage on March 23, 1888.[52] The next day, over Captain Frank Jones' signature, a blank railroad pass for the Mexican National Railway-Texas Division was filled in, instructing agents and conductors to allow C. G. Aten, Company D, Frontier Battalion, free passage from Laredo to Realitos, the closest railroad connection to the Rangers' camp.[53] It would be no joke on April Fool's Day 1888; Calvin Grant Aten was formally enlisted as a Ranger private by Captain Jones,[54] that is, after paying 25¢ to a local public official legally certified to administer oaths.[55] Purportedly, and there is not reason to doubt it, Cal Aten had reported for duty at the Ranger camp totally unarmed, conspicuously embarrassed in a crowd of hardened men all wearing at least one Colt's six-shooter and their well-oiled Winchesters nearby. Ira Aten rushed to his brother's aid, handing him a cartridge-belt, scabbard, and six-gun, barking a 1st Sergeant's helpful command: "Put it on!"[56] Private Cal Aten was now—by any standard—circulating in some pretty tough company. But, according to Captain Jones, he now had "the best and most honest lot of men that I have ever known. Not one of them owes a cent that I am not authorized to settle."[57]

With investigative work and fugitive hunting on temporary hold for Aten, the sergeant turned his mind to administrative chores, one of which was transporting some surplus state-owned mules to Fort Worth for transfer to another Ranger company. No doubt the Company D noncom had a couple of specific beasts at the top of his list. Those two were "very wild and almost dangerous when frighten [*sic*]." Sergeant Aten was familiar with the mules he wanted to keep for Company D—the cream of the crop—but the others might prove troublesome to round up. They were "running in a 10,000 acre pasture & very brushy. I seen them all a few day's since." In any event, the good sergeant was charitably volunteering to make the trip: "I will take the mules to Ft. Worth my-self as there are so few men in camp besides me knowing the runs of the train."[58] Ten days later, Sergeant Aten was sitting in the posh Hotel Pickwick's lobby at the corner of Main and Fourth Streets. The Pickwick was Fort Worth's finest hostelry, "complete with gas lighting, first-class restaurant and bar, and private bathrooms with some rooms."[59] Aten penned a letter, reporting to Captain Sieker that he had safely delivered the mules, but was apologetic that the train had been delayed forty-eight hours because of "two wrecks close to Taylor." For Mr. Austin Ira Aten, where better for two trains to wreck than Taylor, Williamson County? Close to home, by sheer coincidence.[60]

That was the good news. What wasn't was the turmoil Sergeant Aten was going through trying to straighten out the confusion concerning the Mexican National Railway-Texas Division and its convoluted policies regarding the issuance of cost-free or discounted passes for Texas Rangers, their horses and pack mules. Battling with governmental or cooperate officialdom while struggling in the swamp of red tape is and always has been perplexing for the policing fraternity. Ira was on a crusade. The thoroughly piqued Sergeant Aten puffed: "I have had them telegraphing around but they only make a bad thing worse. The agents on this road don't appear to have sense enough to pound sand down a rat hole."[61]

Sergeant Ira Aten had sense enough to keep some rats in the hole. Duval County in the nineteenth-century has been depicted as "wild and lawless." That is fair. There was a long history of banditry in the area, one going back at least as far as the birth of the county in 1858. Three years before the county had been officially organized in 1876, one *bandido* was strutting and crowing like a south-of-the-border gamecock. "In 1873, Mexican outlaw Alberto Garza set up shop in Duval County and began to trade in stolen horses. Garza sent word to the citizens of San Diego to 'bring enough money to buy the stolen hides or enough men to skin the hide peelers.' This, it seems, was just the kind of challenge the Anglos in San Diego liked, so they chose to skin the hide peelers and followed up with a raid that scattered the bandits."[62] The Company D camp near Realitos, in the southern stretch of Duval County, was not situated so the Texas Rangers would be convenient for attending area ice-cream socials or taffy pulls. Though by the late 1880s the county seat, San Diego, was somewhat settled-up, Duval County was yet, from a law enforcer's

Wood Saunders, left, and Texas Ranger Corporal J. Walter Durbin. Durbin said he
had some fifteen good men in Company D, though a few could be a "little fussy and
dangerous" when drinking. Private Wood Saunders measured up splendidly—on
both counts. Their Colt's six-shooters are carried just forward of the hip, butt to
the front, easily permitting a strong-hand cross draw. *Courtesy Nita Stewart Haley
Memorial Library & J. Evetts Haley History Center.*

judgment, near as rough as on old weathered boot—rawhide tough.
The two-story jail on the southwest corner of the county square,
built of brick with a stucco finish, wasn't the gemstone of an artistic-
minded architect. It looked like a big box. Nevertheless it was compulsory home to some mean men. So, when State District Court was
in session, Sheriff Linton Lafayette Wright was in want of good help,
lest a jailbird use the judicial commotion to fly, with or without the
aid of a free-world accomplice. The state of affairs at San Diego were
so dicey that Sergeant Aten took it upon himself, rather than trust
the assignment to a subordinate, to personally guard the jail while

the sheriff and his deputy served as bailiffs; overseeing order in the courtroom, lining up witnesses, and tending to juries, etc. With but one Ranger as backup and relief for catching a catnap, Sergeant Ira Aten provided security at the Duval County Jail—nine days' worth.[63] Afterwards he returned to camp for a few days.

But then Adjutant General King ordered Sergeant Ira Aten to Austin. Donning his traveling clothes and gathering his necessary law enforcing paraphernalia, Ira left camp on the twenty-fifth day of July 1888.[64] He would not be back for 104 days.[65]

Arkansas-born and leather tough James W. "Jim" King was a fiddle-playing whiz. The thirty-two-year-old former Zavala County cowboy had laid down the catch-rope and picked up his Descriptive List, the paper document Texas Rangers carried identifying them as lawmen in lieu of an officially authorized or issued badge. Private Jim King, in addition to being a state salaried lawman and bang-up musician, was also a chronic devotee of strong drink. King could pull from the hip-flask or the holster with dexterity. Whether it was whisky or war Private King was always ready—and more than able. Already Ranger Jim King had been through many "hardships" and "difficulties" with Sergeant Aten, at least so said Ira. For those salient reasons it is presumed Ira drafted and had Adjutant General King instruct King to meet him in Williamson County. Some detective work was on tap.[66] Jim King, technically speaking, could have declined—but he didn't.

Chapter 9

"Wild boy among the villains"

An infectious disease, until it is stamped out for keeps, undergoes periods of incubation between outbreaks. For North Texas the outburst of another fence-cutting epidemic broke forth during the spring and summer of 1888. Ranchman R. A. Davis had decided it was finally time to fence his Ellis County (Waxahachie) pasture—one thousand acres. Laboriously, and at no little expense, holes were dug, cedar posts planted and tamped, and four strands of barbed-wire were tacked in place. It was a fine fence—for two days. Knights of the Nippers went to work under the cover of darkness, and by morning Mr. Davis surveyed their handiwork. Methodically working between every other post the gang of cutters had snipped wire in 3,500 places. Typically, along with the cutting were the not-veiled threats. Should the dear Mr. Davis opt to rebuild he just might find it would be a recurring nightmare, nippers would persistently nip, his pasture might be burned, and if that was not good enough, his earthen water tanks drained—depriving cows of hydration and health. Cattleman Davis was stubborn. He rebuilt.[1] Like his anti-cutter predecessor, John Ireland, Governor Ross was not happy.

The state's chief executive was even more upset after learning that the cutters also *had been* busily at work in Navarro County (Corsicana), Ellis County's neighbor to the south. Private John R. Hughes caught the assignment. His task was simple—on paper. Go to Navarro County on the sly and catch cutters in the act: Easier said than done. Hughes did proceed to Corsicana and met with Judge Samuel R. "Sam" Frost and C. S. West (not Sheriff West).[2] Somehow, and in reasonably short order, undercover operative Hughes had ingratiated himself with and was "staying with" a man suspected of "cutting wire." The hotbed community for Navarro County's fence-cutters was Richland, a dozen miles south of Corsicana. That's where Hughes was taking leave, engaging in petty criminality and tolerantly waiting for the alleged crook to spill the proverbial beans, naming all

R. A. Davis, a prominent Ellis County agriculturalist, had one of his huge pasture fences cut in 3,000 places—four snips of wire between every other post. Here, Mr. Davis (in the middle with white beard), and others of the Waxahachie, Texas, volunteer fire department, respectfully pose before the body of "Frank," one of the fire-wagon's team who suffered an apparent heart attack while responding to a fire or during a training exercise. *Courtesy Ellis County Museum.*

of his fence-cutting pals and telling him when and where they would next snip.[3]

Private Hughes' plan went awry, somehow. During the middle of June—after he had safely made it to Waco—John R. Hughes penned Captain Sieker at Austin a note: "I was getting along very well with the fence cutters until some one made a confident of the wrong man and gave the whole thing away.... they are the best organized band that I ever worked after. They keep spies out all the time.... The big pasture men live in town and the people in the country are almost all in simpathy [sic] with the wire cutters."[4] Ranger Hughes' cover, for whatever reason, had been blown. He returned to the Company D camp in South Texas, but one does not have to necessarily be clairvoyant to translate the unadorned cynicism in Captain Frank Jones' snarky notation: "Prvt. Hughes returned to Camp from Navarro County.... to try and work up some fence cutting cases, failed to accomplish anything, out 34 Days, Marched 1000 miles."[5] Private John Hughes' lack of success—no reflection on due diligence, undercover work is always a thorny proposition—had been the precursor episode for Sergeant Ira Aten's command appearance at the adjutant general's office during July of '88. Rangers Ira Aten and Jim King were to do what Ranger Hughes hadn't done.[6]

Leaving true identities behind, Ira Aten—now Ira Wheeler—and his partner boarded a train in Williamson County, and shortly thereafter stepped out onto the busy depot's platform at Waco, McLennan County. After some comical horse-trading with the state's money the Rangers closed the day possessing "a small mule, a one-eyed horse, [and] an old, light, ramshackle wagon...."[7] Then the itinerant farm boys set off. Plodding along, gradually working their way northeast to Mexia, Limestone County. Reading freshly inked newspaper reports, the Rangers picked up an item of particular interest—a shocker. The industrious sheriff of Navarro County, Hezekah P. "Ki" West, had "waylaid a fence & caught some fence cutters in the act of cutting Judge Frost's pasture fence."[8] Rightly inquisitive, Sergeant Aten left Ranger King and their "outfit concealed near Mexia in the brush." Hopping a train the sergeant quietly slipped into Corsicana to learn more. During a hurried confab with some of Navarro County's officialdom he ascertained that the arrested fellows had "been given away by some parties who had cut fence heretofore with them."[9] He also was told that these cutters were "not in the neighborhood of where they want me to work & they were not bad-men at all, like the ones they want us to work after. The ones that were captured was only petty cutters."[10] Not injudiciously Sergeant Aten wondered if the sheriff's good fortune would negate their undercover ploy: "It is a question now whether the fence-cutters will let up on their midnight work or not."[11] Ira was harboring doubts and disgust. Before leaving Corsicana and creature comforts of the Commercial Hotel, Sergeant Aten drew to an inside straight on his political capital with Captain Sieker:

> We will do our best, although it may-be a failure, nobody knows. However, I will ask it as a special favor of the Adjutant General Office never to ask me to work after fence cutters again under any & all circumstances for it is the most disagreeable work in the world & I think I have already done my share of it for the State Texas & her people. I don't see that I get any credit at the Adjutant General Office for such work, although I am satisfied they do the very best they can under the existing circumstances of the small appropriation made by the legislature. I would rather be at camp & only get $30 per month than get $500 per month & have to work after fence-cutters. If it was any other detective business besides fence-cutting where I would not have to be as guilty of the same crime as themselves I would like it. However, being I have consented to try these villains I will ask for plenty of time so don't get out of patience with me if we don't do anything right away....[12]

Certainly Sergeant Aten was more-or-less begging the Texas Ranger front office not to become impatient with his and King's pending undercover efforts, but in light of his asking their indulgence for a favor, Ira's next remarks ring of overconfidence: "I intend to quit ranging next March & wanted to get out of the courts. Their [sic] is only one thing that will keep me in longer than March & that is a commission & unless the Adjutant General department can give me that by that time you can have my name dropped from the rolls Feb. 28th 1889."[13]

Threatening Ranger headquarters with an ultimatum, trying to extort a lieutenant's or captain's commission shines the spotlight on Ira's conflicted uneasiness. Undercover work, with all the skullduggery and lying, interrelated travel, and rushing from one court appearance to the next was extracting its toll—or—little Mr. Ira Aten was

Aside from hard-core law enforcing duties, Ira, according to family lore, found time to notch Cupid's arrow. He introduced Turner Winfield Owen, who he knew favorably from the Texas Ranger days, to his cousin Isodora "Dora" Aten. The outcome was predictable as evidenced by this delightful old-time image—Dora's husband and three children. *Courtesy Gordon D. Turner.*

exhibiting uncharacteristic cockiness. He had been a Ranger sergeant little more than a year, in the big picture not very long. On the other hand Captain Sieker was a charter member of the Frontier Battalion, a hardened fighter and a well-seasoned leader. A token of whining he could understand. Most enlisted men and noncoms bitched. Being held an administrative hostage, though, especially by a subordinate in regards to a promotion was not in his personal psyche or a part of his tough no-nonsense managerial style. In this instance Lam Sieker would bite his tongue, overlooking such a spurt of childishness: Sergeant Ira Aten was a good Ranger.[14] One who knew him—rightly or wrongly—said, "Aten was also rather high-strung."[15] Perhaps this was one of those times and places in a young man's life where he played Jacks thinking they were Aces. Aten's bluff and bluster were but fleeting. The sergeant had a job to do. Austin Ira Aten, whatever else may be said of him, was never a slacker. In the brush outside Mexia he reunited with Jim King and the pair went to work.

The out-of-work "wagon hoboes" at long last pulled through Worthham and a dozen miles later into Richland.[16] Cognizant they were in desperate need of a viable and believable excuse for remaining in the area, the innovative Rangers hatched their plan. Next morning on the outskirts of town—and out of sight—the boys "accidentally, on purpose" disabled their wagon so it was in need of repair. Using a cedar fence post, inserting it behind the rear axle in place of a wheel, the undercover men laboriously cajoled their one-eyed horse and little mule to drag them and the crippled wagon back near Richland. Fortunately there was a blacksmith shop. Unfortunately the boys had no money—so they said, and the blacksmith was away on a "spree." To maintain a plausible undercover story there was but one alternative: Remain close by Richland, find work and earn enough to pay the village smithy for fixing their already rickety but, now near immovable vehicle—whenever he returned home. Slyly seizing upon the opportunity of being stranded—as planned—Private Jim King broke out the fiddle and in the evenings entertained locals gathering at his and Aten's campfire. Soon the Rangers were invited to lively dances. King fiddled, Aten finessed. The Ranger sergeant was not hoodwinked into overrating phase one of their criminal investigation: "We were having a great time at these dances, but not catching many [none] fence cutters. We were with the fence cutting bunch all right, as they would tell us all about the fence that had been cut and who was in their gang."[17]

Working absent a "shadow of suspicion" the undercover Rangers found piecemeal employment doing odd jobs, picking patches of cotton, and building or rebuilding a rock furnace around the cotton gin's boiler at Richland. Assuredly this construction chore was much more labor intensive than what full-time lawmen were accustomed to, but Rangers Aten and King "never grumbled in the least but went at it like we [they] were raised to it."[18]

What they weren't raised to was attending a protest meeting six miles up the road between Richland and Corsicana, at the little wide-spot of Angus. There, some angry Navarro County folks—no doubt cutters among them—had a sharp bone to pick with the sheriff. Rumors were rampant that the boys arrested on the fence line had been plied with liquor, and after they were drunk, induced to cut Judge Frost's fence by two of their heretofore co-conspirators in the nighttime nipping business. Sheriff Ki West and his intrepid posse had lain in wait, in a specific pasture at a specific time with specific intent. The two informants were desperate to work forthcoming criminal cases off their backs, and had allegedly entrapped their supposed pals in a profitable deal to turn state's evidence, plus pocketing a reward.[19] According to Aten, he afterwards learned, some of the most vocal attendees at the meeting were making "big war talk." There was even hyperventilated prattle of "going to Corsicana in arms & taking them fence-cutters out of Jail." Storming the jailhouse came to naught, as Aten predicted it would. For Sergeant Aten there really was a black and a white. Sheriff West, the best that he could determine, "was a good man." Solidifying that assessment in Ira's mind was the signal fact that "these fence-cutters hate him & can't say too many mean things about him."[20]

Conversely, Sergeant Aten couldn't, wouldn't, and didn't say nice things about alleged fence-cutters populating Richland and the area's cool shaded creek bottoms: "These fence-cutters are very near as hard as my Brown Co. fence-cutters & when they once suspicion us they will no doubt try & murder us…. They are a hard set of men in here & they are thieves as well as fence cutters…. villains of the deepest dye & death would be too good for them…. These fellows are not beardless boys but men from 26 to 40 years of age & never was knowed to do any thing but steal & have always lived here."[21] Thinking their investigative ploys might at some point scorch into fireworks, Sergeant Ira Aten was toying with the idea of asking headquarters for additional six-shooter backup. Aten smartly considered their detective assignment "risky business." If there was going to be a dustup it would be with villains that were "hard men & go well armed." He wouldn't mind having Private John R. Hughes covering his and Jim King's backs—if wires snapped and guns popped.[22]

Another hard fact not missed by Ira was elementary—in the extreme. Sergeant Aten and Private King were working a long-settled area. Those cutters who had "always lived here," were clannish, wedded together by kinship, marriage, and shared hardships. Whether all were thieves might be debatable, that they were thicker than thieves is not. Therein was the dilemma. What could the undercover Texas Rangers bring to the table? Ira Aten was no dummy, especially when he mentally walked in the fence cutters' boots: "We are slowly getting acquainted with the villains but it will take a long time to get their confidence sufficient to cut fence with them as I have heard them say after that their crowd dident need any help to cut fence & an out-fit was a fool to take in any outsiders to help them. Lots of such talk I have heard them make."[23] Seventeen days later the situation remained unchanged. Ira reiterated his and Private King's untenable predicament to Captain Sieker: "I have drop[ed] the idea of ever getting their confidence or even any body else getting it, so as to go out & cut fence with them. As I wrote you before, they don't need any help to cut wire & they will not take any one in but just their own gang who they Know & have lived & stole with always."[24]

Speaking of loose talk: Sergeant Aten was making some "war talk" too. Writing to Captain Sieker, the good 1st Sergeant looked into the crystal ball. "You may hear of a killing if every thing works right up here but it may-be some time yet."[25] Eleven days later Aten posted the Austin-based captain: "Nothing will do any good here but a first class Killing & I am the little boy that will give it to them if they don't let the fence alone."[26] Making sure his legal bases were covered Sergeant Ira Aten requested that he be sent an updated oath of office, as he "may have to make a Killing," further emphasizing his undercover standing with the suspects by declaring, "I am the wild boy among the villains...."[27] Two weeks later Sergeant Aten again chirped, telling Captain Sieker: "We have a double barreled shot gun a piece & if the villains cut the fence we are guarding & they don't surrender when call[ed] upon some body will most likely go away with their hand on their belly.... If such a thing is possible I want to take the villains without killing them but I think a little more of my life than theirs & I will stand a trial for murder before I will stand up & be shot down like a fool."[28] In other words—in a policing idiom—he'd rather be tried by twelve than carried by six. There is no doubt while Ira was slipping and hiding in Navarro County he had heard of a well-publicized shotgun blast coming from South Texas. Still adhering to a smattering of law enforcement jargon, a Texas outlaw had been "bought and paid for," meaning he was fair game, shoot first if necessary—he'd kill you if given the chance, at the drop of a hat.

Captain Dick had been lured to his doom by deception, and so too walked Bill Whitley, Ira Aten's nemesis from bygone days. A trickster had tipped off United States Marshal Rankin that Whitley would make a show at the Harrell Ranch near Floresville, Wilson County. The tip was solid—gold. With a posse consisting of Deputy U.S. Marshals William Van Ripper, Duval West, and Eugene Yglesias the trap was set, double-barrel shotguns loaded for bandits not birds. On the evening of September 25, 1888, Bill Whitley rode in, unsaddled and went into the ranch house, sat down in a chair, laying a Winchester across one of two beds. U.S. Marshal Rankin stepped from his lair—a backroom—and purportedly said, "Be quiet, throw up your hands." Whitley didn't reach for the sky, but did grab for a six-shooter. Rankin's charge of buckshot assured Bill Whitley would be quiet—evermore. After the inquest, and displaying his dead body in San Antonio for hundreds to gawk at, the deceased outlaw was shipped back to Lampasas.[29] Though the Whitley family understandably asserts that Bill's taking off was an assassination, the marshal's family was glad daddy had come home for dinner. Six-shooter games with lawmen is a hard game. Whitley's chief partner in crime, John Barber, found that out the following year when he was cornered and killed in Indian Territory.[30] In the meantime, Rangers Ira Aten and Jim King were not wasting time mourning any desperado's demise. They were playing a hard game, too. Blown cover could result in a shovel full of dirt in the face, or buzzards feasting on flesh. That Aten and King were gutsy Rangers is indisputable.

Ira may have overreached about being bestowed a Frontier Battalion's officers' commission, but the plucky 1st Sergeant's demonstrated grit in a gunplay was not claptrap. Aten's and King's biggest problem, however, was not being forced to do six-shooter battle with Navarro County's clannish fence cutters. The Rangers' stumbling block was an insurmountable hurdle—there really were no fences to cut, which made it difficult to catch a fence cutter in the act. Sergeant Aten summed up historical reality, though in the retellings it is frequently glossed over: "As I wrote you before, there has been no wire cut since we have been here, simply because all the pastures we[re] already cut down.... I have been trying through Mr. C. S. West to get the good-men to put up their fence.... The hardest and most disgusting Job I have had since I have been here is trying to get these good men to put up their fence. They say it will be cut then as many times here-to-fore & financial circumstances will not permit putting up their fence one day & going out the next morning & finding it cut to the ground...."[31] "Many have took down their wire

& rolled it up to save it from being cut.... there are no fences up that these wire-cutter want cut down. Unless the good citizens put up their fence again there will be no more fence-cutting in this section for there are no fences to cut."[32] Now, for hardened men of action, Rawhide Rangers, the sad state was lamentable. Lawmen, especially young lawmen wallowing in a pool of inaction, bogged by too much spare time, find themselves in a near intolerable suspension. Loathsome fence cutters had "let the fence alone" because there was not fence to bother, no nighttime nipping, and no villains to cross paths with Rangers Aten and King; no monkey business, no gunplay, no arrests—nothing. "There was a casualty, however. Sergeant Aten was dying—of boredom."[33] Aware that their forced inactivity was a waste of precious manpower at a critical time, Sergeant Aten dispatched Private King back to Company D's camp. Trouble was brewing on the border.[34] Ira would stay behind in Navarro County, mapping out a workable exit strategy.

While Sergeant Aten was industriously cogitating in Navarro County, most of his fellow Company D colleagues had been rushed to Rio Grande City, Starr County. Victor Sebree, U.S. Customs Inspector, had shot and wounded the well-known political activist Catarino Garza. Sebree then sought refuge behind the barrels of a spit-polished Gatling gun manned by American soldiers at the nearby military base, Fort Ringgold.[35] Sixty armed "Mexicans" demanding justice surrounded the Valley fortress.[36] According to a blip in the *Laredo Times*, "Colonel Clendenin, commanding at Fort Ringgold, had received orders to use his force if necessary to protect lives and property from mob violence."[37] Induced to disperse or watch rotating barrels spit lead, the highly agitated crowd moved back into Rio Grande City—where a full-scale riot held sway. Adjutant General King forthwith telegraphed Captain Jones, Company D, with a succinct but easily understood message: "Call in all near detachments to join you at Rio Grande City, and proceed without delay to that point with such men as you have with you. Take your entire camp."[38] Captain Jones began messaging and marshaling his scattered detachments for the march. One Ranger was making a hurried turnabout trip. Earlier, Cal Aten had taken seriously sick while on a routine scout through Starr County. The illness struck him with such acuteness that he had to be left in Rio Grande City, unable to ride horseback by order of Dr. Kennedy. Later Private Aten recovered his health, at least well enough to board a stagecoach and return to camp.[39] Now, Cal found himself back in the saddle again, hard pounding to the rescue of Rio Grande City—from the Ranger's perspective. Company D Rangers, most of them, rode into Rio Grande City on September 29, 1888.[40] There Rangers found that there was "still a strong undercurrent of excitement and Americans do not feel safe, that is those who have families."[41] Shortly thereafter Lieutenant Brooks with a Company F detachment arrived at Rio Grande City to work in conjunction with Company D's Texas Rangers.[42]

Although he had picked up on the border turmoil in newspaper accounts, Sergeant Aten had opted to remain undercover in Navarro County, ingeniously winding down that investigation, rationally forgoing a helter-skelter trip to the border: "I could not much more than get to Rio Grande City until I would have to come back to Edwards Co. [for court] & besides it take lots of money to ride on that stage from Peña to Rio G-C.... I will not be down until the first part of Nov. unless ordered to do so."[43]

Private Jim King, however, had made it back to the new Company D station just in time to partake in a Ranger roundup at riotous Rio Grande City. Coordinating with Lieutenant Brooks' Company F boys, the Company D Rangers fanned out through town. In a one-day sweep on the twenty-second day of October 1888, the task force arrested twenty-three persons for Conspiracy to Murder, and three for Assault to Murder. Moving a few miles upriver, Corporal J. Walter Durbin led a five-man detachment of Rangers into the little Rio Grande settlement of Roma, arresting another half-dozen surprised folks, charging them with Conspiracy to Murder.[44] Unfortunately Private Wood Saunders—another fine Ranger—missed out on the arresting entertainment. He'd been having a whale of a good time in the border *cantinas*, one buying him a ticket out of Company D for drunkenness, courtesy Captain Jones.[45]

Meanwhile back at the Navarro County ranch—the Love ranch—the gears cased inside Ira's cranium began grinding, picking up momentum with each passing day. The whirling wheels of a "diabolical" proposal would soon spin him out of the county and into the history books—on both counts, just as Ira Aten had planned.[46] It was, then, the perfect scheme.[47]

Early on Ira had been laying the ground work, explaining his inability to infiltrate the gang of Navarro County wire-cutters. Sometimes even the best intentioned lawman falls short, though no fault of his. Ira's reasoning was not ill-founded. Sergeant Aten knew—as

THE SHERIFF OF NAVARRO COUNTY, TEXAS, AND HIS DEPUTIES.

Navarro County Sheriff Hezekah P. "Ki" West. Sheriff West and his deputies, dissimilar to the Texas Rangers' best undercover efforts, actually made fence cutting arrests in Navarro County. *Courtesy Navarro County Sheriff Leslie Cotten.*

nearly everyone else—that the brunt of hard-core fence cuttings had taken place before he and Private King had even been sent to Richland, logic he shared with Captain Lam Sieker: "Long last spring when they were cutting very near every night & taking in everybody to help them it would have been an easy trick to have worked in with them."[48] Illegal fence cuttings had dribbled to near nothing. Generally it was accepted that the lull was attributable to identifiable dynamics—two in number. First and foremost Sheriff Ki West actually catching three fellows in the act of cutting a fence was disheartening to any would-be nighttime nippers. Sneezing at felony charges was asinine. Secondly, the sheriff had not been taciturn in saying that Governor Ross had or would send detectives to Navarro County if cutters continued their illicit surgeries. Such a pointed threat—preventive enforcement—was a sound policing tactic then, and is today. Ira failed not to see the sheriff's wisdom, its effectiveness, and its measurable impact: "But now, after being frightened with detectives time & again & the Sheff. catching some on the fence being given away by their own party when at one time they cut in good earnest with them, how can we be expect to work in with them this late in the day after the scares they have had[?]"[49] Unlike the Lampasas fence cutting case where the culprits were but teenage boys, and dissimilar to Brown County where a private citizen like Joe Copeland was taken under the fence cutters' wing with a premeditated plan, investigative circumstances in Navarro County were much tougher, more complicated. There wire cutting had come to a screeching halt. Hearsay evidence was valueless, inadmissible for past crimes. Catching a cutter in the act was not viable. Pointedly, too, was Ira's disillusionment with undercover work:

> These are my last fence-cutters, whether I catch them or not. I don't want to make a failure in this but when I see that nothing can be done, rest assured I will report such to the Adjutant Gen. office, for I would rather be in h—l than here. We have had to tell ten thousand lies already & I know we wont get away without telling a million. Hereafter it will take more than $50.00 per month to get me to go out & see how many lies I can tell or to be placed in a position so that I will have to tell them to keep from being murdered. I will do my best this time for these good citizens deserve assistance of course & if I can render it to them I will do it if my life pays the forfeit....[50]

Bluffing his way into a lieutenancy or captaincy had simply failed. That not subtle nudge had miscarried. Ira's next proposal would not backfire, but would scorch the ears and fears of the Frontier Battalion's and Lone Star State's high-command. Wholly exasperated, Ira began implanting—not implementing—the ruse for an exit from Navarro County. With ingenuity that has been characterized as diabolical on the one end had it been executed, to just flatly illegal on the other, Sergeant Aten set his course—candidly knowing when, where, and how the noisy journey would end at Ranger headquarters. With time on his hands and not an active fence cutter standing by, Ira sat down by a creek, pencil in hand, and waxed eloquently—intuitively, too. What would be the outcome? Ira knew that from the get-go.

At this juncture in Texas Ranger history Sergeant Aten's proposal is well known. In certain circles it is gobbled down with folkloric relish. Ira, so he led management to believe, was resiliently intent on acquiring the necessary components, manufacturing, and then placing "booms" along Navarro County's fence-lines. The wicked little plan, to be fair, was imaginative—and in the end implicitly effective.

Certainly with an abundance of free time, Ira could perfect his blueprint for bidding Navarro County adieu.

The design for a "boom" was rather simple. Ira made sure Captain Sieker did not miss the salient point, that even a lowly Ranger sergeant could make one:

> I can-not explain the working of my boom thoroughly, but can give you an idea how it works. It is simply taking an old shot-gun or musket put some powder in it as if for shooting, then slide down a dynamite cap on the powder & then the dynamite on top of cap until you think you have enough. Put cap on gun ready for shooting, fasten wire to trigger & then to the bottom of a post that is not in the ground place gun in a box made for the special purpose & place the box just under the ground & cover up so it can't be seen. Of course cock the gun when you put it in the box & a fellow will have to handle it carefully. So you see by this post being very crooked & not in the ground and only supported by the wire & when wires are cut or torn down the post will fall & the end will fly up giving the wire at the bottom end of the post a jerk sufficient to shoot the gun off. The powder explodes the dynamite cap & the cap explodes the dynamite & then small piece of that gun will be found all over Navarro Co. Well, if it don't Kill the parties that cut the fence, it will scare them so bad that they will never cut another fence. Thinking it was a mere scratch shot they never got Killed (and it will be a near scratch if it don't Kill them or cripple them). When one of my booms once explodes all fence-cutters will hear of it most likely & then all a pasture man has got to say to secure the safety of his fence against these midnight depredateors. I have dynamite boom upon my fence. Why if the talking of this is not sufficient, he can have them put there at a small expense & his fence will never be cut but once afterwards...[51]

Sergeant Aten was ruefully forced to acknowledge there hadn't been a fence cut during the whole time he'd been in Navarro County, through August, September, and into October. Ira's discontent was growing, day by day, month after month.[52] He was a man of action, and headquarters wasn't listening. Too, he was thoroughly disgruntled with the pasture-men for not rebuilding their downed fences, and woefully admitting those same ranchmen were cheapskates when it came to spending money, not wanting to spend "a cent in the world, only in paper & stamps to write the Gov. & Adj. Gen. long-winded & scary tales how they are imposed upon...." Ira Aten, then, would take it upon himself to build a few "booms."[53] Perhaps if management believed that, there'd be an order to cease and desist and he could forthwith return to Company D's campground and start Rangering again.

Sergeant Aten's wordy campaign was full of hyperbole, but Ira was literally begging for managerial intervention before he was actually forced by big talk to follow through, actually building and placing a few "booms." "Should the Gov. or the Genl. disapprove of this all they have got to do is to notify me to that effect." Adding to the high drama, Ira made sure bureaucracy knew that when he placed a "boom" and after the fence was cut: "'Why, they will hear of it at Austin.'.... I would just as soon set dynamite booms the balance of my ranging days (which are numbered) as to do any thing else.... I have to go to Edwards co. to attend court which is the 10th of Nov..... Not that I want to stay here any more than having hopes of my boom getting some of the villains by that time.... Keep your ears pricked, you may hear my dynamite boom clear down there. Don't be uneasy about my actions for I will use the greatest precaution with my booms & see that no innocent man gets hurt with them. There are dangers in setting them unless a man is awful careful. How-ever, if I get blowed up, you will know I was doing a good cause."[54]

The anticipated reaction was forthcoming—fast and furious. Sergeant Aten was forbidden to construct or install any "booms" on anybody's fence-line. Ira Aten had skillfully outwitted headquarters: "Your letter was very much appreciated as you have written exactly what I thought you would & what I wanted you to.... Now I have your order to show them that I am forbidden to set booms & they will not expect me to do it.... You say I have failed. It is true. I have not cut fence with any of the villains & I don't want to as I would be harassed in the courts for years, but the failure part was not because we did not try to work in with them simply because the Adj. department has asked some-thing of me which is an impossibility to do, hence I invented my boom racket to keep from making a failure.... Of course I am forbidden having any-thing to do with the dynamite boom directly & the order will be strictly obeyed as I said here-to-fore."[55]

Sergeant Aten, an dutiful Ranger, would comply with orders, but there was a loophole of sorts, at least in Ira's mind. He had not and would not personally resort to the use of dynamite bombs, but there was nothing at all preventing him from sharing that knowledge with area stockmen who might wish to do it themselves. Ira would be a willing teacher.[56] Just as Sheriff Ki West had hinted that the state's detectives might be lurking about in Navarro County, shrewdly suggesting that illicit fence cutters could be blown to smithereens were preventive overtures to beware. So, once word leaked out that area ranchers just *might* have hidden bombs along their fence lines, it was near as valuable a deterrent as if a real bomb had been buried. Sergeant Aten from the start had not been blind to that: "You will see yet my boom racket having the effect to put a quietus on fence-cutting in Texas." He was right. Fence cuttings waned.[57] Realizing there was more barking than biting with Ira's "boom racket" should not depreciate a good Texas Ranger legend.

After departing Navarro County and after an absence of 104 days, Sergeant Aten returned to Company D's camp on November 4, 1888. Again, the notation by Captain Frank Jones seems to bear a measure of displeasure with all this unproductive undercover business. Summarizing his 1st Sergeant's clandestine work in Navarro County, the captain tersely recorded in the Monthly Return, that he "accomplished nothing."[58]

Whether or not Ira Aten was actually one of the seven Rangers accompanying Captain Jones to Roma to keep a lid on any troubles during an election day is nebulous. If he did, this complement of Texas Rangers managed to pull off their peace-keeping duties absent a hitch—or gunplay. Additional Company D Rangers, Private Cal Aten for one, were stationed at Rio Grande City, while other Rangers were deployed to Salineno and added points along the lazily meandering Rio Grande.[59] Post the elections of '88 orders from Austin shifted the Company D camp back to Uvalde County, Camp Leona again.[60]

Relocating Company D's camp from deep South Texas to the bottom edge of the Texas Hill Country was a welcome move for Sergeant Ira Aten, who had had, it seems, "to have borne a roving commission form General King to operate against fence-cutters." While it is true Ira Aten by now was fed up with "secret service" work, a categorical assertion that he "basked in the laurels it brought him," may perhaps be stretching historical psychoanalysis a little too thin.[61] In reality Ira's star was not shining that bright with the Texas Ranger's command structure. The lengthy sojourn in Navarro County had netted no confirmed and countable results, other than scaring the wits out of Governor Ross with a foolhardy plan of blowing up unwary folks. A touch of redemption was in order. Texas Ranger Sergeant Aten needed an arrest.

Ed Foster gave Ira the key to workplace salvation. At Eagle Pass the dimwitted Foster purloined a most valuable gold pocket watch, one valued at $250. Justifiably the timepiece's owner was livid, red-faced, and wanting to wring blood out of the badman. Fortuitously for thief Foster he boarded the train at Uvalde, hoping to very soon alight at San Antonio, and then smartly blend into anonymity. For-tuitous, too, was Ira Aten's luck. The locomotive was towing the same Pullman for the Ranger as it was for the rascal. Having already been forewarned of the criminal offense and the suspect's physical description, when Sergeant Aten espied Foster his suspicions were aroused. He accosted the fellow, demanding he submit to either a pat down or full body search. Saying no to a Texas Ranger, especially this Rawhide Ranger, was not even a viable option. Whether the letdown Foster was spread-eagled or simply reached into his own pocket is unimportant. Regardless, Sergeant Ira Aten "found the watch on his person." The arrest was instantaneous. Hauling his prisoner back to Eagle Pass, Ira turned him over to Maverick County Sheriff William N. Cooke. Normally the wheels of justice grind slow—excruciatingly slow. This time it was different—a fast track prosecution. The arrest had taken place on November 20, 1888. During the following month, on the fourth, Sergeant Aten "appeared against him" in State Dis-trict Court at Eagle Pass. Caught flatfooted with the fruits of the crime on his person, Ed Foster caught time, hard time: five years in the penitentiary.[62]

The focus of Sergeant Ira Aten's next big-time criminal investiga-tion would have been glad to do a nickel, sweltering beneath a Texas sun busting rocks at Huntsville.

The first in a delightful series of five staged photographs made at Company D's Texas Ranger camp near Uvalde, Uvalde County. As no doubt intended, when placed in chronological sequence the photos tell a story—somewhat crudely but a story nevertheless. Here, Sergeant Ira Aten in dark suit, second from left, and other Texas Rangers are depicted in general camp life, some performing a few necessary chores: dressing wild game, washing dishes, and tending to a Dutch Oven. *Courtesy Nita Stewart Haley Memorial Library & J. Evetts Haley History Center.*

Capt. FRANK JONES with 11 Rangers, getting ready to leave camp for scout.

This, the second photo in sequence, is inadvertently mislabeled. Company D was, indeed, at this time commanded by Captain Frank Jones, but he appears in none of the five captivating images, suggesting he was away from the Uvalde camp on assignment or furlough. These Company D Texas Rangers gather their horses and begin saddling and lashing provisions on the pack mule for the upcoming theatrical scout. Standing L to R: Baz Outlaw, Charley Fusselman, Sergeant Ira Aten, Walter Jones, Cal Aten, John Hughes, Jim King, and Ernest Rogers. In background, already mounted, L to R: Jim Robinson, J. Walter Durbin, and Frank Schmid. *Courtesy Research Center, Texas Ranger Hall of Fame and Museum.*

The Company D Texas Rangers, preparing to take off on the mock "scout" after desperadoes, fortify themselves with hot coffee and biscuits before hitting the trail. Sergeant Ira Aten, standing with cup, issues the marching orders. Seated L to R: Jim King, Frank L. Schmid, Ernest Rogers, Cal Aten, Walter Jones, Charley Fusselman, J. Walter Durbin, Jim Robinson, John R. Hughes, and Baz Outlaw. *Courtesy Jeri and Gary Boyce Radder.*

Fourth in the chain of photos is this image wherein Sergeant Ira Aten, artificially detecting outlaws nearby, halts his Company D Rangers, cautioning them to exercise extreme vigilance and unlimber their weapons from saddle scabbards. Note John Hughes bringing up the rear with pack mule, a not subtle indicator that he had yet to gain the prominence later awarded his lengthy Texas Ranger career. Also take note of a horseback Baz Outlaw in foreground, an atypical image of the gunfighter normally photographed not mounted. *Courtesy Jeri and Gary Boyce Radder.*

The fifth and last photo in the set has the Company D Rangers locked and loaded, Winchesters pointed at their sham adversaries, with Sergeant Ira Aten, .45 Colt's six-shooter in hand leading an illusionary charge. Whether these Texas Rangers filled coffins or packed the county jail with disgruntled prisoners is left to the imagination. Perhaps, as it should be. *Courtesy Jim Ryan.*

Chapter 10

"Would as soon go to a fight as a frolic"

Through a grab bag of Motions, Continuances, and Changes of Venue, the Brown County fence-cutting cases bounced back and forth between Brown and Bell Counties (Belton). Factionalized politics and tinkering legalese forestall easy clarity. For the most part, it may be said, absent concrete acceptance of jurisdictional responsibility the cases were pushed south on the docket on or about January 14, 1889. Afterwards, the criminal actions—the wire-cutting cases—withered to nothingness, dying on the judicial vine.[1]

Though he had closed and opened the year at Camp Leona, by February 2, 1889, Sergeant Aten and a five-man detachment had established themselves at Barksdale in the southeastern quadrant of Edwards County, roughly forty miles north of Uvalde.[2] The scenic grandeur of the Texas Hill Country was something to behold, but Ira Aten and his men were not on a sightseeing trip. At once they went to work, first, locating and arresting John Sweeten for Theft of Cattle, turning him over to Sheriff Ira L. Wheat.[3] Shortly thereafter Aten and one Ranger made a scout into Kinney County searching for Frank and Britt Stewart who were allegedly holding a herd of cattle of questionable ownership—certainly not theirs. Unfortunately, for the short term, the badboys gave these Texas Rangers the slip.[4]

Now that he was out from under any disagreeable detective work, Sergeant Aten and his Rangers shone. On a March 1 scout to the headwaters of the East Nueces, Ira and two men ran on to two brothers, Richard H. "Dick" and George Taplin "Tap" Duncan, along with H. Walter Landers. Apparently the fellows had poor excuses for being where they were. Sergeant Aten supposed them to be horse thieves, but if his hunch was right he had bumped into them before, rather than after their having time to pull any dirty thieving deeds. At any rate, they possessed not a single stolen horse, but all were carrying six-shooters—an infraction of Texas state law, but admittedly, selectively enforced. In this instance the letter of the law was to be

Ira Aten. As the Company D 1ˢᵗ Sergeant he would take the
investigative lead in solving a genuine whodunit—a quadruple homicide.   *Courtesy Jeri and Gary Boyce Radder.*

obeyed. The prisoners were hauled before Edwards County Justice
of the Peace Steiber who allowed the defendants to post bond for
Unlawfully Carrying Arms. A few days later Sergeant Aten latched
onto J. W. Beck and Frank Kiuzie, each wanted for Aggravated
Assault. The next day he arrested Al Hanley who was sought because
he had assaulted someone with intent to murder on his mind.[5]
Edwards County, it would seem, was absolutely brimming with fellows in critical need of a dose or two of judicial comeuppance and
Sergeant Ira Aten had more than a spoonful to dispense.

Then it happened: A real newsmaker, a multiple murder case with
unknown perpetrators. And who better to investigate than Ranger
Sergeant Ira Aten?

For most Company D lawmen the first inkling of a misdeed came
from ex-Ranger Ben Lindsey, who with his partner ex-Ranger W. W.
Collier were now operating the Tariff Saloons, with imbibing loca-
tions at Uvalde and Eagle Pass. Ben Lindsey's letter from Eagle Pass
to Captain Frank Jones was informative, and horrifying: "There has
been within the last 4 days four dead bodies taken out of the Rio
Grande river six miles above Eagle Pass. All white—three women

and one man."[6] Sadly, the saloon proprietor was dumbfounded. No one was making a rigorous stab at investigating. As far as local policing authorities—on either bank of the *Rio Bravo*—were concerned it was if nothing untoward had happened, at least according to Ben Lindsey. Separate reports are at variance with his cold assessment. Nevertheless, the ex-lawman was appealing for Captain Jones to put a good Ranger on the case; he would be doing the county at large a big favor if he would. Pointing out to Captain Jones that there were populated settlements along the river, it was Ben Lindsey's idea that someone should "have the country in this neighborhood thoroughly examined for some clue to this horrible murder.... and some effort Should be made to ferret out this murderer...."[7]

Captain Jones was in a quandary. Assuredly the murderous crime called for a competent and thorough investigation. At first blush it seems the Company D boss believed the murderer or murderers to be "Mexicans," which because of the border area location is not really all that outlandish. In fact, there was a disturbing faux pas when two of the bodies were identified as a Mrs. Lopez from the south side of the river, and the young girl that lived with her. Mexican *policia* even had two suspected murderers in custody. The Spanish speaking lawmen were disheartened to learn that they had made an error when the Lopez lady and her companion were found "alive and well." There's no room for doubt the fellows under arrest were not downhearted when apprised of the Mexican officials' pronouncement that they'd be turned loose—without delay.[8]

Jumping to conclusions is not attuned with what a first-class investigator should do: Keep an open mind. Besides false leads, Captain Frank Jones, too, was worried about the quality and leadership capabilities of the local Maverick County sheriff: "I do not consider the Sheriff of that Co. at all reliable and [he] is moreover an enemy to the Ranger force...."[9] The Texas Rangers would make an investigation, adeptly and absent favoritism or prejudice, hopefully solving the crime and legally standing the perpetrator—one or more— before a hangman representing the Blind Mistress of Justice.

Not unexpectedly Sergeant Aten got the call; he had the tenacity of a ferret and the nose of a bloodhound to bring a killer—or killers—to bay. The sergeant was to be assisted by Private John R. Hughes, his ever affable pal and a man by now owning the makings of a first-rate Texas Ranger, Ira remarking: "whenever I had a bad case I always took Hughes with me."[10]

Arriving in the border country the Rangers brought themselves up to speed with the facts—meager as they were. Quickly they learned that on the river seven miles above Eagle Pass, Jacob Meyer had fished a snagged body from the current on February 27, 1889. It was a female, well past middle-age, and she had been not too effectively weighted with a large stone tied to her waist. She was not a local lady, none were missing. And, no one could identify the dead body as anyone they knew in the area. The next day the body of another female was found, a twisted apron around her neck, and a heavy rock dangling at the end of a rope tied around her waist. "Her head was fearfully gashed behind." Four days later, and further upriver, two more bodies had been discovered—a young woman "badly decomposed" and a young man, "five feet seven inches, slimly built." They too had been anchored with rocks tied to their waists, but natural buoyancy had overridden the sinister plot to feed them to the fishes. These three dead folks, likewise, were just as unidentifiable as the first body recovered from the river. The cause of death—at least at first glance—seemed to be head trauma due to a bludgeon of sorts. Yet absent proper names Justice of the Peace G. B. Dunn fittingly ruled the deaths homicides, committed "by party or parties unknown"[11] Public display at a local mortuary (or courthouse lawn) had failed to produce any leads as to who the victims really were. Without much ceremony the deceased had been reverently buried at public expense. Who they were was a mystery. Who killed them and why was a mystery. It was, truly, a whodunit.

Though forensic technology was yet in its infancy Sergeant Aten observed some basic criminal investigative protocols, ordering the plow-line-type ropes used to secure rocks to the bodies held as evidence, as well as the rock weights themselves. He too made note of the physical descriptions of the deceased, particularly that the younger of the two grown women had an artificial dental plate and unusually large and protruding bunions on her feet. The young man, Ira was told, had a noticeable gap between his front teeth, and "the canines were very pointed."[12]

Unlike undercover operations where the case is worked forward, an act of murder is the terminal element constituting the criminal offense. Homicide investigations, then, are customarily worked with a backwards approach, reconstructing the crime scene and tracing last known movements of victims and/or suspects. At this point, Sergeant Ira Aten did not have a crime scene, or any identifiable victims, or any feasible suspects. Deciding their first avenue of clue hunting would focus on finding the site of the murders, the befuddled Rangers began working the river banks looking for signs of a struggle, a blood trail, or an outcropping of rocks that would match those affixed to the dead bodies. Too, they would check with area merchants in case someone had recently sold a lengthy section of plow-line. The leads were skimpy. The outcome was vague. But that is what they had.

Although there is a generous helping of vagueness as to just when it happened, the figurative light bulb sparked on—in Private Hughes' head. John R. recounted a tidbit of information to his sergeant, and it was noteworthy—extraordinarily so.

Earlier, before the bodies had been discovered, but after Sergeant Ira Aten had arrested the Duncan boys and Walter Landers for Unlawfully Carrying Arms, Hughes had seen them also. Scouting along the West Fork of the Nueces he had encountered Dick Duncan, and a fellow introduced to him as Picnic Jones. These two were riding ahead of a wagon driven by a young man with widely spaced front teeth and an infectious grin, along with two grown women and a teenage girl as passengers. During a polite by the trail visit Dick Duncan asserted the young man was his brother-in-law, husband of the young girl, and the other two ladies were his mother and sister, respectively. The procession was headed for Old Mexico, where Dick Duncan's kinfolk were to take up residence on a small scale rancho, he said. The small-talk, at that time, registered no suspicion or surprise. Private Hughes did remember, though, that the wagon was brand-new, a Mitchell, painted green. For some reason, almost subconsciously, he too recalled it had the seller's brand burned into the tailgate: Sold By J. S. Clark, San Saba, Texas.[13]

Sergeant Aten could have been bowled over with a feather. Hughes had offered a workable clue—one crying for follow-up. Leaving John Hughes to scout the Rio Grande continuing to search for a murder scene, Sergeant Ira Aten hit the high road for San Saba. There, Ira began unscrewing a strongbox of evidentiary leads, and nailing tight a murderer's coffin. First and foremost, the San Saba County Sheriff, S. B. Howard, had some real hot news. Dick Duncan was already in jail. The Williamson family, the widow Williamson, her widowed daughter Lavonia Holmes, a teenage daughter, and her twenty-year-old son were no longer in San Saba County, they had— one and all—departed to take up residence in Old Mexico. No, they

The prime murder suspect had purchased a brand-new wagon at the Joe S. Clark Hardware & Wagon Yard, San Saba, Texas. The clue helped focus the Ranger investigation and led to a killer's undoing. *Courtesy San Saba County Historical Commission.*

hadn't been seen or heard from since, Ira was told. Barroom chitchat and backyard gossip was wafting throughout the whole county that it was the Williamsons' who had been found floating facedown and dead in the Rio Grande. And it was no secret just who had helped pack their bags and shown them the way south: Mr. Dick Duncan and Mr. Picnic Jones. The crime was so heinous that the general public, even faraway from the border, was becoming "aroused." Whispers were increasingly growing loud and fingers were pointing, particularly at Duncan.

Dick Duncan, a twenty-two-year-old "red-headed, dancing, idling, singing cowboy" voluntarily surrendered. He had been urged by Berry Ketchum, brother of one of the deadliest outlaws in the Old West, Tom Ketchum, and now by marriage loosely affiliated with the Duncan family, to flee. Dick had spurned his advice and offer of cash to make the mad dash for sanctuary in Old Mexico or South America.[14] After clandestinely huddling with a local lawyer on the outskirts of San Saba in a secluded spot, Picnic Jones decided he'd run, saying "I will leave before sundown." He mounted his horse and "rode away to the west.... He disappeared as if he had ridden into a solid wall which opened to receive him and closed behind him instantly." Dick, on the other hand, had opted to take his chances with the law. "'I'm going to San Saba in the morning and surrender,' which he did. Next morning he entered town, walked up to the Sheriff, and said: 'You know me; I'm Duncan. I have come in to surrender,' and went to jail, where he has since remained."[15]

Sergeant Aten visited with his chief suspect, now provisionally held in the local lockup, as was brother Tap Duncan. Dick Duncan told Ira that if it was, indeed, the poor Williamson family that had been murdered, perhaps it was some "Mexicans" who killed them to get the money the old lady was flashing after selling him that little piece of San Saba County land. When he had last seen them they were alive and kicking. Dick Duncan's story sounded fishy. Ira cast his investigative net, seining around town, reeling in more information, and it was not flattering:

These folks [the Williamsons] were kind of shoddy people. The widow and daughters were permitting fellows to drop in, and this boy was a kind of simple boy and didn't pay attention, and the people in the neighborhood wanted to get rid of them on account of their character. Dink [sic] Duncan was laying up with this girl, who about sixteen or seventeen…. Dink Duncan was laying up with her and she was in a family way. That was proved by the information we had.[16]

Even by a San Saba lawyer's account Dick Duncan, who "had been known all his life as belonging to the class that would as soon go to a fight as a frolic, and a little rather," was purportedly giving in to some raging hormonal issues, not hatching a premeditated murder plot: "The old lady was all right. Her boy Benjamin was all right. One of the daughters was Mrs. Lavonia Holmes, a grass widow. The other was named Beulah. They were not of the best character. This was common knowledge in San Saba County. Duncan knew them well. He was no more virtuous than any other young rough rider. He followed them for an immoral purpose…."[17]

The three women and young boy were, in fact, not Dick Duncan's kin, Ira quickly learned. Why had Duncan lied to Private Hughes? And, most valuable for the moment was the fact that the widow Williamson, her widowed daughter Lavonia Holmes, her son Ben, and her teenage daughter Beulah, had in the dead of night loaded their belongings and had lit out for Old Mexico, escorted by Dick Duncan and Picnic Jones. There had been, after discovery of disfigured bodies, growing rumors of foul play naming a crew of San Saba County's folks. Dick Duncan had been at the top of that sullied list. After gos-

San Saba County Jail, San Saba, Texas. Outside a wandering cow ambles by. Inside a murder suspect is artfully interrogated by Texas Ranger Sergeant Ira Aten. *Courtesy San Saba County Historical Commission.*

sip implicating Dick had swirled around him with a rip-tide's unrelenting embrace, the doubly scared fellow had turned himself in saying something quite similar to: "Prove it!"[18] Sergeant Ira Aten had picked up the gauntlet.

Now with his investigative antenna adjusted to a starting point, San Saba County, Sergeant Aten could begin piecing the puzzle together, witness by witness, clue by clue. It was not to be easy, but with typical confidence and characteristic doggedness Ira Aten thought he could trail movements of the deceased and suspects from San Saba to the Rio Grande then track the guilty parties back to the San Saba country. Sergeant Aten set to sleuthing. He learned a book full.

The blacksmith at San Saba, Tom Hawkins, posted Sergeant Aten about an earlier conversation he had had with Dick Duncan: "Yes, I'm taking your neighbors away, taking them down to Mexico to locate them on some land down there." Purportedly Mr. Hawkins retorted, "I hope you will never let them come back." To which Dick, according to Ira, replied: "By God, they will never come back."[19]

For a sum of $400 and a new wagon, Dick Duncan had purchased the widow Williamson's farm, her deceased husband's headright, plus an additional forty acres. Sometime prior to the twentieth day of January 1889, at nine o'clock at night, neighbors noticed that Dick Duncan and Walter Landers, aka Picnic Jones, had driven up to the Williamson homestead in a brand-new Mitchell wagon, saddle horses tied behind. The commotion was noisy, attracting no little attention as "boxes, beds, furniture, etc. was being placed in the wagon." Before midnight the wagon had been packed full with household goods. Duncan and Jones mounted up. Dick was riding a bay horse and Picnic was atop a "handsome sorrel pacing horse with a striking appearance."[20] Young Ben Williamson slapped reins across hindmost quarters of the bay and roan horses pulling the wagon, urging them to keep up with the two horsemen, now heading south—toward Old Mexico.[21] The fateful trip was then underway.

One day, on February 8 or before February 10, 1889, near the Nueces River, about two miles north of Brackettville, Mr. Tom Salmon had met the travelers, all six, alive and well. They were yet heading south. On Sunday the tenth and the following Monday, Dick Duncan and Picnic Jones had been seen in Brackettville by none other than the sheriff, J. W. Nolan, as well as others, namely Mr. Ballantyne, Mr. Staler, and Mr. Coleman. In fact, Ballantyne, on Monday morning had seen all six travelers pass by his residence, and had even seen Dick Duncan put something into the wagon's bed.[22]

Later, on Monday afternoon, the whole party had been seen passing through Spofford Junction, still heading south. Riding into town, Dick Duncan even conversed with a Mr. Yates and a Mr. Collins, while making purchases at George Hobbs' general store. One of the items he bought was a lengthy section of plow-line. Noticeably, but not all that unusual for the place and time, Dick Duncan was carrying a Winchester carbine—in perfect working order. As late evening closed in on the voyagers, they had made camp at a ranch twelve miles south of Spofford Junction. Camped nearby, too, had been the observant Howard Lavering, situated close enough to get a good—and memorable—look at everyone.[23]

The next afternoon, about eighteen miles south of the previous night's camp, Theodore Wipff had observed the party still making tracks south, but now not too far from the Rio Grande. Mr. Wipff knew it not at the time, but he was the last living person—except for the killer or killers—to see the Williamsons alive.

During his substantive follow-up investigation, Sergeant Aten had learned more. On the seventeenth of February Dick Duncan had ridden back to Spofford Junction, from the direction of Eagle Pass. He had been followed by Picnic Jones sitting in a Mitchell wagon's seat. Later, at Bracketville, witnesses recalled that Dick Duncan's rifle was out of whack, the barrel and tubular magazine were bent—gruesomely so. The next morning the furtive pair left Brackettville, but it was a feint. Picnic Jones drove the wagon southwesterly to Eagle Pass, while Dick Duncan stabled the sorrel horse he was now riding and trying to trade. He then boarded the train that ran from Spofford Junction to Eagle Pass. Once there, he and Picnic promised to discount $35 off the asking price of a certain sorrel horse, if Shad White would but pilot the Mitchell wagon—still packed with bedding and furniture—across the river to the Mexican side.

On the twenty-second, Dick was back in Mr. Hobbs' general store at Spofford Junction. When asked how he had damaged his Winchester, Duncan replied that he had had big trouble crossing a donkey to the other side of the river, and in a fit of anger had whacked the beast between its long floppy ears. After retrieving his horse Dick Duncan struck out in a northerly direction. Thirty miles later he hauled in at the Brown Ranch, inquiring if the owner had seen a man and wagon—a Mitchell wagon—he was supposed to meet him in the vicinity. Answering in the negative, Brown invited Duncan to camp for the night. Also traveling the border country was a Mr. Perry, who likewise camped overnight at the Brown Ranch. Though he did not know who he was at the time, Mr. Perry had seen Picnic Jones earlier, telling Dick Duncan where the man was then camped. Allegedly, an uptight Dick Duncan quipped: "He didn't camp where I told him, but next time I'll learn him to camp where I tell him."[24]

Behind the suspects, circumstantial evidence of their complicity in the murders kept unfolding. Particularly, W. W. Collins, during his interview, declared he had personally observed the burro that Duncan claimed to have beaten with his Winchester. The animal bore no such marks of injury about the head or any other place on its anatomy.[25]

On the twenty-fourth day of February, Duncan's brother Tap and their father, made an appearance in Spofford Junction, looking for Dick and Picnic. They were driving a wagon, too, and had traded a weaned colt to store owner George Hobbs before they headed north, in search of Dick and Picnic. In the northern reaches of Kinney

County, Dick Duncan and Picnic Jones met and traded with a "Mexican" an old quilt for six bushels of corn. Too, they tried to sell him a feather bed and an old gun for $20, but he balked at that deal.[26]

By now a seasoned investigator, Sergeant Aten recognized that any criminal case against Dick Duncan was only circumstantial, but if ample circumstances dovetail, that is good enough. Still, he would give basic forensics a try: "and got the rope and all the evidence we could. We come back with that rope, took our trail back.... We took this rope to Spofford and the other end of the rope fitted right into the end of the coil where it was cut off. It fit to a 'T' with that rope that they had bought there."[27] Although he was sure the dead bodies were of the Williamson family, neither Sergeant Ira Aten, nor anyone else, could truthfully testify to that. For successfully prosecuting murder defendants it is obligatory to prove just who had been killed. Although the technique is common today, when Sergeant Aten brainstormed for disentangling his conundrum the methodology he employed was not widespread. This *may* be the first time the procedure was ever used in the Untied States. Certainly it was the first time Texas Rangers availed themselves of this forensic application: Ira would try to match dental work to deceased.[28] Profitably for his murder investigation Sergeant Aten contacted a former San Saba dentist, Dr. A. E. Brown, a specialist familiar with the widow Holmes' dental layout. Ira Aten finally traced him to El Paso where he was then practicing dentistry. Yes, he knew the Williamson family. He had made a dental plate for Lavonia Holmes. The good tooth doctor was very well acquainted with young Ben Williamson's dental framework and the wide gap between front teeth, conspicuously accented by those pointed canine teeth. A trip to Eagle Pass was on the agenda.

There, Sergeant Ira Aten had the bodies lawfully exhumed and examined by the dentist. Not to anyone's astonishment Dr. Brown confirmed the identities of the deceased, good enough to stand the test in a Texas courtroom. Too, Private John R. Hughes had not been asleep. Steadfastly he had scoured during daylight hours along the Rio Grande, until "he came to an abandoned ranch and despite the rains which had fallen intermittently since February, he found what the frontiersman calls a 'drag'—the unmistakable rut made by passage of some heavy object. The drag led from the old ranch to the river. *And along the bank at its end were stones similar to those which had weighted the bodies!*"[29]

Frontier Battalion fellows pose in a now classic Texas Ranger photograph. Standing L to R: Robert "Bob" Speaks and Jim Putman. Seated L to R: Alonzo Van "Lon" Oden, and John R. Hughes, who accompanied his 1st Sergeant, ably assisting Ira Aten during part of the headlined murder investigation. *Courtesy Research Center, Texas Ranger Hall of Fame and Museum.*

Armed with an overabundance of circumstantial evidence, backed up by as many as forty separate witnesses, and a sampling of physical evidence, rudimentary as it was, Sergeant Aten was bristling with confidence that Dick Duncan and Walter Landers, aka Picnic Jones, were the heartless murderers. In point of fact he notified Captain Sieker that "circumstantial evidence pointed at these parties & when I came to investigate the matter it is one of the plainest circumstantial evidence cases I have ever known."[30] On the other hand, there was a whopping shortage of evidence—circumstantial or otherwise—to convict Tap Duncan.[31]

Even at that Sergeant Aten was worried. Having long suffered the sometimes asinine theatrics of courtroom melodrama, Ira feared that one of the defense lawyers hired to represent Dick Duncan had the state district judge "hoo-dood."[32] Aten was likewise thoroughly of a mind that Walter Landers was just as guilty as Dick Duncan, but that manhunt was sticking Ira akin to a scratchy burr in his long-johns. Landers had fallen from the face of the earth as far as Texas Rangers and county sheriffs were concerned. And there was seemingly a convincing explanation—other than his adopting an alias and hitting the owlhoot trail. Sergeant Aten thought that if he could just capture Landers that the boy would "tell the whole thing & I will bet my hat [on that]. I think I can make him squeal...."[33] Others were reading tea-leaves too. If little Mr. Picnic Jones was dead he couldn't snitch his way out of trouble and he certainly couldn't implicate anyone else. In fact, according to one of Dick Duncan's attorneys, the best suspect for the killings was, indeed, Walter Landers, certainly not his client sitting in jail.[34] Lawyer Leigh Burleson told a nosy newsman: "As for Landers, the man who hauled them to the river under contract with Duncan—that is a different matter."[35] A juryman needed but a *reasonable doubt* to hang his hat on. Blaming Landers might just do the trick. Picking up on a possibly prompted theme, Dick Duncan was inferring as much to Sergeant Aten, who was not necessarily being taken in by the contrived blather: "The two Duncans are laying it all off on Landers & says he is the one that done the murder....we never heard of Landers any more. The supposition is that Dink [*sic*] Duncan had Landers killed. I don't know whether that will hitch up with it or not. That was Landers' home. He had never gotten there from Mexico after this trip. The supposition is that Dink Duncan killed him on the way back."[36] While tracing the true fate of Walter Landers is lost in the dustbin of history, Duncan's story may be moved forward with clarity for the reader, but bleakly for Dick. No longer was his incarceration voluntary; legal paperwork had been filed. He was now unwillingly ensconced in the jailhouse—a Preliminary Hearing at Burnet, Burnet County, on tap.

Sergeant Ira Aten was hustling: "There will be a world of witnesses for the defense from San Saba Co. & two worlds of witnesses from Kimble, Edwards, Uvalde, Kinney & Maverick counties for the State. They can be trailed through all of those counties with the women & man that were murdered & they can be trailed back without them.... Besides a world of evidence what they said to people as they went along about these women and man…. they [lawyers] expect to get them placed under a light bond & they will jump it. Their relatives have got money & are putting it up…. I have worked on the case until I am very near worn out…."[37]

Sergeant Aten knew the outcome at Burnet would be revealing: Dick and Tap Duncan would get out of jail—or they wouldn't. As far as Ira was concerned, the case against Dick was airtight. He had doubts, however, about Tap's actual involvement. Apparently, so too did the judge: "When it did come up I [Aten] had all the witnesses I could get and was there at Burnet, Judge Blackburn held Dink [sic] Duncan without bail and Top [sic] Duncan he released. We were satisfied from the information we had that he had nothing to do with it. Doubt whether he knew anything about it or not. Dink was held without bail and the sheriff was ordered to take him to Eagle Pass." Ira read Tap as not being "such a bad man." But Dick was "a real bad man."[38]

After testifying at the Burnet hearing, Sergeant Aten returned to the Company D camp in Uvalde County. He had been working the Williamson homicide case for thirty straight days without rest, and had racked up about 1500 miles during the investigation.[39] Dick Duncan may have been stretched out on a steel bunk, waiting for his big day in court, but Sergeant Aten still couldn't seem to rest. A persnickety little thorn was troubling the 1st Sergeant. Would or would not the governor honor his commitment to pay a reward for the conviction of Jack Beam? Ira thought he was entitled to it. He penned Captain Sieker a missive: "I sincerely hope the Gov. will pay the reward with-out further delay…. If collected, keep out enough of money for your trouble & expenses if any, and send me a check here for the balance."[40] No sooner had he returned to camp and fired off that letter, than word came he was needed in Batesville, Zavala County, for a court appearance. After testifying there, he was off again, this time to Edwards County: more days tied up with offering sworn testimony.[41] On this occasion, according to Ira, jumping the legal hurdles was worth any temporary aggravation: "We had a fine court at Leakey. The noted cow-thief of Kickapoo Springs, Campbell Tucker, better known as the 'Yellow Wolf' was convicted two years for cow stealing…. Bill Turner of South Llano was also convicted for two for Manslaughter. The killing was six years ago."[42] After winding up his court appearance in Edwards County, it was right back to Eagle Pass for Dick Duncan's legal mess.[43] Not only were the ends of justice to be served, there was a $200 reward check waiting for Sergeant Ira Aten at Eagle Pass. After acknowledging appreciation for the money, Ira posted headquarters about his status, declaring, "Court is in full blast here at present."[44]

During the first week of June 1889, the Maverick County Grand Jury met for its scheduled session. Naturally the most noteworthy business on their agenda was the Williamson murder case. A quadruple homicide is a major newsmaker—anywhere—Texas for sure. Not surprisingly, after hearing testimony from a string of witnesses, Sergeant Aten included, the grand jury returned Indictments against Dick Duncan for the murders. Though Duncan's purchase of the plow-line did have forensic implications, in truth, at the time, there was no expert capable of swearing in court that the rope bought at the store and the rope used to weight down the bodies was an *exact* match. Nor could it be proved *absolutely* that the murder weapon used to bludgeon the stunned Williams family to death was Dick Duncan's dreadfully mangled Winchester carbine. Dentist Brown could positively identify the deceased, but once that prickly little quirk had been ironed out, so could a whole host of folks from San Saba County—and they had. As long as defendant Dick Duncan stood pat, denying his guilt, unless Walter Landers could be found and flipped, there'd be no eyewitness testimony to "the most horrible crime ever perpetrated in Texas." Although there was an outstanding murder warrant for his arrest, no one actually expected to find Mr. Landers—or a Picnic Jones—alive. Both prosecutors and defense counsel knew that the case hinged almost wholly on circumstantial evidence. Armchair detectives may somewhat undervalue circumstantial evidence, but its admissibility in court has long been accepted and, at times, it is an irreversible screw that shuts tight the criminal case's lid. Some frontier folks thought it matchless: "It is an axiom of the legal profession that circumstantial evidence is the best kind of evidence, for the reason that it cannot be confused by a bullying lawyer and cannot perjure itself." Other legal scholars and casual observers looked askance: "It is a very beautiful theory. Sometimes it does not work in practice."[45] In practice, it was going to have to work in the Dick Duncan case.

Pending a series of expected and routine legal Motions filed by defense lawyers, Dick Duncan was moved from Eagle Pass and lodged in the Bexar County Jail at San Antonio for safekeeping until his murder case was to be called for final resolution.[46] One lawful but absurdly out-of-the-ordinary Motion was filed by a San Antonio attorney. His contention was that the entire Penal Code of Texas was invalid, and therefore Dick Duncan's criminal charges were also null and void and his incarceration patently illegal: False Imprisonment, if you will. The underpinning of his theory was that the criminal code as approved by an act of the 1877 state legislature failed to adhere to constitutionality under state law because there had not been a third reading of the bill as required by the amended 1870 Texas Constitution. In plain talk, he charged that Duncan's case and all others should be purged from the dockets—the state's Penal Code was impotent, emasculated. Although there is a degree of smirking comedy associated with this brouhaha, it did take a decision of the United States Supreme Court to untangle the sometime rubbish of legalese and restore justice to Texas' courts. Though the legal she-nanigan fell flat, it did buy Dick Duncan time.[47]

While Sergeant Aten had been busily engaged with the Grand Jury at Eagle Pass, other news broke involving a Company D Ranger, one of Ira's subordinates. The news flash and subsequent official reports were clear indicators that lawmen always walked—then or now—a perilous path. In but a heartbeat the humdrum can morph into horror.

Chasing after a more lucrative paycheck, three of Captain Jones' "best men" resigned. Corporal J. Walter Durbin, Privates John R. Hughes, and Bazzell Lamar Outlaw could better fill their pockets in the cooperate world—guarding mines in Old Mexico. South of the border they went. Though lacking in experience, Charles Henry Van-valkenburg "Charley" Fusselman was promoted to corporal, the lead man for a Company D Ranger detachment in far West Texas. Charley was twenty-two years old, and feared not a bear or a badman.[48]

Brewster County (Alpine) Sheriff J. T. Gillespie, himself a for-mer Texas Ranger, had received a report that one Donaciano Bes-langa was on a rip-roaring tear at Haymond Station a few miles east of Marathon. The guy was either staggeringly drunk or was lost in berserkville. Whether it was liquor or lunacy was not relevant to Sheriff Gillespie or Ranger Fusselman. Donaciano was shooting at folks, and had even slightly wounded an innocent bystander.[49] The newly named corporal jumped in: He'd arrest the man terrorizing the northeastern reaches of the Big Bend Country. For the initial investi-gation the sheriff had assigned a deputy to accompany Corporal Fus-selman, but after failing to locate Beslanga where they thought he would be, the Brewster County lawman retuned to the comfort of his office at Alpine. Quitting was not in Fusselman's makeup. He learned that Beslanga's residence was near Maxom Springs. Knowing sooner or later the man would return home—sane or senseless, sober or smashed—Charley Fusselman staked out the abode. Unfortunately for a Ranger sitting outdoors waiting to make an arrest, a horrendous thunderstorm blew in; wind whipped and lightning popped.

Captain Frank Jones updated Captain Sieker: "C. H. Fusselman killed a Mexican in Brewstar [*sic*] Co. yesterday while resisting arrest. I will give particulars as soon as I hear from Fusselman."[50] And, Charley Fusselman had a few (minimally edited) particulars:

> I borrowed a mule and went to Maxom Springs, found he had left at sunrise. I lay & watched his wife until 10 at night when a heavy storm blew up which drove now deceased into his home for shelter. I run on him but he slipped me as it was so dark. I followed his course to water tank & as I was looking under the tank for him lightning flashed & he shot at me at about 100 yds. I did not see where he was until he fired second shot then I run toward him & returned the shot. Lightning flashed & he was down on tracks & fired several shots & run & I lost him as it was dark & raining so hard. Next morning I got a rifle & took his trail at daylight when about ¾ mile from Station, I heard him cough. I went toward him & the instant I saw him he saw me & sprang to his knees. I could see there was no chance of his giving up as he had a bad expression on his face so I fired as he did, both at same time. Witnesses said the two shots were so near together that they could just be distinguished. Then about 15 shots were exchanged, all this happened in about 20 seconds. I emptied my gun, run in on him grabbed his gun & shot him once with pistol before he would give up. He was hit 8 times. 5 shots were fatal, he would of fought ten minutes longer if I had not grabbed his gun & took it away from him. I then wired Gillespie who came at night with Justice & held inquest & we returned to Alpine. The officers all say I am justifiable in the killing as it was in self defense in the discharge of my duty. Please excuse this long explanation.[51]

Later, in a letter to his brother Calvin Grant, Ira Aten would most favorably comment on Charley Fusselman, characterizing him

Another of the classic Texas Ranger photos: Company D. Standing L to R: Jim King, Baz Outlaw, Riley Boston, Charley Fusselman, Tink Durbin, Earnest Rogers, Charles Barton, and Walter Jones. Seated L to R: Bob Bell, Cal Aten, Captain Frank Jones, J. Walter Durbin, Jim Robinson, and Frank Schmid. Statistically the odds were stacked against this unsuspecting cluster of lawmen. At least five of these Rangers would die violently at the hands of others. *Courtesy Research Center, Texas Ranger Hall of Fame and Museum.*

as honorable and a capable Ranger, but a lawman that took too many chances.[52] Just like the 1st Sergeant, Charley Fusselman would step to the mark. Ira had a good protégé.

With the trial of Dick Duncan on hold, and Fusselman's gunplay relegated to the ash heap of an idiot's folly, Sergeant Aten once again bounded into action—with zeal. He went on the hunt. Though he didn't have to travel beyond Uvalde County, Ira soon racked up another arrest: Lou Buck, charged with Horse Theft. Sergeant Aten turned his handcuffed prisoner over to the county sheriff and received another thanks for a job well done.[53]

The year 1889 was little more than half over, and already two Lone Star peace officers had paid the ultimate price: Potter County (Amarillo) Constable M. M. Givens had been mortally gunned down by the county sheriff, James R. "Jim" Gober, who claimed an accidental discharge during an uncalled-for verbal dustup. Robert L. "Bob" May, the Grayson County (Sherman) sheriff was fatally ambushed at the little North Texas community of Howe, by the Isom cousins, Benjamin and Mandrew, after an attempted arrest had soured.[54] Before the end of summer two more Texas lawmen would give up the ghost during gunfights. Sergeant Austin Ira Aten would be on the ground and up close when dueling Democrats piped the Grim Reaper's death march.

Chapter 11

"Venison is better than no meat at all"

Fort Bend County, geographically blessed with rich Brazos River bottoms gradually giving way to alluvium soils in the flatlands as the winding watercourse amplified, was near perfect farm country—in the western slice of the county, productive cattle growing country, too. Herds of insect-resistant Brahmans stood near belly deep in salt grass, fattening, dependably dropping droop-eared calves for replacement and the market. Cotton crops thrived throughout the area. Fields of rice flourished in the marshlands. In the semi-tropical coppices stalks of sugar cane prospered. During the fall as winter overtook northern states, flights of honking and quacking and colorful wildfowl flocked for refuge in this Gulf Coastal region's wetlands. If 1889 Texas yet owned an Old South plantation culture, its heart beat at Richmond, the county seat. Fort Bend County's eastern neighbor was Harris County and her unremittingly expanding metropolis of Houston, just thirty miles away. Fort Bend County's southwestern flank bordered Wharton County, home to the bustling town of Wharton, which would also play an integral role in the biographic profile of Sergeant Austin Ira Aten—and the Texas Rangers.

Named for a bend in the Brazos River where some hearty folks from Austin's colony had earlier settled, though they had not been the very first, Fort Bend County could trace its organized birth to 1838, but a reasonably short time after Texas had declared her independence, wresting a whopping share of real estate from Mexico.[1] Within Fort Bend County's line, tradition mattered. Fort Bend County was one place where political philosophy and political loyalty were, if not everything, close to it. During the Civil War most Fort Bend County residents were heart and soul, brawn and blood, fervently committed to the Confederacy. Fort Bend County could also rightly claim another distinction. Afterwards, in Fort Bend County the hated Yankee-imposed era of Reconstruction was an utter fiasco—a failure from the get-go. A not trivial wedge of the section's adult population had not been reconstructed at all. They purposefully kept a death's grip on Old South mentality and were mulish about maintaining it.

Demographically the white folks of Fort Bend County were radically outnumbered. Freedmen held the majority and they voted—regularly and in bloc.[2] Though not particularly wielding too much economic power, politically the black denizens of Fort Bend County were powerhouses—or so it would seem to an uninformed outside world's spectator. There was a wicked little secret, though. Although blacks held many of Fort Bend County's elective offices, behind-the-scene white power brokers were—in most instances—actually pulling, sometimes jerking local government's administrative and tax collecting strings. An entrenched cadre of whites—a minority—were personally profiting and politicking for no disruption of the status quo.

Occasionally it is mentioned that the growing rift between Fort Bend County's county seat rivals during the late 1880s was but a case of *Republicans vs. Democrats*. Such incorrectness is understandable—and fixable. There really were no white Republicans in Richmond, save one, David Nation. "In Richmond one had to be a Democrat or nothing."[3] Wearing a political nametag in Fort Bend County was near mandatory—physical wellbeing demanded it. Though they may have given off the aura of radical Republicanism, and did control county and city government, the minority white Woodpeckers were Independent Democrats, while their arch enemies, the Jaybirds, were the Straight Democrats: the Conservative Democrats, traditional prewar Democrats.[4]

Retracing Ira Aten's footprints in Fort Bend County will not necessitate an opus on the postwar intrigues and infighting for two decades preceding his deployment to Richmond, although the machinations and maneuvering, plots and subplots, as well as the droll political jockeying for dominance in Fort Bend County during the late 1880s is truly fascinating. For recapping Ira Aten's role in the Jaybird-Woodpecker feud and resultant bloodshed it only insists that the finer points be recapped—and all so briefly.

A historical nut cracks open with realization that what the Jaybirds could not do with ballots, they would do with bullets.[5] That was a hardcore fact decipherable by a newspaperman jotting for the *San Antonio Daily Express*: "The Jaybirds have determined that negro supremacy shall cease to exist in Fort Bend county. They have been robbed, taxed and ground to the very earth ever since the late war and will stand such government no longer, but have determined so long as blood is in their veins to fight democracy's opposition to the bitter end."[6] Richmond, when it came to settling differences man to man, was a boiling cauldron. If one wished to test the grit of his manhood or sought a fight, a quick trip to Richmond would fit the program. Old South gentlemen generally behaved like gentlemen until pressed with a perceived affront—be it intentional or not, be it just or not. Then the gloves came off and the pistols came out. Writing for the *Houston Post* one newshound particularized the readiness of Richmond's dueling class:

> There is probably one fact about Richmond that will not be disputed by any sane man and that is that there are more men there who will stand up before shotguns and pistols than any town of its size in the United States and if anybody don't believe it, just let the doubting Thomas go over and proclaim himself "Bad Medicine from Bitter Creek" and make a gun play and if somebody don't call him, it won't be at this time or generation.[7]

The driving force—at least the most identifiable and colorful—behind the Jaybird faction was Henry H. "Red Hot" Frost, proprietor of Richmond's illustrious Brahma Bull and Red Hot Bar. Frost's somewhat bizarre nickname was no misnomer. He was no backdown man.[8] Nor was he inclined toward tranquility—or sobriety. Not according to his vocal personal and political enemies. Red Hot Frost could get drunk with the best of them and when so, if there was nobody available for target practice, well, the lights in his saloon would do just fine. They were his fixtures.[9] His, too, was a following of "the young bucks of Richmond—the high spirited, often pugnacious young men who knew there would have to be a fight and wanted to get it over with."[10] To be sure, Red Hot Frost was not too hot for Jaybird firebrands.

Red Hot Frost, though, was not immune to buckshot. One night, while opening a yard-gate, he caught a charge of "blue whistlers" but survived, barely. He named three freedmen as his potential assassins: John and Mitchell Ewen and a schoolteacher named John Donovan. They were arrested along with an alleged co-conspirator, Jackson "Happy Jack" Randall. Subsequent to his arrest, Happy Jack posted bond and disappeared, leaving open the question as to whether he

willingly departed Fort Bend County for keeps, or was now peacefully resting six feet deep under a shading live oak—somewhere? The
ambushing of Red Hot Frost "did serve to bring the Negro question
into the open."[11] Not insignificantly, nor racially tolerant, at least
seven black men were told to gather their families and trappings,
then vamoose, at once: Leave Fort Bend County or pay the fiddler—
buying a ticket to Hell.[12] Wisely, the black men left the county, but
not the story.

Lining up on the opposing team was the sheriff of Fort Bend
County, Jim Garvey, kin to the previous sheriff, Thomas M. "Tom"
Blakely, who had taken over from his relative, J. W. "Jake" Blakely.
Jaybirds were not necessarily surprised with the appointment of Jim
Garvey after the resignation of Tom Blakely; they were, however,
flabbergasted at how fast it had happened. Jim Garvey, Woodpecker
to the core, was like Red Hot Frost capable of tying one on, tipping
the bottle and becoming dangerous—some say, even cruel. Vocal
personal and political enemies said so anyway. Sheriff Garvey was
by his own declaration King of the Woodpeckers, so Jaybirds showed
little surprise at the continued touch of nepotism. Sheriff Garvey
staffed the position of chief deputy with his brother-in-law, Thomas
Calton "Tom" Smith, a genuine tough cookie and already a proven
gunfighter with a cut on his notch stick.[13]

Tom Smith had formerly been the city marshal, at Taylor, Williamson County, which leaves open the door to suggest Sergeant
Aten was already acquainted with him. Tom Smith was the proto-
typical man of the Wild West, "a good rider and roper, a fine shot
with a six-shooter, and a very graceful dancer." He owned the nerve
of a lion, the ferocity of a grizzly bear. Purportedly, while wearing a
badge in Williamson County he suggested that the notorious—and
not overrated—gunman Ben Thompson take the long way around
his bailiwick. Mr. Ben actually obliged. Another time, during a dustup
at Taylor, a "saloonkeeper reached for a gun but Smith beat him
to the draw and the saloonkeeper died with a bullet in his body."[14]
Regardless any political partisanship, when Chief Deputy Tom Smith
decided on a course of law enforcement action he was more than
capable and competent. Deliberately poking a stick in Tom's eye was
brainless folly.

Volney Gibson and his three brothers, Guilf, Ned, and Jim, sons
of a medical doctor, were well-known throughout Fort Bend County.
They were Jaybirds. Volney, it is asserted, was the best pistol shot in

Thomas Calton "Tom" Smith, Fort Bend County Deputy Sheriff and later a U.S. Deputy Marshal. Tom Smith was an intrepid fire-eater during a gunfight. *Courtesy Robert Ernst.*

the county. The Code of the Duello suited the Gibson boys just fine, and in the saloons of Richmond during an argument they were considered "cool customers."[15]

What was not cool was the Woodpeckers' continual hold on county government, a strangle hold in the minds of Jaybirds. They were being taxed heavily, represented poorly. Woodpeckers were quietly happy with the status quo; they were Fort Bend County's caretakers of power and profit—elected by the people. The election, then, of 1888 had been a do or die proposition for Jaybirds. Adopting a proven tactic they had decided to do what Woodpeckers had been doing for years—capitalizing on black citizens' votes. Freedmen and their voting age descendants were honored guests at super grand affairs, the financial bills footed by Jaybirds. The visitors were plied with promises, succulent barbeque, expensive cigars, drams of whisky, and more whisky and more whisky—and then some more whisky. The supposed unawares revelers listened to the speeches, feasted on the freebies, puffed on the stogies, and drank and drank and drank some more. The sea of whisky did not turn the tide. Election day the Woodpeckers, as always, claimed the prize—full control of Fort Bend County's purse strings and the ancillary clout that complemented electoral victories. Woodpeckers were whooping it up. And one in particular, J. W. Parker, the former Fort Bend County judge, was chiding: "The darkies were nearly fattened on Jaybird beef, light bread, cigars and whiskey."[16] Drowning in sorrow the Jaybirds opted to shed their state of mourning and rekindle their spirits with a grand supper and ball. No Woodpeckers invited. Whether an in-your-face insult, or a token gesture of reconciliation, will swing on the hinge of perception. The Woodpeckers would, too, sponsor a nighttime gala. To make sure bereaving Jaybirds knew they would be welcome, fancy invitations were printed and mailed. The Jaybirds were not thrilled—not flattered at all. Playing a childish game, the Jaybirds had derisively readdressed and again mailed the invites—to the black prostitutes on the north side of Richmond's railroad tracks. The whores were surprised—and amused. The Woodpeckers weren't.

Taking particular umbrage was the newly elected tax assessor, J. Kyle Terry.[17] Kyle Terry, like the other cast of characters in the unfolding tragedy, was capable of holding a grudge—and stewing and shooting. Terry could bide his time, but Jaybirds would pay for their silliness—with blood.

In a historic context the time was short. For Terry the months were agony. Then, perhaps thinking, "venison is better than no meat at all," he decided to kill Ned Gibson, since he had not advantaged himself of whacking brother Volney, the real hothead of the Gibson clan. On June 21, 1889, Kyle Terry arrived in Wharton with a breakdown shotgun disassembled, wrapped in newspaper and tucked under one arm. He passed the time of day with chitchat inside the Malitz and Barber Saloon. After lunch, about 1:00 P.M., Ned Gibson left the Fort House and began marching up the busy street to the Wharton County courthouse. He had afternoon business to conduct—he was a lawyer. Kyle Terry had business to take care of, too. He assembled his shotgun, dropped two shells in the chambers, and waited in the doorway's recess. When Ned Gibson came within range, Kyle Terry emerged and let loose with both barrels. The buckshot tore into Gibson's shoulder, mouth, and arm, pummeling him to the street. He screamed and died within a matter of hours. Somewhat pleased with himself, it seems, Kyle Terry had whipped out a silk handkerchief and wiped off the barrels of his yet smoking shotgun. Then, with a smirk on his face, he handed the shotgun over—butt first—to Wharton County Sheriff J. W. Jones who had rushed to the sound of gunfire. Terry was arrested without resistance and placed in the Wharton County Jail. Realizing the potential for a boneheaded attempt by incensed comrades to liberate Kyle Terry, the sheriff cordoned the jail yard with an extra complement of deputies. Later, for safekeeping and a safe-state-of-mind, Sheriff Jones transferred Kyle Terry to Galveston, taking advantage of the better security afforded at the Galveston County Jail. The murder of Ned Gibson was the tipping point. Though there had been an occasional killing and a bushwhacking or two over the previous twenty years, now it had come to a head. No longer was there room enough for both Jaybirds and Woodpeckers in Fort Bend County or the surrounding Plantation Country. It was now open warfare. Too, it was a bugle call for Sergeant Austin Ira Aten and the Texas Rangers.

Sergeant Aten was scouting near Barksdale when he got the call. Captain Frank Jones in a letter to Captain Sieker confirms: "Your telegram is rece'd. I will start a man to Edwards County at once to call in Sergt. Aten and detachment...."[18] Three days later Captain Jones telegrammed Adjutant General King at Ranger headquarters: "Am on train for Richmond with seven men."[19]

After but the briefest stopover at Richmond the Rangers moved to Wharton on a peace-keeping and court security assignment. Kyle Terry's Preliminary Hearing for the homicide of Ned Gibson was on tap, along with the local court's other docketed cases.[20] The judge really had no other choice than to bind Kyle Terry over for a District Court felony trial, the Probable Cause was there. At least he could let the grand jury do its work. He could have denied bond, but he did not. After posting the acceptable percentage of a $5000 bail bond, Terry walked out of the Wharton County courthouse, temporarily a free man. He opted to wile away his time away from Fort Bend County. Kyle Terry began hanging out in the Houston hotspots—where he had earlier killed a Houston policeman—and walking the beaches of Galveston searching for seashells and salvation.

That Captain Frank Jones did not have a crystal ball or was adept at reading Tarot cards is evidenced by lifting a sentence from his

Richmond update to AG King: "Myself and men are on very friendly terms with both partys [sic] and there is no doubt but that our presence here has a soothing effect...."[21] Captain Jones was justifiably concerned with the deteriorating health of his wife, and sought to take leave and rush to her bedside at Boerne, Kendall County, just northwest of San Antonio. Wise to the ways of bureaucracy, Captain Jones wanted to make sure he was covered should Fort Bend County's political affairs flare into any barefaced nastiness during his absence. "I would respectfully suggest that Sergt. Aten and three picked men be left in this section until after District Court in this County and Wharton which will be in September and October. Everything is, and has been, remarkably quiet and orderly since we came here.... I am under the impression that it would not be a prudent idea to remove the entire force for some time. The men are on excellent terms with both factions...."[22]

Singling out Sergeant Aten was, indeed, prudent. He was a good Ranger. Aside from being a workaholic, Austin Ira Aten was now a young man of impeccable credentials in matters of law enforcing astuteness. He, too, was a principled man in issues of honor or with money—his or that belonging to the state. Ira Aten had the makings of a first-rate noncom too, one with promise of earning a captaincy—with a little more experience and when the time was right. He could—as he had already demonstrated—stand tall during gunfights and other dicey dustups. Ira Aten didn't have to run in a pack like a snarling and teeth-gnashing wolf to draw his courage. In a crisis he was levelheaded, not at all inclined to trade good sense for recklessness, suffering a mental lapse and surrendering to emotion when conditions really turned "Western." Nope, he didn't have "fight on the brain." There can be little argument—really none—that Preacher Aten and his whole family, as well as the Texas Ranger front office personnel and Company D's enlisted ranks, were proud of Aten. He had not turned out like some Old West lawmen, those who were really no more than shysters, gamblers, sometimes pimps, sometimes policemen—usually contentious—eternally controversial.

What was a touch controversial though, at least according to Ira, was Captain Jones' avowal that Texas Ranger presence at Richmond was universally appreciated. "The sheriff was one of the political leaders of the Woodpeckers and his office was the controlling point of the whole situation. I [Ira] am sorry to say that I could not get any cooperation from his office. The sheriff, J. T. Garvey, told me he had not asked for the Rangers to come to Richmond, as he could handle the situation himself."[23] All too soon it would be plain that Sheriff Garvey could not "handle the situation himself," but neither could the Texas Rangers.

The Ranger quartet was domiciled in a rented house on the outskirts of Richmond, thus skirting around staying in the typical outdoor camp, the habitually stingy state having to spring for healthier accommodations. Sergeant Aten and his fellow Rangers would alternate patrolling Richmond's streets, their mere presence thought to put the damper on any outbreak of corporeal hostility. Regrettably the Rangers could not control the balmy weather of August in a subtropical zone—the high humidity coupled with the rising mercury was punishing—near torturous. Private J. R. "Jim" Robinson came down sick—if not with malaria, something similar. Unable to shake the fever and chills, the Ranger was confined to his bedroll on a cot, wholly dependent on his buddies for nursing him back to par. Subsequent to the 25 percent manpower reduction, Sergeant Ira Aten and Privates Seth Roberson and Frank Schmid had to pick up the slack.[24]

As the August 16 sun began making its timeless decent toward the western horizon, an undercurrent of uneasiness crept over Richmond. It was nothing to quantifiably put one's finger on, but an overall pall of eeriness nonetheless. Sergeant Aten felt it.[25] Sheriff Garvey felt it.[26] Cautioning Privates Schmid and Roberson to be vigilant in his absence, Sergeant Aten left Richmond and returned to quarters. Dutifully looking after Private Robinson, Ira was attentive to administering the sick lawman a scheduled dose of quinine, and perhaps preparing him some nourishing broth, if he could keep it down. After comforting the Ranger, he would return to Richmond.

Ira Aten didn't know it then, but when he went back to town it would be at the gallop. Richmond, with help from hotheads, was in process of shedding its short-lived skin of dormancy. Shortly in front of six o'clock the aforementioned former judge, J. W. Parker, and his nephew by marriage William T. "Witt" Wade, a deputy sheriff, were horseback, riding toward Parker's home. Unbeknownst to them, paralleling on a side street were Volney and Guilf Gibson, who believed with passionate fury that Parker was the instigator—the man behind the scene—the scoundrel who had pushed Kyle Terry to off their brother Ned. Long had many Jaybirds thought Kyle Terry should have been burned at the stake or drawn and quartered or fed to the hogs.[27] The same for Judge Parker would be just fine, too.

Wade and Parker turned into a cross-street. Volney and Guilf tuned into a cross-street: the same one. When the two parties were nose to nose gunfire burst forth. Who fired first? Well, the answer to that persnickety little question wholly rested with political affiliation, depending on whether one was a Jaybird or a Woodpecker. Although it is measurably skimpy, there is a smidgen of common ground.

Volney Gibson had jumped off his horse to use his Winchester "to better advantage," and then fired a shot at Witt Wade. Depending on the version Wade fell from his horse or skillfully dismounted, but a bullet had not touched him. Volney then shot again, at Parker, but missed, maybe because the judge was now racing toward the courthouse, turning in the saddle, shooting at Guilf with a six-shooter as his startled horse leaped and lunged beneath him. Guilf, like a greyhound after a rabbit, was following close behind, only this dog had a Colt's six-shooter in his paw. Deputy Wade fired not a shot, but was trying to talk Volney out of further mischief, albeit with a revolver in hand. On the other hand, the Gibson brothers and Judge Parker were spitting lead, wildly. One bullet plowed into Parker's back as he continued his madcap dash for the courthouse. Reeling in the saddle he regained balance, sustaining his ability to twist and fire at the pursuing Guilf, who sensed blood in the water—on the street. There was, however, a heartbreaking and lamentable sidebar to this madness.

Robie Smith, an adolescent black girl, was running an errand for the M. Newell household. The eruption of gunfire had burst forth without warning, taking Robie off guard, right in the middle of Jackson Street. She was trying to get to the other side, either taking something to or picking up something from the J. M. Moore residence. Tragically, Robie Smith never made it across the street. Robie caught a bullet to the brain. An unfortunate accident to be sure, but nevertheless she lay motionless in the street, her life's blood painting crimson puddles beneath her head. The poor child was dead.[28] For the moment no one ventured into the street to check on or volunteer medical aid for Robie. Who knew just who the next wildly spent bullet would mark?

Not unexpectedly the sound of gunfire catapulted the curious to peep outside, but more germane for Ira Aten's story it spurred committed Jaybirds off high-center. Though most everyone in Richmond went armed with a pistol or two, their Winchesters and shotguns had been stashed in various business houses for just such an emergency. Many young fellows kept their long guns at Frost's Brahma

Fort Bend County courthouse, the bloody scene where besieged Woodpeckers took refuge. *Courtesy Fort Bend County Libraries, Genealogy and Local History Department.*

Bull and Red Hot Bar. A few others, Guilf Gibson and Keane Feris in particular, maintained a stockpile of arms at the McCloy Drugstore. No matter where the arms were salted away, now owners began fishing them out of hiding places and readjusting cartridge belts. The opening salvo for a real battle had been fired. Jaybirds were rushing to the war front, falling into place behind their main man, Red Hot Frost.

Barely ahead of Guilf Gibson, Judge Parker's lathered horse deposited the wounded fellow at the courthouse, a refuge for Woodpeckers and, too, the site of their squirreled away arsenal. Parker was no doubt hopeful to have finally found kindred Woodpecker spirits in the forms of Sheriff Garvey, Chief Deputy Tom Smith, Deputy Harry

S. Mason, and the Fort Bend County Judge, J. M. Weston, who was also a medical doctor. At the courthouse, in his upper floor office, Judge Weston examined Judge Parker's bullet wound to the back, determining it survivable. Downstairs Fort Bend County's legally empowered, but not necessarily popular, cadre of lawmen made ready for the worst—anarchy.

Sergeant Aten may not have been in town, but the Ranger quarters were within earshot of the echoing crescendo of gunfire. After tendering Ranger Robinson an explainable farewell, Ira Aten stepped into the stirrups and kicked for Richmond. He had two Ranger privates there, perhaps needing backup. If there was to be a fight involving Texas Rangers he would sure be a part of it.

As he dashed into town it was easy to discern two distinct groups squaring off for who knew what, excepting it all spelled trouble. Reining to a fetlock bumping stop in front of Sheriff Garvey, the young Ranger sergeant got an earful: "Aten, I am sheriff of this county, and am going to handle this situation myself. You keep out of this." Taking Garvey at his word that he would not be trifled with, Ira cued his horse with one spur, arced into a spinning half-circle, and sprinted up the street toward the crowd advancing on the courthouse in quick lockstep behind Red Hot Frost. Sergeant Aten came near colliding with Volney Gibson, who was now atop his big sorrel. Reaching out with his left hand, keeping his gun hand free, Ira grabbed the yet warm barrel of Volney's blue-steel Winchester, trying to bring sanity to the lunacy uncoiling at Richmond. My goodness, a girl child had already been killed. Courage Sergeant Aten owned. So, too, did Gibson. Absent even the hint of a gutless blink, Volney had a message for Mr. Ira, a hard message, spoken in a mild-mannered but assertive and self-assured tone: "I don't want to hurt you, Aten, but you can't take my gun or stop this crowd. We are going to clean them all out of the courthouse this time!"[29] Then, from the crowd, from the courthouse, and from a sniper's nest at the McFarlane house, bullets began raining on Richmond, pelting the town with absurdity and pandemonium and devastation that only death can issue. Ira Aten remembered:

> When the shooting commenced I said, "Boys, this is not our fight, save yourselves!" There were brick buildings on that side of the street. On the opposite side there was an opening about twenty feet wide. The sidewalk goes in from the hotel,

slopes down, a wide board sidewalk. I just run my horse right across the street, the only opening there was, made him jump that sidewalk, getting out of the shooting line. When I got there I looked behind and Smidt [Schmid] had tried to follow me, and he was shot down on the street. Robertson [Roberson] was there and there was some chinaberries (trees) and he just dropped behind them and wasn't hit. Smidt tried to follow me and that was why he was hit in the fire. Yes, Frank was a good boy. The bullet hit him in the stomach, must have been looking toward the firing line. It was a spent ball, had hit the ground, and hit him there, and that was what knocked him down, and when he turned, looked around, I guess, a ball hit him right here in the thigh and just grazed that bone and poisoned it and the doctors couldn't do a thing.[30]

While Sergeant Aten was aiding a seriously injured Private Schmid, and while Private Roberson was smartly ducking for cover behind chinaberry trees, the bullet-popping war between Jaybirds and Woodpeckers scorched forth. Sheriff Garvey and Red Hot Frost

The McFarlane house, a snipers' nest during Richmond's infamous Jaybird/Woodpecker War. *Courtesy Fort Bend County Libraries, Genealogy and Local History Department.*

were standup fighters, facing and glaring at each other over their rifles' iron sights. After the trigger pulling, sharp recoil, and levering fresh rounds into their respective Winchester's chambers, both went down—bleeding and broken. Sheriff Garvey died on the spot. Frost would linger for a few more hours, then he too would go. Ex-sheriff Jake Blakely, unarmed, went down for keeps, by most accounts a victim of Frost's unerring fire before he had collapsed to fight no more. Behind a waist-high wrought iron fence encircling the courthouse grounds Deputy Harry Mason and Chief Deputy Tom Smith were giving the Jaybirds fits. That is until Deputy Mason was knocked out of action by a Jaybird's supremely accurate marksmanship—or darn good luck. Deputy Mason's wound was not fatal, but was incapacitating. Tom Smith was no shrinking violet, not on the dance floor, and certainly not on the battleground. Sergeant Aten graphically recalled that the gunfire was so prevalent it seemed as if "Hell was puking."[31] Though a newspaperman would put it down somewhat inaccurately, Tom Smith's already gritty reputation soared with a stroke of exaggeration: "He was a leader of the Woodpecker faction in the race war.... It is said of him that in one battle he killed seven men without removing the Winchester from his shoulder."[32] What wasn't overstatement was Tom Smith's doggedness. Assuredly the recounting is weighted with partisanship, but listening to Tom Smith's voice is worthwhile in taking measure of the man:

> [I] went into the sheriff's office and picked up my shotgun.... I emptied the gun that I had and reloaded it, then I picked up Mr. Garvey's gun that was lying on the ground and walked out in the street firing. Mr. Garvey [before he died] said: "Don't go out there, they will kill you." I walked back to the railing. Mr. Garvey fell about four or five posts this way from the corner of the yard. Do not think that Mr. Garvey shot more than two or three shots. The gun he had only holds about eight cartridges and I shot about five of them. I then stooped down behind a post and loaded it again with cartridges I had in my belt. The cartridges I had were winchester [*sic*] cartridges. I then came back to the courthouse after exhausting my ammunition....[33]

What Smith omits is significant. Short on ammo after Deputy Mason had been knocked out of action, Tom Smith borrowed Harry's six-shooter and cartridge belt. Rearmed he continued the Woodpecker barrage the best he could, by himself. He might have had a little help, if a newsman writing for the *San Antonio Daily Express* got it right: "It was stated to-day on the streets that Ike Womble, a prominent colored Woodpecker, was in the court-house during the riot and was firing all the while at the Jaybirds from the windows."[34]

An open window also provided Jaybirds with opportunity and stardom. Although in the broadest sense but youngsters, Dolph Peareson, Earle McFarlane, and Syd Peareson had assumed their position as snipers in an upstairs bedroom of McFarlane's house. Once through with the cursory medical examination of his bullet wound, Judge Parker tucked his shirt, pulled up his trousers, adjusted his suspenders, and stepped out onto the courthouse steps—six-shooter in hand.

The bullet coming from the McFarlane house was true, tearing into Parker's groin, felling him where he stood.[35] The wounded man crawled back inside the courthouse before another ball could find its mark. Below Parker, on the lower courthouse steps, Tom Smith stood ready and willing for more action. During a lull in the firing Sergeant Aten noticed—and recalled: "Smith was standing alone, rifle in hand, apparently ready to renew hostilities."[36] Tom Smith was a staunch Woodpecker, but Jaybirds would, one and all, readily admit he was good during a gunfight. Tom was not a wolf in sheep's clothing, but a maneating tiger—dressed in human attire.

After the expenditure of pent-up energy and several hundred cartridges, the deaths of Robie Smith, Sheriff Garvey, and Jake Blakely, with Red Hot Frost so seriously wounded it was guessed he'd soon die, and with Judge Parker's injuries serious—touch and go— keenness for a continuation of fireworks ebbed from Jaybirds' and Woodpeckers' psyches. Throw in a few more wounded folks like the ever feisty Volney Gibson who suffered a shot to the jawbone, the projectile yet lodged in his neck, and the deputy with a damaged arm and shoulder, Harry Mason, and a clearer picture begins to emerge. Mix in Will Andrus's limping due to a bullet-damaged leg, along with Witt Wade's minor wound and hard reality began coagulating like the lost blood splotching the courthouse yard and running down Richmond's streets. And that does not take into account the badly injured Frank Schmid, who would eventually succumb to the bullet-inflicted and mortally infected left leg.[37] After all, young Schmid was a salty Texas Ranger, precious to his law enforcing comrades, but not of too much consequence in minds of Jaybirds and Woodpeckers caught up in their own bloody brand of havoc and hollowness. Texas Rangers were forever tough and resilient, theoretically.

Sergeant Aten, however, didn't fathom chancing something else—a further outbreak of indiscriminate gunfire. Though it somewhat depreciates cooked up modern-era mythology—one riot, one Ranger—Sergeant Aten didn't put any stock in such. Ira needed help! He wired Governor Ross: "Altercation among Jaybirds and Woodpeckers; several shot, Sheriff Garvey included—send militia."[38] Following up before midnight of August 16, Sergeant Aten again updated the governor, and correspondingly his Texas Ranger headquarters:

> Sheriff Garvey and Blakely dead. Mason and Parker, of the Woodpeckers, are badly wounded. Frost badly wounded of the Jaybird party. Also others slightly wounded. One of my men wounded and a negro girl killed, both accidentally. Everything seems quiet and further trouble not apprehended to-night.[39]

Without delay upon receiving Aten's telegrams the governor jumped into action. The Houston Light Guard, under the leadership of Captain E. A. Reichardt, absent any wasted ado was deployed to Richmond. Placed on standby notice was Captain George Wilrich's Fayette Light Guard from LaGrange, about halfway between Houston and San Antonio, and the Sayers' Rifles from Bastrop, Bastrop County, southeast of Austin, commanded by Captain R. L. Batts. Also put on the alert were Captain Charles A. Krause's Sealy Rifles from Austin County and J. B. Aquillo's Washington Guards. Governor Ross, accompanied by Texas Ranger Captain Lam Sieker and the Brenham Rifles, would coordinate and follow, making their presence felt at Richmond on the first available train.[40] The morning after the big fight—riot—at 8:36 A.M., Sergeant Ira Aten blissfully wired Adjutant General King: "Militia arrived last night. Everything quiet this morning."[41]

By the time the Texas Chief Executive arrived, all was quiet. The Woodpeckers were holed up in the Fort Bend County courthouse nursing their injuries and gauging reality. Jaybirds, licking their wounds and sniffing a political change in the wind, were scattered throughout Richmond. A segment of the population, the demographic majority, the blacks, sensing a Jaybird takeover of county government, were on the run. "At the sound of the first shots, most of them within hearing took off for the Brazos bottom and, for a time after the battle, none came back, not even to view the scene of the shoot-out."[42] One in particular, that "prominent colored," Ike Womble, "left town after the sun went down yesterday and has not been seen since. He has evidently gone west to grow up with the country. No doubt his course was the better for his future welfare and he is not expected to return soon."[43]

Though peace on Richmond's streets was within reach, its preservation was but tenuous. Fort Bend County, now that Garvey was dead, was without a sheriff. Such a deplorable and shaky state of affairs was altogether unacceptable to Governor Ross. Before he would leave Richmond, the governor would see to it that the county had a sheriff, at least one temporarily appointed until the next regular election cycle rolled around—when he could be accepted or rejected by voters. Therein was an inherent—and legal—dilemma for Ross. He did not have an executive privilege of naming the new sheriff; by statute that was the county commissioner's responsibility. Make no mistake though, Governor Ross, a former Ranger and Indian fighter, was no mealy mouthed politico timorously hiding behind indecision. He'd make it work, one way or the other. The governor's fundamental conundrum was rich: a candidate suitable to the Woodpeckers was, not surprisingly, unsuitable for Jaybirds—and vice versa. The sticking point, aside from the philosophical, was salient. Woodpeckers controlled county government and by virtue of that were charged with filling the vacancy. They could not in the aggregate come up with enough money to meet the necessary posting of a sheriff's bond. The Jaybirds could easily top the financial mountain, but their power to appoint a sheriff was nil. A *Galveston Daily News* on-scene correspondent pegged it to the wall: "Of course it would do them no good, or rather nothing tangible would be accomplished by the appointment of a sheriff who could not give bond, and on the other hand a bond is no good without a sheriff." After meeting with an elite seventeen-man committee of Jaybirds the governor was still at his wit's end. Compromise was not a Jaybird option, not at this juncture. Woodpeckers were obstinately stuck, too. Finding any legitimate takers for the job was difficult, as noted by that same sharp-eyed newspaperman writing for the *Galveston Daily News*: "Despite the fact that the office is worth between $4000 and $5000 a year, it is a financial plum that nobody grabs for."[44] One potential candidate acceptable to both Jaybirds and Woodpeckers was Ranger Captain Lam Sieker. There was a small rub though: he didn't want the job.

Captain Sieker's refusal to become the agreeably appointed sheriff of Fort Bend County was not based on his dislike for any particular Jaybird or any specific Woodpecker, but because of their wives. Earlier, and it was no well-kept secret, some Jaybird women trying to humiliate a surplus of fence straddling fellows had fashioned presents for those of a faint heart. Resourcefully, but belittlingly, the dear ladies had gathered about forty little draw-string bags, filling them with coarse sand. To each pouch was fastened a note: "If you haven't any grit, we are sending you some."[45] No, Captain Sieker, although tolerable to both parties, "would not accept under any circumstances on account of his wife, whom he might bring here but for the bitter feeling between the ladies of the respective sides."[46] Back to square one.

Another name, a Ranger's name, surfaced as a doable conciliation entrant: Sergeant Aten. Ira may not have been the Jaybirds' first choice, but he was good enough. Perhaps in some small way, if it is true, because during the street fight when out of ammunition "some Jay Birds drew bullets from the cartridge belt of one of the Rangers and continued firing."[47] Again, whether it is actually valid or not, it has been confidently asserted that proper consideration of the Company D's 1st Sergeant reflected a "high regard which the Jay Birds had for Aten—their Texas Ranger."[48] The Woodpeckers, if they could not get their own man, were not adamantly opposed to Ira Aten, but they were concerned that he was "too youthful to make a good officer. This was said to be their reason."[49] Unquestionably owning the inside track, maybe it is best to hear from Austin Ira Aten:

> They did not put Ft. Bend County under Martial Law. Ross threatened to do that. He come down after the killing. I wired him, and he and assistant attorney general Harrison. Hogg was attorney general and couldn't come. They [went] into a conference right then with the two factions, and they couldn't agree on a man in the county for sheriff, would suggest this or that man. No, he would be partial to one man or the other. For two days they hung fire that way. The Governor, of course, couldn't stay long. He said, "If you can't agree, I am going to put the county under martial law...." Finally, I had got along with both factions pretty well, hadn't taken any part in anything, and the Woodpeckers suggested, "What is the matter with your sergeant," to Governor Ross. No, they didn't say that either. Governor Ross, he suggested me himself. Then, the Wood Peckers

says, "That is all right, think that will be satisfactory with our crowd." Governor Ross said, "This is my last chance with you. You will appoint Aten sheriff of this county or I will call martial law. I have spent two days here.... You know Aten. Appoint him or I will put you under martial law." Governor Ross went out. Attorney General Harrison staid [sic] there with the commissioners court. They wrangled awhile and said, all right.[50]

On the twentieth day of August 1889, Austin Ira Aten was a Rawhide Ranger no more.[51] At Richmond a dozen men acting in Ira's behalf pledged a whopping $40,000 for three separate and mandatory assurance bonds. And, ostensibly, "No county official, before or since, has ever made such secure bonds. The wealth of the bondsmen was well over two million dollars."[52] Captain Frank Jones also signed an official document, a Certificate of Discharge, honorably absolving Ira Aten of any further duties with the Texas Rangers, by reason of "Being appointed Sheriff of Fort Bend County, Texas."[53] Just a few days shy of his twenty-seventh birthday Sheriff Ira Aten gained a generous boost in monthly income—and preeminence. A special correspondent for the *Houston Post* sought and was granted an immediate interview, also carried in the *Galveston Daily News*:

> I fully appreciate the unusual responsibilities thrown upon me in this case and hope to be able to fill the position satisfactory to all parties. I feel that the appointment must be backed by the people and if I thought it was not the wish of both sides I should not touch it. My earnest intention to act justly and rightfully induces me to accept it because I believe I can succeed by the faithful and impartial performance of duty. I believe that is the only way any man can take this place and succeed. I am not dependent upon, nor driven to it for a livelihood: but friends and the state officers here have urged me to accept it, that the painful situation now existing may be relieved; and for this purpose, more than anything else, I take it. Should there be any mistake made at anytime, it will be an error of judgment and not of the heart.[54]

Sheriff Aten rented a room at Richmond's National Hotel, a hostelry with large "sample rooms" and keeping up with advancing plumbography, a bathroom. At once Sheriff Aten set to work. Through

the graciousness of Captain Jones, two Ranger privates were assigned
to Sheriff Aten as temporary deputies until he could amply staff his
office, one being his brother Calvin Grant Aten.[55] For a more permanent staffing Sheriff Aten had two fellows in mind. Ira knew his
formal education was lacking when it came to "keeping those books."
The first was John T. Olive, the ex-sheriff of Williamson County. Ira's
other choice was an ex-Texas Ranger, A. B. Coffee of Burnet, Burnet
County. Olive was preparing his (successful) bid to regain the sheriff's office in Williamson County, but Coffee began winding down his
business affairs in Burnet, traveling to Richmond to lend Ira a helping hand—in the short term.[56] Sometime later (October '89) Sheriff
Ira Aten put on the Fort Bend County payroll deputy P. E. Peareson.[57]
At the conclusion of Private Aten's provisional deputyship, Ira pulled
his brother aside prior to his leaving Richmond. The sheriff had sage
guidance for young Cal: "If you ever need advice go to John Hughes.
He has the soundest judgment of anyone I ever delt [sic] with."[58]

With his steady no-nonsense approach to matters of business—police business—Sheriff Aten made sure everyone was aware
he would not tolerate any unruliness, remarks echoed by a judi-
cious newsman: "Sheriff Aten stated that he can arrest any man in
the county now without assistance, the people thus showing their
respect for the law and its officers."[59] Of course, if it should come to
pass that Sheriff Aten did need a little help, well, he knew where to
turn: "The men of both factions have every confidence in their young
ranger sheriff, and he will be sure to preserve the public peace at all
hazards, even if the whole ranger force of the state is called on to aid
him."[60]

Sheriff Aten's contemporaries would never question the young
man's nerve, nor would they openly pass any negative judgment
on his personal behavior during the August 16, 1889, street fight.
Already he owned a sterling reputation for standup bravery when
Colt's six-shooters were unleashed to bark and bite. At Richmond on
that bad day the Texas Rangers under Ira's watch exhibited common
sense, applying smart discretion. Private Frank Schmid had failed
to quickly remove himself from the crossfire and that hesitation—
gutsy as it was—cost him his life, though it was an unfortunate accident, not murder. Previously, when it was down and dirty, Ira Aten's
mettle had been tested—and he passed each time. He would do it
again, too. Well into the twentieth century an admittedly well-known
lawman, continuing to nurture hyped Texas Ranger mythology,

Civilian visitors and Company D Rangers in camp after the Richmond fireworks. Note Private Frank Louis Schmid, third from left and supported by crutches: He would later die as result of the gunshot received during the Jaybird/Woodpecker madness. The Rangers standing, L to R, starting with Schmid, are John O'Grady, Baz Outlaw, Captain Frank Jones, and W. W. Jones. The individual standing at far right is unidentified. Seated on the ground is "Hous" the company cook and teamster. *Courtesy Research Center, Texas Ranger Hall of Fame and Museum.*

would manifestly find a compelling need to rehabilitate Ira's actions at Richmond.[61] Those in the know didn't.

There may have been peace in the bending Brazos River country, but the crop of acrimony was thriving. Formal Complaints were sworn to and warrants issued. Captain Sieker, still in town, arrested Volney and Guilf Gibson, brought to heel by Woodpecker allegations, but had also taken into custody Judge Parker and Deputy Wade due to formalized Jaybird accusations.[62] The filings and cross-filings were almost comical, had it not been for the fact a few folks were actually dead as a result of the pigheadedness that had uncorked at Richmond. Captain Sieker returned to Austin. As a matter of courtesy—and friendship—Sheriff Aten updated his Texas Ranger mentor: "I had 23 Jaybirds arrested during the examining trial, but did not do as I promised you and the Gov. because I did not have room for them in the jail, and they, Woodpeckers, sworn out warrants for some of the oldest, & best citizens in the city & they had no more to do with the fight then you did. However, I arrested them all, had them at the courthouse very promptly every day & they were guarded loosely every night...."[63] Interestingly, in lieu of posting bond, Volney and Guilf Gibson, Jaybirds to the core, chose confinement under loose supervision in the Ranger's house on the outskirts of town.[64] For awhile—a long while—the judicial furor, Motions, Continuances, and lawyers' saber rattling would prolong any final legal disposition. Postponements are but routine.

Sheriff Aten's seemingly casual comment about avoiding the housing of arrested Jaybirds in Fort Bend County's jail has an innocent ring. But, not to be overlooked is the contemporary snippet which hints of another reason: Jaybirds' overt intolerance. Racial equality, even when locked in the jailhouse, would prove an unbearable insult for a diehard Jaybird, and Richmond was plumb full of diehard Jaybirds: "The county jail has fourteen negro prisoners confined in it, and the prisoners arrested this evening are under guard of the rangers and therefore not locked up." [65]Too, the earlier news item concerning such narrow-mindedness and fanaticism bears repeating: "The Jaybirds have determined that negro supremacy shall cease to exist in Fort Bend county. They have been robbed, taxed and ground to the very earth ever since the late war and can stand such government no longer, but have determined so long as blood is in their veins to fight democracy's opposition to the bitter end." [66]

An abrupt bitter end was in store for another, at least his career in the fêted Texas Rangers. If not saddened, surely Sheriff Ira Aten was worried about his wobbling Ranger buddy and fellow Navarro County undercover operative, Jim King. Unfortunately for Private King, he couldn't stay away from the bottle; the amber current was now flowing through his veins. It was behavior Captain Frank Jones could no longer tolerate; although King was not "disorderly," he was usually "too drunk to be efficient and it is impossible to keep him sober." At Richmond, Private King was handed his walking papers and a ticket back to Uvalde where his "outfit" was kept.[67]

The same newsman interviewing Sheriff Aten on first taking office also remarked that Ira had been a Ranger for several years and during that time he had "been in numerous tight places."[68] Ira Aten, although no longer a Texas Ranger, still had an electrifying schedule of "tight places" on his law-enforcing dance card: legal nightmares and more close calls, a bucking six-shooter in his hand with poisonously dangerous *mal hombres* falling at his feet.

Chapter 12

"Celebrated Xmas day by killing the two Odles"

Sheriff Aten had advised Captain Sieker that Fort Bend County would have a Jaybird government. He was right. Woodpeckers, what few were left, resigned public office and moved on, most leaving the county for good. A tip-off to either Ira's sense of humor or political tilt may also be drawn from his missive to Sieker. Sheriff Aten was hopeful of maintaining peace for his county, but with the scheduled murder trial of Kyle Terry yet docketed at Wharton, he wasn't as sure: "The next peckerwood & Jaybird riot will be at Wharton, if any more."[1] Captain Frank Jones, too, was reasonably confident the Fort Bend County feud was winding down, unless or until Kyle Terry or Judge Parker showed their faces, then "there is no doubt but that they will be killed...."[2]

Though it may knock sideways preconceptions about sheriffs in the Old West era, most of their time was devoted to administrative and tax collecting duties—when not actively engaged serving the District Court's every whim. Overseeing the jail was a headache. Actually enforcing the law, making arrests and leading hard-riding posses was work normally left to the "outside" deputies—or raring-to-go Texas Rangers.[3] It is easy to recognize that Sheriff Ira Aten was not always boot-top high in enviable glamour and glory. Sometimes it was just mundane everyday work—tiresome and boring. Such as the time he dutifully escorted a "crazy colored woman" to the state's mental-health asylum at Terrell, Kaufman County, just east of Dallas.[4] Or when he was forced to rush headlong into a jail cell: "Aten was notified that a prisoner in the county jail was hanging himself. Repairing to the jail Aten found a young man by the name of Harris hanging by his neck, and to all appearances dead. Severing the rope, Harris dropped to the floor in a heap. Medial assistance was obtained, and after a few minutes the would-be suicide was brought back to life."[5] Or on the very next day when he had to put down Fort

Bend County work and jump to the request of Harris County Sheriff George W. Ellis from Houston. In this instance Sheriff Aten did make an arrest, methodically locating and latching onto Scott Jordon, indicted for Theft, holding on to the prisoner until Sheriff Ellis rushed to Richmond, assuming custody.[6] On another occasion, although he was based in Richmond, far away from the Texas Hill Country, Ira received information about a cavvyard of stolen horses being driven west from Round Rock. Sheriff Aten notified his brother Cal who had retuned to Company D duty in the Upper Nueces River country near Montell, Uvalde County. Tipping off Private Aten that it "was likely they went that [your] way."[7] In one manner or another, day or night, weekday or weekend, exhilarating or monotonous, fruitful or fiasco, tired county sheriffs' everyday workload went on and on. Too, a sheriff was responsible for finding prospective witnesses and executing subpoenas, lining them up for a command court appearance, guaranteeing the wheels of justice turned, maybe slowly, but grinding forward nevertheless.

There is, also, that other touchy and inexorable facet with regard to holding down a county sheriff's spot. It is a political job. Although Ira Aten's ascension to Fort Bend County Sheriff had been more-or-less orchestrated absent his doings, actually plugged in by Governor Ross, it would be the electorate that kept him or any other sheriff in office. A county sheriff unable or unwilling to keep his constituents reasonably happy is a sheriff with a saliently predictable future—a loser. Sheriff Aten, even though a young man, was no dummy. It will be recalled that while working undercover in Navarro County he openly declared that only a commissioned officer's title would keep him in the Texas Rangers, else he would resign on a given date. Ira's ambition is explicable and acceptable and not atypical. He wanted a big job and he now had it. To hold it would require keeping the electorate content, and in this instance that meant Jaybirds. Jaybirds had guaranteed his approval bonds putting him into office, and it would be Jaybirds who would keep him there—or not.

Austin Ira Aten was a product of his place and times. Clichéd? Maybe, but it is meaningful. That said, after acknowledging he had been a "good Ranger" and was generally a "good man" it should come as no surprise to learn Ira was no progressive vanguard rider championing equality and justice for all men. Most Texans were not, not in the nineteenth-century Lone Star State. When brought to the lick log—a Texas colloquialism meaning it is time to act, not talk—Sheriff Austin Ira Aten jumped headfirst.

He became a charter member—as were nearly all Jaybirds—in the newly created Jaybird Democratic Association of Fort Bend County—A White Man's Union.[8] Jaybirds had long thought Radical Republicanism—in the form of quasi Democratic Woodpeckers—had unfairly dominated and injudiciously taxed them into the poor house. The August 16, 1889, street fight had tilted the political applecart upside down. Jaybirds controlled Fort Bend County now. And they were sure bent toward safeguarding their newfound clout. Extracting but Article 15 from their freshly worded constitution is illustrative:

> The object of this Association is to combine and unite the white people for the advancement and prosperity of this county—for the purpose of securing a faithful and honest discharge of official duty by all public servants and to prevent forever this county from relapsing into the disastrous and disgraceful administration of public affairs which has operated this county for a quarter of a century. We, therefore declare that any white man residing in the county or who shall hereafter acquire citizenship in this county who shall undertake to lead against this association any political faction or voting population opposed to the principles and objects of this association, shall be considered and treated as a social and political outcast.[9]

Sheriff Ira Aten's actual comfort level as member of the Jaybird Democratic Association of Fort Bend County is marked by a paucity of hard evidence. As for any peace officer, his was an untenable position. Subsequent actions seem to suggest he was getting a belly full, but before there was any discernible change of heart or conscience or ethical untidiness tinkered with, there was unfinished police and prosecution work on Fort Bend County's blotter.

For the most part the criminal cases originating in Fort Bend and Wharton Counties from the Jaybird/Woodpecker hullabaloo, on Changes of Venue, had been docketed for the court crier's call at Galveston. Kyle Terry's killing of Ned Gibson would be heard there, as would be the case against Judge Parker for killing Robie Smith, a charge instigated by Jaybirds. During late November of 1889, Sheriff

Aten and nine others, including Guilf and Jim Gibson, along with three of Ira Aten's bondsmen, Clem Bassett, Yandel Feris, and H. R. Farmer, made the trip to Galveston as witnesses. Predictably the case was postponed.[10]

December would be a news making month for the law-enforcing Aten brothers, Ira and Cal. Their Christmas holiday would be marked by gunplay and/or detention, not at the same locale, but on the same day. Sheer irony of the messes would cause each to realign their sights, not those on their Colt's six-shooters and Winchesters, but on their chosen profession.

The first day of the last month, however, would roll around prior to the Aten boys' yuletide carnival of fun and frolic—and unsolicited salutations. Alleged murder suspect Dick Duncan's day in court was at hand. The presiding judge overruled the spate of routine motions for a Continuance and a Change of Venue. No longer would there be delay. Before there could be a trial, however, a jury had to be questioned and seated. That procedure, in and of itself, was not easy— not in the early stages—although it was constitutionally necessary: "It was a tedious process. From a venire of 73 names but five jurors were obtained, but the remaining seven were found from less than thirteen talesmen." District Attorney Walter Gillis wisely was going after Dick Duncan for but one murder, that of Lavonia Holmes. Should the defendant by an unexpected quirk be found Not Guilty of her homicide, the companion cases could be reeled out, one by one if necessary until the defendant would be convicted by his peers. Though Duncan's trial was but for the one murder, everyone, the public, spectators, witnesses, newsmen, judge, and trial lawyers, well knew the wholesale story. Forty witnesses testified under subpoena for the prosecution, including Sheriff Ira Aten. Defense attorneys R. H. Lombard and Leigh Burelson called but five, and of them "the father and brother of the defendant gave the only important testimony." Their attempt to establish a plausible alibi for Dick fell on the jury's deaf ears in light of believable and quite contradictory testimony spoken by prosecution witnesses. During closing arguments Duncan's two attorneys harangued expressively, but in trying to plant that crucial seed of Reasonable Doubt, "their efforts were very feeble." The prosecution, too, waxed eloquently, spending several hours "detailing the damning chain of circumstances that connected Duncan with it [the murder]." Having the last word, District Attorney Gillis "with clear statement, and connected narrative and relentless logic proved to a demonstration that Dick Duncan had murdered the Williamson family in cold blood."[11]

District Judge Winchester Kelso, after closing arguments, issued his obligatory legal charge to the jury. In turn they thoughtfully deliberated—for an hour and a half. Or smoked cigarettes and jawed and joked, making it look like they had mulled it over passably. At any rate, shortly after receiving the case, the jury trekked back into the packed courtroom to render their finding. The verdict, as it had to be, was unanimous: "We, the jury find the defendant guilty of murder in the first degree and assess his penalty at death."[12] Transferred back to the Bexar County jail at San Antonio for extra special safe-keeping, the convicted Dick Duncan would helplessly live one day to the next—repetitiously—while the mandatory appellate process for capital cases slogged its way through the Texas judicial system. Duncan's march to the scaffold, if to take place at all, would be at a snail's pace. For a newly installed sheriff and a Texas Ranger—both named Aten—the tempo of upcoming law enforcing business moved at antelope speed. Figurative tigers were after both men. Since the timing was near exact—even to the hour—chronology demands making a pick: Sheriff Ira Aten first.

Unbeknownst to the fine fellows at Richmond and throughout Fort Bend County, some former residents with a little help from the federal government had cooked up a holiday recipe. On Christmas Eve a train rolled into Richmond. Stepping out at the depot was the United States Marshal for the Eastern District of Texas, J. J. Dickerson, former Fort Bend County office holder, and a heavily armed squadron of deputies, many carrying sawed-off shotguns. Their mission was uncomplicated.[13] The Federal Grand Jury for the Eastern District of Texas, impaneled at Galveston (now the Southern District), had returned a string of criminal Indictments. The number was staggering. Although the register of proposed defendants would not be near as large, each defendant was facing multiple charges, which had propelled the total number of Indictments to near 500, according to a recap in the *Galveston Daily News*.[14] Marshal Dickerson and his men were to execute the arrest warrants; it was not their job to question the legitimacy or merit of the grand jury's work. They were but officers of the court at this point.

Twenty-two of the Indictments were for murder and those twenty-two folks were arrested, maybe not without fanfare, but certainly absent any physical resistance. Included in this bunch of taken-aback fellows was the sheriff of Fort Bend County, Austin Ira Aten.[15] Alleg-edly, according to the indictment, Ira Aten was guilty of participating in the cold-hearted murder of his predecessor in office, J. T. Garvey and, too, with killing Jake Blakely. Two former deputy sheriffs, Tom Smith and Harry Mason, in conjunction with Judge Parker and W. H. Gayle, Jr., a former Fort Bend County District Clerk, had partly—but only partly—instigated the criminal filings.[16] Woodpeckers were yet capable of being peckerwoods, it seems. Additionally Sheriff Ira Aten found himself squarely looking at another charge: Subornation of Perjury.[17] Others had been charged under federal civil rights stat-utes dealing with the election of 1888 and the disenfranchisement of potential voters, to be precise the "colored" voters. In all, the number of Fort Bend County denizens taken into custody for the Christmas party racked up at fifty-four.[18] Placed on a train the flabbergasted Jay-birds were escorted through Houston, then to Galveston. At Galves-ton, in deference to simply locking the astonished fellows in jail, their physical custody was maintained in the United States District Court's courtroom, guarded by Marshal Dickerson's posse of deputies. The courtroom was a beehive of activity as bondsmen buzzed around making the requisite postings. Slowly the defendants made bail and exited that honeycomb dripping with legalese.

The federal court system had assumed its jurisdictional role in the prosecution based on Complaints filed by—or at least on behalf of—the seven blacks earlier expelled from Fort Bend County under the threat of death. Their civil rights had been violated, they asserted, and that made it the federal court's business—clear and simple. The murders of Garvey and Blakely during the Richmond street fight were but criminal offshoots of that conspiracy, so they too, qualified for settlement in federal court. That was the claim, anyway. Indeed, in certain cases it was a stretch, especially accusing Sheriff Aten of murder. Newsmen picked up on that post haste. One writing for the *Galveston Daily News* scolded:

> The sweeping character of the indictments under which these parties are held is being generally commented upon by their friends in this city. This comment applies with particular force to the indictment against Mr. Ira Aten, the sheriff of Fort Bend county, who, as a state ranger at the time of the Rich-mond riot, was doing all he could to preserve peace at even the risk of his life. He rushed in between the rioting factions on the

eve of the fight and commanded them to desist, and finding his interposition fruitless he got out of the way as a matter of self-preservation, and if he fired a shot during the riot no one has yet been found to testify to the fact. Under these conditions Mr. Aten regards the indictments against him as rather far reaching.[19]

The penman writing for the *Austin Daily Statesman* was more concerned about the usurpation of state's rights by the federal government—all at the hands of "ex-negro office holders" dragging to the foot of federal power "half a hundred of the leading white citizens of Fort Bend County." A sagacious editor of the *San Antonio Daily Express*, conversely, particularized Sheriff Ira Aten's plight, and the injustice:

> If the indictments against the Fort Bend prisoners are none of them more strongly backed than the affidavits charging Sheriff Aten with murder and subornation of perjury, the subsequent proceedings will be more of a farce than anything else. At the time at which it is stated these offenses occurred Aten was a state ranger and was in nowise connected in the faction fight which resulted so disastrously. In fact, he was chosen sheriff after Garvey's death as a compromise candidate, one who had no special interest in either jaybirds or woodpeckers.[20]

Likewise the Subornation of Perjury charge, at least in Sheriff Ira Aten's individual case, was shaky—wobbly—unsupportable. Earlier during a shooting phase of the Jaybird/Woodpecker feud Mr. J. M. Shamblin, a Jaybird, had been viciously and fatally shotgunned through a window in his residence while a toddling daughter was playing at his feet. [21] A black man, William Caldwell, was arrested (and later legally hanged). Purportedly, Charles Ferguson, a black man, and also a former Fort Bend County District Clerk, was implicated in the Shamblin killing—at least in the minds of agitated Jaybirds. Many Jaybirds, while they generally respected his brother Henry, also a former Fort Bend County official, thought Charles an outright crook. While holding office he had amassed a 1,500-acre plantation on Jones Creek, $50,000 cash, and a lavishly well-appointed brick home in Richmond. That was pretty nifty work for a fellow knocking down a tax-paid salary of $2,000 per year.[22] Charles Ferguson had been one of the blacks forced to flee Fort Bend County. After a year's absence from Texas, returning, he filed a civil suit in federal court during October '89 for a redressing of that wrong, financially. Needless to say, Jaybirds were not happy with Mr. Ferguson. Pricking the tenderness even further, bringing it to an inflamed head, was when—rather than taking legal risks—an out-of-court settlement with Jaybirds was negotiated and made with Ferguson and his fellow plaintiffs: Ringing in at about $40,000.[23]

Therein exposes the festering rub that scratched the sheriff. Indicted with Sheriff Aten for this alleged federal violation were Yandel Feris, John C. and T. E. Mitchell, A. E. Peareson, W. D. Fields, and D. F. McLaughlin. They were supposed to have concocted an evil scheme, to wit: Inducing a convicted criminal to perjure himself by implicating the said Ferguson as being one of Shamblin's cowardly murderers. The payback or payoff was ludicrous on its face: "The specific alleged charge in this indictment is that these parties attempted to induce a colored man (J. W. Davenport, since convicted in this county of burglary) by bribing him with six cigars of the total value of 30 cents and five bottles of whiskey of the total value of $2.50, to swear before the grand jury that Ferguson was one of the murderers of J. M. Shamblin and one who attempted the murder of H. H. Frost. Ferguson being one of the colored men who claims to have been driven from the county and who in consequence has filed an extensive civil suit for damages in the United States courts against some forty-odd citizens of Fort Bend county. Ira Aten, the present sheriff of Fort Bend county is among those indicted for murder, as well as being named in the indictment for subornation of perjury."[24] Though there is vagueness as to just who furnished collateral for the sheriff's bail bond, there is nothing vague about what happened to Cal while Ira Aten was for the short go indisposed as an inmate at Galveston's federal courthouse.

Back in the Texas Ranger service were Messers' John Hughes and Baz Outlaw. Scratching out a living south of the border had not proved inviting or rich enough to hold them—and none too romantic. Hughes had re-upped on December 1, 1889, the same day the Duncan trial began, and Outlaw three months before then on September 1.[25] Cal Aten, as mentioned earlier, after his short stint as a temporarily assigned deputy for his brother Ira, was back on duty with the Texas Rangers—working out of Company D's Camp Leona, near Uvalde.

Christmas Eve found Privates Aten, Hughes, and Outlaw on a stakeout in Edwards County. It goes without saying, at least it should, Cal had not one iota of an idea his brother at that very instant was under arrest and being hustled off to Galveston. Meanwhile, the Rangers, accompanied by local deputy sheriff Will Terry and a few more Edwards County citizens serving as possemen for Sheriff Ira L. Wheat, shivered and waited and waited. Christmas could come and go, they'd stay anchored, stay hitched, if you will. The targets of their around-the-clock surveillance were two of the Odle boys, Will and Alvin.

The Odle brothers, yet in their twenties, had racked up a rather impressive record for hooliganism, horse theft, and homicide. Acting alone or together the Odle boys had burglarized the homes of L. P. Rhoads and W. H. Beatty, and had stolen horses from J. H. Hale, George Jackson, and J. H. Shaw. Alvin had tried unsuccessfully to kill T. J. Hallomon. They were much better at that type work the next time around. Although the motive is mysterious, Will and Alvin Odle killed their brother-in-law, John L. Stroope, leaving their sister Lizzie a grieving widow—or, perhaps, just a widow. Besides doing exactly as they pleased, whenever it suited them, the Odles' method of livestock thievery was uncomplicated. They would steal stock in Texas and race for Mexico; steal stock south of the border and rush it back to the Texas Hill Country. Add jail breaks to their portfolio and the picture becomes quite clear. Will and Alvin Odle, despite their ages, were fairly big-time outlaws—and thoroughly dangerous men.[26]

The brothers, already familiar to Sheriff Ira Aten due to an aforementioned arrest, were on the loose once again, wanted on numerous charges—including Murder. Sheriff Wheat on the quiet had made an under the table—but not underhanded—deal with an informant. Leniency would be traded for tacking two hides to the wall. The snitch knew where the outlaws were to be spending part of their '89 Christmas holidays. He willingly blabbed. The Odle brothers would attend a party—big feed—near Vance, aka Bull Head Mountain.[27]

Along about 8:00 P.M., after dark, horses could be heard approaching the site of a Christmas Day celebration. Will and Alvin Odle may have been daydreaming—maybe euphorically daydreaming—but they never dreamed they had been given up by a spy. In the dark Rangers and helpmates kept time to the approaching beat, and then on signal and in sync—and ever so quietly—eared back the hammers on Colt's and Winchesters and perhaps a shotgun or two. Will and

Alvin didn't hear that part of the tuning. But they would face the music. Whether the obligatory challenge to "Throw up your hands, you're under arrest," was issued prior to or post the shooting is up for grabs. There is an official version—well, two official versions.

Captain Frank Jones in his first letter to Captain Sieker was rather cavalier about the shooting, so it seems: "I guess you have seen in the papers where some of my men celebrated Xmas day by killing the two Odles in Edwards County. It is a great strain off that country and the good people are rejoicing. John Hughes, Outlaw, and young Aten and some citizens did the work."[28] In a second letter, two days later, Captain Jones draws back a touch from the celebratory tone, making sure a base was covered: "I have no particulars of the killing of the Odle's except that they drew their pistols when commanded to surrender and the firing began. Hughes, who is in charge of the Edwards County detachment, simply stated that they made a hard fight and they (the Rangers) were compelled to kill them."[29] Plainly Captain Frank Jones was getting his details second-hand, as would any commander not on the ground when the shooting blistered forth. At least two of the three Rangers that were there reduced their versions to writings, Privates John Reynolds Hughes and Calvin Grant Aten. Hughes' official report is herein cited—in full:

> Vance, Edwards Co., Dec. 25th 1889. Ten O'clock P. M. With the assistance of Deputy Sheriff Will Terry and a few good citizens, we succeeded in trapping Will and Calvin [sic] Odle who are wanted for murder and theft. They resisted arrest and made a hard fight and we had to kill them in self defense, also killed one horse and shot another through the neck. It took place about 8 o'clock tonight. We will hold an inquest in the morning. Outlaw & C. G. Aten were with me.[30]

Cal Aten remembered it somewhat differently. Cognizant of reality about getting in the first lick, the Rangers and Deputy Terry, along with the citizens posse—most of them—were not about to give the ever dangerous Will and Alvin Odle any opportunity to inflict damage. This was not a jovial sporting event; survival mattered. In a letter to Ira, Cal cut the meat off the bone: "There is another happening that comes out of the (Battle of Bull Head Mountain). I am responsible for [missing word] but you will understand that it pertains to the time when the Odle boys were assassinated. That is all it was just plain legal assassination. However there would have been someone else assassinated if we hadn't got in the first shots."[31] Cal Aten's simplistic logic is easy to grasp. It was a case of them—or us—and better them. According to at least one report, Mr. Jim Rhodes, a member of the civilian posse, hadn't or didn't want any part of the apprehension or ambush. After the gunfire abated he "ejected every cartridge from his Winchester to prove that it had not been fired."[32] Private Aten was in the dark as to whether or not an Edwards County Grand Jury would bring forth any Indictments charging the Rangers and others with shooting too quick. Not knowing for sure either, Sheriff Aten pledged to peddle his influence in his brother's behalf: "I will write to Ira Wheat about not having you boys indicted in Edwards co: I wish I had time I would go up there & could tell in a short time which would be best, to have you indicted now or not. I expect Wheat would like to make some fees in the matter."[33] Though from the purely practical standpoint Cal Aten knew his actions were defensible, the killing troubled him, at least minimally—but not legally. Later, writing memoirs Cal reflected:

> I have held a dying outlaw [Alvin Odle] in my arms. One of the worst ever-known in the Southwest. Took his pistol out of his dying hand. The same pistol I keep under my mattress now. It was a wonderfully beautiful gun then without a blemish on it, beautiful engraving. I was sorry for that boy. Just a few years older than I and I have often wondered what he would have done had our positions been reversed. Just rode off and left me like a dog, I think, but this would be another story and I intended to tell you of my first scout.[34]

What Cal Aten, modestly, failed to mention is that taking out the Odle brothers, as least in the mind of Captain Frank Jones, put the kibosh on an Edwards County crime wave: "and as the detachment in Edwards County is not especially needed there since the Odles are killed, I would suggest that they be withdrawn and sent to Presidio County."[35] Exactly when Sheriff Aten had learned of his brother's dalliance with danger goes unrecorded. He had troubles of his own, and they were not going away. The mistletoe, strings of cranberries, and twisted holiday ribbons may have been taken down, but when the Texas winter sun shone down on New Year's Day 1890, Sheriff Austin Ira Aten was yet tangled in the trappings of misplaced legality.

Not only did he have his own neck to worry about, but others' legal predicaments as well. One particular matter, a case styled the *State of Texas vs. Kyle Terry*, would prove to be troublesome.

Terry's murder trial for killing Ned Gibson was to take place at Galveston. So, too, was the trial of Judge Parker for killing poor Robie Smith—though unmistakably an accident Jaybirds were making hay with the poor child's demise. Resultantly, with big trials on tap, the Galveston County courthouse was literally packed with folks from Fort Bend County on January 21, 1890. Though there had not been any gunplay since the August 16, 1889, disaster, tempers between Jaybirds and Woodpeckers had not cooled. Aside from the political acrimony another factor was at play. When Kyle Terry gunned down Ned at Wharton he did more than kill a Gibson. Texas was feud country and Kyle Terry had drawn blood. Ned had brothers. An equitable settlement, in their minds was, maybe short-sighted, but clear as crystal. It was now Terry's turn to give blood.

Sheriff Aten returning from business away from Richmond made a railroad connection at Houston. There he joined and traveled to Galveston with a contingent of Jaybird witnesses. At Galveston, Ira was in or near Sheriff Patrick Tiernan's office with an assortment of Jaybirds, Volney Gibson included. Purportedly Gibson told Aten that he did not want to inadvertently bump into Terry, as the man had made death threats against him and he would have to respond in kind. Therefore, having the best interest of everyone at heart, Sheriff Aten left Volney Gibson and his cohorts alone, while he wandered upstairs in search of District Attorney Oliver to help secure arrangements—keeping fellows on the warpath apart. And almost if by prearrangement—though it was but coincidence—the curtain of catastrophe came down. Kyle Terry walked into the courthouse. Feud mentality equates to revenge, and Volney Gibson would have his. Espying Terry cross the rotunda and climbing steps heading for the second-floor courtroom, Gibson withdrew his pistol, an improved Colt's revolver, and employing a steadying two-hand hold aligned the front sight with Kyle Terry's heart and touched the trigger. Volney's bullet flew true. Kyle Terry didn't hear the gunshot; he just collapsed to the polished marble floor—trying to unlimber his six-shooter, but "the hammer of the man's pistol caught in the loop of his drawers." A quick-witted journalist later penned: "His was one life that had literally hung by a thread."[36] Kyle Terry's earthly life didn't hang long—he died on the courthouse floor. The echo of gunfire reverberated throughout the hall of justice alerting others that something was really amiss at seaside Galveston. Others may or may not have fired a round or two themselves, but Volney Gibson is credited with the kill. He stood pat, gun in hand, seemingly dazed until approached by Sheriff Tiernan who put a hand on his arm. That broke the spell. Voleny Gibson ran, pursued by the sheriff. The chase was short. A Galveston policeman, Detective Cahill, was in Volney's flight path and snared the pigeon. In addition to his handgun, Gibson had been armed with a big double-edged bone-handled knife. According to most accounts, the local newspapers included, near everyone in the courthouse was armed with at least one six-shooter—some maybe even two or three.[37] The local press was outraged. Local lawmen—and Sheriff Aten is on the list—were scrambling for answers and piping excuses. For his interview Ira Aten said:

> The inferno has been drawn from the report of the killing, as published in The News to-day, that I brought a lot of armed witnesses to Galveston for the purpose of doing mischief. As a matter of fact I did not bring them here at all. The witnesses were under bond and came here in obedience to the requirements of that bond. They were not in my custody and I did not turn them over to the sheriff of Galveston county. I had not been in Richmond for a week before these witnesses left and did not come from Richmond with them, but joined them in Houston. They were in no way under my charge, and I merely went with them to the courthouse to witness the trial, and be of any assistance I could to Sheriff Tiernan. It was merely as a matter of courtesy on the part of Mr. Tiernan that they were permitted to occupy the sheriff's office. I had conferred with Mr. Dick Tiernan [deputy sheriff] in reference to placing them in a room to themselves, as we had done before, and he was preparing to do this when the shooting occurred. Gibson did not want to meet Terry, and asked me to go up and see Oliver and arrange so that they should not meet, and I was on this mission when Terry entered the building and the shooting occurred. I did not know that any of them were armed.[38]

Regardless the justifications—a few rather lame it seems—the fact Jaybirds and Woodpeckers were still at it, this time in a supposedly neutral courthouse, was not boding favorable publicity for

Galveston's gendarmes—and that ever sticky and souring side-dish of close association was oozing off onto Sheriff Ira Aten's shirt-sleeves as well. Though it has yet not irrefutably surfaced, it may be at this point Sheriff Aten began questioning the wisdom of trading a noncom's stripes for a top dog's gold bars and the linked supremacy. He was under indictment for two felonies, hounded relentlessly by newspapermen, swamped in the bottomless quagmire of admin-istrative red tape, trapped in the jungle of reconciling tax receipt errors, overseeing a jailhouse full of suicidal nitwits, and now and then having to lay everything aside while he took some hopelessly psychotic person to the insane asylum. This sheriff's business was wearing thin. Shooting it out with the likes of Wes Collier or Brown County's fence cutters or investigating Dick Duncan right into some grim-faced hangman's hands was in spades easier and more pleasur-able than the untidy confusion relentlessly billowing from Fort Bend County. And besides all that, the girl he had an eye for, Miss Imogen Boyce, did not propose to have any truck with a lawman. A lonesome young sheriff's widow she would not be—and that was her answer.

After but a one-day breather the courtroom theater at Galveston resumed. Judge Parker's case was on the docket. Any further post-ponements were not merited. Impatience for resolving the criminal charge had surged—fatigue had set in—hardened for disposition no matter the verdict.

Sheriff Tiernan this time around would take no chances: "The constabulary forces at the courthouse were doubled and quadrupled." Stationed at every doorway were special deputies. None entered the courthouse until they first stood a thorough pat down search, and if they left one room and went to another, they were searched once again.[39]

Unquestionably studying the trial testimony is fascinating, but for moving Ira Aten's story not necessary. The most spectacular word from the witness stand came from Volney Gibson who was brought in irons from a cell deep in the bowels of Galveston County's dun-geon. Particularly witnesses noticed that Gibson was "a correct reflex of the character of the man, bold and daring and apparently straight-forward." Witness Volney Gibson did not shy from the truth, cold as it was. During cross-examination he unequivocally declared: "I always go armed as I think I have good cause for it; when we [Guilf Gibson] met Parker we were all going home, can't say that I did or did not turn into the street Parker was on to meet him, in fact I turned in to meet him; I expected trouble from Parker, he had made a demonstration toward me with a shot gun down town, I wanted to give him a chance to do what he was going to do; there was deep enmity between us, at least there was on my part."[40] After detailing the exchange of gunshots that kicked that horrible day into gear, and after hearing a string of conflicting testimony, it was plain as day the prosecution was barking up the wrong or at least a tree too tall. There was no way to prove just whose bullet was responsible for the little girl's death. In a somewhat surprising move District Attorney Oliver asked for a verdict of Not Guilty—and obligingly—"The jury did not leave the box, and Major Frank Spencer [Assistant District Attorney] wrote the verdict, 'We the jury find the defendant, J. W. Parker, not guilty.' To which they all assented.... Judge Parker was discharged."[41] Volney Gibson was not. The alleged murderer remained a prisoner, temporarily held without bond by the sheriff in Galveston County's austere lockup.

Doubtless Sheriff Ira Aten was glad to scamper back to Richmond, as the folks in Galveston County were not at all pleased that a cadre of feudists from Fort Bend County had brought their fight across the county line.[42] Conversely, the Jaybirds of Fort Bend County were not thrilled that a federal grand jury at Galveston had chosen to indict fifty-four of them for sundry violations of the U.S. Penal Code. For Sheriff Aten, the Murder and Subornation of Perjury charges were of little concern, as reflected in a letter to his close personal friend Lam Sieker:

> You have no-doubt noticed in the papers that our cases in the Federal court was continued by the Judge him-self. Our lawyers argued jurisdiction on the cases & the Judge took them under advisement until next court. While on the bench the Judge just as well as admitted he had no jurisdiction in the murder & subornation of perjury cases, but continued them with the balance. He continued all of the cases so it would keep the people quiet here next election. The cases will all be dismissed next court beyond a doubt as our lawyers had some kind of agreement with the Judge. I don't think we will have to ever go to Galveston again on this account.[43]

Sheriff Aten may not have had to return to Galveston on account of the Indictments lodged against him, but he did find it necessary to make his reappearance: As a witness for defendant Volney Gibson's Writ of Habeas Corpus hearing. With such hullabaloo continuing to garner widespread notice, Sheriff Aten's arrival on the first of April cried for a newsman to elicit a comment or two from the now high-profile official. Just how were things over in Fort Bend County? Assertively Aten replied. A newsman jotted: "The people of his county are busy with their crops just now and that prospects were never brighter. The negroes, he says, are hard at work and that all of the best negroes who left the county during the trouble there have returned and gone to work. He says the records of the courts show that the county is now one of the most quiet and orderly in the states."[44]

That afternoon, Sheriff Aten, but one of a lineup of witnesses summoned by the defense, took the witness stand. Aten testified that, yes, he knew Kyle Terry, having met him once. He, too, knew Volney Gibson quite well. Moreover after learning that Terry was making death threats to kill all of the Gibson boys, he personally warned Volney to be on guard, but he had never heard of him make any threats against Terry. Certainly he expected that at sometime there might be trouble between the parties "owing to the general bad feeling." Sheriff Aten most assuredly did not know that any of the witnesses subpoenaed that day were armed; furthermore "he heard no threats that led him to believe there would be any trouble at the time Terry was killed."[45] Ira Aten's testimony, backed up by other witnesses, was enough for state Judge Cleveland to hang his hat on. Gibson's bail bond was set at $10,000 which was without unnecessary delay posted by three of Volney's Fort Bend County cronies. Gibson would never have to stand trial. A year later he was cut down by deadly tuberculosis.[46]

That Ira Aten was holding a good hand and was in on the know is smugly mentioned in a letter to his brother Cal, still a Texas Ranger, but now stationed in far West Texas in Presidio County, PO Marfa:

> All of our cases in the federal court was dismissed on the 3rd [April] inst. But new indictments found against about 50 of the citizens here for running the negroes off before the election. Of course, I was not indicted for that. The murder & perjury cases are disposed of for good as the Judge decided the federal courts had no Jurisdiction on them. I am free again.[47]

And free he was. Out from under the legal cloud, Sheriff Ira Aten, as subsequent events reveal, began having second thoughts about the mosquitoes and marshlands and misadventures of a sweltering life in high-humidity Fort Bend County. He was rethinking, as he had been for a year or two, about the unsettled and uncertain life expected of Texas peace officers. No sooner had he returned to Richmond than the message was driven home, again.

Charley Fusselman had replaced Ira as Company D's 1st Sergeant. Both Sheriff Aten and his brother Cal were favorably disposed toward the young Ranger. The news from El Paso was a shocker. While attending court there, an occasion arose where Sergeant Fusselman and ex-Ranger George Herold (involved in the 1878 Sam Bass shooting), then an El Paso city policeman, and an area stockman, John L. Barnes, were compelled to give chase after cow thieves. Outside of town at Smugglers Gap in the Franklin Mountains, the hastily fashioned posse of three picked up the trail. They also picked up owlhoot Ysidoro Pasos who had fallen behind his thieving comrades in crime. Unfortunately the lawmen did not pick up on the fact they were close to the *bandidos*, right on top of them. When they rode into the loosely milling livestock, Fusselman and the others thought the outlaws had abandoned four-legged prizes, but they were wrong—dead wrong. The posse had ridden straight into the thieves' dinner camp. These desperadoes were desperate, opening fire on a very startled Fusselman and party. When the shooting stopped, Sergeant Charley Fusselman lay dead, knocked from the saddle by two bullets to the head. Not knowing just how many gunmen they faced, Herold and Barnes—really not unwisely—retreated, hurrying to Hell Paso for reinforcements.[48]

Back at Richmond, Ira Aten was sickened by the bad news. He was literally sick, too. Whether he actually meant it or not—there is really no reason to doubt him—Ira quickly shot off a letter to brother Cal at Marfa: "am not well yet or I would have come up to El Paso to see what could have been done about catching the murdering assassins. I want to come awfully bad but I would sure enough get good & sick if I exposed myself right now. I am glad John H. [Hughes] has gone to El P & I think he will be able to do something towards catching the villains. I am very sorry to hear of Charley being killed for he was a good boy & good officer but always risked too much. I am satisfied John H. will do something if any-thing can be done towards catching the villainous murderers. It seems like the rangers are getting the worst of things recently."[49] Fusselman's death reiterated just how perilous was the tightrope lawmen walked. The tiniest misstep could get you killed.

Sheriff Aten's remark that Rangers were recently getting the "worst" of it ties directly to another 1890 event that had recently unfolded. The tragedy was personally trying for Ira. His old-time Ranger buddy Jim King, after being cut loose from the Rangers for his unmanageable bouts with the bottle, had given up the ghost—violently. Earlier he had worked undercover in Zavala County, *playing* the part of a fired but disgruntled Ranger. This time around it was no joke—he *was* a dishonorably discharged Texas Ranger. The Zavala County cow stealers thought it was the same old game. On the eleventh day of February they "foully assassinated" him.[50]

Unfortunately for Ira that sad news would be followed by more. Unexpectedly, five weeks after giving birth to a son, Luke Victor, Ira's oldest sister Angie Kimmons died of undetermined but natural causes. Whether Sheriff Aten attended the funeral is indeterminate;

The Americus Jerome "A. J." Kimmons family. Ira's oldest sister Angie and her husband, along with their children sit for a photographer. The children are, L to R: Samuel Austin, Ira's favorite niece Virgie, standing behind little brother Albert Floyd, then Myrtle Imogen and Elmer Clarence. Angie would succumb to illness at an early age, leaving Virgie to care for her siblings. *Courtesy Bruce Archer.*

surely he must have wanted to. Ira's favorite—well, one of his favorite—nieces, sixteen year-old Virgie, was now tasked with stepping into her deceased mother's role as devoted caregiver for her five younger brothers and sisters.[51]

Clearly by midyear Sheriff Ira Aten was toying with the idea of throwing in the law enforcing towel. He did attend the Texas Sheriffs Association meeting at Abilene, Taylor County.[52] But either on this mini-vacation or shortly thereafter Ira was planning for his future in West Texas, not sultry Fort Bend County. County commissioners had not been kept in the dark. Compassionately they allowed Sheriff Aten a thirty-day relocation furlough, perhaps hoping he would change his mind.[53] He did not. In a June 28, 1890, letter to his brother Cal, Ira made no secret about what was up, and it was not operating a jail or serving as a court's bailiff or sneaking up on someone with a subpoena in hand. Richmond was—if things went right—to be but a memory. Ira was a Western man. After purchasing two mules for $210 at Gainesville, Cooke County, and a wagon and harness at Wichita Falls, Wichita County, Ira Aten was off on an exploratory trip with two others. He was looking for land, not only for himself, but for his brothers Cal and Eddie, if they were so interested: "I will look for you a section close to me & if I locate up here.... Eddie wants to come up here to & I am going to get him a section also. I think that we will be able to find some nice country west of here. We will go to Baylor Co. then west to Dickens & Crosby & if we don't find a place to suit us we will come back a line of counties higher.... It will be hard work up here a year or two but will get it all back after a time if he [we] manage properly. I want John H-to come also...."[54]

Though the Democratic Jaybird Association had earlier put Ira's name in the hopper as their candidate for sheriff and tax collector, which would have shooed him into office, it seems that he quite literally had enough fun dancing to political tunes. Later, he confirmed and admitted: "At the end of my term of office I left the county. It was quiet and peaceful; many of the principals of both factions had left, but those remaining were not entirely reconciled to each other."[55] Bracketing the timeframe he was actually in Fort Bend County—as a Ranger and a sheriff—is best drawn from Ira's voice: "I staid [sic] their [sic] from July, 1889, until December, 1890."[56]

Sprinkling what a smart newcomer to Fort Bend County should do with a dash of humor, Ira delighted—so it seems—repeating a story with a wink: About that time a new resident farmer was plow-

Ira Aten's oldest brother, Thomas Quinn and his children, Fred and Allie. The date and the location of the photograph suggest they may have conferred with Ira in Wichita Falls, Texas. *Courtesy Betty Aten.*

ing behind the mules, momentarily hesitating at the turn-row, with two mean-looking strangers standing nearby watching his every movement. Each caller had Colt's six-shooters strapped to their sides, Winchesters nestled in the crooks of their arms. One spoke, snarled, to the nervous man of the soil, "Are you a Jaybird or a Woodpecker?" The farmer was perplexed. Were these nasty looking guys Jaybirds or Woodpeckers? Spitting out the wrong answer could prove awkward—hazardous for one's health. Seconds seemed like eternity. Shrewdly—plowing a middle-ground furrow—the noncommittal but distraught farmer replied: "Well, gentlemen, I guess that I am a Jaypecker!"[57]

That surviving Jaybirds wanted and commanded political power in Fort Bend County is easily evidenced by the monument erected honoring their brethren at the courthouse in Richmond. *Courtesy Fort Bend County Libraries, Genealogy and Local History Department.*

Before lucking into, falling into, or being pushed into the Fort Bend County job, Ira Aten had written about his aspirations and plans for the future:

I expect to some of these days to stand up before a fire & shake off my six shooter & Winchester & Kick them in & watch them burn & go up in the pan-handle & settle down upon a little farm and go to nesting, be a better boy & read my Bible more. When I am called up-on by an officer to assist him in making an arrest, I will go out to the barn & get a pitch-fork or the hoe & follow in behind the officer like old grangers do....[58]

From the historical perspective, dissecting Austin Ira Aten's prophecy for a good life is a snap. Indeed he would wind up in the Texas Panhandle—but it was much too early for him to shake off his six-shooter and Winchester, kicking them into a consuming fire. Gunplay and gunfire were yet on Mr. Ira's calendar of upcoming events.

Chapter 13

"He fell like a beef"

For whatever reason Ira forewent establishing himself in Dickens or Crosby Counties, but he did opt for settling in one of those "line of counties higher": Castro County. Although it may seem that the 1876 state legislators had been on a drunken spree or fertility drugs when it came to birthing new counties, such had not been the case. Their rationale was fitting. In one fell swoop, for economy's sake, freethinking lawmakers had created fifty-four separate counties in or just below the Texas Panhandle, aka the Llano Estacado. There was at the time insufficient population to actually organize the counties with installation of local governmental officials, but that would soon change. Railroads were advantaging themselves of Texas' liberal land grant policies. Once the steel ribbons were laid, locomotives and boxcars would be chugging across the grasslands. Commerce would come—then the jaunty homesteaders.[1] Lawmakers would bet—and were betting—the farm on that.

Castro County was some thirty-odd miles west of a north/south line connecting Amarillo and Lubbock, at the midpoint; about forty-five miles east of the New Mexico Territory borderline. Its sheer isolation is amplified by noting that for the 1880 census enumeration Castro County registered zero residents.[2] While Ira was winding up his 1890 business affairs at Richmond, the whole population of Castro County measured a whopping nine.[3] Needless to say, the county was yet to be organized. There was no local regime, no county seat, no taxman, no sheriff, and no jail. There was plenty of space and solitude in Castro County, just the ticket for a former Fort Bend County Sheriff and ex-Texas Ranger looking for peace and quiet.

In a general sense the section, though hardly populated, had seldom seen peacefulness, nor had it ever been any too quiet. Comanche and Kiowa warriors had made exploration and occupation of the area a health hazard, until pushed off the Llano Estacado and beyond during the Red River War of 1874–1875. The U.S. Army had interdicted the Indian threat, the first barrier to the section's settlement. Anglo entrepreneurs would ably knock down the next hurdle. Industrious hide hunters did what an industrialized nation does best: squeeze the applicator of technology until the desired result is realized. Killing the buffalo—on a commercial basis—was business, not some vacationing lark. America's marketplace had demanded durable tanned leather for belting the machines in Eastern industrial plants and for finished buffalo robes as warm buffers from cold weather and/or floor coverings: A near insatiable want. Perhaps the most famous hide hunter of them all, J. Wright Mooar, took strong exception to any suggestion that the role he played in clearing buffalo from the Southern Plains was wanton destruction or a casual pastime: "Buffalo hunting was a business and not a sport; it required capital, management and work, lots of hard work, more work than anything else. Many magazine and newspaper articles claim the killing of the buffalo a national calamity and accomplished by vandals. I resent their ignorance."[4] Capitalism and a finely honed transportation system had brought an efficient killing machine to the project. Plains Indians had long been trafficking in surplus hides, but their commerce had never been resourcefully sluiced onto the conveyor belt of a big business model. Eastern-based capitalists provided the coin and outlet, while unrelenting Anglo hunters underwent the labor intensive hazard to life and limb. Millions of buffalo equated to millions of dollars. Americans were money making experts. In but remarkably short order the Llano Estacado was wholly littered with bleaching skeletons, even that scavenged commodity making a few enterprising bone collectors and fertilizer manufacturers rich.[5] The booming roar of the Sharps big .50s and the stinking aroma of acres of shaggy hides pegged to the ground was but a memory—a recent memory, but a memory nevertheless. With Castro County worry free from raids by hostile Indians and/or the unwanted trampling from millions of wandering buffalo, her doorway to settlement opened wide. There were few takers—not in the beginning, not until the early '90s. Not unexpectedly there were absentee land owners holding title to Castro County real estate, but possessing a piece of legal paperwork and actually parking oneself on the surveyed plot are patently diverse undertakings.[6] The first long-term pioneer who had chosen Castro County as home was James W. Carter, who had planted his domestic roots as early as 1884, purchasing from the state of Texas and/or railroad rights of way, 46,080 acres. At first he lived in a makeshift tent and dugout abode. Two years later his

Ex-Texas Ranger Ira Aten horseback in the Texas Panhandle. *Courtesy Research Center, Texas Ranger Hall of Fame and Museum.*

wife Ellen gave birth to a precious daughter, Lizzie, purportedly "the first white child born to a permanent settler in the area." Carter, who had brought a herd of cattle with him, quickly became a dominant county personality. His 7-UP brand was well-known throughout the region.[7]

There are two versions of why Ira Aten had opted to remove himself from the denser populated sections of the state. One is meritless.[8] The other is true, at least in part. Ira Aten wanted to go somewhere that he did not have to concern himself about "having any more deadly enemies on my [his] trail than what I have already got."[9] There also is another reason—one with sound logic and practical pocketbook inducement. Land was cheap. Ira grasped a good deal when he saw it: "I took up some state land. That was when the state was allowing you to take land under this state land act. I had to pay one dollar per acre for it, maybe a dollar and twenty-five cents.... they allowed us to take [a] section instead of 160 acres at one dollar and a quarter per acre. I took 640 acres. Had a number of years to pay it, twenty years, I think. So much down."[10] At any rate, Aten patented 160 acres from the Castro County Number 30 survey, Block M 10A, and school section Number 34.[11] Ira Aten, as December 1890 closed, was a land owner. Mr. Aten was something else, too. Tucked into his pocket was a handy little document, the Descriptive List, that piece of paper awarding him law enforcement status. Ira was a Special Texas Ranger, unpaid, but nevertheless a legally empowered state peace officer.[12] He was also a bachelor—not an eligible bachelor though.

Actually when he had begun courting Imogen Boyce is not precise. But make no mistake, somewhere along the timeline of '89 or '90 she had swept Mr. Austin Ira Aten off his feet. Imogen also knocked Ira off his chosen career path. She'd not marry a lawman. Rangers rambled too much for the likes of Imogen, and sheriffs and deputies were never at home much either, even if most of their work was conducted inside far-flung county lines. Law enforcers, state, local, and U.S. Marshals, ever walked the tightrope of peril, too. Unfortunate circumstances—accident or illness or murder—might make Imogen a young widow, but having only a badge and a Colt's six-shooter as keepsakes was not in her future. Mr. Austin Ira Aten, if he wanted her hand, could find another line of work. He could choose.[13]

So, then, Ira had made the choice. Whether or not he told Miss Imogen Boyce about his law enforcement commission as a Special

John Ely Boyce, Imogen Boyce's brother, accompanied Ira Aten to Castro County (Dimmitt). *Courtesy Jeri and Gary Boyce Radder.*

Texas Ranger is enigmatic. Was it a nifty little secret? Kept from the bride-to-be? There are concrete truths, however. Ira would establish his admittedly small Castro County stock farm in the Texas Panhandle, away from outlaws and misfits, and when there was a home—a good home—Miss Imogen Boyce could and would change her name and address. Then, life would be but a bowl of cherries.

Ira Aten did not make the trip to the Panhandle alone, however. Accompanying Ira was Imogen's brother John Ely Boyce, who would also claim a piece of cheap state land.[14] As the sheriff of Fort Bend County, Ira had fostered a reasonably favorable relationship with a jailhouse inmate, a "colored man," Lewis Epps. Somehow the fellow had earned Ira's trust. So much so that Sheriff Aten had made him a trustee while working off his debt to the county. When Aten left for the Panhandle, Lewis and his wife, Amanda, went along, too, a fact confirmed by Ira: "I brought from Fort Bend County a negro family with me for cook, you know, a man and his wife, to do my cooking and kinda keep the ranch."[15] Though Ira is no doubt mistaken with regards to one assertion, the second may very well ring true: "He was the first negro that was taken to the Panhandle. Some of those fellows, I thought was going to mob me for it."[16]

Settling in two and a half miles east of the fledgling community of Dimmitt, Aten became one of perhaps only a hundred voting-age adults who had now drifted into Castro County to carve their niche of prosperity from the sometimes harshly unforgiving Texas Panhandle.[17] Ira set to work improving his place and anticipating the day Imogen could join him. It was hard work. Aten then owned two yoke of oxen, and "a little bunch of cattle." Although Ira was all too familiar with fences and fence cutters and spools of those curling steel tendrils, he chose to string barbed wire around part of his land, that 160 tract. For fence posts Ira had to yoke the oxen and travel east into Swisher County (Tulia) scouring the canyons for the right-sized cedars. Then, after several of the sixty-mile trips, he kept "breaking land" until he had something over a hundred acres under cultivation.[18] Unluckily it was dry that first year and "nothing came up."[19]

Something that did come up, however, was Ira's twenty-one-year-old brother Eddie. Somewhat stepping out of the mold forged by Reverend Aten, Eddie owned a propensity for getting into a little trouble due to "reckless habits." Apparently Daddy Aten's fire-and-brimstone architecture for living life did not beguile Eddie. He was fascinated by the unruly "distractions of frontier life in Texas." If any of the Aten boys had a "wild streak," it was Eddie. Though they could not actually make him go, Austin Cunningham and mother Kate suggested that Eddie give living in the Panhandle with Ira a try. Ira, as earlier noted, had finding Eddie a piece of Panhandle land one of his priorities. Ira gladly welcomed him, not only because he loved him, but Ira supposed hard outdoor work would snap the cockiness right out of Eddie, just as surely as Castro County ice-storms snapped a scarce tree limb—if there was one.[20] Preacher Aten may have lost another son to the Wild West, but in reality it was but a trade. On August 31, 1890, Calvin Grant Aten discharged from the Ranger service at Marfa, Presidio County, returning to the familiar home environs of Williamson and Travis Counties.[21] Even though he saw the practical wisdom of sometimes getting in the first lick, perhaps Cal was a tad uneasy with forging a lifelong career as a quick-triggered Texas Ranger.

On the other hand, Ira just could not seem to give it up. Reconciling what he might or might not have let Imogen in on at this late date is yet tricky. On the fifth day of May 1891 Adjutant General Woodford Haywood Mabry signed Ira Aten's Descriptive List. Ira Aten's commission as a Special Texas Ranger had been updated under provisions of Special Order No. 6, AGO. Ira was maintaining his status as a Special Texas Ranger, continuing to serve without drawing pay, but nevertheless a Texas Ranger. Ira Aten was again assigned to Company B, at least for paperwork purposes. And he could still legally carry a six-shooter on or about his person.[22] Had he clued Miss Imogen in? Or did Ira yet have a little secret? Aten was still trying to enforce the law despite Imogen's qualms or orders.

Before the month of May 1891 was history, Special Texas Ranger Ira Aten was on the hunt, and it wasn't for quail or pheasant. He was after horse thieves. Due to typical brevity of Texas Ranger reports, the details are somewhat obscure, but Special Ranger Aten, although he did not end up arresting the thieves, did press them so hard for five days that they abandoned the four stolen horses. Recovering stolen property, while not as glamorous as cuffing up a thief, is an important part of the lawman's job—the horses' owners thought so anyway. Particularly in this case, Ira Aten made doubly sure that AG Mabry at Austin knew that once livestock was stolen in the Texas Panhandle and quickly driven west into New Mexico Territory, recovery was next to impossible. Proximity to the boundary line was a niggling problem—and would continue to be for Ira Aten.[23]

Folks did not stream into Castro County; a dribble would better characterize the build up, but nevertheless 1891 was a banner year for the yet unorganized county. Ira Aten was on the make, a not negative comment about a fellow intent on bettering himself. Ira and R. A. Roberts teamed up in the land and insurance business under the name Roberts & Aten, *"General Real Estate, Rental and Insurance— Agents."* On printed letterhead stationery the budding businessmen proudly stated: "We Have Town Lots in Plainview, Tulia, Canyon City, and LaPlata. We Are Sole Agents for Lots in Castro City.... We Have an Uncommonly Well Selected List of Farming Lands in Each of the Plains Counties. Call and Examine Maps, Correspondence Solicited."[24] While ardently extolling the availability of land in the Panhandle, Messer's Roberts and Aten downplayed or forewent underscoring a touch of harsh reality.

Life in Castro County was hard. J. E. Turner and his wife, Rosalla Ann, and their five children, before they had a home "used a wagon bed as a bedroom, and stretched a wagon sheet between four posts set in the ground to form a second one. The cook stove and the table were set up nearby in the open." Thornton Jones and his brother Will built a dugout in the north bank of Running Water Draw, all four rooms, curtain partitions providing privacy. Once during a snowstorm, the dugout was completely shrouded by winter's white blanket, the only evidence of a habitation being the lonely black stovepipe seemingly gasping for air. Thornton Jones was away on business, and when Will Jones and Ed Kiser realized the direness of the circumstances, they then went to the home, knocked on the jutting stovepipe as if it were the door, and ascertained the condition of the wife and three children trapped inside. Learning the prisoners below were alright, and had plenty of food to eat and wood to burn, and due to the snow continuing to drift too badly to dig them out, the decision was made to let the family nestle below ground like badgers until the storm blew its last frosty breath. Several days later, and after Mrs. Jones was near exhausted from singing songs and telling stories to keep the children entertained, they were rescued.[25]

Someone that was not rescued was Mr. Dick Duncan. Time and defense motions had run their course. On the morning of September 18, 1891, at the Maverick County jailhouse, Duncan "ate a light breakfast and after taking sacraments of the church and being baptized he devoted himself earnestly to his prayer book and listening to the words of the priest." He was, then, a completely different man than the one sitting in the courtroom eighteen months before, when he seemed "cool and unconcerned." Crime reporters knew Dick Duncan to be "possessed of a most violent temper which at times during his imprisonment broke out in uncontrollable fury." He was especially embittered—according to newsmen—against the officers of the law who he declared were in league against him."[26] Citizens were in league against him too, after the inordinate string of legal shenanigans. A reporter writing for the *El Paso Daily Times* noted: "The citizens of Eagle Pass, where Duncan has been incarcerated were indignant at this official interference [a governor's stay of execution] and it has been by the greatest effort of cooler heads and by the presence of numerous guards that judge lynch has been prevented from following the bent of his mind."[27] Shortly after 11:00 A.M. the condemned Dick Duncan was escorted to the top of the scaffold, where he "paid the penalty for his crime...."[28] As a lawman Ira Aten had been instrumental in solving and bringing to justice the perpetrator of one of the state's most heinous crimes. Now, as a private citizen Ira had had little desire to watch Dick Duncan wiggle and strangle or drop hard with a resounding thud as his neck snapped. Ira Aten did not personally witness the hanging, although for public consumption he remarked that he "Always wished I could have seen him hung."[29]

The few citizens calling Castro County home were in need of liberation, too. They needed an organized county: A geographical subdivision with an official county seat, courthouse, and sheriff—a sense of order, a conventional form of local government—for the mutual benefit of Castro County people. Theoretically it sounded good. Practically speaking—in this instance—the prospect quickly became nightmarish. Ira Aten nostalgically remembered that even though the population was decidedly sparse, "everybody in the county knew everyone else, and it was just like a big family."[30] Yes, but a dysfunctional family. Two spots, each with fervent supporters, were vying for selection as the new county seat: Dimmitt and Castro City. The competition was fierce.

Castro City, lying about two and a half miles southeast of Dimmitt, was principally owned by the aforementioned Thornton Jones, according to Ira. Other sources also mention S. L. Richardson and Lycius (Lysius) "L" Gough as lively promoters and lot owners at Castro City.[31] There was a "town company" proposing that Castro City should be Castro County's new county seat. Their desire was not uncontested. Mr. Hilory Green "H. G." Bedford, Reverend William

Currans "Will" Dimmitt, and Parson H. M. Bandy were the chief land owners, and therefore among the chief supporters of Dimmitt as county seat. Ira Aten favored Castro City.[32]

Two of the most vocal adherents for awarding Dimmitt shire-town honors were the McClelland brothers, Andrew and Hugh. Originally from the Volunteer State, Tennessee, the boys had come to Dimmitt intent on making their fortune, Andrew a practicing attorney and Hugh a land speculator. Adding to the opposing din was the strident—at least to Ira—voice of that old-time cowman and early Castro County settler, J. W. Carter, whom Aten unhesitatingly classified as "one of my worst enemies there."[33]

The brouhaha was spiraling nasty, but bloodless. Thought by many to be outsiders, the McClelland boys were in the driver's seat if Dimmitt was chosen as the county seat. Andrew might run unopposed for the position of county judge. If so, patronage and pecuniary affairs would be his to oversee—manage—dominate. Castro County's movers and shakers began rethinking their stratagem. With the selection of Dimmitt almost assured due to the stellar maneuverings of the Bedford Town and Land Company, but the electorate somewhat diluted if a complement of voters remained wedded to the idea of Castro City as county seat, the compromise pitch and buyout was made "two or three months before election."[34] Several folks, Ira Aten included, were traded town lots in Dimmitt for withdrawing their sponsorship of Castro City from the contest. Ira's share, the best he recalled: "I think I got twenty-four lots to support Dimmitt."[35] J. W. Carter, an ardent supporter of Castro City fumed, particularly mad at Ira for—in his mind—selling out.[36] Now, with but one choice for county seat, efforts turned to fielding a stalwart slate of county officers in opposition to the McClellands' ticket, that is, subsequent to the formal application of Castro County's organization getting the obligatory thumbs up.

Carrying a formalized written petition listing 150 names to county commissioners in Oldham County (Tascosa), who had the authorized legal say-so over nearby unorganized counties, were John R. Griffin, J. H. Griffin, and W. F. Cooper. The Bedford Town and Land Company had guaranteed them smooth title to 100 city lots for steering Dimmitt through the bureaucratic maze of becoming Castro County's seat of government.[37] After receiving the long anticipated go-ahead, an election for Castro County officials was scheduled for December 21, 1891. Ballots would be cast and counted in the little local hotel at Dimmitt. Not surprisingly, for nearly everyone except the McClelland brothers, was the election of L. Gough, one of Ira Aten's newfound friends, as county judge.[38] Judge Gough, who later became a rather respected Texas author and poet, had a philosophy for life that had earlier served him well during his days as a cowboy herding livestock to market centers throughout the West. It was a set of values not foreign to Ira's upbringing. Judge Gough's advice for cowboys trailing to the cowtowns was simple: "If you want to get back with a whole hide you must be born in the middle of the week looking both ways for Sunday."[39] Suffering defeat at the polling place, Andrew McClelland was crestfallen, angrily so. Charles Isom "C. I." Bedford, twenty-three years old and a native Texan, was elected Castro County's first sheriff. H. G. Bedford's second son now held title to a salaried county job, but owned not a lick of law-enforcing experience. Too, at this point, Castro County owned not a courthouse or jailhouse. The election, after the haranguing and hollering, had really come off absent a hitch. The next item on the newly organized county's agenda, well, that would wash out a different story. It would be a gunfighting drama starring an ex-Texas Ranger as protagonist. Or, if one were looking into the muzzle of his Colt's six-shooter, that dark hole seemingly the size of a whisky barrel, maybe he could just be classed a nasty piece of work. Ira Aten was not inclined to brook abuse or insult.

The seat of Castro County and her roster of officialdom had been decided. What was yet to be fixed were matters dealing with implementation of school board matters—also a hot topic for any community, budding or long established, on the frontier or in towns already tamed. Gaining or maintaining the power to dictate what educational banquet school children are spoon fed is—and always has been—a relish savored for those in authority, but bitter repast for those with no say-so. Ira Aten confirmed the acrimony: "After the compromise over the county seat site, the feeling died down, but school trustee election came up and it got very nasty."[40]

Intent on settling in Castro County, marrying and raising a family, Ira took an active interest in community affairs. From hard work or civic service Ira Aten was no shirker. He attended a nighttime public meeting at Dimmitt regarding school trustee issues. Though what he said remains buried, he was vocal. And so, too, was Andrew McClelland. In response to Ira's recommendations or suggestions or tirade, Andrew objected, loudly. He called Aten a liar. A hush fell over the meeting hall. There was not even a sliver of space for misinterpretation. Ira Aten was a liar, and Andrew McClelland would stand by that—till the day he died. The crowd was aghast at what they had just heard. No doubt some folks expected an immediate response and mêlée, then and there. Ira demurred from instantly taking action, saying, "One night at a meeting one of them called me a liar, and I could not resent it there in a crowd...."[41] But he could resent it—and did.

Andrew McClelland's caustic remark—thoughtless remark—for several reasons put Ira on destiny's collision course. His overall make up was not tuned to suffer fools or bigmouths, no matter who they were. The equation was also complicated by the fact his reputation as a man was at stake, in a community he wanted to dub his home. Had it actually happened faraway, in New York or New Orleans, perhaps it could have been forgiven and forgotten or swept under memory's rug. Not in Dimmitt though. What would his brother Eddie think? How would his fiancée Imogen see him after she heard the news? Or, her brother John E. Boyce, who was also now calling Castro County home. What would Rangers like Lam Sieker, Frank Jones, and John Hughes believe—and Cal Aten, too? Gossip spread like Johnson grass in a flower garden. Ira needed to nip this weed in the bud.

After stewing all night, the next day, two or three days before Christmas 1891 (reports vary), Ira grabbed his Winchester and buckled on his Colt's six-shooter. Then he harnessed traveling stock to the wagon, climbed aboard and took off for Dimmitt—and resolution. Upon arrival in town Ira left his rifle in the wagon and went in search of Andrew McClelland. It only took a moment to find him, standing in front of his office. Ira's inquiry was sharp: "Andrew, you called me a liar last night. Can you still say it?" Andrew McClelland stood fast, without a second thought saying he would stand by his words, no take backs. Then Aten, by his own admission, cursed at Andrew, who in turn told Ira that he was unarmed. Ira's reply was blunt: "Go get them." By this time Hugh McClelland appeared on the scene, a Colt's .45 in hand, telling Ira, "I'm ready for you." Giving himself some fighting room, Ira backed up a step or two into the street and said: "Shoot, you son of a bitch," and holding his hands out away from his body, daringly boasted, "I'll catch the bullet!"[42] Owing to the unfolding high drama, maybe it is best to hear from Mr. Aten:

> I did not think he could hit me. He shot and hit the ground
> at my feet and then turned to run around the corner of the

house. I shot at him as he went around the corner, and I shot
to kill. I cut a gash in the flesh clear across the small of his back
just under the skin. A half inch or more would have broken his
back. Parson Bandy said you could just lay a pencil down across
in the wound. He stopped around the corner and would stick
his head around the corner, shoot at me then dodge back. I
could not get a shot at him, as he would jump back around so
quick, and he shot at me two or three times. About that time
Andrew was coming back down the street with a six-shooter
in both hands and I knew I was going to have to get rid of one
of them, so I could give my attention to the other. I figured
about how far Hugh must jump back from the corner of the
house after he shot. I figured he would jump back about one
step, so I shot through the corner of the house about where I
thought he would be and hit him in the back of the neck, but
it was not deep enough to kill him and he tore out and ran
past Parson Bandy, who was coming up and said as he went
by: "If you want to save that fellow Aten's life, you had better get down there or I am going to kill him." Andrew had a
small six-shooter and a large one. I backed off a little way and
he brought up both guns and shot. It is the only time in my
life, in all my experience on the frontier, that I ever saw a man
try to shoot with both hands at the same time. After shooting, he dodged around in front of a team of mules that was
hitched to a wagon and I shot at his heart as he ran around. I
thought I had hit him in the heart as he fell like a beef, but he
had turned as he went around the team and I had hit to the
left of the heart in the shoulder. When he fell, his six-shooter
flew out from him. I thought I had killed him, but he began to
kick around in a minute and crawled around and got his big
six-shooter and began shooting at me from under the mules. I
began thinking about getting some evidence on account of the
fact that I was the aggressor that day. "Get up, Andrew, I don't
want to kill you while you are down," I called. I called again.
Judge Gough was standing on the porch and saw and heard all
of this. Then Andrew crawled around and took a rest off the
wagon wheel, and holding his six-shooter in both hands, prepared to shoot again. We both shot at about the same time and
his six-shooter flew out of his hands right straight up, and I
thought I had hit him between the eyes, but I hit his hands.

Old Man Bedford ran out crying: "Mr. Aten, don't shoot again! Don't shoot again! You've killed him!"[43]

While he had noticed Judge Gough watching the gunfight, Ira had not seen Kenneth Turner, but Mr. Turner had seen him. Particularly, Turner was keen on discerning Ira's gunfighting demeanor. Accordingly Turner said and could testify that "Aten was in no hurry, and took the time to fire his gun with both hands like with a rifle."[44] Ira was a devotee, then, of sage gunfighting advice: "Take your time, quick." Unleashing hellfire that barks but does not bite is mindless—deathly so.

Current Castro County (Dimmitt) Sheriff Sal Rivera holding one of his predecessors' historic Six-shooters: Ira Aten's Colt's .45 with a 4.75-inch barrel. *Author's photo.*

Aten had not killed either of the McClelland boys, but he had sure knocked the fight out of them. The Dimmitt street fight is more than a little revealing about Ira Aten's psyche and his aptitude at coping while under life threatening pressure. In the first instance, Ira was wholly capable of acting alone, not finding it necessary to impregnate his reservoir of raw nerve by drawing on a gang's help and gang mentality. Hyenas hunt in packs, one going for the hamstring, others for the neck. Ira, when he had to—or thought he had to—wore the stripes of a tiger, the solitary hunter, a maneater. His absolute coolness during the heat of battle is confirmed by his acknowledgment that he had carried the fight to the McClelland brothers with overt premeditation. Ira was the aggressor—and he realized it. Once aware that Judge Gough was an eyewitness, Aten's motive changed from "I shot at his heart," to "Get up Andrew, I don't want to kill you." Ira's abrupt about-face, harkening the wisdom of damage control, speaks to coolness.

Although no longer a state-paid Ranger, Ira Aten was still tough as rawhide. Two fellows who knew him in the Panhandle, R. J. Frye and C. F. Vincent, characterized Ira ever so simply: "Aten was a scrapper."[45] He, too, was pliable, malleable enough to know his actions were maybe justified, but by the letter of the law, illegal. The young and tenderfoot green Sheriff Bedford made his first felony arrest, Ira Aten, charge: Assault to Murder. Aten quickly made bond and waived the optional preliminary hearing. Ira Aten grasped that a Castro County Grand Jury would have but little trouble—really need to—return an indictment. He was ready for trial—by jury.[46]

He may not have wanted to be, but Ira made ready for something else—an explanation, an excuse to Imogen why a man who had pledged to set the six-shooter aside had reneged. Ira may have been a cool customer in a gunfight, but Miss Boyce might be cool—cold as ice—to the idea of taking up with a six-shooting man. She had made it clear lawmen impressed her naught. And for this dustup business at Dimmitt, Mr. Aten had no peace officer's badge to hide behind, at least as far as Imogen knew. Either way, the gunplay was not a legitimate line of duty shooting. Hadn't it been a feud, a duel, madness? Did name-calling really justify gunplay? Had he plainly run amok? Nevertheless Imogen loved Ira, and now with a pending trial haunting his future—and the possibility of prison—maybe he needed her more than ever. Would he give her an assurance—a sterling promise—that he would "never again accept public office or

C. I. Bedford, Castro County Sheriff. He would place Ira Aten under arrest for the Jones Street shoot-out at Dimmitt. *Courtesy Castro County Historical Museum.*

hunt down criminals?"[47] Mr. Ira bent to her fancy. Yes, she would marry him.

On the third day of February 1892, hardly a month after the Aten/McClelland shoot-out, Ira stood before the pulpit at Austin's Central Christian Church. Twenty-four-year-old Imogen Boyce, "the bride, a handsome, bright, charming young woman," her head held high, adoringly stood beside her groom, "her pure and holy love, the first, the last, the only love." Though a church wedding, Ira's pending legal difficulties had hurriedly forced the couple's nuptials: There were no bridesmaids or a best man, only ushers. After remarking that this marriage was no lottery as the couple had long known each other, the

Imogen Boyce and Ira Aten's wedding photograph. *Courtesy Jeri and Gary Boyce Radder.*

newspaperman writing for the *Austin Daily Statesman* encapsulated
public sentiment, joining with the "many friends of the happy couple
who attended the wedding and the thousands of friends of the popular groom all over Texas in wishing them a long life of happiness."[48]
And to be sure, the Aten/Boyce wedding was a newsmaker. Besides
the respective families, which were both well thought of throughout the Williamson/Travis County corridor, guests included such
statewide notables as John D. McCall, the Texas State Comptroller,
former Adjutant General Wilburn H. King, Sheriff Emmet White of
Travis County, and Ira's old pal and mentor from Ranger days gone
by, Lam Sieker, now Assistant Adjutant General.[49] The honeymoon,
well, it would be delayed. After the two o'clock wedding ceremony
the newlywed Atens boarded a night train bound for Amarillo, fifty
miles above Dimmitt.

Exactly what Imogen thought about her new home, a dugout, more than a long walk east of Dimmitt, is not known.[50] On the other hand it is plain that she knew her husband would have to dig himself out from under the imminent criminal case. Although Ira believed that one of his "worst enemies," J. W. Carter, had had a hand in "arousing" the McClelland boys to kill him, solid evidence— if there is any—is yet veiled by obscurity.[51] Likewise is the shortage of proof to implicate the McClelland brothers in a grandiose murder conspiracy. Who knows? The prosecutor, District Attorney D. B. Hill, was not blind to the fact that it was Ira who carried the fight to the McClelland boys, not the other way around. The simplest measure for Castro County folks to get themselves off the hook was just charge all three—and thus it was: The system could sort it out. After Dimmitt's holiday season shoot-out the McClellands had abandoned the Castro County ship, setting an eastern course and sailing across a sea of grass, finally making port in their native state, Tennessee. Ira Aten would be the first to weather the legal storm.

Quite brilliantly, for one-half of his defense team Ira hired W. B. Plemons, a thrice-wounded Confederate veteran, and a powerhouse Panhandle lawyer whom many believed was an unstoppable force in adversarial contests before juries, absolutely refusing to be "derailed, denied, or defeated."[52] Another remarked that lawyer Plemons "believed there were two sides to every question—his side and the wrong side."[53] Accordingly, "His client could do no wrong, nor could the enemy ever do right.... As a lawyer he was pugnacious, zealous for his client's interest, vigorous, and untiring. His method was that of the gladiator—defying all who came to measure strength with him—and thumbs down for the vanquished."[54] Sitting in the second chair would be attorney Green Wilson of Plainview, Hale County, forty-five miles southeast of Dimmitt. The tongue-in-cheek rejoinder "Don't take a knife to a gunfight," is good guidance. Likewise, unless a district attorney wanted to spar in a down and dirty legal dogfight—tooth and toenail—he best not lay a criminal case in the laps of defense attorneys Plemons and Wilson. Plemons particularly "gloried in agitation and dispute and was never excelled in repartee."[55] Although by nearly all accounts young Mr. Aten was extraordinarily well-thought-of in Castro County, the lawyers' safest bet, in their minds, was to seek a change of venue.[56] Successful with their motion, Ira Aten's criminal case was moved to Tulia, Swisher County, Castro County's eastern neighbor. Now, Ira could but sweat

out the slow grind of Texas' criminal justice system—his case docketed for the December 1892 term of District Court.

Whether Ira's future in Castro County was hanging by a chain
or a thread the young man had no way of knowing, but Aten was
never, ever, idle. He had a wife to support and a child on the way.
He had a farm and small ranch to see after. And, from time to time
he supplemented his uncertain income with seemingly menial labor,
though managing a team pulling a heavy load did entail skill. Not
only did he work hard, so too did his baby brother Eddie. Castro
County was in want of a courthouse and the construction, which is
well documented in county records, also mentions payment to the
Aten brothers for hauling lumber from Amarillo to Dimmitt: Ira was
paid $30.99 and Eddie knocked down a bigger check, $59.51.[57] Too,
it was in this timeframe that the county did not have a jail and there
was no place to house prisoners. Though there is no record of Ira
smiling at Sheriff Bedford's solution, he knew it was but a stopgap
measure. Resorting to necessity, when the sheriff had a prisoner—
which was not too often—he just took the man home with him. If
Charley Bedford thought the prisoner could be trusted the honor
system was invoked. If not, for escape risks or unruly prisoners, the
sheriff just handcuffed himself to the inmate and the pair snuggled
under the same pile of warm blankets till morning.[58]

Some other fellows weren't burrowing with the sheriff, however.
Castro County was in big ranch country. Dimmitt was "settling up."
Nearly everywhere in the American West, for a myriad of sociological reasons, when towns finally dotted the livestock landscape, cow
thieves were guaranteed to follow. Castro County was no oddity. All
too soon young Charley Bedford was overwhelmed. The wholesale
stealing of cattle had shifted into high gear, and the thievery was
gaining "momentum." The brazenness of a few cow thieves—that is
what ranchers knew them to be, not something as politely benign as
a rustler—was incredible.[59] On one Sunday morning while Dimmitt
folks were singing hymns and pitching pennies in the offering plate,
outside, those cow thieves were pitching loops around the necks of
"milk pen calves." By the time the preacher got around to shaking
hands and saying "See you next Sunday," the pens were empty and
Dimmitt kids were crying for sweet milk.[60] Away from town it was
worse.

There is an anecdotal tale that Eddie Aten had a fondness for
poker. Supposedly in a Panhandle area saloon Eddie found himself

Castro County's first courthouse. Ira and Eddie Aten would earn extra money by hauling lumber for its construction. Like so many of Texas' wooden courthouses it would be destroyed by a devastating accidental fire. *Courtesy Castro County Historical Museum.*

in a difficulty with someone during a card game that had morphed into a gunplay. If it is a true story there is the untidy nuisance with authentication due the paucity of evidence, an out-and-out scarcity of proof. Coupled with the story, however, is a hard truth. Ira suggested or coerced or begged Eddie to straighten up his errant ways. Using his influence with Ranger Sergeant John Hughes, Ira secured Eddie a private's slot as a member of Company D, then headquartered at Ysleta, El Paso County. On the sixteenth day of September 1892, Edwin Dunlap Aten, twenty-two years of age, became the third Aten brother to enlist with the Texas Rangers.[61]

Conceivably Ira was quite enthusiastic about Eddie becoming a Texas Ranger. Imogen, if guess work is allowable, was not. And more especially accenting her displeasure would have been knowledge of Williamson County's Sheriff John Olive's demise in the line of duty, just four days prior to Eddie enlisting in the Rangers. Ira's longtime friend and law enforcing comrade had been fatally ambushed while standing on the depot's platform at Echo, Bell County—presumably the culmination of revenge for fellows he had killed twelve years earlier. Too, Imogen was not unaware of the fact that just a few months before, another Williamson County lawman had been killed. James Burrell Gunn, a forty-seven-year-old deputy sheriff, had been fatally shot—three times—during a dustup in front of the Mankin Saloon at Georgetown.[62] Imogen Aten could well see, on that eastern edge of the Texas Hill Country, the longevity of a peace officer could be snuffed out in an instant. She was not unawares, either, that one of Ira's law enforcement buddies, the former Burnet County sheriff, John Wolf, but then Burnet City Marshal, had been mortally gunned down during a volatile dispute.[63] Who knew what kind of hard characters were roaming and hiding in "no man's land," the Texas Panhandle? No, there is no doubt Mrs. Imogen Aten was thankful she had extracted from Ira a promise to forevermore forgo any law enforcement work. Perhaps, she did not know that even Special Rangers were obligated to submit activity reports. Nine months after his charming Travis County marriage ceremony, Special Texas Ranger Ira Aten—in writing—notified Adjutant General Mabry: "No scouts or arrest for Oct."[64]

There may have been trouble enough along the Texas/Mexican border, but things were popping in the Texas Panhandle. Sheriff Bedford never could—and it was an impossible task for a rookie lawman—to get a handle on the rampant thievery washing over Castro County. At election time he was turned out.[65] His replacement at the polls was a former XIT cowboy, Perry Cox. Just like Fort Bend County wherein black voters could swing an election, in the Panhandle, wage-working cowboys voting in a bloc could often slide their man into office. Ira Aten, a well-seasoned Texas lawman, sized up Sheriff Perry Cox rather quickly and pithily: "He did not do anything with the outlaws."[66] During a separate interview, Ira described Perry Cox as "a good boy, but his sympathy was rather with the cowboys. He was a rough and ready cowboy, and that was what caused the trouble."[67] The "trouble" was that Sheriff Perry Cox's bondsmen were having second thoughts.

For Ira and Imogen, life was pretty merry, all except for those storm clouds of legality looming on the horizon. Aside from the mundane chores, occasionally there were collegial debates on interesting topics at the newly constructed clapboard school house in Dimmitt. On the outskirts of town "once in a while" cowboys competed in cow pasture rodeos, roping steers and riding wild four-year-old broncos gathered from the range. Wolfing—killing wolves—was good sport too, and necessary. Castro County folks also enjoyed dances, but they never were as popular at Dimmitt as elsewhere, not according to Ira.[68] Dimmitt never was a noted saloon town, full of parasitical gamblers and good girls gone bad. To be sure one could dabble in sin, but a sparse population was not a good draw for that "bottom-of-the-bucket" crowd, not like Tombstone or Silver City in the paired territories. Really, in or near town peacefulness was more common than rowdiness. Farther out, however, those cow thieves were working with madness and impunity. Several outfits were fashioning quite large herds of "off color" cattle. Ira Aten's primary tribulation was not in Castro County, though. He had some thorny business at Tulia.

Defense lawyers Plemons and Wilson had but little wiggle room. Ira, already armed, had taken the fight to Andrew and Hugh McClelland. Ira had told an unarmed Andrew to go and get his gun or guns and be quick about it. And, by his own admission Ira had called Andrew a "dirty lying son-of-a-bitch," and told Hugh, "Shoot, you son-of-a-bitch." No one was silly enough to believe Ira could have caught the bullet as he had cheekily parried, but it was clear he had audaciously bared his chest, tempting trouble. Was Andrew McClelland's calling Aten a liar—in public—provocation enough?

Attorneys representing criminal defendants frequently shifted blame—or tried to. Ira Aten's lawyers for the December 20, 1892, trial followed suit. The McClelland brothers, according to the lawyers' arguments, were not longtime residents of the state, but from Tennessee. They had come to the Lone Star with a precast objective—bulldoze Texans out of their hard-earned money. Castro County Judge Gough testified in Ira's behalf. Summing up, the defense contention was that the McClelland boys' misfortune had been to run up against Aten acting as if they were "bad men." And, as Plemons expressively harped, "they had got a hold of the wrong man, and got the worst of it." Now, that line of reasoning would make sense to a Westerner, a Westerner living in cow country. In light of that logic District Attorney Hill was at a loss. He knew the prosecution's case was floundering. Lawyer Hill fumbled and stumbled then said: "Your Honor, it may be a crime to be born in the State of Tennessee: but if so, I plead guilty to the offense."[69]

Texas Rangers assigned to the Texas Panhandle. Back row from L to R: Jack Harwell, John L. Sullivan, Bob Pease, Arthur Jones, Edward Fulton "Big Ed" Connell a particular friend of Ira's, and Lee Queen. Seated L to R: Billy McCauley, Bob McClure, Wesley Cates, and Ben Owens. *Courtesy Research Center, Texas Ranger Hall of Fame and Museum.*

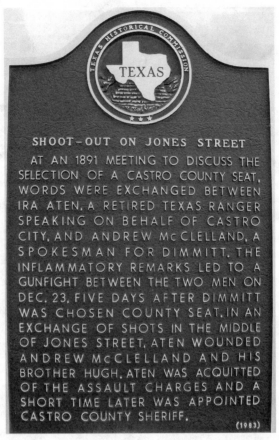

SHOOT-OUT ON JONES STREET
AT AN 1891 MEETING TO DISCUSS THE
SELECTION OF A CASTRO COUNTY SEAT,
WORDS WERE EXCHANGED BETWEEN
IRA ATEN, A RETIRED TEXAS RANGER
SPEAKING ON BEHALF OF CASTRO
CITY, AND ANDREW McCLELLAND, A
SPOKESMAN FOR DIMMITT. THE
INFLAMMATORY REMARKS LED TO A
GUNFIGHT BETWEEN THE TWO MEN ON
DEC. 23, FIVE DAYS AFTER DIMMITT
WAS CHOSEN COUNTY SEAT. IN AN
EXCHANGE OF SHOTS IN THE MIDDLE
OF JONES STREET, ATEN WOUNDED
ANDREW McCLELLAND AND HIS
BROTHER HUGH. ATEN WAS ACQUITTED
OF THE ASSAULT CHARGES AND A
SHORT TIME LATER WAS APPOINTED
CASTRO COUNTY SHERIFF.
(1983)

Texas State Historical Marker commemorating—highlighting—Ira's
shooting mêlée with the McClelland brothers at Dimmitt. The marker
is on grounds of the Castro County courthouse.   *Author's photo.*

The judge may or may not have been amused. He sent the state's
case to the jury. Defendant Aten was somewhat concerned after
learning that two of the jurymen had Tennessee roots—and they
were farmers not cowmen. For awhile, it seemed those two fellows
were to throw in the proverbial monkey-wrench and hang the jury.
In the end, however, they came around and voted for acquittal along
with the other ten jurymen. Ira Aten was formally found Not Guilty.
After the verdict every man sitting on the jury came over to Ira and
shook his hand, even the two temporary hold-outs. They could not
resist, however, telling Ira that they thought he "was a little hasty in
shooting two men for only calling you a liar, but we were not willing

to send you to prison for it."[70] Hasty or not Ira Aten was a free man, a man who had best hasten home—big doings were astir.

Two days after the trial, on December 22, presumably at the Atens' dugout, Imogen presented Ira with their first child, a boy, Marion Hughes.[71] Assuredly the birth of his first son had been a splendid Christmas present. Ira Aten was a family man. He was also an admirer of folks that could eke out a living from an agricultural lifestyle. Ira, then, while in Castro County was—among other things—a small time livestock man and minor league dirt farmer. As 1892's midnight clock chimed its last second, little did Ira know he was fixing to have a hard row to hoe.

Chapter 14

"I'll break them up on lawyers' fees"

A new year blew in with its characteristic winter blast. Castro County citizens, many yet living in dugouts, burrowed deep anticipating a desired thaw. Springtime would bring forth the warmth, but not a welcoming respite for many Dimmitt area folks. With the good weather came the bad. Cow thieves were at work, again. A sparsely populated range—mostly unfenced—was prime territory for those bent toward building their herds with running-irons, that nondescript piece of steel that could be used to duplicate a brand. In honorable hands the straight iron with a curved hook could be used to properly mark livestock of an absentee owner gathered during a roundup. In devious hands it was a tool of the trade, good for artfully blotching an old brand, or copycatting a new one.[1] Panhandle brand burners were hard at work, that spring of '93.

Something else was hard at work, too: grasshoppers. Hardly any rains had fallen during 1892, and now if hardscrabble farmers weren't handicapped enough, hordes of pesky and ravenous insects invaded Castro County chewing the profit from plowed fields. Particularly Ira Aten noted the tribulations of those earliest Panhandle years: "1891, '92, and '93 were all dry years. I kept planting every year and nothing came up until about '93; and then Millet, johnson [sic] grass, and maize all came up together."[2] Scratching a living from the ground was a hard go. Law enforcing paid little better. The loss of even one cow or calf, for the everyday folks, was not trivial.

Ira Aten said, and it is not exaggeration, that Castro County people were at the crossroads: They could either move out of the county or run the thieves out of the county. As with nearly any brewing acrimony there was more talk than action—at first. Dimmitt folks, as a community, were grumbling. Imogen Aten missed much of it. Understandably the new mother was proud of her bouncing bundle of joy, delighting in the opportunity to make the train trip home and show off baby Marion Hughes to both sets of grandparents. Ira could

Although his prominent moustache somewhat masks his actual age, Ira at this juncture was a seasoned law enforcement veteran: Rawhide tough. *Courtesy Castro County Historical Museum.*

"bach" while she was away. He was a big boy—a grown man. But Imogen was in for a surprise.

The dissatisfaction with Sheriff Perry Cox had erupted. The XIT cowboy-turned-lawman was not pleasing his constituents, including his bondsmen. Their solution was straightforward and irrevocable. Fellows who had guaranteed his sheriff's performance bond withdrew their support morally, but more importantly, financially. A sheriff absent the mandatory bond does not a sheriff make. Castro County had a vacancy. County commissioners turned to Ira Aten, that former Texas Ranger with a deservedly high profile, that ex-Fort Bend County sheriff with administrative know-how. Of all the Castro County folks, Mr. Ira Aten was the one best qualified—the most experienced—at dealing with owlhoots and outlaws, murderers and cow stealers. Ira's conundrum was real. Proverbially he was between the rock and a hard place. Practically he was between the community's wants and a wife. Ira had promised Imogen. Ira broke his promise.

On the ninth day of May 1893, Austin Ira Aten was made the sheriff of Castro County, knocking down $50 per month. The appointment would stand good until the following year when voters would be given a chance to accept or reject their county commissioner's interim choice.[3] Adhering to the standard policy of the day, Sheriff Aten deputized his brother-in-law John Boyce, guaranteeing himself at least one loyal face in the ever tumultuous trench of county politics.[4]

Ira Aten in certain respects was a wise man. In this instance he opted to tell Imogen of his going back on his word, in writing. To him that sounded much better than a face to face meeting. Her reaction was not heartening. Imogen's words were plainspoken. Ira remembered: "so my wife almost quit me when I accepted the appointment as sheriff. She was down at Austin and I let her know and she said that she would not come back until I resigned."[5] In response, for this long-distance battle of willpower Ira penned another letter, explaining: "After you have returned home and looked over the situation, and still insist that I resign, I will resign."[6] Ira's powers of persuasion may not have altogether worked on their own merit; he did have some help. In the end, Imogen's father and her father-in-law, Preacher Aten, convinced the headstrong girl that her place was with her husband. In fact, on the return trip to the Panhandle, Imogen and infant Marion Hughes were accompanied by Ira's dad, an adept mediator and doting grandfather.[7]

Not being privy to pillow talk it is out of the question to reconstruct the verbal interchange between Sheriff Ira Aten and the letdown Imogen. Imagination should suffice. Ira had calculated the odds and had made his move back into law enforcement. Imogen Aten, then, was brought to a hard truth: She could accept it, or seek divorce, or depart Castro County for an awkward estrangement until she or Ira capitulated, brokering the impasse. In the end, Imogen stepped to the plate after internalizing the sad state-of-affairs then unwinding in the birthplace of her first child. Honest folks were on the defensive; cow thieves, fugitives, and ne'er-do-wells were gaining the upper hand in that section of the Panhandle. Unless someone put the kibosh on the meanness and outlawry, Castro County would be depopulated of law-abiding people. Imogen consented to

Ira becoming sheriff. Not only that, perhaps excepting her brother John, she was Ira's most reliable and trustworthy deputy, unofficially, of course. From time to time she would wear a six-shooter and guard an occasional prisoner in the less than secure structure passing as a county jail.[8]

Imogen Aten was not the kind to say, "I told you so." But just shy of two months after taking office, Ira was posted with heart rendering news, also learning that an Aten had been drawn into the bloody affair, too. In far West Texas, along the Rio Grande in El Paso County, Texas Ranger Captain Frank Jones had been leading a scout after the Olguin boys, Jesus Maria the father and Severio the son, both charged with "horse and cattle Stealing and with assault with intent to commit murder."[9] Riding with the captain were Corporal Carl Kirchner, and Privates T. F. Tucker, Robert Edward "Ed" Bryant, the previously mentioned Wood Saunders who had been allowed to reenlist, and Ira's youngest brother Eddie Aten. The long and the short of the story is simple. On a sandbar known as Pirate Island the Texas Rangers ran into trouble—big time. Corporal Kirchner reported:

> We had searched several houses & were on our way back when we saw two men approaching us when they saw us they began to retreat with all possible haste, of course we followed at once & only ran them about one half mile when myself & Private Saunders overtaken them & demanded a surrender by this time we were not six feet from an adobe building on the road side[.] Two shots were fired at me from the house & about four at the rest of the party[.] One of the shots fired at me struck my Winchester but only ruined the magazine[.] We all at once dismounted & opened fire on them[.] Capt. Jones was hit the first volley, his thigh was broken but he continued to shoot until shot in the breast & killed dead on the spot about 15 ft. from the door[.] We continued to fire on them until they retreated & hid in the building[.] Just then a friendly Mexican who was with us in search of stolen horses told me we were in Mexico in the outskirts of Tres Jacales a small Mexican town & that the people had sent for the Mexican soldiers who would be there in 15 minutes[.] My first decision was to stay with our dead Captain & Kill or capture the Mexicans but after waiting about 45 minutes I saw from the appearance of every-thing we would be overpowered & murdered so we retreated to this side....[10]

Ira was particularly disturbed by this tragic turn of events. The death of Frank Jones was sad. [11] Realization that Eddie had undergone baptismal fire as a Texas Ranger was brought close to home for Ira and Imogen. This law enforcing business was chancy. Yet Ira and Eddie were willing to gamble. There would be other gunplay on Eddie's schema of life.

Meanwhile, in Castro County, Sheriff Aten was up against the wall. Thieves were stealing cattle and horses with remorseless gusto. Catching criminals is but half the job. Attaining convictions in court was where the wagon wheel hit the rutted road. All too soon Ira learned that many of his law-abiding constituents were loathe to bear witness. "They [thieves] just had the people bulldozed, and to a person saying anything about it they would say: 'Don't say a word about it. They will steal me out.' It looked a mighty little thing to send a man to the pen for stealing a cow or calf. Even good men on juries were slow in coming to this, though horse stealing was more serious."[12]

Seemingly it was but par business for defense lawyers to "get one or two men to hang the jury in every case...."[13] Coming up short with actual courtroom convictions Sheriff Aten adopted the previously mentioned law enforcement tactic, maybe questionable, but nevertheless often effective: "You might beat the rap, but you can't beat the ride." Immodestly Ira declared that he would just break the gangs up by forcing them to fork over illicitly earned dollars to perpetually hungry defense attorneys: "If I can't put them in the pen, I'll break them up on lawyers' fees."[14] Continuing with the mini-autobiographical narrative Ira Aten swanked: "I began to arrest the ring-leaders of the gangs on every hatched up charge by which I could make any kind of a case, as the juries would not convict anyway."[15] Now, to a cow thief this seemed underhanded. On the other hand, the Panhandle area defense lawyers loved it, and at least one—probably more—favorably remarked, "If it were not for Aten we'd starve to death."[16]

Particularly Sheriff Aten was intent on stopping alleged nefarious activities of the Cordel brothers, Fred and Oscar. The boys had established a ranch six miles northeast of Dimmitt. According to Ira their reputation was not good, as their increasing herd of cattle was "off color." The brothers coming up from Palo Pinto County about 1891 had barefacedly established their ranch as a headquarters for some of the toughest characters riding the Llano Estacado. "Every thief that passed through the country stopped with them," so said

Sheriff Aten.[17] He also mentioned that at their ranch one could frequently—*always*—find a hanging beef waiting to be butchered, but there was never a telltale branded hide drying in the sun.[18] For a cowman that was a naked clue—the evidence had been hidden—buried or burned.

Although there are not supplemental details—which is a historical shame—Sheriff Aten and the Cordel brothers apparently squared off. Ira Aten's comment is epigrammatic and nebulous: "I never had any shooting scrapes with them, though once we stood with our hands on our six-shooters and cussed one another."[19] What he might

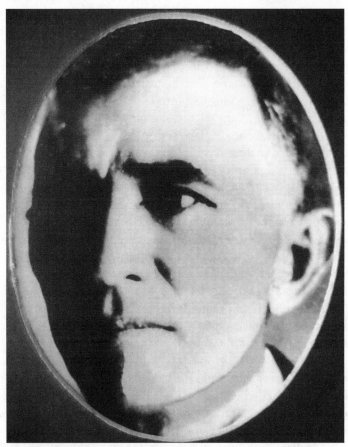

Sheriff Frank Scott, Swisher County's (Tulia) very first sheriff. He successfully accompanied Castro County Sheriff Ira Aten across the Panhandle and into the Indian Territory in search of cow thieves. *Courtesy Swisher County Sheriff Emmett Benavidez.*

have wanted to do with a Colt's pistol in regards to the Cordels, Ira did with their pocketbooks. A case in point is illustrative.

With a new sheriff in town the Cordel brothers opted to move their clandestine livestock operation east into Indian Territory. With the help of some cowboys of questionable repute they gathered, all in all, several hundred head, moving them onto the new range along the Washita River.[20] Perturbing to Panhandle cowmen was the fact that some of the cattle, most of the cattle, came off of several prominent ranches: the JA, the T-Anchor, the Long S, and the XIT.[21] The loss from the XIT was especially noteworthy to Sheriff Ira Aten. His wife Imogen's cousin, Colonel A. G. Boyce, was the ranch's general manager.[22] With the help of Frank Scott, Swisher County Sheriff, and Bob Bishop, foreman of the JA, Sheriff Aten set off in pursuit of stolen cattle, returning them to their rightful owners, and arresting a gang of contemptible cow thieves. The trio trailed and tracked and interviewed their way across Swisher, Briscoe (Silverton), Armstrong (Claude), Donley (Clarendon), Collingsworth (Wellington), and Greer (Oklahoma) Counties, "the latter belonging to Texas at the time" and across the state line onto Indian lands.[23]

In the end, grueling days in the saddle augmented by investigative drudgery and an utterly mulish mindset yielded its big dividend. Without a fight the lawmen managed to slip up on three of the cowboys "loose herding" the stolen cattle.[24] At the point of Winchesters desperadoes became detainees. The prisoners were lodged in the Roger Mills County jail, at Cheyenne, pending ironing out of extradition matters. Two of the owlhoots, William "Bill" Burkett, a former Panhandle well driller, and an unidentified twenty-one-year-old, agreed to waive extradition proceedings and return to Texas. The third, an inflexible fellow named Howard Thatcher, however, wanted to advantage all legal recourse, and rebuffed any waiver.[25] According to Sheriff Ira Aten, the foremost targets of his unflagging efforts were not rounded up: "I think the Cordels were coming back after more cattle when we got there."[26]

Ira Aten watched as, over time, Rangers of the Frontier Battalion had steadily marched down the more than bumpy road to professionalism. The metamorphic transition from wild-eyed youths—Indian fighters—chasing after the chance to scalp a Comanche or two, to a reasonably effective crime-fighting machine had taken place. Texas Rangers were now lawmen, and lawmen were entrusted with obeying the law. Sheriff Aten through that experience with the Rangers and as Fort Bend County Sheriff knew firsthand the importance of dotting the legal i's and crossing the statutory t's. Suspected cow thief Thatcher could only be brought back to Texas after a legally drawn requisition from the governor, since the alleged crimes had taken place in the Lone Star State, not Oklahoma or Indian Territory. To legally hold Thatcher, Sheriff Aten needed to work—expeditiously.

Sheriff Aten assigned Sheriff Scott and Bob Bishop responsibility for rounding up the herd of stolen cattle. Once shaped into a herd for the trail, they were to hold them in readiness for a drive back to the Texas Panhandle. In the interim, Sheriff Aten would by stagecoach haul Thatcher to Guthrie, Oklahoma Territory, where he could confab with the governor—begging for time. He would catch up later. Sheriff Aten's meeting with the governor went well: "I saw the Governor, told him my story, and asked him to give me thirty days to go back to Texas and get extradition papers for this man. He gladly consented to hold him, saying, 'We have too many of that kind of men in the Territory already.'"[27]

With a thirty-day deadline hanging over his head, Sheriff Aten jumped into overdrive. First he traveled to Cheyenne and picked up the two prisoners. Then he rejoined his comrades loose-herding the beeves. Sheriff Aten matter-of-factly explains everyday mechanics of the trail herding trip. "I did not fear these two prisoners very much. I would handcuff them together at night, but we three had to stand all the guard around the cattle at night, which made a long guard. We always rode the best horses, so if the prisoners undertook to get away we could overtake them without the necessity of shooting them.... We gave them sorry horses to ride and let them drive the drags."[28]

Sheriff Aten's overhanging dilemma was nightmarish. The Texas governor would not engage in extradition matters short of the proposed defendant actually being indicted by a grand jury. A mad citizen or eager lawman simply swearing to a Complaint was not sufficient, not for extradition purposes. Sheriff Aten, therefore, was desperate to find an appropriate grand jury then sitting. The district courts were not in session in Castro, Swisher, Randall (Canyon) or Armstrong Counties. Luckily, such was not the case at Clarendon, Donley County. Rushing to Clarendon where he knew not a soul, Ira hurriedly conferred with the district attorney and the district judge. Though the cattle had not been stolen in Donley County, the alleged thieves had passed through the county on their way to the Indian

Territory hideout. That was good enough, believed the court's stewards. Ira appeared before the grand jury—for an hour—laying his case before them. If there were any, Indictments would not return until the grand jury's session ended. Sheriff Aten could but cross his fingers, leave Clarendon, and rejoin his boys and the herd.[29]

Word of Sheriff Ira Aten's success spread quickly. Panhandle area ranchers—big and small—sashayed out to meet the returning champions, cutting the herd for their missing cattle. Those that could properly identify stolen livestock were allowed to regain custody of their walking and bellowing assets. Sheriff Aten had proved the Castro County commissioners right. He was the man for the job. After an extended absence from the county, Ira rode back into Dimmitt, glad to be home. The pleasure was short lived. The clock was ticking on the Thatcher matter. Fortunately, the Donley Grand Jury had indicted the fellow and the district attorney had forwarded the necessary paperwork to Texas Governor Hogg, who had in turn notified officialdom at Guthrie. Without delay Sheriff Aten left for Oklahoma. He got there just in the nick of time, one day before the thirty-day grace period expired. He now had his stubborn prisoner— legally removable back to Texas.[30] Transporting a supposedly treacherous prisoner, by himself, was no cake walk. Ira elucidates:

> This man was a dangerous criminal, having several other charges against him. I took no chances with him. I had brought along handcuffs and leg irons, which I used on him during the return trip. In the daytime I would have one side of the leg irons on one leg, draw the other up under his pants by a light chain about twelve feet long, and let the prisoner carry the chain in his hand, or put it up his sleeve, so that no one would know he was a prisoner. I always had a horror of shooting a prisoner for running away from me. I came back to Vernon on the train, getting there at 8 o'clock at night. As the Amarillo train would leave at 5 o'clock the next morning, I decided to go to a nearby hotel instead of the jail, as I was afraid I would not get my man out of the jail in time to catch the train. I asked the proprietor of the hotel to give me a room next to his as I had a prisoner and might need some assistance. I handcuffed my left hand to the prisoner's right. Then I asked the proprietor to skackle [sic] us together with the leg irons and take the keys and my pistol, saying I wanted to catch the 5 o'clock train next morning.[31]

Successfully Sheriff Aten returned to Castro County, where, according to Ira: "Right after I came back from the Territory, I arrested the Cordels at their ranch. They made no opposition; they just figured on beating their case, which was easily done in that country at the time."[32] The criminal prosecutions, however, were not quite so triumphant. Fearing that he could not get convictions in Castro or Swisher Counties because the cow thieves had too many friends and honest jurors could be intimidated so easily, Sheriff Aten also sought criminal Indictments in the heavier settled Armstrong County, "further east," where it "was more civilized."[33] Using the twenty-one-year-old arrestee as a state's evidence witness, Sheriff Aten and the prosecution team were victorious in obtaining convictions against the other two, Burkett and Thatcher. As is so often the case, however, the big boys, in Ira's mind, skated in a direction other than one leading to the Huntsville penitentiary. He had secured Indictments in several counties charging Oscar and Fred Cordel. Cleverly the two brothers—with the facilitation of incredibly persuasive defense lawyers—had completely shifted the blame from themselves to the three cowboys. In the end, though, the Cordels' band was broken up, even absent their convictions.[34] A man is wholly innocent until proven Guilty. But even the Not Guilty fellows sometimes pay the fiddler. In essence, then, they had "beaten the rap, but not the ride." The Cordel brothers' freedom had come at a high price—their Panhandle attorneys were flush. Sheriff Aten's investigative tactic of "breaking them up on lawyer's fees," had done the trick—at least for this bunch. Charitably it has been written that due to Sheriff Ira Aten's stellar work "all traces of the bad element had been eliminated" from Castro County.[35] When it came to enforcing the law Sheriff Ira Aten was a whirlwind. Perhaps reading between the lines hints at the wide-ranging scope of Ira's dragnets. Fellow lawman Edward Fulton "Big Ed" Connell recalled: "I came to the Panhandle in 1893. When Ira Aten heard I was in Amarillo with the Rangers he had me gather his prisoners a time or two, which were scattered all over the Panhandle, and bring them to court at Dimmitt. He was sheriff there."[36] Panhandle pirates, many sallying forth from the interior regions, were not to be keelhauled by but a single skipper. The Panhandle Plains were awash with buccaneers, maybe not outfitted with a sword in one hand and a black eye patch, but assuredly with a long rope and running iron and saddle-gun. There was plenty of work.

Someone else still carrying a gun, besides the Panhandle's desperadoes, was that "wild in his ways" brother, Eddie Aten. Finding his niche, law enforcing was Eddie's forte. Like his brother Ira, Eddie had become a "good Ranger." Whether for fight or festivity Eddie's Texas Ranger cohorts could count on him. He had grit. Private Aten was yet stationed in faraway El Paso County working under the command of Company D's new captain, John R. Hughes, who had replaced the slain Frank Jones. For the second time in less than six months Ranger Eddie Aten would be involved in a gunplay.

Shortly after Thanksgiving Day, 1893, Ranger Privates Eddie Aten and Frank M. McMahan were casually enjoying a game of billiards at an Ysleta saloon. Captain Hughes had not placed the establishment "off limits," due to his logic, for very sound reasons. First because there were "so few places to go for recreation in Ysleta," and secondly, the billiard hall portion was "the very best place to learn the news."[37] Law enforcing work grinds on the axis of solid criminal intelligence, so Captain Hughes' reckoning was not faulty. The purposeful leak of a clue or the inadvertent slip of a tongue in a setting where alcohol dampens inhibitions and/or eggs on thoughtless talk can be and often is an asset—for the lawman. There is no way of now knowing the spirits of the two Rangers or how much spirituous liquor they had or had not consumed by 2:00 P.M. on the thirtieth day of November. They did, however, hear a hellacious argument taking place on the street. Aten and McMahan responded.[38]

The Rangers made an after-incident report to their commander. Captain Hughes in turn updated Adjutant General Mabry:

> The facts are about as follows. The two Rangers were playing billiards when they heard a lady's voice screaming murder. They ran out into the street and saw two women in a buggy, one trying to climb out over the back of the seat and screaming he is murdering us. The other (a Mexican woman) laying in the bottom of the buggy apparently dead, with blood on her head and shoulders and Jose Apodaca beating her with the gun [rifle]. They supposed the woman was dead and called to the man to surrender when he turned and pointed the gun at McMahan....[39]

Pointing guns at Texas Rangers is idiocy with a capital I, and perilous with a big P. The outcome should come as no surprise. Privates Aten and McMahan dropped the hammers on their Colt's six-shooters and Apodaca just dropped.[40] Luckily for Apodaca—though wounded—he had sidestepped the Grim Reaper. As was but criminal justice business as normal, Rangers Aten and McMahan were placed under bond awaiting outcome of an El Paso County grand jury investigation, which was due to convene on December 11, 1893.[41] When the grand jury met they opted not to indict the Rangers, though they did have an invitation for Mr. Apodaca: He could answer to formal charges of Aggravated Assault as the victim had, in the end, survived. A warrant issued. On the evening of December 30, 1893, Captain Hughes and Private Ed Bryant latched on to Mr. Apodaca, delivering him in irons to an El Paso County deputy sheriff.[42]

Meanwhile back at the ranch, the Ira Aten ranch, the young sheriff of Castro County and his sometimes gun-toting bride were beginning to rethink their future. Little Marion Hughes was underfoot and Imogen was pregnant as that last day of 1893 rolled around.[43] Sheriff Aten was but now and then home, always subject to call out, and fully aware that brigands sailing on that undulating sea of Panhandle grama grass were foully proficient at murder.

Exactly describing the role Lewis Epps, the black man initially accompanying Ira to the Panhandle, played in the lives of the Atens is shadowy, but not purposefully so. From the sketchy data at hand it would seem the relationship had remained favorable—on an even keel. Mr. Epps and his wife, Amanda, had filed on and been granted title to 160 acres in Castro County. Later, June 13, 1891, for a fee of $75 Mr. Epps and his wife had sold the 160 acres to Ira's brother Frank Lincoln and his wife, Josie. Frank held the land until April 28, 1892. Then for a compensation of $250 Frank and Jose sold the tract to Ira and Imogen. The final title on this real-estate transaction passed to Ira and Imogen on January 15, 1894, according to records maintained at the Texas General Land Office.[44]

Whether or not Ira accompanied Imogen to the Austin area is unknown. Perhaps wanting to be closer to home when the baby arrived, Imogen had sought comfort at her family's old homestead, surrounded by loved ones. On March 7, 1894, apparently with ease, Imogen gave birth to her and Ira's second son, Albert Boyce. And again it is murky regarding Ira's presence, but there is a likelihood that the sheriff put Castro County business on hold for a day or two and scooted down to the Williamson/Travis County vicinity for a family visit. Younger brother Cal was to be married. On the second

Calvin Grant Aten and Mattie Jo Kennedy. A wedding photograph. *Courtesy Betty Aten.*

day of May 1894, Mr. Calvin Grant Aten walked eighteen-year-old
Miss Mattie Jo Kennedy down the aisle at Round Rock.[45]

Although as a Texas Ranger he had witnessed and been a first-
hand player in many historic Lone Star events ranging from troubles along the Texas/Mexican border, to a key figure in the bloody
fence-cutting wars, as well as a supposed nonpartisan participant
in the Jaybird/Woodpecker political feud, Ira had yet to find himself embroiled in a labor union's disputes with big business. He had
been lucky. So much could not be said for his brother Eddie. While
Ira and Imogen were surviving on the meager—but typical—pay
of a Texas Panhandle sheriff and looking after infant and toddling
sons, trouble was brewing just up the road from Round Rock—in
Bell County.

Traditionally railroad executives cleaved to their pinstriped vests an affinity for Texas Rangers. The Rangers' bosses were politicians. Politicians listened to corporate America. When there was a disagreement between labor and management—a strike or threat of a shutdown—bureaucracy's wheels turned, and in Texas that equated to rolling out the Texas Rangers. Union reps and the rank and file saw the Texas Rangers as strikebreakers. In management's eyes they were but dutiful and devoted peace keepers. In fairness, lawmakers and forward-thinking bigwigs recognized the importance of protecting railway commerce, the artery connecting Texas with the fast-moving outside world of American trade. Citizen Texans demanded free access to reasonably priced imported goods, and farmers and ranchers banked on dependable railway traffic to export their commodities. Standstills were expensive for consumer and producer.

During July 1894 labor turmoil sparked at Temple. A strike was on. Company D's Captain John Hughes rushed to the scene, leaving orders for Eddie Aten, as of May a brand-new corporal, to gather more men and come at once. Obediently Corporal Aten made the necessary arrangements and the next day he and Privates Will Schmidt, Ed Palmer, and Jim Latham boarded a West Texas train, hurrying to Temple. The Company D Rangers were soon joined by Captain J. A. Brooks and a few men from Company F. Breaking into smaller deployment units the eighteen stern-faced Texas Rangers traversed the steel rails, carbines in hand, Colt's six-shooters visible in the scabbard. In between scheduled runs the Rangers guarded railroad yards, a front line of defense against vandalism. There are two quantifiable outcomes as a result of Texas Rangers rushing to Temple. A dozen and a half strong-willed Winchester Warriors riding the trains and protecting the railway yards for a few days until local officers and private guards set up their security blanket had the desired outcome: little to no violence at Temple.[46] The second and most familiar result was occasion for a photo op: an omnipresent feature of Texas Ranger diversion—for posterity's sake, of course.

By not even one account—at least as of yet—is there indication that Sheriff Ira Aten was performing the duties of his office in any manner other than splendidly. Many cowboys in the Panhandle somewhat stood in awe of Sheriff Aten's standup deportment. One fellow summed up succinctly, stressing that Ira Aten "was a gun man."[47] Aside from gunfighting gumption, part of the sheriff's

Rangers from several Frontier Battalion companies came together at Temple, Bell County, in response to a possibly violent railroad strike. Ira's youngest brother Eddie is standing poised for trouble in the back row, fourth from left. *Courtesy Texas Ranger Hall of Fame and Museum.*

From L to R. Albert Gallatin Boyce, Civil War veteran and cowman extraordinaire, a relative of Ira's wife and General Manager of the XIT Ranch; John V. Farwell from Chicago, Executive Director of the gargantuan and historic though not particularly well-liked XIT Ranch in the Texas Panhandle. *Courtesy Nita Stewart Haley Memorial Library & J. Evetts Haley History Center.*

popular success was born in his work ethic. Euphemistically, Ira Aten would only tell a person how much fence he had built yesterday, not how much he was *gonna* build tomorrow. Intentions were okay, accomplishment counted.

Two folks were taking especial notice of Ira. Both were relatives by marriage, second cousins of Imogen Boyce Aten. Both had high-profile reputations in Texas. Rube Boyce the notorious Lone Star shootist, jail-breaker, sometimes man on the dodge, alleged stagecoach robber, and always dangerous ne'er-do-well, was one. Reportedly when defending his lack of education the illiterate Rube said he didn't go to school because he had spent his formative years dodging bullets.[48] Earlier in his Ranger days (mentioned in this text) Ira Aten had even arrested Rube Boyce on misdemeanor violations and placed him in jail. Now, Rube had much of his wayward days behind him and was looking for a home, according to Ira. "Rube wrote me out here when I first come and wanted to come out here, and I always liked Rube pretty well.... I showed the letter to my wife. She said, 'Don't you get him out here. He will get us in trouble, he will disgrace us.' And I never answered his letter."[49] The other Boyce making an entreaty to Ira conquered Imogen's worries—for a little while—and received a thoughtful hearing.

Albert Gallatin "A. G." Boyce was well known, a well-respected cowman and trail driver. Albert was a native Texan, born in Travis County, later moving to Round Rock, and then on to Burnet County. During the Civil War A. G. Boyce had been a Confederate combatant in several battles for the Southern cause, and for awhile a Union prisoner at Fort Douglas, in Chicago. After an exchange of military prisoners soldier Boyce fought and was wounded in the engagement at Chickamauga. Later, the toughened old warrior contested on the very last Civil War battlefield, Palmito Ranch, at the southernmost point of Texas, in Cameron County. After the war Boyce earned his initial claim to cow country fame by bossing a crew of cowboys on a tortuous two-year trail driving trip to California. At the time Ira made his move to the Panhandle, A. G. Boyce was already there, although the ex-Ranger didn't know him then.[50] When and why they met impacted both their lives. A touch of historical backtracking is germane.

Nineteenth-century Texas was rich in land, but cash poor. So, when obligation and desire coalesced into need for finding financing for a new state capitol there was but one common-sense solution: Trade somebody a pot full of land for constructing a spectacular granite state house. Legislators thought that a plot 3,050,000 acres in size should even the balance sheet, and thus the legendary XIT brand became known throughout the world, a whopping empire with real-estate holdings in ten Texas counties, all adjoining and all in the Panhandle. Texas had a commodious capitol building and foreign investors had an enormous cattle setup—sparsely watered.

Actual ownership of the sprawling cattle kingdom belonged to the Capitol Freehold Land and Investment Company of England and its shareholders' £3,000,000 ($15,000,000), leased to the Capitol Syndicate (American investors), John V. Farwell, Chicago, Illinois, Managing Director. Of primary concern to Ira Aten's story is Mr. B. H. "Barbeque" Campbell, the ranch's general manager so nicknamed for his brand—BQ. Barbeque Campbell was a character. XIT foreman Mac Huffman pegged him right and tight: "Barbeque had the gall of a government mule. He was a great big fellow with a big face, was overbearing, talked lots, and might meet you for the first time and before he got away try to bulldoze you into something."[51] Campbell was frugal with personal funds, extravagant—even wasteful—with the ranch's assets.[52]

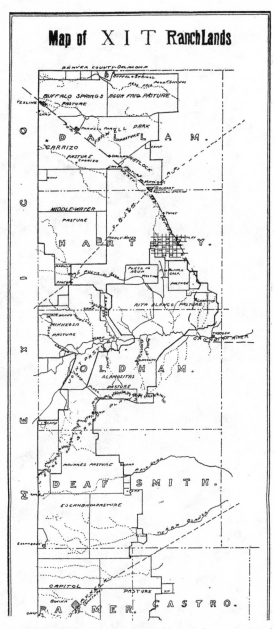

XIT Map. Note the Escarbada Division situated in southwestern Deaf Smith County and the location of its headquarters just inside the Texas boundary line with New Mexico Territory. This spot, lonely as it might have been, would be home to Ira and Imogen for approximately six years.   *Courtesy Nita Stewart Haley Memorial Library & J. Evetts Haley History Center.*

Escarbada Headquarters complex. A lonesome world to its own. *Courtesy Nita Stewart Haley Memorial Library & J. Evetts Haley History Center.*

He too was reckless about the company he kept, a troubling predilection that oozed into the selection process of the workforce and idlers he was hiring—or just letting hang out sopping up free gravy. Somewhat concerned, John V. Farwell engaged attorney Avery L. "A. L." Matlock. He was to make an investigation into the ranch's books, business practices and hiring principles. For blustery Barbeque Campbell the jig was up. "Matlock talked with the cowboys, saw men working there—or upon the payroll—who had been run out of other sections of Texas, saw the ranch harboring horse thieves, saw lax business management, evidences of theft, and general lawlessness."[53]Barbeque Campbell's "loose herding" of the syndicate's cowboys, all carrying six-shooters, had over but a short spate of time allowed the ranch to become a safe haven and rendezvous for cow thieves, outlaws, and "hard cases of all kinds."[54] In but short order, because the ranch was infested with pure-quill desperadoes, the XIT gained distinction as "the hellhole of the West."[55]On one section of the ranch (later the Escarbada Division, meaning Escarpment, Scrapings), cutthroats and gamblers were gathering with regularity, "where they had a regular monte bank, where men from the distant parts of the ranch, and from long distances off the ranch, came to gamble and stayed for days at a time, at the expense of the Company.... that the regular gamblers go down from Tascosa to Escarbada to gamble with the men...."[56] The section, wild and isolated as it was, beckoned caution for lawmen—few as there were. Texas Rangers riding the vast Panhandle, due to the potential for serious trouble, were mandated by one of their bosses to "carry 120 Rounds of ammunition on ever[y] Scout we [they] went on."[57] The horrid and unprofitable mess was wholly unacceptable to John Farwell. His directive to attorney Matlock was clear and curt: "Go take charge of the ranch and run it as though it were your own."[58] Barbeque Campbell was out. A. G. Boyce was in, the new general manager.

Reorganization of the XIT was then underway. It was a man-sized job. The ranch was gargantuan. In this instance 3,000,000-plus acres—the way it was surveyed—equated to a chunk of real-estate 200 unbroken miles long on its western border with New Mexico Territory.[59] The ranch, by this time encircled and cross-fenced by 6,000 miles of barbed wire, maintained a not immodest carrying capacity of between 125,000 to 150,000 head.[60] General Manager Boyce fired cowhands with dubious reputations and subdivided the ranch into seven separate divisions or pastures, each with their own

James M. "Jim" Cook, a one-time Escarbada Division Manager,
genuine tough *hombre*, and the first sheriff of Deaf Smith County
(Hereford). *Courtesy Deaf Smith County Historical Museum.*

superintendent, each autonomously responsible for their assigned
bailiwicks—fiefdoms within themselves. The Escarbada Division
was situated about midway between the northern and southern
points of the XIT, naturally bordering New Mexico Territory. This
specific 937.5-square mile, 600,000-acre cross-fenced province was
somewhat geographically apart from the other divisions. It was not
pancake flat. The Escarbada hosted the "Canadian [River] breaks,
with their creeks, canyons, hills, and scrub timber...."[61] The topography was near perfect operating territory for cow thieves, and they
were eating up the Escarbada, running stolen cattle west across

Escarbada's main house. Imogen Aten traded an upgraded residence over the Dimmitt dugout for seclusion on the XIT's most troublesome division. Here the Aten family gathers before a fireplace: Imogen and Ira, and children L to R: Ira Dunlap, Albert Boyce, Imogen, and Marion Hughes. Note the window is covered to prevent a would-be assassin's unobstructed view inside.   *Courtesy Jeri and Gary Boyce Radder.*

the line into New Mexico Territory, then yet unfenced open range country—and from there who knew where? Old-timer J. E. Moore noted brusquely: "Thieves bothered a great deal around Escarbada." One day XIT men riding the western fence found a green yearling hide with an XIT brand hanging on the top wire, with a welcome note: "We're camped over here in the canyon. Come on over and eat some XIT beef—if you feel lucky." The cowboys opting to exercise common sense had "no appetite for an ambush" and did not try to invade the canyon in some foolhardy puff at machismo. James M. "Jim" Cook, a sure enough tough two-gun man, was put in charge of the Escarbada. He was "eternally at odds" with those cow thieves across the XIT's western fence. Jim's fighting reputation was fierce. So, too, was his affinity for perfume and skirts. "Femininity and cattle mix poorly." Jim was out, Mac Huffman was in, quickly replaced by Jim McLaren.[62]

Losses continued nonstop, financially dragging the XIT's bottom line into the red inkwell. A. G. Boyce was not happy, but he was a fixer. Although he was tough-as-nails, Boyce was the general manager, much too busy to focus on a single division, even one with substantial troubles. He was in need of a real tough *hombre*, someone rawhide tough. The Castro County Sheriff got the call—a division manager's position awaited Austin Ira Aten at the Escarbada.

Chapter 15

"I'll shoot you right through the middle"

Ira mulled over A. G. Boyce's proposal. At first Imogen was not enthralled with the idea. It would necessitate relocation. More troubling from her perspective was the fact her husband was being promised the moon and was not being courted for his cow sense, but for his gunmanship. In fact the clever Mr. Boyce was glossing over that pesky aspect and had promised "that he did not intend to manage the ranch very many years, as he was getting old, and that when he retired he would have worked me [Ira] into the general management."[1] Clearly nearly everyone in the Panhandle saw Ira as a standup lawman, but in the cow camps he wasn't necessarily seen as an expert stockman—not by all: "Aten wasn't much of a cowman."[2] Yet, for Sheriff Aten the offer was tempting. Not unwisely Ira hedged his bet. He would stand for reelection and then decide.

For a majority of Castro County voters there was no dispute; their man was the incumbent. On November 6, 1894, Ira Aten by virtue of the election had his sheriff's contract renewed. For this go-round. Ira's political tenure was short. It has always been best to quit at the top of one's game. In January 1895 Sheriff Ira Aten tendered his resignation to the Castro County Commissioners. Did he have a temporary replacement in mind? Sure, his deputy brother-in-law John Ely Boyce would make a fine sheriff, if given the chance. And, so it was.[3]

Imogen and Ira and their children Marion Hughes and Albert Boyce took up residence at the XIT's Escarbada Division headquarters, located in the recently organized Deaf Smith County (Hereford). By any measure Deaf Smith County was a cowboy county. The first county seat was La Plata (formerly Grenada, created by the XIT) and was so at the time the Atens moved to the Escarbada. Big ranch influence controlled Deaf Smith County politics. The ground had been home base a decade earlier for disorganized waddies in their ineffectual try at unionizing during the legendary cowboy strike of '83. At the time Ira and Imogen removed onto the huge Escarbada

281

Division, Nathan Edgin was the second county sheriff, occasionally housing disheartened prisoners in his "single iron cell of indeterminate manufacture." Beyond doubt at the time, lonesome Deaf Smith County was at the "fringe of civilization" jutting up right against the ever-turbulent New Mexico Territory line. In the less than populous county, a person unfortunately taken ill was treated through a third-hand analysis most of the time. A hard-riding cowboy would race for Amarillo, near eighty miles away, carefully guarding the list of symptoms tucked into his shirt's buttoned-tight pocket. A couple of days later the messenger would at the gallop return with the good doctor's diagnosis, the soup drinking and bed rest instructions, as well as the prescribed medicine—if even available in the Panhandle.[4] Compulsory surgeries were more complicated, the logistical nightmares alone maddening, not even taking into account the inherent peril facing the patient. Escarbada necessities—supplies for both home and ranch—were brought by laboriously slow freight wagons continuously inching out their roundtrips—seven days a week, thirty days a month.[5] The Escarbada was for the most part a desolate world to its own: Division Superintendent Austin Ira Aten its metaphorical Master and Lord. Although Ira was managing a working subdivision of the cooperate giant, overseeing as many as 30,000 to 40,000 head of cattle, branding upwards of 10,000 calves every year, he was under no benign storybook illusion: His actual charge was to put the brakes on, and then stop the wholesale thievery underway—by fair means or foul. Talk, threats, and gentle intimidation was okay, if it worked; stronger methods, Colt's and Winchesters if it didn't.

Division Manager Aten took over administration of the Escarbada from Jim McLaren. According to Ira, "they [thieves] were giving so much trouble that he could not seem to cope with the situation."[6] A young cowboy, William "Billie" Timmons, while certainly not disputing Ira Aten, suggests another or additional reason for McLaren's separation from the XIT, one he personally witnessed. In preparing for a trail drive to the XIT's Montana finishing range Jim McLaren was inventorying supplies as they were loaded into a wagon for the journey. General Manager A. G. Boyce was nearby, observing. One of the items McLaren marked off his list were two pairs of collar pads for the mules. On the previous year's trip wet pads due to sweat and rain had galled the team's shoulders, causing nasty sores. Billie Timmons recounted the exchange between Boyce and McLaren:

Seeing the pads, Mr. Boyce asked, "What're you going to do with them?" "I'm going to protect these mules' shoulders," Jim replied. "I swore last year if I ever drove another herd I'd do something so I wouldn't have sore-shouldered mules." "Jim, if you drive a herd for me," Mr. Boyce declared, "you'll put those collar pads back and drive just like you did last year." That got Jim. "Well, then, I won't drive your damned herd," he said. Boyce replied calmly but with finality. "That's good, Jim, there're a lot of damned good men looking for a job as trail driver." "Yes," Jim said heatedly, "and there're men looking for a damned good trail driver, and I'm that." I [Timmons] told Jim good-bye and never saw him again.[7]

Soon after taking over his $75-per-month managerial duties at the Escarbada, Ira tendered his Descriptive List to Texas Adjutant General Mabry: It was not voluntary. Special Rangers were required to file those niggling monthly reports highlighting their activities and Ira had been remiss: "Herewith please find my descriptive list as requested & am sorry that I have neglected to make a monthly

Though there are many photos of XIT cowboys, these were some of the toughest: They actually rode for the Escarbada Division. *Courtesy Deaf Smith County Historical Museum.*

report as the law required. How-ever accept thanks for you kindness in the past & hope you will not think too hard of me for my neglecting a required duty."[8] Though he now held no official law enforcement commission, XIT Division Manager Aten had not laid aside an interest in the work just because he had taken up residence on the Escarbada. Quite the contrary.

First and foremost boss Aten was a "protection man." It was not then some funny terminology. A protection man did just that: protect the ranch and its property from interlopers and long-ropers. General Manager A. G. Boyce gave Ira Aten two things to facilitate his assignment: Winchesters and a free hand. In turn Ira Aten took several steps he thought necessary—practical. He doubled his life insurance policy to $5,000 and had windows on the ranch house painted dark green, indemnity against would-be assassins lurking about the headquarters complex. Then he looked over his workforce. Next he put out the call for trustworthy backup. He had a couple of fellows in mind. Successfully—in a manner of speaking—he recruited two topnotch fighting men with Texas Ranger backgrounds, Wood Saunders and Big Ed Connell. The Escarbada was of such gigantic proportion that five subcamps had been previously established, two of which were critical in Ira's estimation. Wood took up position in the Trujillo Camp, west, over on the New Mexico line north of headquarters; Big Ed, still holding a paid Ranger's commission, was stationed at the Tombstone Camp, on the Escarbada's eastern flank. Besides some regular Texas Ranger work, Big Ed was tasked with guarding that section called "the strip," an area where the "little men" would slip into the pasture stealing XIT livestock, almost at their leisure.[9] Ranger Ed Connell backs up Ira's averment that there was a great deal of depredation taking place on the Escarbada's cow herd, and that the state's Texas Rangers lending a helping hand to heavily invested stockmen was but par business. Ranger Connell corroborated: "The Syndicate needed some officers stationed out here [XIT] to keep down the stealing. I got in a lot of criminal work here."[10] That particularly cozy relationship between the big cowmen and the Texas Rangers, and Ira Aten's political savvy and efficacy, are again evidenced by the remarks of Big Ed Connell:

> He [Aten] quit the sheriff's office to run the Escarbada and in less than thirty days he had A. G. Boyce take the matter up

Ex-Texas Ranger Wood Saunders got the call from Ira to help rid the Escarbada Division of ne'er-do-wells and cow thieves. He intrepidly reported for duty armed and ready for war. *Courtesy Nita Stewart Haley Memorial Library & J. Evetts Haley History Center.*

with the Captain of my Ranger Company, Captain W. J. McDonald, to have me stationed out on his division. I never did [cowboy] work with the hands of the XIT, though I kept a camp and the Syndicate paid me twenty-five dollars a month besides my salary as a Ranger.[11]

In speaking of that Escarbada section bordering New Mexico Territory, worked from the Trujillo Camp, Ira was plain about how wild and woolly it really was: "I never kept a married man at Trujillo, as they were so tough around there. Ed [Connell] was afraid to eat with the fellows over there, afraid they would poison him."[12] There was a standing operating procedure for Escarbada cowboys while assigned or visiting at the Trujillo Camp. In Aten's words:

We always kept heavy curtains on the windows at the Trujillo camp. When a man rode up there at night and said, "Hello,"
the camp man would not go out until he recognized the man's
voice or found out who he was. Then when he went to the door,
if he was not sure, he would try to get the drop on whoever was
outside or have the advantage. A man never went out of that
camp without his six-shooter. I went to Trujillo one night, rode
up and called, and thought the man recognized me. I walked in
the door and White, who was there, had a six-shooter sticking
in my belly as I stepped in. "Why," he said, "Mr. Aten!" "Yes," I
replied. "I thought you recognized my voice."[13]

At both the Escarbada headquarters compound and at the Tombstone Camp, according to Ira, Mrs. Aten and Mrs. Connell always
answered the door—not the men. The likelihood of a woman being
mercilessly gunned down was nil. Ira or Big Ed, standing inside in
the shadows with a six-shooter or double-barreled shotgun in hand
until a visitor or stranger was satisfactorily identified and his business made known, was but smart.[14]

Recapping general information about the Escarbada is useful—
interesting—and pertinent. The division's workforce during winter
months was trimmed by a third, down to about a dozen. Two of
those fellows, Frank Fuller and Charlie Orr, on or about the first day
of January, were put to "wolfing." The XIT furnished them with two
horses, a light wagon, and foodstuffs, but no salary through the winter. Until the spring roundup kicked off in April, the guys were on
their own hook. They could, however, make more money "wolfing"
than "cowboying." The county paid a bounty of $5 for the scalp of
every wolf—little or big, grownup or pup. The XIT added another $5.
On one occasion at a wolf's den, Frank and Charlie drew straws to see
who would crawl in, six-shooter in hand. Charlie came up short. On
his belly in he went, flickering candle in one hand, .45 Colt's in the
other. Mrs. Wolf was not in the mood for company. She saw opportunity and a glimmer of daylight atop Charlie's back. Charlie's first shot
missed. He didn't have time for a second. The clawing and scratching
bitch wolf "undressed him" on the way out of her den. Luckily Frank
was outside, Winchester handy, and though he earned the $10 that
day, he could barely control the laughter—joviality Charlie didn't
come to appreciate. When cowboys other than those officially put to
wolfing by a stroke of good luck ran across a lobo on the Escarbada—

At Ira's behest Texas Ranger Ed Connell was moved onto the Escarbada Division to back his and Saunders' play. Ranger Connell (future sheriff of Deaf Smith County) drew wages from both the State of Texas and the XIT, a pretty nifty financial arrangement. *Courtesy Research Center, Texas Ranger Hall of Fame and Museum.*

there were plenty—a little fun was called for. If the wolf was operating on an empty stomach the chase was on, and on, and on, until miles later some lucky horsebacker finally popped the lucky shot—he got the scalp and claimed the prize money. On the other hand, if the wolf had just feasted, having a belly engorged with mouthwatering XIT beef slowing it down, the catch ropes were uncoiled and real cowboy sports demonstrated their skill, though they did not jump down and deftly tie three paws with a rodeo performer's flair. The wolf was simply unceremoniously dragged to limpness—then scalped. Many children living out on the far-flung Panhandle ranches could ill afford to have dogs as pets due to the large number of poison baited wolf traps. Whether for play or work, wolfing was serious business in the Panhandle.[15]

Perhaps even more crucial was the windmill crew. They worked all year around. There was on the Escarbada very little natural water. There were however, some twenty to twenty-five dirt tanks made by shoring dams across draws and approximately fifty to sixty windmills. A malfunctioning windmill or an eroding dirt tank dam is useless and costly. Consequently, two men were on constant duty, one horse and a wagon, a month's supply of grub, snuff, parts and tools, and elementary school orders: Keep things running and flowing. Come back to Escarbada headquarters once a month, replenish, and then start working the same circuit again till the beans and coffee and tobacco were gone.[16]

Once weather marched the line of dependability, along about April, the cowboy crew was increased—for the Escarbada about thirty-five—and the dawn-to-dusk cow work began. The general roundup and branding went on continuously until about Christmas, as scattered cattle were shaped into herds large enough to make holding worthwhile. Special attention—whenever found—was given to putting a red-hot XIT on mavericks, those animals weaned by nature, but not yet marked by a ranch's familiar logo. If a cow thief got there first, well, it was finders keepers. Ira Aten's orders regarding unbranded calves—even if but one day old—was easy to interpret: "Brand 'em!" His logic may or may not have been as charitable as he told his crew: "You may save some good cowboy from becoming a cow thief." Pocketknife castration, doctoring, and branding was all in a day's work—as was making sure boundary and cross fences were upright and tight. The herds had to be culled, the old and barren cows separated, then shipped or driven to Channing, Hartley County, the XIT's general headquarters. Back on the Escarbada, uncut male yearlings went to the bull pasture, and replacement heifers were trailed faraway enough and held until they reached breeding age. On the Escarbada, in addition to cow work, the breaking of some thirty-odd head of cowponies was necessary for keeping the division's number of using horses at about 150. Sometimes, when there was an especially select horse gathered, the excited Mr. Walter Farwell of the ownership group, during one of his periodic visits to the ranch, would covetously appropriate the animal for his string of polo horses, an act that chafed Ira Aten. He

Division Manager Ira Aten, seated far left, takes a dinner break with other Escarbada Division cowboys.   *Courtesy Nita Stewart Haley Memorial Library & J. Evetts Haley History Center.*

wanted, indeed needed, the good horses on the ranch, his division of the ranch, the Escarbada.[17] There was not a stake of actual owner-ship, but there was proprietary pride. And, Ira Aten owned a plate-ful of pride.

The sheer isolation of the Escarbada is highlighted by enumer-ating three harsh realities: Imogen Aten's nearest female neighbor, Mrs. Rhea, was residing over fifteen miles away in the New Mexico Territory; mail came to the Escarbada but once a week, and some-times three weeks between; and once a year Ira, driving a "big hack," would take Imogen and the children to Amarillo for a shopping spree, a not trivial eighty-mile one-way trip taking three days to manage going, and three coming back. For those trips outside or within the huge ranch property, Ira had expressly outfitted the wagon for his beloved wife and the kids with accommodations for sleeping.[18] Nat-urally the outings were made while Old Man Winter was napping, summertime.

Something else came out with the warm days: rattlesnakes. Since there was very little to do for family entertainment, some-times Ira would hitch the buggy, allowing Imogen and the two boys to accompany him on an inspection trip, not to the Trujillo Camp though. He remembered one such trip in particular, one to the Toro Camp at the northeast corner of the Escarbada. Naturally the daytime trip was an open-air experience, but in this instance the nighttime was to be pleasantly passed slumbering beneath the Pan-handle's moon and stars, listening to the coyotes yelp. Little kids like picnics and sleeping outside. Bedrolls (cowboys called them "hot-rolls") were spread. Imogen shrieked! A big diamondback slith-ered into a hole on the bed-ground. Little Marion and Albert froze in curious bewilderment: stand still or run? Ira had fended off big-ger threats than a snake. Nonchalantly he grabbed a spade, shov-eled dirt into the hole, tamped it firmly with a boot heel, and laid his suggans (blankets) atop the now stopped-up orifice—and sat down, unworriedly saying: "That snake will not bother us now."[19] And it didn't.

Two-legged snakes were also slithering across the XIT's land, the Escarbada in particular; that is what had landed Ira Aten his manage-ment job. By this time in Ira Aten's narrative it is no news that the man of medium physical stature was a dynamo when it came to guts and/or gunfighting. It might stand articulate debate that he could sometime slip off of the half-cock notch, but never that his threats or promises were just "hot air." Ira Aten may have been aging but he wasn't losing his edge. Strangers had no business riding the Escarbada's pastures, not without Ira's okay. One day he bumped into one on the eastern side of the section. The fellow was wearing a six-shooter—manfully—but he was mouthy. In Ira's mind the outsider was "talking ugly." Ira Aten had a clear message for the rascal, whoever he was, even if he hailed from Hell: "Now, you get your horse, saddle, and go. Take that road there and never come back, and when you start don't look back." Grabbing his Winchester, Ira punctuated his warning, "If you look back, I am going to shoot you right through the middle."[20] The suspected cow thief didn't need an interpreter or a chiropractor. He kept his neck straight and his eyes to the front—he never looked back.

From his Ranger days Aten had learned the value of current knowledge in keeping abreast of matters, an especially priceless tool for catching crooks. The cowboy grapevine was not useless, but its

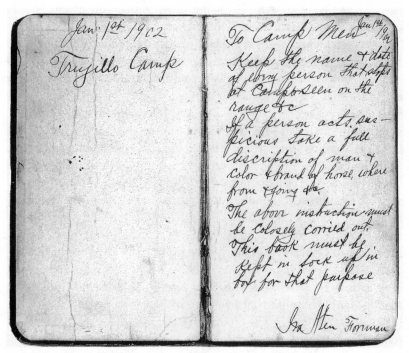

Lockbox notebook for the Escarbada's Trujillo Camp. Note Ira Aten's no nonsense directives to trusted men. *Courtesy Nita Stewart Haley Memorial Library & J. Evetts Haley History Center.*

shortcomings were wholly wedded to what someone wanted to tell—
or not tell. Sometimes a friend got the wink, a stranger the blame.
Mr. Aten had his unfussy solution. At both the Trujillo and Tombstone Camps he initiated the lockbox model for keeping up with the
news. Only trusted personnel were given a key. Their orders were
short in words, tall in meaning: "Keep the name and date of every
man who stays all night, passes camp, or seen on range. If the person is a suspicious character take a full description of man & color &
brand of horse, & where from & where going, etc. The above instruc-
tion must be closely carried out. This book must be kept in lock up
box for that purpose."[21] Therein was a paper record of who was passing through the Escarbada, and what business they had inside the
pasture. And, for Ira's way of thinking, unless he had been overtly
clued-in on that proposed or stated business beforehand, a chap
had no good business inside the Escarbada's wire. A parallel policy,
then, for the Escarbada, was pretty well understood. That troublesome west side of the division, the New Mexico Territory side, where
cow thieves were constantly taking down fence and driving herds
of XIT cattle to unrestricted openness and into the abyss of mysterious disappearance, was subject to Ira Aten's hard diktat: Shoot
first, as a "preventative."[22] Aten was not mealy mouthed with any
mislaid political correctness: "We used to shoot at the boys across
the fence.... whenever we saw them just to keep them scared off &
we did this rather frequently." Division Manager Aten, for this job,
had absolutely no use for the criminal court system in Deaf Smith
County, because "they would not convict for cow stealing." Almost
proudly Ira bragged—not incorrectly though—that while at the XIT
he never, once, "had a man arrested," but "we handled the cases our-
selves."[23] Make no bones about it, Mr. Ira Aten was his own man: "Up
in Hartley County Old Man [A. G.] Boyce had them in court all the
time but rarely got a conviction. But that was not my way of dealing with that class of people."[24] As a point of pride, whether riding
alone or in the company of one or more XIT cowboys, Ira Aten could
look into the mirror and truthfully say: "I never saw an unknown
man in the pasture but that I went to him." When he closed with the
stranger Ira's message was plain: leave the Escarbada as "there was a
danger of getting shot." Just to make sure the meaning was not lost
in translation, Aten would personally escort the wayward sightseer
or scalawag to the closest fence line, but not injudiciously: "I would
ride over to the fence with him talking as we rode along, even though

it might be five or six miles. If he happened to be armed, I would ride a little behind him and to his right, so I could watch him."[25] A false move would have been suicide.

With the stealth of a puma on the prowl Ira Aten roamed the Escarbada pastures, always alternating his routes, never returning on the same trail he had gone out on. Aten was not hesitant to travel the division's vast reaches, alone. His backbone didn't need a splint. Ira Aten would unexpectedly stop in at one of the Escarbada's scattered camps. There he would rest, take a meal, and check the lockbox. Whether the assigned cowboy or cowboys were in camp or not was immaterial. Ira would write down instructions for placement in the lockbox. Ira might mention from which direction he had come and who he'd seen, "but did not write where I was going as I did not want them to know." Aten was cagy. Friendship with the working cowboys was okay by him, but not at the cost of being blindsided by treachery from within. He was being paid to be vigilant. Ex-Texas Ranger (future Deaf County Sheriff) and one of Ira Aten's chief protection men, Big Ed Connell, summed up his *nominal* boss's nose for the hunt. "There never was a better officer than Aten. He could smell the direction a thief went. I don't believe there was ever a braver man that drawed breath."[26] High praise, indeed, from an intrepid lawman on the Panhandle scene, not a wishful thinking mythmaker with novelistic tone hammering out drivel. Big Ed Connell, too, depicted part of Ira's blueprint for survival: "He would never sit around close to a campfire at night but always got back. If a man came into camp he would never sleep until he found out what the fellow wanted and who he was. He was always careful."[27]

He, too, had to be careful with his bookkeeping. Unlike typical Texas ranches of the time, XIT division managers had to cope with prescribed record keeping—it went with the job. Ira Aten minces no words when describing the less than glamorous responsibilities he was tasked with:

> The foreman made monthly reports in which they gave the calf brandings with the number of heifers and the number of steer calves. Also they gave the number of cattle that had died, the number of horses, the conditions of the ranch, a weather report, the number of men whom they worked, the payroll, and the like. These were sent from each division and

tabulated at Chicago. Then each division made an annual report of conditions.[28]

Besides the mandatory monthly and annual reports the XIT's upper-management had formalized in writing the expectations of and prohibited conduct for ranch employees—a working cowboy's manual. Twenty-three rules demanded compliance or discharge. From the everyday cowhand's perspective the rules were easy to understand but not necessarily popular. Particularly the prohibitions against carrying six-shooters, largely ignored on the Escarbada (Winchester saddle-guns were okay), the use of "vinous, malt, spirituous, or intoxicating liquors," and gambling in any form whatsoever, were irksome strictures to free-spirited boys of the range. Other guidelines were for the XIT cowboys normally complied with anyway, such as not abusing their assigned horses; not being allowed to strike the animal over the head or spur across the shoulder. They could run wolves with ranch mounts, but not antelope or mustangs. For ranch work a cowboy was required to use XIT horses, although he could own two private horses—pastured at a location determined by the division manager. Perhaps everyone in the Panhandle could clearly understand the motive for another rule: "Loafers, 'sweaters,' deadbeats, tramps, gamblers, or disreputable persons, must not be entertained at any camp, nor will employees be permitted to give, loan or sell such persons any grain, or provisions of any kind, nor shall such person be permitted to remain on the Company's land anywhere under any pretext whatever." Other rules, however, had a direct impact on Panhandle folks not employed by the ranch, and their implementation was communally abrasive. But two of those little strictures, Numbers 17 and 18, are illustrative:[29]

> Employees of neighboring ranches on business are to be cared for at all camps, and their horse fed if desired (provided there is feed at the camp to spare); but such persons will not be expected to remain on the ranch longer than is necessary to transact their business, or continue their journey.
>
> Bona fide travelers may be sheltered if convenient, but they will be expected to pay for what grain and provisions they get, at prices to be fixed from time to time by the Company, and all such persons must not remain at any camp longer than one night.

For Texans raised in cow country, someone actually having the unmitigated gall to write down such stuff about putting limits on hospitality was exactly what could be expected of "damn Yankees" residing in faraway Chicago, Illinois. To some ranch folks such asinine formality made the XIT "the most unpopular outfit in the Panhandle." A cultural convention of ranching folks' generosity had always been found in the West—the real West—and "no stranger had ever been denied free shelter and food for himself and his horse."[30] "In a single stroke the syndicate had wiped out the code of the old West and pre-scribed a new order."[31] Tradition and cow camp cordiality counted for something, but the XIT's "owners and operators were Eastern finan-ciers who had no intention either of becoming Texans or of adopting the customs of the region. The lax business methods of the majority of the cattlemen were openly frowned upon by the XIT financiers. As a result, they were heartily disliked both by cowboys and ranch-men...."[32] Reading between lines is pointless while checking ex-XIT cowboy Anderson Witherspoon's observations:

> About 1898 I left the X I T's and went to the L X's on the Canadian. I stayed here about two years and then went with the Prairie Cattle Company. Here they had a real cow outfit—the best horses, the best cow hands, the best cattle, and the best boss I ever saw. This boss was Joe Frazier. When I left this Com-pany, I turned in ten head of the best cow horses I ever saw. Here, too, the wages were higher. The X I T's paid $25, the L X's $30, and the Prairie Cattle Company $35. They also fed better and furnished better horses. Once while I was with the X I T's a cowboy took some axle grease and wrote STARVATION in big letters on the side of the wagon. The boss [Ira ?] was plenty mad but never found out who did it.[33]

In fact, although it is indefensible, the XIT was so despised in particular quarters that swiping a steer whenever a fellow got the chance was but fair play—getting back at the condescending nitwits: "Many men considered it more of a crusade than a crime to steal from the syndicate."[34]

One cowboy who was not put off by the persnickety rules or the XIT's less than charitable reputation—and more than happy to draw that $25 a month paycheck—was Ira's brother Cal. Moving his Mattie Jo to the Panhandle, Cal took a job cowboying on the XIT in

Deaf Smith County courthouse at La Plata, before the county seat was moved to Hereford. *Courtesy Deaf Smith County Historical Museum.*

Oldham County, near Adrian, eyeing opportunity and saving funds for the day he could lay cash on the barrel-head, taking up title to his own ranch.[35]

Brother Eddie was yet a Texas Ranger, a good Texas Ranger, at least it seemed so to Captain John R. Hughes. On July 25, 1895, Eddie was promoted to 1st Sergeant of Company D, the position Ira had held prior resigning to take the Fort Bend County job.[36]

Ira's two older brothers, Thomas and Frank, were still making their homes in the interior, as was Preacher Aten and his wife, Kate. In fact Frank, at the time Ira took the XIT position, was Justice of the Peace, Precinct 4, Travis County, but later moved to a farm in Williamson County. Besides raising children, of whom Frank and Josie had six, he was gaining national renown as a beekeeper, collecting honey from 325 colonies. Locally he sold the produce at 6¢ a pound, but had so much that "he found it necessary to ship it out and send it to Galveston to be shipped as ballast to a New York firm. 'It weighs twelve pounds to the gallon and water weighs eight; so it's good ballast.' The charge was ten cents per one hundred pounds."[37]

Bees may have been busy in Williamson County, but thieves were buzzing in Deaf Smith County. Astutely Ira Aten finagled himself or was elected to a precinct constable's position. The title allowed him a law enforcement commission, since he no longer carried six-shooter authority as a Special Texas Ranger.[38] On one occasion he was notified by cowboys working the Yellow House Division's pasture that *mal hombres* were driving cows and calves west toward the New Mexico Territory line. The suspects had "waved around" the two XIT cowboys, meaning that they did not want to be closely approached. The unarmed cowboys had looked up Ira. Division Manager Aten's response was so very typical of his deportment: "I took a boy and loped down there that afternoon, but of course they were gone. I struck them near Sandy Point about ten miles south of Trujillo and about twelve miles from where I had a herd in the Trujillo pasture. They dropped their cattle and got out immediately, of course. They did not expect anybody to come up from the south...."[39]

Between the cow work, paperwork, and protection work, Ira could barely catch his breath. Those outside the Escarbada wire may or may not have harbored ambivalent feelings about Ira and his ruthless methods, but one and all knew him to be diligent—and sharp. While visiting with Big Ed Connell on the Trujillo side, Ira received word from an XIT cowboy that two fellows from across the New Mexico Territory line had passed by driving a herd of thirty or forty horses, no doubt stolen. Connell and Ira set off in pursuit, or as Big Ed said, "We lit out."[40] About sundown the thieves heading northeast into Potter County (Amarillo) were located "fixing to bed their stock for the night" in a barren draw. Big Ed matter-of-factly just said: "Ira, there they are; let's get 'em." Aten was not ready to shift gears prematurely, replying: "Ed, we are working for the Syndicate and we have no papers, and if we do go after them we may have to kill one or both of them and they may take it out on the Company." Though it made sense to Big Ed, he was not happy. But, he did agree to accompany Ira to Amarillo and "get papers" (John Doe warrants). Unfortunately the time delay was to the thieves' benefit; they had given Ira and Ed and even—by then—some Company B Rangers the slip. With pressing Escarbada affairs in want of tending, Ira returned to the ranch. Connell did not. Letting Big Ed finish up the story is best. It is insightful and interesting, maybe with a touch of comedy:

I figured which way the thieves might go and out toward Panhandle [Carson County] and struck their trail about twenty five miles out from Amarillo.... I found that they had not passed Panhandle that day.... When morning came I caught my horse knowing that I was ahead of them—went back about ten miles and saw the fellows ahead breakfasting.... They were in a lake [bed] and not a hoof in sight. They had run the horses off over the hill into another lake. I knew it would not do to go straight up to them as they would have the advantage, so I rode sidling up to them with my left side toward them. I had my Winchester slipped out and was holding it down beside my leg on the opposite side. I eased up and made out like I was hunting a roundup, looking all around. They had their Winchesters in their laps eating breakfast. When I was about a hundred yards from them they slipped their plates off their laps and started to pick up their guns. I jumped off my horse on the right side, threw down on them, and told them to drop their guns. One started to raise his and I yelled to him that I would kill him. All the time I was going towards them as fast as I could. When I got up close I told them to raise up, but keep their hands in the air, and they did so, their guns sliding off their laps. Then I got one of them to come up to me and took his six-shooter off, then I had him back off and the other one up. There I had two men, two Winchesters, and two six-shooters; but my horse had run off when I jumped down and I was afoot. I looked around and saw a man passing down the road and I waved my hat at him. He loped down. I told him my predicament and he loped off and caught my horse. Then I made him bring the thieves horses in and had them make a rope corral and we caught the saddle horses and turned the others loose. I took them to Panhandle and put them in jail. Then I wired to Amarillo and a Ranger came out in a hack to get them. We put them in a hack and started in. The two were sitting there in the hack abusing one another for surrendering to me. One of them said: "Two of us could have whipped him, and now we are on our way to the pen." Out from Panhandle a little piece I saw a skunk sitting on a prairie dog hole a little ways off. I said to the Ranger: "Watch me knock that skunk's head off." I threw down and shot and he flopped over. "Now," said one of the fellows, "Do you see that? He would have killed both of us." They never abused one another after that, but I put up my six-shooter and called it a good shot.[41]

One of the chief responsibilities for cowboys working the Escarbada under Ira Aten's protection was to "ride the line," above all, that territory worked from the Trujillo Camp. The situation on that side had become "tense." Shameless cow thieves, if they were not tearing down fence making it appear as if accidently done by cattle, so they could be driven into New Mexico Territory, were intentionally setting pasture fires. A weary ride of fifty-plus miles a day on the fence line, to and fro, was commonplace. When it was determined that livestock had been "drifted out" the SOP was for Ira to summon his fighting men, Wood Saunders and Big Ed Connell, and broach the state borderline with a chuckwagon and cowboy crew, rounding up every bovine in sight for inspection. Few dared face Winchester disaster. Testing Messrs Aten, Saunders, and Connell was dangerous foolishness, something that was best put on the backburner, although one particular dustup was so steeped in controversy it did, much later, cause the coughing up of a civil lawsuit. During such sorties the XIT cattle were turned back east, the New Mexico Territory livestock left on the range. Quick work normally netted results, keeping losses to a manageable number—though the theft of a single bawling calf would irritatingly grate on a man's—a gunfighting man's—nerves.[42]

Something that else that would get on Ira's nerves was a lazy cowboy, a slacker. Around the first of March every year on the Escarbada the cowboys had to start riding "bog." The dirt water tanks would be low, mucky, and gluey. Cattle trying to escape the torment of a heel-fly by wading or searching for a refreshing drink often became hopelessly mired, trapped as mud sucked to their hocks—and higher. Unable to extricate itself the enmeshed animal would simply die of exhaustion and/or starvation. Its only salvation was that cavalier on horseback, the cowboy riding "bog." The roping was easy. The pulling was hard. Nine times out of ten, if found quick enough the cow brute was freed. On the Escarbada, for those three or four weeks, two special but temporary "bog camps" were maintained until the rains came and put out surface water. One time when near the Toro Camp, on a branch of the Agua Prieta, the good Mr. Aten found seventeen head desperately stuck—immovable absent a catch rope tattooing and a tugging. Ira pulled out five, all that his straining horse could manage. The cowboy stationed in that vicinity was not around, nowhere to be found. He had vanished in the vastness, out somewhere for awhile, a little while. Ira fumed "when the man came along I was so mad I could not talk to him at the time, and I told him to go to Tombstone [Camp] and wait until I got there. I never saw him again. He got his private horse and left. He did not wait to get his pay."[43]

There were other exciting happenings on the Escarbada during March. On the thirtieth day, 1896, a third son was born to Ira and Imogen, Ira Dunlap.[44] Perhaps just qualifying as speculation, nevertheless it is but reasonable to suggest that from time to time the whole Aten family partook of dinner (lunch) at one of the roundup sites. For after wolfing down a plate of son-of-a-bitch stew and drag-

Ira Aten's sons L to R: Marion Hughes, baby Ira Dunlap, and Albert Boyce, yet dressed in a toddler's dress still common for the times. The XIT was a dandy place to grow up—for a boy. *Courtesy Jeri and Gary Boyce Radder.*

ging a cathead biscuit through the greasy but luscious juice, and after a quick cigarette if near a windmill, it was time for cowboys to top off their afternoon mounts. Most would pitch. And it was quite a show, green-broke cowponies pitching in unison, while wildly yipping Escarbada cowboys fought for dominance and a lasting seat in their cinched-tight caque (saddle).[45] After the fun was over, it was back to work tossing loops. Snagging and dragging. Unwilling and bawling calves, tacky slobber grudgingly clinging to their milk-splashed gums, were not politely acquainted with white-hot embers and red-hot XIT irons. The stench of burning hair and the manure-painted ground provided a backdrop that only cowmen, cowboys, and little children could appreciate. It was a dusty, dirty, and stinky business.

There was other business to conduct also, personal business. Realizing there was no probability of them returning to Castro County, Ira and Imogen traded to Allen G. Bell their Dimmitt County property for his 184 acres in Williamson County on September 10, 1897.[46] Ira and Imogen were not, however, mulling over moving off of the XIT, not at that time anyway. The following month the couple entered into an agreement with Ira's brother Frank to buy the newly acquired Williamson County place, with Ira and Imogen carrying the note for two years.[47]

Progress was coming to the XIT, and by default to the Escarbada. Hard as it may be to believe, telephone communication was in vogue, even for a scattered outpost on the edge of civilization. Ira Aten highlights the forward evolution and the recurring headache it triggered:

> We used the top wire of the fences and put the telephone into the camps. Then the cowboys reported in that way instead of by writing. We had lots of trouble with our telephone line on the west side to Trujillo camp. The New Mexican fellows would ground our wires. They would take a real fine wire, and then run this little wire under the bark of the post and down into the ground to ground it. We would sometimes ride the fence two or three times before we found where that ground was, then we would have to peel the bark off the posts to find this small wire. Sometimes this was done for aggravation, sometimes for the purpose of throwing us out of communication with Trujillo while they were stealing cattle. But they soon found out that when we could not get in connection with Trujillo, I would be

out there riding the line looking out for anything that might happen. [48]

Division Manger Aten's suggestion that sometimes tampering with the telephone line was just an act of "aggravation" fits well with the aforementioned declaration that a sizable sampling of Panhandle folks were not enamored with the XIT kingdom in general, the Escarbada operation in particular, and the "strong-handed" tactics employed by one Mr. Austin Ira Aten.[49]

Besides tinkering with phone lines and snipping wire, some folks with a grudge against the XIT or cow thieves wanting to misappropriate cloven-footed assets resorted to the most devastating measure: arson. An uncontrolled inferno on the horizon not only spelled out monetary negatives as valuable grass was consumed, but was also an unwelcome distraction for hardworking cowboys. Firefighting XIT cowboys could ill afford the luxury of being on the lookout for thieves. Extinguishing a fire, or at a minimum controlling its path through backfires and sound firefighting techniques took precedence over all else. That was rule Number 13 in their manual: "In case of fire upon the ranch, or on lands bordering on the same, it shall be the duty of every employee to go to it at once and use his best endeavors to extinguish it, and any neglect to do so, without reasonable excuse, will be considered sufficient cause for dismissal."[50]

Assuredly the point of origin for many Panhandle wildfires could be traced to the tip of a lightning strike or the utter carelessness of someone discarding a store-bought match. On the XIT—at least on the Escarbada—smoking cigarettes was supposedly limited to the area around windmills and waterholes. Nicotine seizes its own authority though. A quick puff or two behind the boss's back would not be unexpected. Ira could live with that. He could take precautions, such as the summer he oversaw the plowing of 150 miles of fireguards along the Escarbada's outer fence,[51] or lookouts stationed at the top of a windmills during periods of high wind, scanning for an orange glow on the horizon when pastures were tinderbox dry, or having response wagons strategically placed, loaded with water barrels, foodstuffs, coffee and coffee pot—and half a dozen fire-brooms.[52] The accidental fire was a hazard to be dealt with. The arsonist was a hellion to be hunted—with vengeance. For a firebug, regardless of the motive, Division Manager Ira Aten had no sympathy.

Escarbada Division Manager Ira Aten, white shirt and black vest, managing the day's branding chores. *Courtesy Nita Stewart Haley Memorial Library & J. Evetts Haley History Center.*

Although in later life Ira Aten would write of infernos engulf-
ing the Texas Panhandle, one particular wildfire boiled his blood.[53]
Following extinguishment of a nasty fire Ira had decided to make
an investigation. Near Endee (Quay County), a "small community
of picket houses, with upright poles forming the walls and sod-
covered poles forming the roofs," on the New Mexico Territory side,
Aten found hoofprints going through the XIT fence—two riders
eastbound.[54]

Subsequent to piecing together a string of damaging clues, Ira
determined he knew who they were; two months before he had
denied one an okay to trap wild mustangs on the Escarbada:

> I had decided to stay at the Trujillo Camp for the night on
> the New Mexico fence line about ten miles from Endee. As I
> was jogging along the road toward camp I saw two men coming
> down the road toward me. Suddenly they whirled their horses
> off the road and went at great speed down a draw. I recognized
> them as the two men I had been told had left Endee for Texas
> the day before, and my suspicions were strengthened.[55]

Those suspicions were reinforced when on the distant horizon
Ira could detect that dreaded amber hue, and it was not a western
sunset. In Ira's mind he was sure—dead sure—who had set another
fire—a second attempt at burning him out so he would "not be able
to hold his job."[56] Aten had reached the breaking point. He would
"put the fear of death in their hearts." With a well-oiled Winchester
in hand and a Colt's six-shooter at his side, the Escarbada's tiger went
on the hunt. What happened next? There are two competing versions, both winding down to matching bottom lines. Ira would claim
that he intended to kill his adversary, no ifs, ands, or buts. Once he
learned of Aten's plan—and he had no reason to discount it—Ira's
target just up and disappeared. Friends had advised him that taking a hiatus at Cripple Creek, Colorado, was smart. This he did for
several years, until it was safe to return to his Panhandle stomping
grounds—once Ira had moved on. The ever straightforward Big Ed
Connell adds his two cents' worth, version two: "Old Man Boyce and
Ira Aten cornered him off over on the Trujillo bull pasture one time
and were going to kill him, but he talked them out of it. They finally
let him off on condition that he would never come back to the country and he did not until Boyce had been killed [next chapter] and Ira

Aten had left."[57] Though he in fact did answer to General Manager Boyce, there is not even the slightest doubt that it was Division Manager Ira Aten who brandished an iron glove on the Escarbada. Not only did he hold midlevel management rule from the XIT, but the multi-tasking Ira Aten owned Deaf Smith County political power, too.

Of course, it was a byproduct of the ranch. County Commissioners are elected by precinct. The Escarbada Division made up one-half of Deaf Smith County's land mass. For that section, then, XIT cowboys were the voting majority—maybe just a bloc of twenty—but solidly behind their boss at election time—and election time—and election time. The office was Ira's to have.[58]

Where and when Ira Aten acquired his business acumen is indeterminate, but apparently he had. For not only was he a Deaf Smith County public servant, but after the little town of Hereford blossomed, Ira was appointed to the Constitution Committee for the Hereford Board of Trade and later was an initial board member when the Hereford National Bank was chartered. Too, Ira Aten had been elected as an alderman when the little town was first incorporated, since he had acquired a little place of his own nearby, running a few cattle and horses carrying their own brands. Meager as it was, the little burg of Hereford offered more amenities for a wife and children than did the lonesome Escarabada. By any reasonable calculation Austin Ira Aten was thoroughly committed to community betterment and taking care of his family.[59]

So while Ira Aten was looking to shoot some fire starter or cow thief, all the time tending to the Ecarbada's ranching interests, and Deaf Smith County's administrative business, as well as commercial interests of his own, and while Cal was riding the XIT range roping and tripping and branding beeves, brother Eddie was having some fun, too.

Although time and mythos have been good to the Texas Rangers for their role in the story, the heaped-on credit may have been, in truth, somewhat overblown. Nevertheless, Sergeant Aten was a key player, and his hard work should not be diminished by an inconvenient fact check. Much hoopla has been written about how the Texas Rangers en masse came together at El Paso to prevent a prizefight. Normally lost in the hollows of retellings is obfuscation—purposely or otherwise—of a single and signal actuality that the proposed fight's promoter, Dan Stuart, once the Texas legislature had enacted laws making the scheduled bout illegal, had openly and publicly and forcefully spouted common-sense talk. Stuart reiterated the fact "he was a law-abiding man and would not conduct the prizefight on Texas soil in violation of the statutes, risking arrest, humiliation, and, of course, a financial wreck."[60] Even the gutsy Captain John R. Hughes, forecast—rightly—that the fight would not take place on Texas soil. Yet, Texas state politicos were pigheadedly determined to roll out the state's corps of Winchester Warriors.[61] Responding to orders, Texas Rangers hustled to El Paso to make sure Stuart was a man of his word. The whole story is steeped with folkloric embellishment, but Sergeant Eddie Aten was a busy fellow—that is indisputable. The Company D Monthly Return reveals: "Sergt. Aten made Scout from El Paso to Langtry to investigate arrangements made by Prizefighters—out 3 days, travelled 600 miles."[62] Unfortunately for anti-fight moralists, as history well records, the boxing match did come off, not in Texas but on a Rio Grande sandbar in Mexico, neighboring the waggish Judge Roy Bean's iniquitous Jersey Lilly Saloon. Regrettably, when all of the Rangers lined up for one of the most widely published Texas Ranger group photographs at El Paso, Sergeant Aten was elsewhere—doing his job. In the end the prizefight saga explicitly revealed Texas Rangers could be prepositioned in force for preventive enforcement actions, and that individual members would obey orders regardless of personal feelings about the validity of law, but the deployment caught contemporary criticism as being "overkill."[63]

Who was not being killed on the Escarbada were any cow thieves. Division Manager Aten, with the help of Saunders and Connell, had—over a period of several years—put fear into the hearts of would-be thieves and badmen with their "bold and cunning" devices.[64] Their methods, while lauded by XIT upper management, were disparaged by many Panhandle folks as too hardnosed and unwarranted. Ira Aten proffers an excuse—maybe partly true—"it was too quiet for the daring old Rangers, just doing routine cowpunching work and they quit and hunted fields anew."[65]

What was not quiet was the Aten household. Imogen's and Ira's three sons had to make room for another, but this time it would be a girl. On the fourth day of April 1898, little Miss Imogen Aten gulped for air and cried her way into the world. Her parents were ecstatic.[66] There was other news, later, that really was not any too good.

The Frontier Battalion—most of it—assembled at El Paso to put the kibosh on a prizefight that was unlikely from the outset to have taken place in Texas, not after the state legislature adopted prohibitions for pugilistic contests. A proficient and practical law enforcement historian theorizes rolling out Texas Rangers for this brouhaha was "an over kill that should have been avoided." Providentially the image of nattily dressed Lone Star lawmen armed for war added to the Texas Ranger mystique then—and surely does now. Unluckily Company D's 1st Sergeant Eddie Aten was working in far West Texas, shadowing would-be ringside promoters, and riding the rails from the New Mexico Territory line to Langtry, Val Verde County, Texas, as the time his comrades climbed the steps for a terrific photo op. He missed immortalization in the snapshot. *Courtesy Research Center, Texas Ranger Hall of Fame and Museum.*

George Washington Brumley and wife Caroline. Mr. Brumley had two dugouts, one at San Jon, New Mexico, and another in Deaf Smith County near Hereford, Texas. He frequently traveled between the two—crisscrossing the vast Escarbada Division. Often he camped at the Escarbada headquarters or at Twin Wells. Later he bought 9,000 acres of Escarbada Division ranch lands, Twin Wells included in the transaction. *Courtesy Dr. John Baker.*

The writing was on the wall. Profitability for the XIT was sinking. The gist of the XIT's decline is simple; at 3,000,000 acres the ranch was just too big to manage efficiently, especially with the upturns and downturns of the ever volatile livestock markets. The selloff of land began. One of the resilient Deaf Smith County pioneers that ended up with a portion of the Escarbada, 9,000 acres, was the ever-industrious George Washington Brumley and his devoted wife Caroline. Mr. Brumley had located two dugouts, one near Hereford, Texas, another scarcely across the XIT boundary fence, below San Jon, just inside the New Mexico Territory line. His obligatory travels between the two dugouts, geographically, necessitated a jaunt across the immense Escarbada. Many were the times he pleasurably visited and stayed the night at the Escarbada headquarters, or camped at the springs known as Twin Wells, a refreshing site he later acquired for his personal land dealings portfolio.[67]

Across that New Mexico Territory borderline in Quay County, and in line with Ira Aten's remembrances about the locale's strong number of cow thieves, the newly installed sheriff James Alexander Street had his hands full. The newfound county seat was Tucumcari, and Mr. Street, a former Bell Ranch cowboy and saloon owner, had been one of the town's founding fathers. The governor of New Mexico had appointed Street sheriff when the county was formally organized during 1903, and he would sustain that position afterwards through several election cycles. Sheriff Street, a man with a sterling reputation for fearlessness, had several man-sized headaches, namely with those cow thieves operating within his isolated ranch country jurisdiction—and another with bureaucracy's silly squabbling concerning the New Mexico Territorial Mounted Police, an outfit the sheriff would later ride for.[68] Asking the good Sheriff Street if the eastern side of Quay County adjoining the XIT was a hotbed for wide-loopers and brand blotchers would have been pointless. Jim Street and Ira Aten were in rock-solid agreement. That section—for a time—was a greenhouse for growing herds of "off color cattle."

Quay County, New Mexico Territory Sheriff James Alexander Street. His wild and woolly law enforcing bailiwick lay just across the XIT's western fence: Sparsely populated, but home turf to a few unruly cowboys, cow thieves, and pasture burners. Ira Aten and Sheriff Street, with huge territories to cover, were busy wardens. *Courtesy Tucumcari Historical Research Institute & Tucumcari Historical Museum.*

The XIT may have been undergoing a diminishing downsize, but Big Ed Connell's family was on the increase. Just as Aten had done with naming his first child after lifelong friend John R. Hughes, Ed Connell so honored Ira. The strength of that bond is evidenced by the arrival of twins in the Connells' home on May 17, 1904. Big Ed and wife Sophie named one twin E. F. and sometimes called him Bill. His brother was named Ira Aten.[69] No doubt his namesake beamed with heartfelt pride.

During 1904, Ira and Imogen decided to take their delayed honeymoon, traveling on a two-week visit to the St. Louis Fair. Imogen's sister babysat the youngsters while the happy couple vacationed, this "being the first time we [they] had ever been away from home together." Perhaps not fully realizing its captivating significance at the time, the Atens were particularly fascinated by the California Pavilion and the salesmanship of boosters promoting the Golden State. Ira declared to Imogen that whenever they relocated to another home it would be in California.[70] There is little room to doubt, upon their return to the remote and somewhat inaccessible Texas Panhandle, and after reuniting with the kiddos, their minds were working overtime, spinning with possibilities—excuses—justifications—big plans.

Though proffering a smidgen of guesswork might be tempting, reading between the lines of Ira's remarks from an evidentiary perspective is tricky, far short of conclusive. Nevertheless it is engaging. Could Imogen have laid down the law? Imogen was an independent lady. Several years before she had dictated conditions for taking up a life with Ira: lay the six-shooter aside and quit the law enforcement business. In the end she had acquiesced. She had put Ira and Dimmitt County folks ahead of her personal wishes. Later, she had moved onto the XIT where her husband was seldom home, still carried a Colt's .45 and Winchester, and faced down bad men. Now, had loneliness for female company, tedium, and hardships of a pioneering life on the Escarbada given birth to a renewed spirit of autonomy? Did she tell Ira that he had to forgo further employment with the XIT and the risks it held? Was she was just plain sick and tired of her life in the Texas Panhandle? Not surprisingly her innermost thoughts are secret, not randomly broadcast for public consumption. There is a hard truth, a bottom line, according to Ira: Literally, Imogen was really sick and legitimately tired.

In the third quarter of 1904 Division Manager Aten penned Joe Frazier, a fellow ranch manager located near Tascosa, a note telling him of preparations to spend the winter in California, "on account of my wife's health." To another Ira also admitted: "My wife's health began to fail on those high Plains. We had four children and she worried a great deal more than necessary. The doctors told me to take her to a warmer climate." Making ready for the trip, Ira updated Frazier about his personal cattle and horses, the brands they were wearing, and asked him to "be so kind as to Look out for them" should they get into adjoining pastures, or anywhere else throughout the Panhandle, promising: "Should you see anything of mine please put it where I can send after it.... I do not Know just how long I will stay in California that depends upon Mrs. Aten's health." Leaving Tom Reynolds, a "good man" looking after their personal ranch holdings, the Atens left for California on or about the tenth day of November 1904.[71] It would be a fateful, life-changing trip.

Opportunely, three close friends of Ira's encouraged him to join them on an exploratory expedition into Old Mexico. Gold mines were the hot news. During January 1905, Ira, who had been staying in the Long Beach and San Diego areas, traveled by train through southernmost California, scoping out the countryside, particularly the unripe and thirsty Imperial Valley—and he liked what he saw. Nonetheless he continued with his journey to Douglas (Cochise County), Arizona Territory and ultimately met his three Texas Panhandle *amigos*, G. R. "Rat" Jowell, C. W. (or C. G.) Witherspoon, and Lyle Tannehill. Since the Yaqui Indians were "a little bad at the time," the eager adventurers outfitted themselves with sufficient firearms and cartridges for any eventuality. Shying from rumored dangers and bona fide adversity was foreign to Ira's makeup. He still owned guts, gumption, and the wherewithal to successfully chart his family's future. Aten and his associates "rode around for five days, looking over the countryside."[72] For some reason—dry as it was—California's Imperial Valley had magnetically drawn Ira in. Too, it would be good for Imogen's health. After the short sojourn in Mexico, Ira told his prospecting pals that his mind was made up: he was "going to invest in the Imperial Valley."[73]

Chapter 16

"Never worked harder in my life"

Detailing the intricate, tiresome, mundane, and obligatory tasks linked with an out-of-state relocation is not necessary. Especially not for advancing—winding down—the thrilling story of an ex-Texas Ranger and man who had served as a frontier-era sheriff in two Texas counties, throwing in the ten years he spent as a rawhide-tough ramrod on the largest cattle ranch in the Lone Star State—maybe even the world.[1] It was a distinction none could claim.

The door is near swinging shut on Ira Aten's law enforcing life, but it is not quite closed. Divesting himself of property held in Texas, Ira chose to build a comfortable home and establish himself near Imperial, Imperial County, California. Mr. Aten had opted for that location because although the town of El Centro was not there yet, the always resourceful Ira had "got a tip it was going to be here [there]."[2] From the get-go Ira Aten exhibited his enthusiasm for life, a man seemingly never at rest—at home or work.

Over time, Ira, with the help of his boys, began notching out from the desert surroundings a mini-paradise in southern California, "towering eucalyptus trees" and all. He had forsaken the six-shooter and Winchester, returning to his first ambition of "farming and stock-raising."[3] The Imperial Valley was still a "frontier country" but it was being settled-up by a wide assortment of Americans—and not just a few were Texans. While he had known not a soul in the area upon arrival, Ira quickly established himself and family as industrious citizens with a rich tradition of involvement in public affairs. In seemingly no time the Aten clan were an integral component of the Imperial Valley's potential. The community's outlook was bright. So was that of the Atens. The family's joy was peaked upwards again after the birth of the last child to Ira and Imogen, a precious treasure, another girl, Eloise, born December 12, 1908, and nicknamed their "Golden West Baby."[4]

Expanding his farming and ranching operations Ira somewhere along the timeline acquired additional land in the vicinity of Cali-

Eloise Aten, Ira's and Imogen's "Golden West Baby." *Courtesy Jeri and Gary Boyce Radder.*

patria, Imperial County, which he christened the Calipatria Ranch, about twenty-two miles due north of Imperial.[5] There the land was subdivided for his five children, lovingly ensuring they each got off to a good start in life. One of the chief agricultural commodities of this property was the production of flax. However, most of the 1,700 acres was a cattle operation, with a carrying capacity of 5,000 feeder steers through the winter due to the yield and lushness of irrigated alfalfa pastures.[6] Perhaps an extract from the *American Biography and Genealogy: California Edition* furnishes a suitable overall description regarding *part* of Ira's southern California agricultural operation:

> Mr. Aten does a general ranching and farming business, has a choice dairy herd and raises hogs, maturing them at two hundred pounds in eight or nine months. He is the father of the

cotton industry of Imperial Valley having planted cotton three years with success before he could induce the farmers to plant on a commercial scale. A visit to Mr. Aten's farm is a revelation to those who can be made to believe that this section only a comparatively short time ago was an arid waste, non-productive and useless. In his orchard, chiefly maintained to supply his own table may be picked apples, pomegranates, pears, apricots, oranges, grapefruit, lemons, tangerines, figs, prunes, plums, peaches, quinces, grapes, black-berries and dewberries, olives, almonds and English walnuts.[7]

And it was from the Imperial Valley that Ira earned his spot in the "biggest and hardest job" he ever had. Ira was placed on the Imperial Irrigation District's board of directors, a geographical subdivision constituting 612,200 acres, a giant slice of real-estate even larger than the XIT's Escarbada.[8]

Big-time responsibility went with the title. The Imperial Irrigation District's primary function was to do their part in ensuring construction and completion of Boulder Dam and the All American Canal, Colorado River projects with mammoth and lasting consequence for all of southern California. According to Ira, the job was tougher than saddling a widow-making bronc. Particular corporate interests were the entrenched enemy, namely the great "Power Trust." The project at the Boulder Dam alone would generate "a million horse power of electricity." Those already controlling the production of electricity—and its rewards—were antagonistic toward the venture, and that wasn't even counting opposition to the All American Canal's projected "eighty thousand horse power" output of greatly valued kilowatt energy. These partisan interests were continually fighting the undertakings in the U.S. Congress. "In a report of the Federal Trade Commission made to the United States Senate it was stated that the power trust of the United States has spent $22,000,000 to defeat the legislation to build Boulder Dam, the All American Canal, and Mussel Shoals."[9] Ira was a fighter, a fighter determined to win. Water came to the Imperial Valley.

Not surprisingly for a cowboy type, the plain spoken Ira Aten had seen a close parallel between the "Power Trust" boys and cow thieves back in the untamed Texas Panhandle: Both had been taking "an unjust toll" on the honest working folks. The big time electrical boys, by their blatantly immoral, if not illegal, greed, were corporate

The Aten Ranch at El Centro, California: A showplace. *Courtesy Jeri and Gary Boyce Radder.*

monsters sucking blood from those poor fellows struggling for self-improvement in an already tough environment, so thought Mr. Austin Ira Aten. Black hats that gluttonous bunch had worn.

Someone else was wearing a black hat as far as Ira Aten was concerned. In particular it was a fellow from the Texas Panhandle, John Beal Sneed. A love-triangle was in play—a tragic affair of the heart. Al Boyce Jr., son of A. G. Boyce, the XIT's former general manager, had stolen a man's wife. He had run off with Lena Snyder Sneed, a former sweetheart and daughter of Tom Snyder, noted Texas cattleman, and if not a friend, then an acquaintance of Ira's. Needless to say—in this passionate instance—Beal Sneed did not say, "Good Riddance!" He was mad, with bloodlust in his eyes. Naturally, with everyone's dander up, the elder Boyce sided with his son. The senior Boyce made some disparaging remarks about the character of Mrs. Lena Sneed. Such caustic comments made it to Beal's ears and he was infuriated. He went on the hunt, not like a tiger, but a rattlesnake. Beal Sneed got his chance to strike in the plush lobby of the Metropolitan Hotel, downtown Fort Worth, January 14, 1912. Skulking Beal Sneed slithered up to the senior Mr. Boyce, bared his fangs and injected lead poisoning into the unsuspecting Boyce, who was sitting in a chair reading a newspaper. The murder trial was worthy of note, as was the verdict—Not Guilty. A. G. Boyce's earlier letter telling Lena Sneed, "If you will stand hitched, the Boyces will stand hitched," seemed to imply the deceased was part of a giant conspiracy. In Texas, at that time, a "home-wrecker" was fair game. Beal Sneed yet had a score to settle with the fellow that had caused all the trouble and misery in his life, Al Boyce, Jr.[10]

It was time for a vacation, so thought the acutely worried Al Boyce. Where better to go for some fresh air and sunshine: California. The Imperial Valley would be a good spot for relaxation. Boyce had kinfolk living there, Mrs. Imogen Boyce Aten. At her *hacienda* Al could sleep sound. If the spiteful Beal Sneed really wanted a piece of him, well, he would have to go through Mr. Ira Aten, that gritty old-time Ranger first—no easy feat. Fully expecting a spiteful visit from Beal Sneed, Ira reassured Al that if he was indeed followed to Imperial County the solution was childishly simple: They would just kill him.[11] Though there may have been a gigantic ring of hyperbole in Ira's compassionless pledge to Al Boyce, the wisest course of action would have been not to test his resolve—Aten had always proven he could "stay hitched." No brag, just fact.

Thankfully for Ira, Beal Sneed did not make the vengeance trip to California. He would have probably bitten from a plug too hard to chew. Ira would have had to face the legal music. Instead, Al Boyce Jr. danced back to Texas, a mistake. At Amarillo, Beal Sneed leased a vacant house down the street from the widow Boyce's stately mansion. "Here, disguised as a farm hand and allowing his beard to grow, accompanied by his farm overseer, he lay in wait for two or three weeks, hoping that Al, Jr. would show up." Finally, Sneed espied his prey walking toward his mother's house. Quickly Beal Sneed stuffed his sawed-off shotgun into a cardboard carton and stepped outside the rented cottage. Al Boyce suspected naught. When Beal "got within forty or fifty paces of Boyce he pulled out his shotgun and killed Boyce with a volley of buckshot in his back." The slogan "don't mess with Texas" is a familiar refrain. At Beal Sneed's second murder trial the jury's Not Guilty verdict was plain, the implication translucent: "don't mess with another man's wife."[12]

At this juncture it may be reported that Eddie Aten had married, divorced, and remarried. He and his wife, Gertrude (Bacus Aiello) Aten, remained in far West Texas, where Ed, after discharge from the Texas Rangers, worked as a Special Officer for the railroad. That is after his stint as a faro dealer in Ike Herrin's saloon at the then real wild and real woolly Shafter, Presidio County, in the Big Bend Country.[13] Later he bought out Herrin's interest and became the saloon's sole proprietor. Though it may be but anecdotal, it has been reported the ever plucky Eddie survived another gunplay:

> Aten was involved in several shooting scrapes, one of which occurred in Ysleta when a drunk shot at him, but without effect. In returning the fire he shot his assailant through the lung, inflicting a wound that produced a result that was both unusual and amusing; when the wounded man recovered he thanked Aten because the shot had cured his asthma![14]

What isn't anecdotal is twofold. After reinitiating his tenure as a Special Officer with the railroad, Eddie stuck with the job, honorably, for near forty years. Secondly, just like big brother Ira, Eddie maintained an especially warm friendship with that old Texas Ranger warhorse, John R. Hughes. Their personal relationship was tight, so much so that Hughes, who had been given the deceased Frank Jones' pocket watch by the family, passed the heirloom along to Eddie Aten as a gesture of the retired captain's high regard for his ex-Ranger 1st Sergeant.

Unlike his brother Eddie, who had no surviving children, Cal Aten was intent on raising a family. After Cal left the XIT he purchased his own 2,560-acre ranch near Adrian, Oldham County, fourteen-odd miles west of Vega registering the 8N brand. Cal and Mattie Jo greeted eight children into the world: Cassie, Calvin Warren, Darrell Lamar, Rena May, Quinn, and Lannie Lillian, Austin Turner, and Moody Evelyn. Later he moved southeast, where for the remainder of his life Cal farmed and ranched near Lelia Lake, Donley County.[15] Even during middle age, when the need arose Cal took the oath of office becoming a Loyalty Ranger on the first day of June 1918, serving in that capacity into the following year.[16] During that time of service Cal Aten was expected to "assist our government in every way possible during this war.... work under cover as much as possible, and in a secret capacity, and report all disloyal occurrences to this office for instructions." When called on by local law enforcement to lend a helping hand, Cal Aten as a Loyalty Ranger had all the "rights and privileges given any peace officer in the State of Texas."[17]

Calvin Grant "Cal" Aten and family at their 2,500-acre ranch near Adrian, Oldham County, Texas, before moving to the Lelia Lake ranch in Donley County and prior to the births of Austin Turner and Moody Evelyn. L to R: Darrell Lamar, Cal, Rena Mae "Rennie," Lannie Lillian, Mattie Josie "Mattie Jo," Quinn Lacey, Cassie, and Calvin Warren. During the World War I era Cal Aten once again served the State of Texas in a law enforcement capacity: a Loyalty Ranger. *Courtesy Sally Walker and Shirley Aten Roberts.*

Frank Lincoln Aten, after managing the Round Rock Creamery Association, would make a mark as secretary treasurer for the Farmer's Mutual Insurance Association of Williamson County. Afterwards he would serve as the postmaster for Round Rock, retiring from that position. But, if truth be told, aside from his family, he was perhaps most proud and best remembered for his role in chartering the The Old Settlers Association, eventually becoming its president, an office he held for twenty-four years.[18] Frank and Ira shared a love of history, recognizing its importance.

World War I was truly a sad time for the country and for Ira and Imogen Aten, and in fact for the whole closely allied Aten family— brothers and sisters, aunts and uncles, nephews and nieces—and grandparents. Ira's oldest son Marion Hughes enlisted in Great Britain's Royal Flying Corps and fortunately made it though the war, eventually writing a book of his wartime experiences. Unluckily, his younger brother Albert Boyce was killed during the Battle of Argonne Forest in France. Later an American Legion Post in El Centro was respectfully named in his honor. The youngest of the Aten brothers, Ira Dunlap, would eventually migrate to northern

New Mexico and acquire grazing rights to the humongous Vermejo Park Ranch.[19]

The Aten brothers' surviving sister, Clara Belle, had married George O. Bachman, originally from Ohio. The couple, now raising a family, had settled at Goodletsville, Tennessee, just a short distance north of Nashville.[20]

Austin Cunningham Aten, age 90, had been widowed more than a quarter of a century. He was living with his oldest son Thomas Quinn at Round Rock when his health began faltering. The old-time circuit riding preacher who had progressed to presiding over a devout congregation in Williamson County passed away on November 13, 1924. He restfully slipped to the other side knowing he had instilled in his offspring a firm spirit of self-sufficiency and unselfishness.

During 1927 the determined J. Evetts Haley, cattleman and historian, began implementing his blueprint for writing a serious and comprehensive chronicle of the XIT ranch. One tentacle of Mr. Haley's tactical approach was exceptionally smart. Specific ranch paperwork was not subject to change, no matter when reviewed—the facts and figures, receipts and records, would be there. People were the indispensable ingredient if he wanted to get the story right. Time waited for no man. Fortunately for J. Evetts many of the old-time cowboys and ranchmen of the XIT days were yet alive and kicking—and talkative. Faithfully he set his course for interviewing these fellows before an unstoppable calendar robbed his walking storehouses of their treasures. During an almost unparalleled series of personal visits the indomitable historian went to work recording their recollections. For the XIT, and correspondently the Escarbada, there seemed to be a common thread—Ira Aten. Derelict in his historic duty Haley would have been had he not sought out Ira.

Employing common sense Mr. Haley planned an interview with Ira Aten when it was guaranteed to be bitingly cold in West Texas, February 1928. Haley scooted off to sunny southern California, his mind whirling with questions, his writing tablet in hand. Mr. Haley was affably afforded Ira's and Imogen's red-carpet welcome. Hospitably Ira entertained J. Evetts not just overnight, but for days. The two hit it off fabulously. Mr. Haley knew how to talk with cowmen and cowboys; he was one himself. With expertise he could elicit good stories. And, Mr. Ira Aten had a notebook-full. Mr. Haley was wise enough to know there were times when it was not smart to turn off the spigot. This was one. Ira reminisced about his days spent as a Texas

Ranger and sheriff in both Fort Bend and Castro Counties—about gunfights and fence cutters and testifying in court. He told about murder investigations and everyday life in a Ranger camp. There was more to be said than just those ten years on the Escarbada. Mr. J. Evetts wanted it all: names, places, dates, opinions, accusations—warts too. Ira Aten didn't stutter and wasn't shy. When Ira and he parted, Haley's briefcase was full with a 115-page oral history.[21]

The next year, 1929, a masterpiece of Texas cattle range culture appeared: "As I recall only a thousand copies were printed, and none was offered for sale to the public. They were placed in libraries

Striking a dashing pose atop an "honest" horse during his Golden Years, Ira is an idyllic Western man: No bluster, no bluff—legit all the way around. *Courtesy Jerri and Gary Boyce Radder.*

and given as presents by directors of the Capitol Syndicate." Actually 1300 copies of J. Evetts Haley's *The XIT Ranch of Texas: And Early Days of the Llano Estacado* were printed by Chicago's Lakeside Press.[22] The authoritative work was gauged a major contribution to the genre and a huge success—in most quarters. There were a few folks on the New Mexico side of the line who were not happy—they and their kinfolk had been labeled as common cow thieves. They threatened and initiated civil lawsuits—each one filing as individual plaintiffs.[23] Ira Aten, later asserted and perhaps rightly took solace in the fact a civil trial jury failed to award monetary damages to the family, "which vindicated my [Ira's] story."[24] There is a rest of the story, too and it bears mention. But a single paragraph will suffice. A lawyer for the defense appends:

> We were well supplied with favorable evidence, but realizing that might not be so fortunate in other trials, especially where women of the family were plaintiffs, and knowing that we might be harassed by very expensive litigation for the next ten or fifteen years, we were glad to make a compromise settlement, paying the plaintiffs $17,500 in consideration of all other pending suits being withdrawn, and an airtight agreement that they would never bring other suits against us. In this settlement we agreed to refrain from issuing any more of the books which had stirred up all the litigation, which we had no intention of doing anyway. Those which we had on hand in Chicago were destroyed in accordance with our compromise agreement.[25]

Ira could ill-afford tangling his mind too much with any brouhaha taking place in distant Texas. He was busy—as usual. Now, aside from family, personal involvement in public affairs were the axles beneath Ira's drive, the hub of his being. Enthusiastically he was a charter member of the Imperial Valley Pioneer's Association and the Texas Imperial Valley Association. Ira became an officer in the Farmers Union, Chapter Six. Doubling down, Ira was also instrumental in capitalizing the Home Telephone Company so phone service would be available in Imperial County. He did not stop there. A tireless Mr. Aten was on the board of directors for El Centro's Chamber of Commerce and a bank, plus the real estate business and one of the founders for the county's first cemetery.[26]

There were some things one just couldn't get out of his system. The details remain sketchy, but worthy of acknowledgment. From time to time Ira Aten would lend local law enforcers a helping hand, serving in posses. Generally this volunteer work revolved around raiding some local beer hall or saloon or gambling den operating in violation of Federal Prohibition laws, California's state laws, or El Centro's city ordinances. One story cries for retelling.

Once, when an aging Ira was on standby as a witness—or actually testifying—for the local Magistrate's Court, he thought he could detect that the outraged defendant was armed—another illegal infraction, this one even more serious than the matter at hand. Ira caught the attention of a bailiff, or the sheriff in other accounts, tipping him off. The old lawdog had been on point—the fellow was arrested with not one, but two pistols. Purportedly, Ira remarked in relief: "Thank goodness you got him. I was afraid I was going to have to shoot him."[27] And no doubt had he had to, he would have. Austin Ira Aten was always close—back pocket close—to a Colt's six-gun.

Sometimes cow sense is common sense. Assuredly the old-time frontier lawman never put himself in harm's way by going about unarmed while serving in a makeshift posse; he knew better than such imprudence. Too, he wasn't naïve about tall tales and inflated drama. Ira was sensible.

What wasn't common sense was some of what Ira was reading and, yes, by now seeing in the movies—the Westerns. Though it must register as but speculative there should not be too much argument that Ira, a real Old West lawman, was at least mildly disturbed after picking up a 1921 copy of ex-Texas Ranger Jim Gillett's *Six Years with the Texas Rangers*, and the author's recapping of particular historic events he had absolutely no involvement with. Through the years Ira had personally known and worked with dozens—maybe hundreds—of Old West lawmen. Some of them had been exceptionally good officers, some not so good, and a few had been plain sorry. From A to Z, though, none could walk on water, no matter what enterprising movie moguls or book editors palmed off on the public. In fact, rather than glorifying killing, Ira was troubled, so much so that while away on a trip to Texas he wrote Imogen: "Been thinking about bad men shooting and killing all day and my mind is not fit to go to church."[28]

Assuredly Ira wondered after reading Walter Prescott Webb's 1935 opus *The Texas Rangers: A Century of Frontier Defense*, why the distinguished author had failed to even note the tragic shoot-out wherein young Frank Sieker had paid the ultimate price—a gunplay he, himself, had participated in. The fact Ira was taking in the "picture shows" is clearly evidenced by his comments about the misfortune of Ranger Sieker's death: "I never saw a better picture of a man being shot off a horse, even in a picture show. Falling back from his horse. They don't usually fall back from the horse, but forward, but the horse was going very fast, and he fell backward—still holding the six-shooter, you know."[29] Also, during 1935, *Startling Detective Adventures*, a trendy monthly magazine, offered readers opportunity to reexamine one of Texas' most remarkable murder cases, the one Dick Duncan was hanged for, one largely resolved due the superlative investigative efforts of a hard-working young Texas Ranger Sergeant named Ira Aten. For chronological perspective it is germane to note 1939 was a noteworthy year for Austin Ira Aten. It cannot be postulated with absoluteness—absent a ticket stub—the likelihood is that Ira took in the Hollywood classic directed by John Ford, *Stagecoach*, starring John Wayne.[30] The popularity of the Western had swept over the country with the film industry's birth, had been sidetracked by the public's enthrallment with gangster movies, but was now back in the process of ginning out six-shooter epics starring America's best onscreen talent.[31] A cardinal fact certainly not missed by Ira.

J. Marvin Hunter at Bandera (Bandera County), Texas, was publishing *Frontier Times*, a monthly magazine devoted to recapturing history—particularly focused on Texas history. It became a popular and widely circulated publication, and had been since its very first issue, October 1923. Part of what made the periodical a success was perhaps fortuitous; many of the personalities who had lived through, witnessed, and participated in the thrilling Wild West days were yet alive, some quite old, some in their prime. There then was a valuable base to draw from, a gold mine for an editor trying to scratch out a living for his family, but one committed to preserving memories of the not too distant past. Rumors were adrift—at least in the beginning they were rumors to Hunter—that out in California that old-time Texas Ranger was bent towards preserving his story.

Ira Aten, who had laid the six-shooter and Winchester aside, had sometime circa the mid-1930s picked up the ink pen. Apparently reasonably confident that he could hammer out a worthwhile journalistic product, Ira reduced his memoirs to writing in the format of an authentic manuscript, a small, but book-length endeavor

John Hughes and Ira relax in the Atens' comfortable southern California ranch home. Their bond of friendship was solid. *Courtesy Research Center, Texas Ranger Hall of Fame and Museum.*

highlighting his early experiences enforcing the law in Texas and overseeing the vast Escarbada's range lands. There may have been a subliminal message buried in Ira Aten's title: "Six and One-Half Years in the Ranger Service, Fifty Years Ago." Adding that extension of six months to the manuscript's title may or may not have been a thrust in ex-Ranger Jim Gillett's direction. Author Gillett, as previously noted, had haphazardly authored an autobiography, *Six Years With the Texas Rangers*. Was Ira Aten trying to upstage Jim Gillett? Was Ira trying to query Gillett's work, consciously or subconsciously hinting that it was best to write what you lived, not what you were told? With his base foundation laid, compartmentalized chapters within an overall framework of his life's work, Ira was ready, willing, and able to turn the crank. The year 1939 was a banner year for those flipping pages of *Frontier Times*.[32]

The old-styled Texas lawman, turned farmer, rancher, and recognized public-spirited workaholic found time, somehow, to churn out a fascinating string of first-person accounts of happenings he knew about—personally, having been a player. Appearing in the April 1939 issue of *Frontier Times* was his first, "The Jaybird and Woodpecker War." Ira followed up the next month with "Texas Honors a Ranger Captain," a poignant piece about the dedicated monument for Texas Ranger Captain Frank Jones. Never content to rest on his laurels, Ira kept up the whirlwind of writing: for the July edition, "Fence Cutting Days In Texas," followed in October by "Early Day Fires in the Panhandle." Ira's articles were whopping triumphs. They were rekindling fond memories of bygone days, not only for the prolific author and his contemporaneous California friends and neighbors, many from Texas, but old-time Ranger comrades as well. Several of them jumped onto the bandwagon, jotting down their own recollections of what they had seen or heard—or nostalgically thought they had seen or heard. *Frontier Times* was a treasure trove for the readership—then and now—and a most valuable repository of Texas history.

The publishing world seemed never to get enough Westerns. Whether or not Ira was surprised is indeterminate, but there he

Old-time ex-Texas Rangers pay their respects at the Marker memorializing the ultimate sacrifice made by Captain Frank Jones. Standing L to R: Eddie Aten, Ira Aten and Ed Bryant. John Hughes kneeling pointing to the inscription. Both Eddie Aten and Ed Bryant had participated in the gunfight. *Courtesy Research Center, Texas Ranger Hall of Fame and Museum.*

was—all decked out, horseback, Colt's six-shooter, Winchester, and Bowie knife—right there on page 43 in the June 1940 issue of *True Detective*, another monthly magazine, one distributed nationwide and quite popular.[33] The editors were running multi-issue articles that summer about one of Ira's dearest friends, that old Border Boss, John R. Hughes. To write of Hughes meant writing of Austin Ira Aten. To write of Aten meant writing of John Reynolds Hughes.

Ira Aten's article for the April 1941 issue of *Frontier Times*, "Swimming Cattle Across the Canadian," along with his article the following month, "Crossing High Water in a Wagon," may or may not have been an impetus for another visit by the indefatigable chronicler of Texas ranch life, J. Evetts Haley. Accompanied by grassroots historians Hervey Chesley and Earl Vandale, the trio set off on a research trip interviewing old-timers throughout the Southwest. Along the way they boldly settled on extending the July 1941 excursion to the Imperial Valley and a visit with Ira. After traveling through sweltering Texas, New Mexico, and Arizona heat—before automobiles had air-conditioning—the three historic sleuths at long last finally parked in front of El Centro's renowned Barbara Worth Hotel, went inside and signed the guestbook.[34]

Next morning, braving a 118-degree scorcher, the boys were off to see Ira at his place, "north of town, with its towering eucalyptus trees, and the birds flying around in the branches unmindful of the terrific heat."[35] Characteristically Ira bounded out to greet the visitors with unbridled zeal, parrying to Haley, "Have you come for another million dollar story?" Aten was making a not veiled allusion to *The XIT Ranch of Texas* lawsuit of twenty years before. It was all taken in good fun, cowboy humor—a good natured jab.[36] Ira's delighted Texas guests were treated to a few creature comforts—good food, good seating—and best of all, good conversation. As the morning waned and after lunch, the old ex-Ranger assumed his afternoon ritual, perhaps best put to words by one of his interviewers, Hervey Chesley: "Aten's custom at the time and during the hot weather was to lie in his bedroom in the afternoons, stripped off and covered by a sheet, under the breeze from an electric fan. From this posture he told his story without the necessity for much interrogation."[37] The Aten interview broadened to several days, even though J. Evetts Haley had to shorten his stay due to pressing cattle business in Texas. The end product, a 160-page unpublished typescript is, and certainly has been, a not guarded but underused historic resource.[38] A condensed version did find its way into Hervery Chesley's *Adventuring With the Old-Timers: Trails Traveled—Tales Told*, but only after the typescript had been significantly chopped to make way for recounting the remembrances of other frontier era folks.[39]

The following year J. Marvin Hunter published a letter from Ira to brothers and sisters, one of those Christmas type round-robin epistles stuffed with family news and personal observations about first one thing and another, this and that. This letter and another, written but not published the following year, while basically more valuable to the genealogist, do offer patchy and interpretative use-fulness for the historian and/or biographer.[40] Also during 1942 big news broke about Ira's pal John R. Hughes. The Naylor Publishing Company in San Antonio released Jack Martin's *Border Boss: Captain John R. Hughes—Texas Ranger*. Mr. Ira Aten was one of the key figures in Hughes' biography, a fact not missed at Bandera.

J. Marvin Hunter, ever the consummate journalist, recognized the worth historically and financially of capitalizing on Ira Aten's experiences. It was truly a story of historic merit, a legitimate Old West saga. Mr. Hunter learned of Ira's dormant manuscript, the big one. J. Marvin had an idea. He sought and was granted permission to carry Aten's work in *Frontier Times*, a four-part serialized piece, starting with the January 1945 issue and concluding with the April edition. The absorbing articles were so well-received by both the general public and scholars that the astute Mr. Hunter saw the wisdom that same year of combining the stories—with supplemental material—into a small book, *Six and One-Half Years in the Ranger Service: The Memoirs of Sergeant Ira Aten, Company D, Texas Rangers*. It was quickly gobbled up by interested family members, general readers of Western literature, and book collectors. It was soon on the out-of-print list.[41] That wasn't all. That same year the editors of *Readers Digest* in their September issue carried an article on the famous XIT—again Ira was spotlighted for his work in clearing nests of despicable cow thieves out of the Texas Panhandle.

Increasingly as Ira began putting on a few pounds with age he developed a somewhat predictable routine for beating the heat of southern California. He would vacation—between planting seasons—at Burlingame, not far south of San Francisco. Imogen, her health slipping, lived there with her two daughters, Imogen and Eloise, the latter having married Roland William Radder. Daughter Imogen never married, but was almost a fixture at Stanford University, serving as secretary for the Student Body, an absolute delight to all who knew her. Particularly drawing Ira's regular visits to Burlingame, besides seeing his ailing wife, daughters, and son-in-law, was the opportunity it provided the old Ranger to dote over Gary Boyce Radder, his only grandchild. Almost with a girlish giddiness Ira recalled taking his adored grandson to the San Francisco Zoo: "We took our lunch along and the baby had the time of his life looking at the animals and birds and asking questions.... San Francisco has a wonderful Zoo and play-ground attached for the children and is kept up by the city and is free...." In the evenings Ira fondly recalled that Aunt Imogen would get down on the floor playing with baby Gary, acting as a tutor. Time was taking its toll. Ira was no dummy to that. The elderly Aten could see it plainly as baby Gary played beneath his feet, learning "a little more each day, and I am forgetting what little I ever knew."[42]

In a fitting October 1944 tribute Ira was honored at El Centro's American Legion Hall, the post named after his son Albert Boyce. In commemoration for his long law enforcement life, not only in California, but Texas as well, the Imperial County Sheriff, Rob-

Ira and Imogen Aten enjoying their twilight years. *Courtesy Jeri and Gary Boyce Radder.*

ert W. "Bob" Ware, had a surprise. The eighty-four-year-old champion of gunfights and horseback chases, a veteran of boring nights passed on surveillance suddenly interrupted by sheer terror when an arrest finally went down, was *partially* given his due. Sheriff Bob Ware made it official; he deputized Ira Aten, the newest—but not a rookie—Imperial County Deputy Sheriff. Hugh T. Osborne, one of the program chairs, extolled Ira Aten's nature, portraying him as "a courtly gentleman, a loyal friend, a distinguished citizen, and a fearless fighter for what he believed in." Hugh Osborne was right on target, on all counts.[43]

With all the unasked-for accolades being heaped upon him while he lived, it is difficult to imagine that Ira wasn't knocked back on his heels in disbelief when news reached him from Texas. Since those early Texas Ranger days he and John Hughes had been tight—thicker than thieves if an inappropriate analogy is played. As aging men, Hughes had visited with Ira in California several times, and Ira had

A doting Ira Aten with his one and only grandchild, Gary Boyce Radder, the apple of his eye. *Courtesy Jeri and Gary Boyce Radder.*

visited with Hughes on numerous occasions in Texas. There would be no more get-togethers. On the third day of June 1947 the Border Boss picked up his pearl-handled Colt's six-shooter and stepped into his sister-in-law's garage at 4215 Avenue H, Austin, Texas. A single gunshot echoed throughout the neighborhood. Despondent and with failing health, John R. Hughes had taken his own life.[44] Ira Aten was crestfallen upon learning the news.

There would be no room for misgiving, Imogen would cry, too. Her husband was a realist, he knew sometime in the not too distant future he would meet his Maker. Father Time was unsentimental. In preparation for the inevitable, Ira instructed hired hands at the Imperial Valley ranch to chop down two of his prized eucalyptus trees. The hewn and dressed stumps—close together—would serve perfectly as platform for his casket.[45] And so it was. When called, Ira was ready. Although she would outlive Ira by four years, Imogen and the girls perhaps knew the end was near when during one of his annual visits to Burlingame, Ira contracted pneumonia. After ninety-one years Ira Aten could fight no more. On August 6, 1953, he quietly slipped to the other side.[46]

Quite interestingly, a New York-based journalist, Harold Preece, during the early 1950s picked up on the potential value of Ira Aten's published memoirs—if reworked into his style of dramatic prose— which, to be fair, really was in vogue at the time. The same year that saw the passing of Ira, saw the melodramatic penmanship of Preece in a three-link chain of articles for *Zane Grey's Western Magazine*. Later, the sidebar for Preece's article in *Real West*, "I Fought These Masked Rustlers," while perhaps true in part, is perhaps somewhat misleading: "On his death, Ira Aten, one of the greatest of all Texas Rangers, bequeathed to Harold Preece, the noted Western writer, his memoirs, and among these was this interesting article on fence cutting, which was the cattlemen's last desperate attempt to destroy the barbed wire fence."[47] Circumspect readers may judge the genuine merit of an assertion that Ira Aten "bequeathed" his memoirs to writer Harold Preece. On September 8, 1941, the remarkably well known Western writer J. C. Dykes, in writing, asked Ira Aten for authorization—permission—to make copies from the as of then yet published, *Six and One-Half Years in the Ranger Service, Fifty Years Ago*. Aten's written response to Mr. Dykes on the thirteenth day of September is informative. It seems Ira had evidently "bequeathed" quite a number of copies:

The Atens' residence at the much cooler Burlingame, California. Imogen spent most of her time here, while Ira divided his time between this commodious abode and the El Centro ranch. Unlike some Old West lawmen spending later years in poverty and obscurity, searching for speciously inflated stardom, Ira's industriousness and business acumen had paid its worthwhile dividends. *Courtesy Jeri and Gary Boyce Radder.*

Your of the 8" inst. is at hand and note your request which is gladly granted. A few years ago some of my old Ranger Comrades got after me to write up some of the happenings of our Ranger Life. I only made about 15 copies for the boys and dear friends. Some of the stories have got into the magazines— "Blue Book" and Frontier Times of Bandera, but none are copyrighted....I have no copies of my stories not even the original as it is loaned out.[48]

During September of 1960 Harold Preece, through his New York publisher, Hasting House, released *Lone Star Man, Ira Aten: Last of the Old Texas Rangers.* According to Preece's Introduction many capable writers had earlier approached Ira Aten wanting to write his neat story, but he had turned them all away, of course with his standard gentlemanly manners and humility. Luckily for Mr. Preece—according to Mr. Preece—it was he who finally became Ira's close confidant, personal friend—and chosen biographer. Curiously, Mr. Preece's biogra-

phy of Aten was published seven years after Ira's death.[49] No doubt
Mr. Preece hoped it would stand the test of time at face value. Dis-
passionate scrutiny was not then a coin of the realm for Westerns.
Journalistically constructed dialogue was but commonplace. Citing
key source material was not. All Ira Aten would have ask for, maybe
even asked for, was that the truth be passed on—all of it.

Even in old age Ira had taken pride in staying busy, not trying
to beat someone out of something for nothing. Ira Aten was by any
standard head and shoulders above several of the speciously puffed
Old West lawmen of that sullied ilk—despite what their apologists
might pen. Unquestionably those off-color guys garnered—grabbed
the spotlight—and could bank the much more recognizable names,
but Mr. Ira Aten was "legit" all the way around. Counterfeit or cor-
rupt or conceited he certainly was not. Ira remarked prior to his
death, taking his own personal measure, but not in a boastful way:
"It is natural for people to say to old folks in meeting them 'How do
you feel?' I come back at them. 'Never worked harder in my life, nor
felt better.' There is a lot of truth in it, too!"[50] In the end age may have
overtaken Austin Ira Aten's aging body, but not his indelible spirit.
Mr. Austin Ira Aten was boot-strap tough. He had been a good Texas
Ranger: a Rawhide Ranger.

Reposed at last in eternal peace: Mr. Austin Ira Aten, son, brother, husband, father,
grandfather, businessman, agriculturist, philanthropist, XIT Division Manager,
sheriff of two Texas counties, and Texas Ranger: A Rawhide Ranger. *Courtesy Jeri
and Gary Boyce Radder.*

Endnotes

Notes to Chapter 1

1 Rick Miller, *Sam Bass and Gang*, 241–62; Miller's is the seminal work
   on the life, adventures, misadventures, and death of Sam Bass; Karen
   R. Thompson and Jane H. Digesualdo, *Historical Round Rock, Texas*,
   110–15; James Bradley Warden, in later life, contributed an essay to
   Williamson County, Texas: Its History and Its People, Jean Shroyer, ed.,
   titled, "I Saw the Shooting of Sam Bass," 44–45.

2 Ibid.; Robert W. Stephens, *Texas Ranger Sketches*, 55–58.

3 Ibid.; Frederick Wilkins, *The Law Comes to Texas: The Texas Rangers,
   1870–1901*, 165–66.

4 James Gillett, *Six Year with the Texas Rangers, 1875 to 1881*, 124: "He
   [Jones] was armed with only a small Colt's double-action pistol…";
   Stan Nelson, "American Double Action Pocket Revolvers, 1875–1900,"
   Minnesota Weapons Collectors Association News 23, no. 1 (2009): 12–16;
   Phil Spangenberger, "Colt's Rivals," *True West*, June 2005, 34: "these
   'self-cockers' were light, handy and popular on the frontier with
   many notables, including Billy the Kid, John Wesley Hardin and Cole
   Younger."

5 Harvey N. Castleman, *Sam Bass, the Train Robber: The Life of Texas'
   Most Popular Bandit*, 23.

6 Chuck Parsons and Donaly E. Brice, *Texas Ranger N. O. Reynolds: The
   Intrepid*, 224–27; Leona Bruce, *Banister Was There*, 34; Chuck Parsons,
   John B. Armstrong, Texas Ranger and Pioneer Ranchman, 70; Robert M.
   Utley, *Lone Star Justice: The First Century of the Texas Rangers*, 185.

7 Ibid.; Bill O'Neal, *Encyclopedia of Western Gun-Fighters*, 36.

8 Ibid.; Thompson and Digesualdo, *Historical Round Rock*, 113.

9 Gillett, *Six Years with the Texas Rangers*, 126; Stephens, *Texas Ranger
   Sketches*, 41; Miller, *Sam Bass and Gang*, 373; Parsons and Brice, *Texas
   Ranger N. O. Reynolds*, 233–34; Robert W. Stephens, *Texas Ranger
   Indian War Pensions*, 44–45.

10 Dora Neill Raymond, *Captain Lee Hall of Texas*, 160; Parsons and Brice,
   Texas Ranger N. O. Reynolds, 226; Parsons, *John B. Armstrong*, 69;
   Bruce, *Banister Was There*, 34–35; Thompson and Digesualdo, *Histori-
   cal Round Rock*, 67; Miller, *Sam Bass and Gang*, 241–46.

11 Miller, *Sam Bass and Gang*, 255.

12 Ibid., 258; Thompson and Digesualdo, *Historical Round Rock*, 114.

13   *Galveston Daily News*, July 21, 1878; [Morrison ?] *Life and Adventures of Sam Bass: The Notorious Union Pacific and Texas Train Robber*, 84. Noted Old West bibliophile Ramon F. Adams asserts the author of this 1878 publication was a Dallas newspaper reporter.

14   Miller, *Sam Bass and Gang*, 259; Clara Stearns Scarbrough, *Land of Good Water: A Williamson County, Texas History*, 298; Edna Goodrich, "Legend of Sam Bass," *Students' History of Williamson County*, ed. Estelle Mae Norvell, 45.

15   Thompson and Digesualdo, *Historical Round Rock*, 114.

16   Parsons, *John B. Armstrong*, 70.

17   *The New York Times*, July 21, 1878; James D. Horan, *The Outlaws*, 224: "The news of the capture of Sam Bass flew across the frontier"; Scarbrough, *Land of Good Water*, 296. The author reports, locally, in the *Williamson County Sun*. The hot news item was carried inside the folds.

18   James Bradley Warden, who was ten years old at the time Sam Bass was killed and was in Round Rock at the time, would later write: "My daddy and me had met the Rangers four miles out of town. When they found that they had missed the fight after riding for two days and two nights, they were mad and cussed and stamped their feet. I thought daddy and me might be in as much danger from the Rangers as we were from the outlaws." See Warden, "I Saw the Shooting of Sam Bass," 45.

19   Utley, *Lone Star Justice*, 186: "George Herold got close enough to send a Winchester slug slicing through Bass's back and kidney,"

20   Dan Thrapp, *Encyclopedia of Frontier Biography*, vol. 1, 70–71; Leon Claire Metz, *Encyclopedia of Lawmen, Outlaws, and Gunfighters*, 16–17; Charles L. Martin, *A Sketch of Sam Bass, the Bandit*, 157.

21   Miller, *Sam Bass and Gang*, 260; Stephens, *Texas Ranger Sketches*, 15–20.

22   Ibid.

23   Harold Preece, *Lone Star Man: Ira Aten, Last of the Old Texas Rangers*, 22. Seven years prior to the 1960 release of *Lone Star Man* and eight years after Aten's memoirs "Six and One-Half Years in the Ranger Service" were published in the *Frontier Times* series, Harold Preece published a strikingly similar three-part sequence for *Zane Grey's Western Magazine*. Smartly the author's attribution is for Ira Aten, with the caveat "as told to Harold Preece." Part I, "I Rode with the Texas Rangers: Hell on the Border" appeared in the May 1953 edition; Part II, "I Rode with the Texas Rangers: War on the Salt Grass" made the edition of June 1953; and the concluding Part III article "I Rode with the Texas Rangers: Lawman Till I Die" was carried in the August 1953 copy. Readers may judge the historical merit of these articles for themselves.

24 Maude Wallis Traylor, "Two Famous Sons of a Famous Father," *Frontier Times*, November 1933, 304.

25 E. M. Ainsworth, "Old Austin and Round Rock Road to Fort Concho," *Frontier Times*, July 1929, 406: "He [Sam Bass] was buried in the cemetery in Old Round Rock and his sister put up a stone monument later; it was literally chipped away by gruesome relic hunters, and a second stone was put up, but it has also felt the hand of the abnormal collector of relics, and when I saw it about two years ago, it also was bady [sic] mutilated."

26 Bruce, *Banister Was There*, 37. Author Bruce quotes a letter written by Texas Ranger John Banister to his mother on July 22, 1878, posted at Round Rock:

Dear Mother:

We are both [John and Will] well. The notorious Sam Bass died yesterday at 4:20 P. M. He made no request. Two minutes before his death he said, "This world is but a bubble—trouble wherever you go." And after saying this, in two minutes his soul was launched into eternity. I have a relic which he gave me, his six-shooter, belt and scabbard. The shot that killed him passed through the top of the scabbard and through the belt. An awful excitement prevails over the little town of Round Rock. Dick Ware killed Barnes and George Harrel [sic] killed Bass. Harrel is one of our Company. The Ex-Ranger [Moore] is still alive. The wagon started with the body of Bass twenty minutes ago to the graveyard. I think we will return to San Saba soon. Well, I will close. Write to S. A. From your dutiful son. J. R. B.

Placement of the comma after "six-shooter," in the above cited letter has created confusion. Absent the comma it could be interpreted that Sam Bass gave Bannister the six-shooter belt and scabbard, not the handgun. Also present when Sam Bass was interviewed by the *Galveston Daily News* reporter was Texas Ranger Lieutenant John B. Armstrong, although it is unlikely that as a commissioned officer he would be serving as a guard. A snippet in the May 1926 edition of *Frontier Times*, 45, reports the University of Texas ended up with the Sam Bass cartridge belt.

27 Preece, *Lone Star Man*, 23.

28 *Round Rock Leader*, February 27, 1986.

29 Ira Aten interview with Earl Vandale, Evetts Haley, and Hervey Chesley, July 1941, El Centro, California. Courtesy the Haley Memorial Library and History Center (HML&HC), Midland, Texas. Hereafter Aten-1941, HML&HC. "Us boys would go to the window and peep in," 5; Ira Aten to Imogen Aten, November 20, 1936: "I was a boy of fifteen when Sam Bass was killed.... We boys would sneak up to the windows when the rangers were not watching and peep in. There he was

stretched out on a mattress, boots and spurs at the foot of the bed. I often wondered if that had anything to do with me joining the ranger service." From a series of nine 1936 letters from Ira Aten to Imogen Aten, Courtesy Research Center, Panhandle-Plains Historical Museum (PPHM), Canyon, Texas.

30 Bob Alexander, *Winchester Warriors: Texas Rangers of Company D, 1874–1901*, 26.

31 Preece, *Lone Star Man*, 23. Acceptance or rejection of the verbatim dialogue in Preece must be left to the reader's discretion; Noel Grisham, *Tame the Restless Wind: The Life and Legends of Sam Bass*, 89.

32 Aten-1941, 5, HML&HC. In an unidentified newspaper clip (thought to be June 1957) with a Round Rock dateline, Frank Lincoln Aten seems to suggest another motive for brother Ira's infatuation with the Texas Rangers: "My brother Ira, he was 16 then, and another boy kept looking in the window at the robber lying there on the mattress, and a Texas Ranger run them off. The second time he run them off he said: 'Next time, I'll put you in the jug over there.' Ira told him 'When I grow up, I'm going to be a Ranger and tell other people what to do,'" VF-Aten, courtesy Texas Ranger Research Center, Texas Ranger Hall of Fame and Museum (TRHF&M),Waco, Texas.

33 Miller, *Sam Bass and Gang*, 262; Bruce, *Banister Was There*, 37; Sam Bass Café, *True Story of Sam Bass the Outlaw*, 9: "Yet knowing death was near, he refused to give any of his friends away and died game to the last"; The fact that the Sam Bass Café was commercializing the Round Rock shoot-out well before publication of its 1950 booklet is evidenced by Ira Aten to Imogen Aten, November 25, 1936, in PPHM: "The first large sign you see driving into this little town [Round Rock] on the highway is, 'The Sam Bass Café.' The people here pride themselves it was here Sam Bass and his gang met their Waterloo. However I did not know it was being commercialized here. If my brothers will let me eat out in town, I am surely going to eat there for the romance that is in it."

34 Aaron P. Aten to Reverend Thomas G. Aten, September 13, 1897; also, Austin Cunningham Aten to Ira Aten, November 26, 1921, courtesy Betty Aten.

35 Ira Aten, Typescript, "Our Ancestors of Another Day": "Now we will go back to the year 1651 and another forefather, Adrian Hendericks Aten (or Van Auton) before they left Holland and migrated to America," courtesy Betty Aten; B. Morando, "Ira Aten: Texas Ranger," *Famous Lawmen of the West*, A Special Collector's Edition published by *Real West Magazine*, Fall 1965, 18; Telephone interview with Gary Boyce Radder, Ira Aten's grandson, September 9, 2009; Personal interview

with Betty Aten, Frank Lincoln Aten's granddaughter, September 22, 2009; Handwritten summary signed Ira Aten, "My father's side of the house": "My Grand Mother Margaret Quinn Aten was a Christian church deciple [*sic*] & raised her family in that faith. She was a strong-minded woman both in religion & politics. She died in 1891 at the age of 94. Her husband Peter died in 1842, at the age of 49. He was in the War of 1812, and died from the effect of a wound many years later & his widow drew a Gov. pension on that account until her death." Courtesy Betty Aten.

36 United States Federal Census, 1860; Alan J. Lamb, *An Aten Genealogy*, 31–32.

37 Aten-1941, 8, HML&HC: "[father] joined the Union Army. That caused a rift between my father and mother's family. My grandfather never spoke to my father or invited him back there for years and years.... My grandfather on my father's side was dead when the Civil War come on, all of his family was of the Union. Mother's folks sympathized with the South."

38 Janet B. Hewett, *The Roster of Union Soldiers, 1861–1865: Illinois*, "Aten, Austin C. 77th Inf. Co. I Cpl," 35; Janet B. Hewett, ed., *Supplement to the Official Records of the Union and Confederate Armies*, Part II—Record of Events, Vol. 13, Serial No. 25, 105–31.

39 Preece, *Lone Star Man* gives Ira Aten's place of birth as Cairo, Illinois, rather than Peoria, see page 24; Primary source records in the Texas State Library and Archives Commission (TSA), Austin, Texas, and TRHF&M records reveal Ira's POB as Peoria County, Illinois. One example: *Descriptive List*, Ira Aten, May 5, 1891; also, *Imperial Valley Weekly*, August 10, 1953: "A native of Peoria, Illinois, Mr. Aten spent his early life in Texas...."; and, *Imperial Valley Press*, August 23 1984, byline Peter R. Odens: "He [Ira Aten] had been born in Peoria, Ill., on Sept. 3, 1862"; in a January 1, 1930, typed letter to his siblings Ira reveals and confirms: "Through the courtesy of our cousin, Earl V. Aten, of Houston, Texas, has sent me on request, a copy of the record (which he has in his possession) from our Grandmother Aten's old Family Bible, kept in her day... 'Austin Ira Aten, September 3, 1862, near Peoria, Illinois. Now living in El Centro, Imperial Valley, California,'" courtesy Betty Aten; of course the best voice is that of Ira. During extensive February 1928 interviews by J. Evetts Haley at El Centro, California, Aten unequivocally declared: "I was born at Peoria, Ill," 114. Hereafter cited as Aten-1928, HML&HC; likewise, Aten's name is variously given as "Austin Ira" or "Ira Austin." In the above cited 1930 letter Ira makes several genealogical corrections. He does not, however, make any change to the notation "Austin Ira

Aten." Occasional federal census records also identify Ira as "Austin
I. Aten."

40 John F. Walter, *Seventy-Seventh Illinois Infantry*, rev. ed., July 1997.
"The Seventy-Seventh Illinois Infantry was organized at Peoria, Illinois, during August, 1862. It was mustered into Federal service there
on September 3, 1862." n. p. Courtesy, Historical Research Center,
Texas Heritage Museum, Hill College, Hillsboro, Texas.

41 J. E. Hewitt, cont., "The Battle of Mansfield, LA," *The Confederate
Veteran Magazine* 33 (January–December 1925): 172–73, 198; Hewett,
Supplement to the Official Records of the Union and Confederate Armies,
131.

42 Aten-1941, 2, HML&HC; Andreas, Lyter & Co., *Atlas Map of Knox
County Illinois*, 15: "[Name] Aten, A. C....[Residence] Abingdon....
[Business] Hardware....[Nativity] Ohio....[When Came to Co.] 1849....
[Where From] Peoria Co., Ills."

43 Ibid.: "And sold the farm there when I was five and moved to Abing-
ton, Illinois, five miles south of Galesburg."

44 United States Federal Census, 1870, Indian Point, Knox County,
Illinois.

45 Aten-1941, 2, HML&HC.

46 Aaron P. Aten to Thomas G. Aten, September 13, 1897; Charles C.
Chapman, ed., *History of Knox County, Illinois*, 575.

47 Stephens, *Texas Ranger Sketches*, 18: "The stern religious upbringing
practiced by his father [Austin C. Aten], an old fashioned 'fire and
brimstone' minister, conflicted with the distractions of frontier life in
Texas."

48 Roger Jay, "'The Peoria Bummer'—Wyatt Earp's Lost Year," *Wild West*,
August 2003, 46–52; William B. Shillingberg, *Dodge City: The Early
Years, 1872–1886,* 170; Roy B. Young, "Wyatt Earp: Outlaw of the
Cherokee Nation," *Wild West History Association* [WWHA] *Journal*,
June 2010, 19–29.

49 George Carleton Mays, "Wyatt Earp: Climax at the O. K. Corral,"
Famous Lawmen of the West, Fall 1965, 7–8; Leon Claire Metz, *The
Shooters*, 270: "In truth, historians are not certain if Earp was a
bonafide frontier Paladin, or a scoundrel with a clever biographer.
Right now the evidence leans toward the latter assessment"; Marshall
Trimble, *Arizona: A Panoramic History of a Frontier State*, 273: "the
Fighting Pimps"; William B. Shillingberg, *Tombstone, A. T.—A His-
tory of Early Mining, Milling, and Mayhem*, 137; Joseph G. Rosa and
Robin May, *Gun Law: A Study of Violence in the Wild West*, 120; Steve
Gatto, Neil B. Carmony, ed., Introduction, npn: *The Real Wyatt Earp: A
Documentary Biography*: "Few of them can accept the fact that Wyatt

was a small-time peace officer and a big-time fabulist"; Frederick Nolan, *The Wild West: History, Myth and the Making of America*, 139: "An almost forgotten relic of the old frontier.... Fueled first by books, then movies, and later television, Wyatt Earp—a man who was never more than a deputy sheriff or an assistant marshal—was transformed into the most famous lawman of the frontier West. Controversy still swirls around his name and his life. Was he a saint or a sinner, a rugged frontiersman or a sly opportunist, a pimp and crooked gambler or an incorruptible lawman, a small-time peace officer or a mendacious fabulist?"

50 Bob Alexander, *Fearless Dave Allison: Border Lawman*, 16.

51 Typescript of Virginia (Kimmons) Abbott, April 1, 1961, titled "My Autobiography," 1, courtesy Betty Aten.

52 Aten-1941, 4, HML&HC: "We went into a log cabin. Had each grandmother with us."

53 Shroyer, *Williamson County*, 57; Unidentified newsclip—obit: "Austin C. Aten came to Texas October 29, 1876...."; Aten-1941, 2, HML&HC: "October 1876, when my father moved to Texas."

54 *Austin Daily Statesman*, February 4, 1892: "reared in Travis County...."; *Fort Worth Star Telegram*, November [?] 1924: "Elder Aten came to Texas in 1876, and made his home near where Pflugerville now stands"; United States Federal Census, 1880, Precinct 2, Travis County; Aten-1941, 2, HML&HC: "We come to Round Rock, Texas, and my father went over on Cap Carrington's cotton plantation and ranch there in Travis County"; *Galveston Daily News*, August 21, 1889: "but was brought to this state when a boy by his parents, who now live where they first settled in Travis county, fifteen miles north of Austin....His [Ira's] parents are comfortably located at a good home in Travis county."

55 Aten-1928, 4, HML&HC.

56 Luke Gournay, *Texas Boundaries: Evolution of the State's Counties*, 57.

57 Abbott, "My Autobiography," 9.

58 C. R. Perry, *Memoir of Capt'n C. R. Perry of Johnson City Texas: A Texas Veteran*, Kenneth Kesselus, ed., 28.

59 Gary and Margaret Kraisinger, *The Western: The Greatest Texas Cattle Trail, 1874–1886*.

60 Alexander, *Fearless Dave Allison*, 19.

61 Aten-1941, 4, HML&HC.

62 John H. [Jack] Culley, *Cattle, Horses and Men of the Western Range*, 33: "As a matter of fact there were but few fist fights in the West in those days. Difficulties were generally settled with that useful instrument, the .45 Colt...."

63   *Galveston Daily News*, February 7, 1877.

64   Robert J. Casey, *The Texas Border and Some Borderliners,* 189; Aten-
      1941, 38, HML&HC: "Yes, a great deal of the trouble on the Frontier
      was from whisky, most of the trouble, and from gambling and things
      like that"; William H. Forbis, *The Cowboys,* 217: "Most other gunfights
      occurred not between cowboys but in the Western underworld, among
      the gamblers, toughs, and professional criminals who walk the dark
      corridors of any society."

65   *The Austin Daily Statesman,* February 4, 1892; Betty Dooley Awbrey
      and Claude Dooley, *Why Stop? A Guide To Texas Historical Roadside
      Markers,* 383–84.

66   There is no hard evidence that Ira attended school on Lisso's farm.
      His personal remarks about a formal education leave much to be
      desired. Aten-1941, 2, HML&HC: "I went to school when I was six
      and I was fourteen years old, October, 1876, when my father moved
      to Texas, and in going to Texas I lost my education, because my father
      went on a cotton plantation, and there was no school and I didn't
      go to school after thirteen." It would seem, then, Ira's formal educa-
      tion as a child was from the age seven to age thirteen. A snippet in
      The Austin Daily Statesman of February 4, 1892, clearly—and maybe
      inaccurately—remarks that Ira was "reared in Travis county.... went
      to school."

67   Excerpt from letter of Angie Aten to her grandmother, January 8,
      1882: "Frank & Ira & Brown boys have went up the country on a hunt-
      ing spree, been gone near 2 weeks, have not got back I guess," courtesy
      Betty Aten.

68   Abbott, "My Autobiography," 7.

69   Stephens, *Texas Ranger Sketches,* 18.

Notes to Chapter 2

1   Abbott, "My Autobiography," 5.

2   John Wesley Hardin, *The Life of John Wesley Hardin, As Written by Him-
     self,* 28–29; Leon C. Metz, *John Wesley Hardin: Dark Angel of Texas,* 28;
     Richard C. Marohn, *The Last Gunfighter: John Wesley Hardin,* 26–27;
     Lewis Nordyke, *John Wesley Hardin: Texas Gunman,* 74: "He made it to
     Professor Landrum's school, saw Joe, and attended classes all in one
     day"; Thompson and Digesualdo, *Historical Round Rock,* 460.

3   Rick Miller, *Bounty Hunter,* 96: "By now, the word of Hardin's capture
     had been picked up by the national press, and almost all major news-
     papers had reported it."

4   Shroyer, *Williamson County,* 57.

5   Preece, *Lone Star Man*, 25.

6   Aten-1928, 5, HML&HC: "I have always thought Sam Bass and that incident caused us to go with the Rangers."

7   United States Federal Census, 1880, Precinct 2, Travis County, Texas. Austin I. Aten is enumerated as a seventeen-year-old son of Austin C. and Kate E. Aten, living at home.

8   Preece, *Lone Star Man*, 27–28.

9   Ibid., 14: "Dialogue has been constructed from his [Ira's] correspondence, his memoirs, and from the recollections of people who heard him speak."

10 For a study of Texans in the role of citizen soldiers fighting Indians the vital work is Steven L. Moore's four-volume *Savage Frontier: Rangers, Riflemen, and Indian Wars in Texas*, published by University of North Texas Press.

11 Utley, *Lone Star Justice*, 83; Michael L. Collins, *Texas Devils: Rangers and Regulars on the Lower Rio Grande, 1845–1861*, adds a slight variation: "their [gangs of Mexican banditti] misdeeds were sometimes wrongfully assigned to *los malvados Tejanos*, 'the evil Texans,'" 12; For an insightful recap of the famous Walker Colt's, refer to Philip Schreier, "Walker's Walkers: The Colt Walker Revolvers of Captain Samuel H. Walker, Texas Ranger," *Man at Arms*, no. 3 (1998): 30–35.

12 Alexander, *Winchester Warriors*, vi; D. E. Kilgore, *A Ranger Legacy: 150 Years of Service to Texas*, 3–5.

13 Walter Prescott Webb, *The Texas Rangers: A Century of Frontier Defense*, 24; Charles M. Robinson III, *The Men Who Wear the Star: The Story of the Texas Rangers*, 4.

14 Marion Humphreys Farrow, *Troublesome Times in Texas*, 58. For an informed understanding of the Texas State Police, the researcher should access William Curtis Nunn, "A Study of the State Police During the E. J. Davis Administration," Master of Arts thesis, University of Texas, Austin, Texas, 1931.

15 H. P. N. Gammel, comp., *The Laws of Texas, 1822–1897*, vol. 8, 86.

16 Ibid.; 86-91; Harold J. Weiss, Jr., "Organized Constabularies: The Texas Rangers and the Early State Police Movement in the American Southwest," *Journal of the West*, January 1995, 28–29.

17 Alexander, *Winchester Warriors*, 17.

18 Ibid., 27.

19 General Order No. 2, Frontier Battalion, TSA.

20 Gammel, *The Laws of Texas*, vol. 8, 86–91; Wilkins, *The Law Comes to Texas*, 28.

21 Interview by author with Paul Spellman, Chuck Parsons, and Rick Miller, San Antonio, Texas, July 17, 2009.

22 Kilgore, *A Ranger Legacy*. The handwritten Monthly Return is reproduced on pp. 24–25.

23 Ibid.; Moore, *Savage Frontier: Rangers, Riflemen, and Indian War in Texa*, vol. 1, 8–10.

24 Dayton Kelley, "Ranger Hall of Fame," *FBI Law Enforcement Bulletin*, May 1976, 21.

25 J. Marvin Hunter, ed., *The Trail Drivers of Texas*, 721–22.

26 Hervey E. Chesley, *Adventuring with the Old-Timers: Trails Traveled—Tales Told*, 82.

27 Hunter, *Trail Drivers of Texas*, 722.

28 Scarbrough, *Land of Good Water*, 284. For a succinct look at the Texas prohibition movement in a political context, see Alwyn Barr, *Reconstruction to Reform: Texas Politics, 1876–1906*, 85–92.

29 Thompson and Digesualdo, *Historical Round Rock*, 296.

30 Ibid., 299.

31 Scarbrough, *Land of Good Water*, 284.

32 Ed Blackburn, Jr., *Wanted: Historic County Jails of Texas*, 356.

33 Thompson and Digesualdo, *Historical Round Rock*, 351–52.

34 An assertion that Ira Aten knew Imogen Boyce during school years is drawn from *The Austin American Statesman*, February 4, 1892.

35 Sergeant Ed Sieker to Adjutant General Jones, July 12, 1880, TSA; Bob Boze Bell, "I Should Have Killed Them All," *Cowboy Chronicle*, May 2008, 58; Alexander, *Winchester Warriors*, 157–61. For a comprehensive accounting, see Chuck Parsons, "The Jesse Evans Gang and the Death of Texas Ranger George R. Bingham," *Journal of Big Bend Studies* 20, 2008.

36 Ronald G. DeLord, ed., *The Ultimate Sacrifice: Trials and Triumphs of the Texas Peace Officer*, 54.

37 Preece, *Lone Star Man*, 26.

38 Aten-1941, 4. "I [Ira Aten] wanted to ramble around, wanted to be a cowboy"; Alexander, *Fearless Dave Allison: Border Lawman*, 19.

39 Aten-1941, 6, HML&HC.

40 Abbott, "My Autobiography," 7.

41 Photographs of knife courtesy Robert W. Stephens.

42 Preece, *Lone Star Man*, 28: "I [AG Steel] know a peace officer who speaks highly of you [Ira] and your family—Sheriff Emmett White here in Austin. Yes, sir, Sheriff White is a right close friend of ours"; Sammy Tise, *Texas County Sheriffs*, 494, does not list R. Emmett White picking up the reins as sheriff of Travis County until his election on November 6, 1888, five years after Ira Aten's enlistment with Company D of the Texas Rangers. The discrepancy does not negate the fact White could have written the letter of recommendation, or that the

Austin C. Aten family, Ira included, were well thought of throughout Travis and Williamson Counties.

43   Aten-1941, 5, HML&HC.

44   "Descriptive List," Ira Aten, May 5, 1891, TSA; Ira Aten, Typewritten manuscript, "Six and One-Half Years in the Rangers Service," 60. This document was later reprinted for a four-part series in *Frontier Times*. There are several extant copies of the manuscript, for example: The University of Texas, Center for American History (UT-CAH), Austin, Texas, and the HML&HC; Aten-1928, 7, HML&HC: "And I thought, 'Well, maybe that is pretty good advice.' I didn't crave it [liquor and tobacco], and didn't fall in with any of them. None of them will ever tell you that they saw me do those things—not that I pride myself on it, but it is just an unnecessary habit."

45   Aten-1941, 5, HML&HC; Ira Aten to Imogen Aten, October 31, 1936, PPHM.

46   Peter Watts, *A Dictionary of the Old West*, 262–63: "It [rawhide] could be used for ropes, whips, chaps, or anything else you fancied. It expanded when dampened and contracted when dried. So you could mend a broken wheel with it; use it as joining material in the construction of a corral; make it into hinges for a door or gate; sole your boots with it; even torture an enemy with it."

47   Monthly Return, Company D, April 1883, TSA; Certificate of Pay, State of Texas, Ira Aten, Date of enlistment, April 26, 1883, TRHF&M.

48   Ibid.; Captain Sieker to AG King, May 4, 1883, TSA: "the four recruits sent to me"; the handwritten notation on the Monthly Return is "Enlisted by Gen. King, April 26th 1883," TSA; Stephens, *Texas Ranger Sketches*, 144.

49   Captain Sieker to AG King, March 31, 1883, TSA.

50   Alexander, *Winchester Warriors*, 176; Captain Sieker to AG King, January 13, 1882, TSA.

51   Captain Sieker to AG King, April 24, 1882, TSA.

52   Monthly Return, Company D. April 1883, TSA.

53   Major John B. Jones to Lieutenant Frank Moore, Company D, August 20, 1877, TSA; Lieutenant Moore to Major Jones, September 6, 1877, TSA: "The Company which I now command will want eight of the improved Winchester guns—which you will please forward."

54   Certificate of Pay, State of Texas, Ira Aten, August 31, 1883, TRHF&M: "Balance due on Pistol issued last quarter."

55   Monthly Return, Company D, April 1883, TSA.

56   Ibid.

57   Inspection Certification of Company D property, April 1883, TSA.

58   Captain Sieker to Captain J. O. Johnson, April 21, 1883, TSA.

59 Captain Sieker to Captain J. O. Johnson, May 14, 1883, TSA.
60 Frontier Battalion General Order Number 18, September 20, 1877, TSA; Alexander, *Winchester Warriors*, 133; Company D Monthly Returns and certain contemporary photographs reflect employment of a "teamster," TSA.

Notes to Chapter 3

1   Aten-1941, 7, HML&HC.
2   Captain Sieker to AG King, May 5, 1883, TSA; also, Private W. T. McCown to Captain Sieker, May 3, 1883, TSA.
3   Dr. G. M. Devereaux to AG King, April 28, 1883, TSA.
4   Captain Sieker to AG King, May 21, 1883, TSA. In all fairness to Private Coopwood it must be acknowledged that he requested the discharge rather than suffer humiliation of a forced termination. He would later reenlist in another company; Monthly Return Company D, May 1883, TSA.
5   Gourney, *Texas Boundaries*, 83
6   Captain Sieker to AG King, May 4, 1883, TSA.
7   Ibid.
8   Alexander, *Winchester Warriors*, 187; Monthly Return, Company D, May 1883, TSA; Captain Sieker to AG King, May 29, 1883, TSA.
9   Monthly Return, Company D, June 1883. TSA.
10 Captain Sieker to AG King, June 4, 1883, TSA; Monthly Return, Company D, June 1883, TSA; T. H. Hammer had enlisted with the Texas Rangers on March 29, 1883.
11 Captain Sieker to AG King, June 21, 1883; Captain Sieker to AG King, June 30, 1883, TSA.
12 Paul H. Carlson, *Texas Woollybacks: The Range Sheep and Goat Industry*, 169, 178.
13 Bill O'Neal, *Cattlemen vs. Sheepherders: Five Decades of Violence in the West*, 24.
14 Monthly Return, Company D, September 1883, TSA; Alexander, *Winchester Warriors*, 189.
15 Stephens, *Texas Ranger Sketches*, 83–85.
16 Corporal B. D. Lindsey to Captain Sieker, September 19, 1883, TSA.
17 Ranger P. C. Baird to AG King, December 15, 1883, TSA.
18 Ibid.
19 Captain Sieker to AG King, January 19, 1884, TSA; Monthly Returns, Company D, September 1883 and January 1884, TSA.
20 Ira Aten, "Six and One-Half Years in the Rangers Service: Memoirs of Ira Aten, Sergeant Co. D, Texas Rangers," a 1945 four-part series in

Frontier Times: Part I, January; Part II, February; Part III, March; Part IV, April. Part I, 98: "....I was always expecting the impossible—like we see so often in the moving pictures these days—such as attempting to rescue some pretty girl from the Indians in a daring attack, or from the bandits who infested the Texas border along the Rio Grande."

21   Monthly Return, Company D, January 1884, TSA. As of the time of this writing, after reviewing Company D correspondence files and Monthly Returns, it seems safe to claim the capture of Rickerson was Ira's first arrest as a Texas Ranger. As to a stopover to visit his parents, the conjecture does not seem farfetched, based on a remark in the January 1884 Monthly Return: "Delivered him [Rickerson] to Sheriff of Llano Co and returned to camp via Austin"; Tise, *Texas County Sheriffs*, 344.

22   Captain Sieker to AG King, February 28, 1884, TSA.

23   Captain Sieker to AG King, February 29, 1884, TSA. A reasonably comprehensive article dealing with brand burning—blotching—may be found in the March 1927 edition of *The Cattleman*: "Fifty Years of Battling for Interests of Range Cattlemen," by J. Frank Dobie.

24   Captain Sieker to AG King, March 22, 1884, TSA.

25   Monthly Return, Company D. March 1884, TSA.

26   Captain Sieker to AG King, March 31, 1884, TSA.

27   Aten, "Six and One-Half Years in the Ranger Service," Part I, 101.

28   Ibid., 102.

29   Monthly Return, Company D, April 1884, TSA.

30   Aten, "Six and One-Half Years in the Ranger Service," Part I, 103.

31   Gournay, *Texas Boundaries*, 61, 93, 111.

32   Aten, "Six and One-Half Years in the Ranger Service," Part I, 103. There is a conflict between what an aged Ira Aten wrote, and data in the contemporary Company D Monthly Return for April 1884. Ira remembered he and the other man were "to act as guards for the tax collector of Val Verde county in the territory along the Pecos and Devil's rivers." Notation in the Monthly Return, too, is specific: "Privates Aten and Bargsley went to Devil's river in Crockett County to meet the Deputy Sheriff of Kinney Co. for the purpose of making a tour of Crockett Co. on a tax collecting expedition," TSA.

33   Ibid.

34   Monthly Return, Company D, May 1884, TSA.

35   Ibid.

36   Captain Sieker to AG King, May 31, 1884, TSA.

37   Monthly Return, Company D, June 1884, TSA; Frontier Battalion General Order No. 15, May 13, 1884. Company D 1st Sergeant Frank

Jones was promoted to Company D 1st Lieutenant under this order, TSA.

38   Ibid.

39   Captain Sieker to AG King, June 26 and July 20, 1884, TSA.

40   Monthly Return, Company D, July 1884, TSA.

41   Supplement to Monthly Return, Company D Detachment stationed in Llano County, July 1884, TSA; Tise, *Texas County Sheriffs*, 454.

42   DeLord, *The Ultimate Sacrifice*, 56; Bob Alexander, *Lawmen, Outlaws and S. O. Bs.*, vol. 2, 180.

43   Supplement to Monthly Return, Company D Detachment stationed in Llano County, July 1884, TSA.

44   Monthly Return, Company D, September 1884, TSA; Aten, "Six and One-Half Years in the Ranger Service," Part I, 108.

45   Alexander *Winchester Warriors*, 195–201; Harold D. Jobes knowledgeably recounts the incident in an article, "Fence Cutting and a Ranger Shootout at Green Lake," *Wild West History Association Journal*, October 2009, 39–48; Mike Cox, *The Texas Rangers: Wearing the Cinco Peso, 1821–1900*, 326–28; *The Dallas Daily Herald* of July 29, 1884, also carries the story, and correctly avers that the unfortunate incident was not as cut and dried in favor of the Texas Rangers as popularized histories would lead one to believe.

46   Lieutenant Jones to Captain Sieker, September 26, 1884, TSA.

47   Captain Sieker to AG King, September 13, 1884, TSA.

48   Captain Sieker to AG King, September 29, 1884, TSA.

49   Captain Sieker to AG King, September 30, 1884, TSA. Captain Sieker is referring to a preliminary hearing in a Justice of the Peace Court, not an actual trial in a District Court.

50   Alexander, *Winchester Warriors*, 199–200.

51   Monthly Return, Company D, September 1884, TSA.

52   Ibid.

53   Ibid.; Tise, *Texas County Sheriffs*, 43.

54   Ibid.: "22nd: Private Aten arrived in camp from Eagle Pass." Presidio was a small Mexican village, not Presidio, Texas.

55   Alice Braeutigam, cont., *Pioneers in God's Hills: A History of Fredericksburg and Gillespie County, People and Events*, 9–11; Aten-1941, 45, HML&HC.

56   There is a competing version of the crime, an undated typescript repeating a family's oral history: "Wesley Collier had a fast horse which he raced locally and won all races. He was from the west side of the Colorado River near what was Mud, Texas, in Travis County. He decided to go to Fredericksburg and try his luck there. When he got there, he arranged a race with the fastest horse in the area and large wagers were put up. Collier won the race much to the dissatisfaction

of the locals who had bet a large amount of money against him. It was late in the day and the locals not wanting to give up their money decided to put all the money in a safe in Brandigan's [Braeutigam's] store for the night while they tried to find a way to keep it. Early the next morning Collier went to the store to get his money so he could leave town before the local losers could get organized. Brandigan would not give him his money and an argument arose and both pulled their guns, Collier killed the store keeper and took his winnings and left." Typescript courtesy Chuck Parsons.

57 Aten-1941, 45, HML&HC.

58 Monthly Return, Company D, November 1884, TSA. Although in his memoirs Ira Aten mentions that two of the alleged killers were initially arrested, the Monthly Return enumerates three: Jack Beam, Wesley Collier, and Bill Allison. They were all arrested in Travis County by "Corpl. Baird and Scout."

59 Aten-1928, 85–87, HML&HC; Aten, "Six and One-Half Years in the Ranger Service," Part I, 111: "We took them to San Antonio, to a new jail, the best in the State—fool proof." Further substantiating Aten's assertion that the prisoners were locked up in the Bexar County Jail in San Antonio is the *Writ of Habeas Corpus* filed in their behalf in the case of Ede (sometimes written as Ed) Janes, C. W. Collier, and Jack Beam: "said application for writ of habeas corpus against the Sheriff of Bexar County Texas...." All official court documents relating to this criminal case are courtesy the Gillespie County District Clerk, Fredericksburg, Texas, and Chuck Parsons; Tise, *Texas County Sheriffs*, 204; Blackburn, *Wanted: Historic County Jails of Texas*, 37. The Bexar County Jail had been constructed in 1879 and was a two-story building.

60 Monthly Return, Company D, October 1884, TSA.

61 Monthly Return, Company D, November 1884, TSA; Tise, *Texas County Sheriffs*, 204.

62 Ibid.

63 Ibid.; Tise, *Texas County Sheriffs*, 357.

64 Aten, "Six and One-Half Years in the Ranger Service," Part I, 98: "Baird soon resigned to accept the office of chief deputy sheriff of Mason county [sic], and I was appointed Corporal in his place"; Monthly Return, Company D, December 1884, TSA.

65 Monthly Return, Company D, December 1884, TSA; interestingly, for the pay period closing on February 28, 1885, which would have covered December of the preceding year, is the notation on Ira Aten's Pay Certificate: "2 mos. as Prvt $60, 1 [mo] as Corpl. $35," TSA.

66 Cox, *The Texas Rangers: Wearing the Cinco Peso*, 330.

67 Monthly Return, Company D, December 1884, TSA.

68 Two letters Captain Sieker to AG King, January 31, 1885, TSA.

Notes to Chapter 4

1   Captain Sieker to AG King, February 6, 1885, TSA.

2   Aten, "Six and One-Half Years in the Ranger Service," Part I, 104.

3   Captain Sieker to AG King, February 6, 1885, TSA.

4   Alexander, *Winchester Warriors*, 202.

5   Adolphus Petree to J. Evetts Haley, July 26–27, 1941, 8, HML&HC. At least for some folks Sheriff Joe Tumlinson was not a person to take lightly, not according to Mr. Petree: "But they knew Joe Tumlinson too. He was the same way. He would pull the trigger, and there would be a dead Mexican," 19.

6   Ibid.

7   Chuck Parsons and Gary P. Fitterer, *Captain C. B. McKinney: The Law In South Texas*, 75; Wilkins, *The Law Comes to Texas*, 251; Tise, *Texas County Sheriffs*, 160.

8   Petree to Haley, 21, HML&HC.

9   Parsons and Fitterer, *Captain C. B. McKinney*, 75.

10   Aten-1928, 59, HML&HC.

11   Parsons and Fitterer, *Captain C. B. McKinney*, 75; Blackburn, *Wanted: Historic County Jails of Texas*, 103.

12   Captain Sieker to AG King, February 28, 1885, TSA.

13   Parsons and Fitterer, *Captain C. B. McKinney*, 76.

14   *Daily Index Appeal*, February 13, 1885. The researcher probing border area mind-sets in a law enforcement context may wish to refer to the inclusive study of Erik T. Rigler, "A Descriptive Study of the Texas Rangers: Historical Overtones on Minority Attitudes," Master of Arts Thesis, Sam Houston State University, Huntsville, Texas, 1971. The Appendix is particularly fascinating and revealing.

15   Alexander, *Winchester Warriors*, 202.

16   Governor Ireland to AG King, February 7, 1885, TSA; Wilkins, *The Law Comes to Texas*, 251.

17   Parsons and Fitterer, *Captain C. B. McKinny*, 75–76; Alexander, *Winchester Warriors*, 207.

18   Paul N. Spellman, *Captain J. A. Brooks, Texas Ranger*, 34; Captain Sieker's presence is suggested by his correspondence: "I will go to San Antonio tonight in answer to Capt. Johnson's dispatch." Captain Sieker to AG King, February 6, 1885, TSA.

19   Monthly Return, Company D, February 1885, TSA.

20   Aten, "Six and One-Half Years in the Ranger Service," Part I, 104.

21   Aten-1928, 59, HML&HC.

22   Spellman, *Captain J. A. Brooks*, 34; Parsons and Fitterer, *Captain C. B. McKinney*, assert Company F's Captain, Joe Shely, "remained one step behind McKinney and the others, thereby missing the big event in the

middle of the Rio Grande," 76; Private J. A. Brooks, in unpublished memoirs, places Joe Shely on the scene, see Spellman, 35.

23   Aten, "Six and One-Half Years in the Ranger Service," Part I, 104.

24   Ibid.; Ira Aten's understandable fogginess due to age regarding this issue is readily discernible by comparing his 1928 and 1941 interviews. In Aten-1928, HML&HC, he says on pp. 60–61: "We came to terms for a treaty sitting on our horses in the middle of the stream, with the river running swift to our horses' bellies. We could not write there, but agreed to go over to the Mexican town and write out a treaty.... We went over and wrote the agreement." For Aten-1941, 26, HML&HC, Mr. Aten remembers: "I think five on our side rode into the river to sign it. Captain Sieker, Lee Hall, Charles McKinney and I think Corporal Lindsey. I don't think Sgt. Jones was along. And myself. I went along. They allowed me to go along. And they signed that right in the middle of the river.... [W. W.] Collier, I think, was along. 'Old Man' Tumlinson was with us." Likewise there are discrepancies between Mr. Aten's versions regarding the cast of characters. That Aten was a witness to this part of Texas border history is not in doubt. That he at this juncture of his Ranger career was empowered as a diplomat, a policy decision maker, is unlikely.

25   Raymond, *Captain Lee Hall of Texas*, 220.

26   Alexander, *Winchester Warriors*, 202; Spellman, *Captain J. A. Brooks* has the location identified as Las Ysles Crossing on page 35; Raymond, *Captain Lee Hall of Texas* has it as *Las Islas*; Parsons and Fritter in *Captain C. B. McKinney* particularly address the various identifications of the same piece of ground. See page 80, n. 8.

27   Spellman, *Captain J. A. Brooks*, 33.

28   Ibid. An example of how the event has been journalistically titillated may be drawn from the writing of Preece in *Zane Grey's Western Magazine*, Part I, 99: "I Rode with the Texas Rangers: Hell on the Border."

29   *Dallas Daily Herald*, February 12, 1885.

30   Alexander, *Winchester Warriors*, 202.

31   Captain Sieker to AG King, February 13, 1885, TSA.

32   Two letters from Captain Sieker to AG King, February 20, 1885, TSA.

33   Ibid. The second letter offered Captain Sieker's assessment: "I scouted up the river and found the Ranchmen considerably excited, but I apprehend no trouble at present as the Mexicans will be afraid to come over the river in any force for sometime"; Monthly Return, February 1885, TSA: "established a camp on the San Ambrosia in Maverick County 4 miles fro the Rio Grande and one mile from the corner of Webb & Dimmit Counties."

34   Paul N. Spellman, *Captain John H. Rogers, Texas Ranger*, page 26 for "rustler capital of the world"; Captain Joe Shely, Company F, to AG

King, March 13, 1885, TSA. Details of these crimes may be found in Parsons and Fitterer, *Captain C. B. McKinney*, 84.

35   Captain Shely to AG King, March 13, 1885, TSA.

36   Parsons and Fitterer, *Captain C. B. McKinney*, print the *Dallas Herald* newspaper story in full on pp. 76–77.

37   Ibid.

38   Ibid., quoting Frank B. Ernest to Governor John Ireland, February 8, 1885, TSA.

39   Captain Shely to AG King, March 13, 1885, TSA.

40   Monthly Return, Company D, March 1885, TSA.

41   Petree to Haley, 15, 22, HML&HC.

42   Aten-1928, 86, HML&HC.

43   Ibid., 87; an assertion that the prisoners had first been incarcerated at San Antonio in the Bexar County Jail is not challenged and is taken directly from Aten. Primary source documents, later, will also confirm an escape from the Mason County Jail. For moving Ira's story the real significance is that there was a jailbreak and he was hunting for the escapees. Later Aten would write in "Six and One-Half Years in the Ranger Service" with confidence: "In the meantime another one of the murderers had been captured by other parties and was locked up in the Fredericksburg jail. This building almost immediately and mysteriously burned down upon the prisoner," Part I, 111; Blackbun, *Wanted: Historic County Jails of Texas*, 134: "The new prison was built in 1874 but burned in 1885, and an inmate died in the fire."

44   Aten-1941, 45, HML&HC.

45   Robert Penniger, *Fredericksburg, Texas....The First Fifty Years*, 79.

46   Interview with Dave Johnson, October 10, 2009. Johnson, an exceedingly well-versed expert on crime and criminality in the Texas Hill Country, advises that, although unsupported by primary sources, some oral histories squarely place blame for the jailhouse fire on the prisoner himself during a botched try at escaping.

47   Alexander, *Winchester Warriors*, 269.

48   Captain Sieker to AG King, March 27, 1885, TSA.

49   *Monthly Return*, Company D, April 1885, TSA.

50   John R. Baylor to AG King, April 19, 1885, TSA; Texas Ranger Company D Privates A. P. Barry and W. W. Collier to AG King, April 16, 1885, TSA.

51   Monthly Return, Company D, May 1885, TSA.

52   Ibid.

53   Lieutenant Frank Jones to AG King, May 13, 1885, TSA.

54   Monthly Report, Company D, May 1885, TSA.

55   Captain Sieker to AG King, April 30, 1885, TSA.

Notes to Chapter 5

1   Utley, *Lone Star Justice*, 244.
2   Captain Sieker to AG King, May 31, 1885, TSA.
3   Alexander, *Winchester Warriors*, 204–6.
4   Aten-1928, 52, HML&HC: "They were coming from Catulla [*sic*]
     towards the Rio Grande."
5   Ibid.; there is a slight discrepancy in that some accounts mention two
     pack mules, others but one.
6   Aten-1941, 28, HML&HC; Alexander, *Winchester Warriors*, 204; Ser-
     geant B. D. Lindsey to Captain Sieker, July 10, 1885, TSA.
7   Utley, *Lone Star Justice*, 243.
8   Aten, "Six and One-Half Years in the Ranger Service," Part I, 99.
     Though Aten refers to Lindsey at the time of this encounter as being a
     corporal, he was, in fact, Company D's 1st Sergeant.
9   Aten-1928, 52, HML&HC.
10   *El Paso Times*, June 4, 1885: "Gonzales and his son aged 13 years"; *Dal-
     las Daily Herald*, June 2, 1885: "with Apolonus Gonzales and his son,
     aged about 21 years"; Captain Sieker to AG King, July 14, 1885: "The
     two Mexicans (Gonsales & Son) are in Mexico and are likely to remain
     there unless I can have them extradited," TSA; Alexander, *Winchester
     Warriors*. 205.
11   Aten-1941, 32, HML&HC: "They had six shooters, but they were
     shooting with their rifles."
12   Aten-1928, 52, HML&HC.
13   Aten-1941, 28, HML&HC.
14   Ibid.
15   Affidavit and Personnel File [Frank Sieker] for Texas Peace Officers
     Killed in the Line of Duty, Courtesy Ron DeLord, Executive Director,
     Combined Law Enforcement Associations of Texas (CLEAT), Austin,
     Texas; Aten-1941, 31, HML&HC. In this version Ira Aten does not
     have Frank Sieker dying instantly, but quickly.
16   Aten-1928, 53, HML&HC; Aten-1941, 28. Modestly, Ira Aten does
     leave room for the possibility that Frank Sieker made a telling shot:
     "and the other one ducked down on his horse. Frank or me one had
     hit him on the shoulder...." Aten's description of Sieker's death is
     dramatic: "I never saw a better picture of a man being shot off a horse,
     even in a picture show. Falling back from his horse. They don't usually
     fall back from the horse, but forward, but the horse was going very
     fast, and he fell backward—still holding the six-shooter, you know,"

32, HML&HC; *Galveston Daily News*, June 2, 1885; in San Antonio at the time of his brother's death, Captain Sieker sent a telegram to AG King on June 1, 1885.

17 Alexander, *Winchester Warriors*, 206; *Galveston Daily News*, June 2, 1885.

18 Aten, "Six and One-Half Years in the Ranger Service," Part I, 99; Aten-1928, 53, HML&HC.

19 Aten-1928, 53, HML&HC.

20 Ibid.; Tise, *Texas County Sheriffs*, 43; unidentified newsclip: "B. D. Lindsey says rangers now 'sissies,'" VF-B. D. Lindsey, TRHF&M; Stephens, *Texas Ranger Sketches*, 83.

21 Alexander, *Winchester Warriors*, 206; Utley, *Lone Star Justice*, 244; Cox, *The Texas Rangers: Wearing The Cinco Peso*, 331.

22 Sergeant Lindsey to Captain Sieker, July 10, 1885, TSA.

23 Ibid.

24 Monthly Return, Company D, June 1885, TSA.

25 Aten-1941, 32, HML&HC.

26 *El Paso Times*, June 4, 1885. The newspaper story identifies the senior Gonzales as Pilanus.

27 *Dallas Daily Herald*, June 3, 1885.

28 Aten-1941, 32, HML&HC.

29 *El Paso Times*, June 4, 1885. Not unexpectedly, Preece, *Lone Star Man*, paints Apolonio and Pedro with the darkest of evil brushes, journalistically ensuring foils for the protagonist of his biography, Ira Aten, 47–56. Interestingly, Webb, *The Texas Rangers: A Century of Frontier Defense* somewhat out of character for his venerating historical accounts of Texas Rangers, omits wholly any mention of the death of Private Frank Sieker—and its aftermath. Also quite intriguing is the editorial comment at the bottom of page 30 of the Aten-1941 interview: "Short time after this, Evetts and I talked to Mr. Adolph Petree, down in that country, and he told about the wounded man going to the ranch. It seemed he minimized the fight with the Mexicans, saying they were a 'man and a boy.'" Commendably, although Ira Aten recounts the fight in his published memoirs, he does not make any personal characterizations of his adversaries. It would appear he purposefully refrained from calling them "bandits," or "desperadoes" or "murdering horse thieves."

30 Petree to Haley, 14, HML&HC.

31 Captain Frank Jones to Adjutant General Woodford Haywood Mabry, March 1, 1892, TSA.

32 Sergeant Lindsey to Captain Sieker, July 10, 1885, TSA.

33 Ibid.; Alexander, *Winchester Warriors*, 207.

34 Utley, *Lone Star Justice*, 243; Cox, *The Texas Rangers: Wearing The Cinco Peso*, 331.

35 Aten-1941, 29, HML&HC.

36 Sergeant Lindsey to Captain Sieker, July 10, 1885, TSA.

37 Ibid.; Aten-1941, 29; HML&HC; Utley, *Lone Star Justice*, 245: "On June 1, within thirty minutes of their arrival, the sheriff's kin had been released from custody and all the Rangers thrown into jail, charged with assault with intent to murder"; Seb S. Wilcox, "The Laredo City Election and Riot Of April, 1886," *Southwestern Historical Quarterly*, July 1941, 6–7; Blackburn, *Wanted: Historic County Jails of Texas*, 347.

38 Aten-1928, 58, HML&HC.

39 Abbott, "An Autobiography," 4; Virginia Kimmons Abbott, "Genealogy," typescript, 1925, courtesy Bruce Archer, Angie Aten Kimmons' great grandson.

40 Ibid.

41 Aten-1928, 58-59, HML&HC.

42 *The San Antonio Daily Express*, February 15, 1885.

43 Interesting is Captain Sieker to AG King, August 17, 1885, TSA: "on my way to Cotulla, where I will go in a few days to see some parties regarding the murder of the Mexicans in Dimmitt [*sic*] Co, also some parties Sen. Hall wanted me to see in the Shely matter"; AG King to Honorable E. F. Hall, June 29, 1885, Adjutant General Letter Press Book, September 8, 1884–August 22, 1885, 371. Also see page 376, AG King to Captain Sieker, June 30, 1885, TSA: "Senator E. F. Hall, has presented to Governor Ireland, some charges against Capt. Jos. Shely, and asks that they be investigated....."

44 Sergeant Lindsey to Captain Sieker, July 10, 1885, TSA; Monthly Return, Company D, June 1885, TSA: "They on seeing the Rangers advancing on them at once ran and were pursued. Aten and Riley came up with them first and demanded their surrender to which they agreed and when Riley reached out to take a gun from one of them he was suddenly and without warning shot and the men who were Mexicans began firing on Aten...." Interestingly there is no mention in the Monthly Return concerning the Rangers' stay in jail. It is handled with the nondescript "they were followed by Sergt. Lindsey and arrested and jailed in Laredo. Sergt. Lindsey and scout returned to Camp. Out 30 days and marched 175 miles."

45 Ibid.: "I find by talking with Riley & Aten that they tell substantially as above"; Dudley G. Wooten, ed., *A Comprehensive History of Texas, 1685–1897*, vol. 2, includes a chapter dealing with the Texas Rangers written by Adjutant General W. H. King. Aten's involvement in

the shoot-out with "Mexicans" is handled absent the contemporary controversy, but does include the Rangers being jailed, and comments on the prevailing racism: "but as their victims were of the hated white race, while they and those before whom they were brought belonged to the Mexican race, it is easy to understand why 'the tables were turned' and these guilty men allowed to escape to the land of 'God and Liberty,' while those who were honestly and gallantly serving Texas were held as prisoners for nearly a month, under a false and infamous charge." See pp. 362–64.

46 *Corpus Christi Caller*, June 7, 1885.

47 *Dallas Daily Herald*, June 3, 1885.

48 *El Paso Times*, June 4, 1885.

49 Unidentified printed newsclip titled "Webb County Grand Jury," courtesy HML&HC.

50 Wilcox, "The Laredo City Election And Riot of April, 1886," 7; Aten, "Six and One-Half Years in the Ranger Service," Part I, 100.

51 Ibid., 5-6.

52 *Galveston Daily News*, June 19, 1885, picking up a story from the *San Antonio Daily Express*.

53 Ibid. The twelve members of the Webb County Grand Jury were: E. S. Remington, Foreman, L. J. Giraud, Albert Urhahan, A. V. Woodman, Raymond Martin, Juan Ortiz, A. Scrwabil, L. E. Puster, C. Benavides, James Orfila, J. Deutz, and C. M. MacDonnell; The endorsement on the petition was signed by J. C. Russell; Aten, "Six and One-Half Years in the Ranger Service," Part I, 100.

54 *Galveston Daily News*, June 20, 1885.

55 AG King to Captain Sieker, August 19, 1885. Adjutant General Letter Press Book, September 8, 1884–August 22, 1885, 468-469, TSA.

56 *Galveston Daily News*, August 5, 1885.

57 Private Grant to Captain Sieker, August 22, 1885, TSA.

58 *Galveston Daily News*, June 20, 1885; Captain Sieker to AG King, August 31, 1885, TSA: "I have discharged or rather dropped Baker & Grant as directed...."; Monthly Return, Company D, August 1885, TSA; AG King to Captain Sieker, August 19, 1885, TSA: "....I take it for granted that you have promptly discharged Grant.... The Governor directs me to say that, unless the circumstances of this case are totally opposed to those detailed in the 'Times' and entirely in favor of private Grant, in every particular, you will drop him from your roll at the last of this month if not already discharged, and that you will take the same course with private Baker, who is indicted for criminal libel."

59 Aten-1941, 33, HML&HC; AG King to Captain Sieker, July 22, 1885: "In reply to your letter of 20th inst., I would say that you are hereby

instructed to move your company to some point in the vicinity of Uvalde, Tex"; Adjutant General Letter Press Book, September 8, 1884–August 22, 1885, 423, TSA.

Notes to Chapter 6

1 Monthly Return, Company D, July 1885, TSA.
2 Captain Sieker to AG King, July 20, 1885, TSA.
3 Monthly Return, Company D, August 1885, TSA: "Lieut. Jones and 3 men made scout to Jaidin and other points on Rio Grande after Pendencia Herrera and other parties, failed to find them. Out 2 days. Marched 60 miles"; *Galveston Daily News*, October 30, 1885; Tise, *Texas County Sheriffs*, 503, 526: "Dario Gonzles SPELLING? .... and served until sometime in 1886 when he was ousted as sheriff."
4 Captain Sieker to AG King, March 27, 1885, TSA; Captain Sieker to Captain Johnson, March 27, 1885, TSA.
5 Frontier Battalion, General Order, No. 85, October 12, 1885, TSA.
6 Lieutenant Jones to Captain Sieker, October 27, 1885, TSA; Lieutenant Jones to Captain Sieker, November 1, 1885, TSA.
7 Monthly Return, Company D, October 1885, TSA.
8 Monthly Return, Company D, December 1885, TSA; Lieutenant Jones to Captain Sieker, November 1, 1885, TSA.
9 Monthly Return, Company D, September 1885, TSA: "Corporal Saunders and 2 men made scout to West Nueces via Brackett to intercept if possible 'Collier and Beam' Escaped prisoners from Mason County."
10 Ibid.; Monthly Return, Company D, January 1886, TSA: "Aten and Sheriff Wheat followed trail of Collier and Beam who broke jail at Mason, Texas."
11 Ibid.
12 Ibid.
13 Monthly Return, Company D, February 1886, TSA.
14 Ibid. Prisoner Redman was turned over to the sheriff of Uvalde County.
15 Aten-1928, 85–87, HML&HC.
16 Ibid., 88; Monthly Return, Company D, March 1886, TSA: "Private Ira Aten made scout to Austin, with Capt. Sieker's horse." The fact that Ira Aten would, at some point, be delivering a horse to Captain Sieker was not unexpected. See Lieutenant Frank Jones to Captain Sieker, November 30, 1885, TSA: "Aten thinks that he will get back from Laredo about the 15th Dec. and would like to ride your horse to Austin for you if that time will be soon enough"; Lieutenant Jones to Captain Sieker, February 28, 1886, TSA: "Aten will leave with your horse on 2nd if the weather is favorable."

17 Ibid.; Monthly Return, Company D, June 1886, TSA: "under orders for Genl. King...."

18 Monthly Return, Company D, June 1886, TSA.

19 Aten-1928, 89–90, HML&HC; Addendum to Monthly Return, Company D, June 1886, TSA.

20 Ibid.

21 Addendum to Monthly Return, Company D, June 1886, TSA; Tise, *Texas County Sheriffs*, 494.

22 Aten-1928, 92–93, HML&HC; Aten, "Six and One-Half Years in the Ranger Service," Part I, 111.

23 Ibid.

24 Ibid.

25 Aten to AG King, April 3, 1886, from "Hughes rancho," courtesy of Hervey E. Chesley Collection, HML&HC.

26 Aten-1928, 91, HML&HC; Monthly Return, Company D, June 1886, TSA. After gunplay with Collier: "Then to Austin and reported to General King and was ordered back...."

27 Ibid.; for the 1945 publication of Aten's memoirs, Ireland's instructions to Ira were somewhat toned down: "Bring those murderers in dead or alive." See Aten, "Six and One-Half Years in the Ranger Service," Part I, 111.

28 Ibid., 96–97; Dane Coolidge, *Fighting Men of the West*, 1932. While the author does seemingly parrot folklore inspired by twentieth-century creative journalism, he asserts that the fugitive was initiating or maintaining an illicit relationship: "Then the Ranger [Aten] discovered a weak-minded fugitive from justice and, by playing on his fears and promising him immunity, discovered the clue he was looking for. Although Roberts [Collier] had a wife, he had been sparking the daughter of a nester [Dayton]; but the next time he came to see her they [Aten and Hughes] trapped him, and in the fight that followed he was killed," 142.

29 Ibid.

30 Ibid., 98–99; unfortunately the facts regarding the killing of Wes Collier have, over the years, been journalistically corrupted. Ira Aten's reminisces—on the whole—are solidly backed up by primary source documents. Perhaps the first secondary attempt at "juicing up" the story is the semi-fictional string of stories carried in *True Detective Magazine*, a four-part series by Paul Havens titled "Border Boss: The Saga of Captain John R. Hughes, Texas Ranger," beginning with the June 1940 issue. These stories were verbatim preludes to Jack Martin's *Border Boss: Captain John R. Hughes—Texas Ranger*, which was published in 1942. Perplexing as it may be, the possibility that Jack Martin is a pseudonym for Paul Havens—or vice versa—becomes

palatable. Preece's *Lone Star Man*, published in 1960, not surprisingly then, picks up and regrettably repeats misinformation contained in the preceding works. Thereafter the dominos of half-truths tumble throughout succeeding efforts at telling either the Ira Aten or John Hughes story. Examples are Mr. Ted Shannon's "Ira Aten and the Disappearing Killer" for the February 1965 edition of *The West* and Mr. B. Morando's "Ira Aten: Texas Ranger" in *Famous Lawmen of the West*, a special edition of *Real West*, Fall 1965. But one example of the journalistic chicanery would be the creative birth of Judd Roberts, a notorious outlaw and member of Butch Cassidy's Hole in the Wall Gang. In the above-cited works—wholly disregarding evidence—the fictionalized character Judd Roberts replaces the very real Wesley Collier. In an effort to spice a good story, details of his demise are melodramatically garbled almost to the point of non-recognition. The fictionalized account is carried forward in Hatley, "Ira Aten, Last of the 'Old Time Rangers'." That Wesley Collier even knew any of the so-called Wild Bunch would historically be doubtful. An assertion that Judd Roberts, even though a fictional personality in this instance, was an associate of that crowd falls on its face in light of known facts and a proper application of chronology. For a October 12, 2009, clarifying interview with the esteemed Chuck Parsons, former "Answer Man" for *True West* magazine, confirmation was sought. Mr. Parsons confirmed there is no evidence of Aten and/or Hughes ever coming in contact with a Judd Roberts. Furthermore through his personal contacts with several recognized Butch Cassidy and Wild Bunch historians and authors—experts themselves—there is not a scrap of factuality in associating Judd Roberts with that conglomeration of criminals either. Also see Alexander, *Winchester Warriors*. Aten discusses the manhunt in his memoirs published in the *Frontier Times* series, but does not mention killing Collier. Both Preece, *Lone Star Man*, and Jack Martin, *Border Boss*, have dramatic recreations of this story, but the dead badman is identified as Judd Roberts, 353 n. 311.

31   Ibid.; Wilkins, *The Law Comes to Texas*, 271, mistakenly reports: "Aten rode to the ranch of John Hughes, who was more than willing to help and offered suggestions for capturing the murderer. The two men captured the fugitive without trouble."

32   *Liberty Hill Ledger*, July (exact date unknown) 1886, "Justice Must Prevail," courtesy, J. Evetts Haley Collection, HML&HC. According to the newspaper story, Aten, in addition to notifying Sheriff Olive and AG King, also wired Collier's wife and brother "who live somewhere on the Colorado river," and to his father in Kerr County, Texas. Also, according to the same report he notified the *Fort Worth Daily Gazette* and *San Antonio Daily Express*, May 26, 1886: "Adjutant General King received

a dispatch today from Liberty Hill, stating that a ranger named Aten shot and killed one Collier, who resisted arrest"; *Galveston Daily News*, May 26, 1886: "Adjutant-general King learns that a ranger of the frontier battalion shot and killed a man named Collier, at Liberty Hill, to-day.... He is represented to have been a desperate character."

33 Ibid.; Addendum to Monthly Return, Company D, June 1886, TSA: "and on the 25th of May met and killed Collier who resisted arrest"; Tise, *Texas County Sheriffs*, 544; for biography of Sheriff John T. Olive, see Jim Dillard, *The Noble John Olive: The Life and Death of Willamson County Sheriff John T. Olive*.

34 Ibid.

35 Ibid.

36 Aten-1928, 99, HML&HC.

37 AG King to A. L. Patton, June 19, 1886; Adjutant General Letter Press Book, August 24, 1885–July 22, 1886, 377, TSA.

38 *Liberty Hill Ledger*, July (exact date unknown), 1886; a verbatim reprint of this article was carried in the *Burnet Bulletin*, May 30, 1929, under the heading "From the Bulletin: 43 Years Ago," courtesy of Chuck Parsons.

39 Captain Jones to Captain Sieker, May 31, 1886, TSA.

40 Addendum to Monthly Return, Company D, June 1886, TSA.

41 Ibid.: "Went to Austin and reported and then returned to gather information in regard to Jas. Fannin wanted for Murder in Gillespie Co."

42 Monthly Return, Company D, July 1886, TSA.

43 Monthly Return, Company D, August 1886, TSA; Maverick County Sheriff Tom Oglesby to AG King, July 20, 1886, TSA: "I have been shown letter Captain Jones ordered Aten to Austin. Aten is doing his work here. Will you revoke ordering him away until you hear from us...."; Captain Jones to Captain Sieker, August 18, 1886, TSA.

44 AG King to N. O. Reynolds, August 2, 1886: "I will try to send you a certain man [Aten], belonging to the Front. Batt. who is now going to Comanche County & who will be instructed to go to your town on his return from Comanche. There are no men, that I know of, in the Battalion, who are detectives, and there is no appropriation, with which to pay regular special agents, hence the difficulty of sending a man to ferret out the perpetrators of the fence cutting you mention." See Adjutant General Letter Press Book, July 28, 1886–May 4, 1887, 21, TSA.

Notes to Chapter 7

1 Application for Process, Gillespie County Criminal Case No. 418, *The State of Texas vs. Jack Beam*, August 23, 1886: "an attachment for Ira

Aten, a resident of Travis County, State of Texas, whose evidence is believed to be material for the State in said Cause"; Subpoena, for Ira Aten, August 23, 1886.

2   Charge of the Court, Gillespie County Criminal Case No. 418, *The State of Texas vs. Jack Beam*; Aten-1928, 91, HML&HC: "He [Beam] pled guilty with the understanding that he would get a light sentence."

3   Verdict Form, Gillespie County Criminal Case No. 418, *The State of Texas vs. Jack Beam*.

4   AG King to Col. E. D. Linn, July 27, 1886, Adjutant General Letter Press Book, July 28, 1886–May 4, 1887, 1, TSA.

5   Ernest Wallace, David M. Vigness, and George B. Ward, eds., *Documents of Texas History*, 228.

6   R. D. Holt, "Introduction of Barbed Wire into Texas and the Fence Cutting War," *West Texas Historical Association Yearbook*, June 1930, 66; Henry D. and Frances T. McCallum, *The Wire That Fenced the West*, 3–98; Walter Prescott Webb, *The Great Frontier*, 249–50; Samuel Stanley, "The Fence Cutters' War," *Real West*, August 1985, 18; Walter Prescott Webb, "The Fence-Cutters," *True West*, May–June 1963, 13.

7   Alexander, *Winchester Warriors*, 191.

8   Ibid.; entertainingly, author Katie Lee explores another dimension the introduction of barbed-wire had on the cattle culture in her seminal *Ten Thousand Goddamn Cattle: A History of the American Cowboy in Song, Story and Verse*, 9–11: "The second phase came when the cowboy's life was drastically changed. When the land he had conquered began to have value for things with roots, the nesters and sodbusters came to fence him out of it. Not only did he lose his job, he lost the need to perform his role of the first white man to inhabit the *whole* Western wilderness…. In 1874 some dude had to go invent barbed wire. As this stuff unwound, mile after mile off the spools, Mr. Cowboy's usefulness as a night nurse ended. A short twelve years later his trail-herding days shuffled to a stop. The long drives from Texas to Montana were over. In their place railroads spread like lights in series, dashing across the continent, carrying the cattle he once had driven…. The cowboy's third and most productive musical period begins here. After the fences he had time to do things beside rope cattle, brand, wrangle horses, de-horn steers, and de-ball bulls. He discovered talents he didn't know he had. The bunkhouse replaced the trail camp and in it such items as a fiddle, a jew's [*sic*] harp, banjo, mouth-organ (called a French harp then), a concertina, and even a guitar could be found. He started putting down words about how things *used* to be, and you know what that means—it means he forgot a lot of the bad stuff and waxed nostalgic about the nearly insignificant. No longer isolated, this cowboy caught a dose of creeping civilization and began

believing his press. He even went out and did some of those things just to live up to the image."

9   Ruth Whitehead, "That Bloody Fence Cutting War," *The West*, December 1969, 20.

10 Wayne Gard, *Frontier Justice*, 108: "Soon the work of these saboteurs was the talk of the state. Some ranchmen had their pastures burned."

11 Wallace, Vigness, and Ward, *Documents of Texas History*, 228; C. E. Lee, "The Fence-Cutters War in Texas," *Frontier Times*, July 1931, 467.

12 Ibid.; William C. Stewart, "Days of Free Range in Texas," *Frontier Times*, September 1947, 539.

13 Gard, *Frontier Justice*, 107–8.

14 Holt, "Introduction of Barbed Wire into Texas and the Fence Cutting War," 73.

15 T. R. Havins, *Something About Brown: A History of Brown County, Texas*, 37.

16 Alexander, *Winchester Warriors*, 191; James L. Haley, *Passionate Nation: The Epic History of Texas*, 377: "Those who favored fencing stretched barbed wire across public roads and sometimes cut off whole towns, and some free rangers sought to best the system by fencing in public domain to which they had no claim."

17 Gard, *Frontier Justice*, 104.

18 Gammel, *The Laws of Texas*, vol. 9, 569.

19 Alexander, *Winchester Warriors*, 191; Stanley, "The Fence Cutters' War," 21: "Despite the new law in Texas, cutting resumed with the same vigor."

20 Lieutenant Jones to AG King. June 17, 1884, TSA: "The Sheriff is an utter failure as a peace officer"; Corporal Lindsey to AG King, May 5, 1884, TSA: "I learn from a reliable source that the local authorities in this [Llano County] and Burnet Cos. are very inefficient in their duties and from my same observation of the men am not surprised"; Stanley, "The Fence Cutters' War," 21.

21 Jobes, "Fence Cutting and a Ranger Shootout at Green Lake." Citing the *Llano News*, 40.

22 Captain Jones to AG King, October 7, 1887, TSA. Notation by AG King at bottom of letter: "Write him that the Gov. has a standing reward of 200 for ever case of conviction in fence cutting. K."

23 Webb, "The Fence Cutters," 13.

24 Ibid.; Will Henry, *The Texas Rangers*, 166: "The job [cutting a fence] was done in minutes and there was no evidence upon which to make an arrest."

25 Alexander, *Winchester Warriors*, 141. During the nineteenth century, for many Texas Rangers, the designation "detective" carried a singular and somewhat negative connotation: it meant a covert operative.

Texas Rangers as peace officers would investigate openly. A detective operated on the sly, snooping undetected it was hoped.

26 Ira Aten, "Fence-Cutting Days in Texas," *Frontier Times*, July 1939, 442: "In order to round up these fence cutters it was necessary to be deceitful, to lie, and even to steal, so as to win their confidence...."

27 Ibid.: "It was even an insult to an old-time ranger to call him a 'detective'...." Interestingly, an imprisoned inmate in 1889, perhaps in a rehabilitative tone, warned potential criminals about detectives: "Young man, as you meditate the commission of some crime, I would urge upon you also to take into account the fact that you will be overtaken. A detective will be put upon your track. He may come to you in the guise of a friend, and before you are aware of what you have done you will unbosom yourself to him, who later will appear as a witness against you in a court of justice and be the means of sending you to the penitentiary.... An experienced detective will read the expression in your face." See John N. Reynolds, *A Kansas Hell or Life in the Kansas Penitentiary*, 227.

28 AG King to J. W. Jones, Sheriff, Wharton County, January 28, 1888. "As a matter of law and of fact, we have no right to detail a ranger for service as a 'detective,' as he must voluntarily consent to undertake the peculiar duties expected of a detective.... The amt. of duty required in this case involves extraordinary expenditures, and in addition to our lack of legal authority to 'order' a ranger to assume the duties of a detective, this question of expense becomes one of importance, where the small frontier fund is considered." See Adjutant General Letter Press Book, October 24, 1887–May 24, 1888, 200, TSA; AG King to J. W. Jones, Sheriff, Wharton County, January 30, 1888: "As before said, the State has no lawful authority to assign a Ranger to duty as a detective, but I must have his consent to undertake such work...," in the Adjutant General Letter Press Book, October 24, 1887–May 24, 1888, TSA.

29 Aten, "Six and One-Half Years in the Ranger Service," Part II, 129.

30 Aten-1928, 70, HML&HC.

31 Ibid., 71; Parsons and Brice, *Texas Ranger N. O. Reynolds*, 292.

32 Ibid.: "It was Huling's fence they were cutting. They were put in jail and I was turned loose."

33 Aten, "Fence Cutting Days in Texas," 441–42; Aten-1941, 80, HML&HC: "telling wild stories...."

34 Aten-1928, 70, HML&HC.

35 Aten, "Six and One-Half Years in the Ranger Service," Part II, 128.

36 Ibid.; Wilkins, *The Law Comes to Texas*, appreciably elevates the courtroom drama by having Ira Aten actually striking the fence cutters' defense attorney, see page 268. The author's assertion of an actual

physical assault is not borne out by inspection of the source cited.
Ranger Ira Aten may have wanted to strike the attorney, but he did
not. Aten himself said: "That made me pretty mad and I was about to
go over the table at him." See Aten-1941, 84, HML&HC. Clearly Aten
did not strike the lawyer.

37   Ira Aten, as told to Harold Preece, "I Fought These Masked Rustlers,"
Real West, May 1963, 20–21; Parsons and Brice, *Texas Ranger N. O.
Reynolds,* touch upon this incident, bringing it to a close with: "The
identity of the two companions of Aten was not disclosed," see page
292; Preece's averment that the boys went to prison is clearly discounted by Ira Aten: "In the Lampasas County case the jury acquitted the boys. They had all the neighbors around there and they were
angels and I was a demon." See Aten-1941, 84, HML&HC.

38   John Cogswell, "Installation of Barbed Wire in Texas." *Frontier Times,*
July 1939, 447.

39   Barbara J. Cox, *The Wire-Cutting War of Brown County, Texas, 1883–
1888,* 1; James C. White, *The Promised Land: A History of Brown County,
Texas,* 55–57; J. Marvin Hunter, ed., "'Morg' Baugh of Brownwood,"
Frontier Times, September 1946, 232–34; Ethel Baugh Franke (Morg
Baugh's daughter) to Tessica Martin, February 23, 1975: "It was the
Baugh ranch and was on the part that Uncle Lev and Dad bought."
Courtesy Ed Walker, Brownwood Public Library—Genealogy Branch,
Brownwood, Texas.

40   Winnie Baugh Strait, "The Baugh Families," unpublished 1938
typescript. Remembrances of Washington Morgan Baugh, as told to
Strait: "In 1884, Morg and Lev Baugh began fencing their land with
barb wire fencing. They went to Cisco and bought about 2,000 pounds
of wire. Later they got 7,000 pounds from Dublin. Fenced pastures
were unheard of by most ranchers and was bitterly resented by them.
Then began the days of wire cutting. A regular gang was formed who
cut down their fences seven times," see page 12. Courtesy Herbie
Belvin; Clay Riley, Brown County Historical Society to author, March
19, 2010: "Levin, Morg, and their brother-in-laws (McInnis and
Windham) became sizable land owners during the 1870s and 1880s";
Tevis Clyde Smith, *Frontier's Generation,* tells of the salty cowpuncher
McInnis, who "came to Brown county in 1865.... For his part, McIn-
nis got a job punching cattle for Lev Baugh. It was not easy work, in
the cold wintertime, when the cattle would stray from the range, but
McInnis liked his job. He enjoyed many phases of it, particularly the
chance elements of his work. There was no telling when he would lose
his scalp to some hostile Comanche or Kiowa; on the other hand, the
Indians stood some risk themselves when they brushed up against
McInnis.... Then, there were other kinds of game; an occasional black

bear wandered into the Bayou bottoms. McInnis killed one with his six-shooter. He also had brushes with catamounts. The panthers were a nuisance to the stockmen; they killed many valuable cattle. McInnis shot several of these animals; he killed one near Cross Cut, while the lion was eating a yearling," see pp. 35–36; F. Romer, *Makers of History: A Story of the Development of the History of Our Country and the Part Played in it by the COLT,* 59, credits California lion hunter J. Bruce with killing 218 pumas with his .38-40 Colt's six-shooter.

41 Gard, *Frontier Justice,* 110.

42 Havins, *Something About Brown,* 37; John Henry Brown, *Indian Wars and Pioneers of Texas,* 455.

43 Andrew R. Graybill, *Policing the Great Plains: Rangers, Mounties, and the North American Frontier, 1875–1910,* 141: "Baugh—who was legendary in Brown County for having nearly decapitated an Indian scout in the 1860s with a blast from his .8-gauge shotgun...."; Strait, "The Baugh Families," 12; Cox, *The Wire-Cutting War,* 2.

44 Whitehead, "That Bloody Fence-Cutting War," 32.

45 Ibid., 33.

46 Ibid.; Brown, *Indian Wars and Pioneers of Texas,* 466; Tevis Clyde Smith, *From the Memories of Men,* also confirms that merchant Weakley "sold every firearm he had, and all the ammunition," but may have slightly confused the chronology. See p. 30.

47 Patti Mauldin, ed., *The Genealogy and History of Brown County Sheriffs,* 40–41; Mary Whatley Clarke, *A Century of Cow Business: The First Hundred Years of the Texas and Southwestern Cattle Raisers Association,* 41: "They rode to the courthouse square where they were met by Sheriff Adams who ordered them to lay down their guns. After much objection they obeyed and then followed the sheriff to the district courtroom where they shouted their grievances .... Gradually the crowd quietened. After a long day, the fence cutters secured their guns and rode out of town"; Pattie Lee Cross Weedon, ed., *Early Communities of Lake Brownwood: A History of the First Families Who Settled in the Northern Part of Brown County Between the Pecan Bayou and the Jim Ned Creek,* 1980 edition, 8: "The names of some of the members were: John Matthews, Jeff Johnson, Ace Matthews, Frank Johnson, Charlie Johnson, James B. Lovell, Hog Harris, Bill Purcell, Bill Green, Amos Roberts, John Keesee, Bazel Harper, Bob Parrock, Charlie Byrd, Jim Byrd, Shep Byrd, Charlie Tuckness, and Elijah Robert 'E. R.' Ashcraft, Anderson, Runnels and Lewis"; Tise, *Texas County Sheriffs,* 70; Alexander, *Winchester Warriors,* 192; that the number of wire cutters in Brown County was fairly substantial may also be found in Comanche County Sheriff James "Jim" W. Cunningham's "Sheriff's Experience With Fence-Cutters," *Frontier Times,* July 1930, 459–60; that double-

agents were employed during the fence-cutting turmoil may be found in the remembrances of Edward Baxter Featherston in *A Pioneer Speaks*, Vera Featherston Back, ed., 75–76.

48   Smith, *From the Memories of Men*, 29.

49   Cox, *The Wire-Cutting War*, 3. The author identifies the indicted parties as Amos Roberts, Jake Lewis, Baz Hopper, Charlie Johnson, Frank Johnson, Jeff Johnson. A. S. Mathews, John Mathews, Bob Parrock, and Jim Lovell; this listing of defendants was earlier spotlighted in Havins, *Something About Brown*, 38–39. On April 25, 2010, the author had the agreeable opportunity to interview James Franklin "Jim" Dempsey, at Terrell, Kaufman County, Texas. Mr. Dempsey is originally from Brown County and is a great-grandson of Elijah Robert "E. R." Ashcraft. Mr. Dempsey fondly remembers his great-grandfather giving him $10 to buy his first calf, and the fact that after age thirty-five E. R. Ashcraft never shaved off his beard. Mr. Dempsey also remembers family oral history. Germane to this narrative is the following information he received from his granddad, Simon Franklin Ashcraft. From time to time during the 1880s an unnamed man would appear at the Ashcraft farm located in Brown County, just west of Rattlesnake Draw. After but a brief consultation with the unidentified person, E. R. Ashcraft would catch and saddle his favorite horse, grab his rifle, and disappear for several days at a time. Upon his return E. R. Ashcraft remained mum about his mysterious absence. Could he have been on a fence-cutting mission? Mr. Jim Dempsey does not know. From family lore the disappearances always remained hush-hush. Elijah R. Ashcraft was a member of the Farmers Alliance, many of whom were not sympathetic to the wholesale fence building then underway—and were themselves sometimes fence cutters.

50   Aten-1928, 72, HML&HC.

51   Ibid.; Aten-1941, 87, HML&HC: "We couldn't get any assistance from the sheriff. I gave information to a reporter [after the shoot-out on the fence line] kind of condemning the sheriff. The Brownwood papers gave me the devil, said they had a good sheriff. But the sheriff never gave us [Rangers] any assistance whatever"; Strait, "The Baugh Families," 12: "Morgan and Lev appealed to the local officers for help to prevent this, but the sheriff, Bill Adams, had a brother, Zack, who was helping the wire cutters so nothing was done about it."

52   AG King to Ira Aten, August 26, 1886: "You will proceed to Brownwood for the purpose of investigating lawlessness in that section, and will make such report and recommendation as the facts and circumstances may warrant. Call at the Bank & see Messrs. Coggins, Ford and Martin, or rather see Mr. Ford of said firm, who will indicate parties

and places to be seen." See Adjutant General Letter Press Book, July 28, 1886–May 4, 1887, 69, TSA.

53   Aten-1928, 72, HML&HC; Aten's assertion that Pinkerton men had been on the state's payroll in regards to the fence cutting epidemic was not hollow. See Utley, *Lone Star Justice,* 235: "But Ireland now had a fund of $50,000 and he turned to professionals—Pinkerton's National Detective Agency in Chicago and Farrell's Commercial Detective Agency in New Orleans. He also hired private detectives in Texas.... The operatives identified many culprits but never caught any in the act of cutting and never gathered enough evidence to convict even had a jury been willing to convict"; White, *The Promised Land,* 69–70.

54   Aten, "Fence-Cutting Days in Texas," 443.

55   Aten, "Six and One-Half Years in the Ranger Service," Part II, 129. In this writing Aten does not specifically identify the rancher by name. For Aten-1928, 75, HML&HC, Ira Aten identifies him as Bob Herrick which in fact would be Bob Parrock. See Rick Miller, comp. and ed., *Bell County: Crime and Criminals, 1851 to 1902.* "#3196 State vs. Bob Parrack—change of venue from Brown County for theft of horses; #3199 State vs. Bob Parrack change of venue from Brown County for assault with intent to murder; #3200, State vs. Bob Parrack—change of venue from Brown County for assault with intent to murder"; and other criminal cases transferred to Bell County from Brown County, see p. 266; Cox, *The Wire-Cutting War,* 3, identifies the man as Bob Parrock; Other citations also refer to Parrock.

56   Ibid., 129–30.

57   Aten-1928, 75, HML&HC; Smith, *From the Memories of Men,* 29: "We have been criticized for the course the Rangers took, but the wire cutters were no angels, and something had to be done to make a man's life and property safe. We knew that there was only one way to crack the case. Somebody had to get in with the fence cutters, and gain their confidence. Ira Aten was selected as the man to do the job."

58   Aten, "Six and One-Half Years in the Ranger Service," Part II, 130; *The State of Texas vs. R. C. Parrock,* Brown County Cause Number 3196. Aten took the two stolen horses and left them at the Huling Ranch in Lampasas County. The defense counsel was alleging that the horses were those of Ira Aten and that Huling would testify that "Ira Aten was in possession of the horses alleged to have been stolen by the defendant herein, claiming said horses as his own and that.... Aten left said horses with Huling as his [Aten's] horses." Two factors are evident: the defendant was trying to lay the horse theft on Aten, and Aten, at the time he left the horses at the Huling Ranch, did not disclose the horses were not his, thus maintaining investigative integrity of the undercover assignment. Case synopsis courtesy Rick Miller.

59 Shroyer, *Williamson County*, 57; interview with Betty Aten grand-daughter of Frank and Josie Aten.

60 Ibid.; Awbrey and Dooley, *Why Stop?* 239.

61 Strait, "The Baugh Familes," 11: "One evening while in town, he [Joe Copeland] sidled up to Morgan [Baugh] and traced on the store counter with his knife—'They are going to cut yhour fence tomorrow night'"; Cox, *The Wire-Cutting War*, 5.

62 Aten-1928, 77, HML&HC.

63 Cox, *The Wire-Cutting War*, 5: "The next evening at sundown, eight rangers arrived from Belton on horses"; Strait, "The Baugh Familes," 12: "Lev immediately informed and wired the adjutant general in Austin. Eight rangers were here the next evening at sundown, coming from Belton on horses."

64 Spellman, *Captain J. A. Brooks, Texas Ranger*. Spellman has the Rangers sallying forth from a pre-positioned spot in Brown County, see pp. 44–45. In several other accounts Ranger John Rogers is not listed as a participant in the ensuing gunfight.

65 Strait, "The Baugh Families," 11–12: "Lev [Baugh] met them [Rangers] and took them out to the ranch. Morgan, Elam Thompson, Bill Sloan, Ira Aiten [*sic*] (a detective), Oscar Baugh, Frazier and Snow (two hands on the ranch) had gone over on the fence line and were waiting for the rangers. They all tied their horses back in the brush and stayed together after the rangers had arrived. They had sent Jim Aubrey to town to notify the officers there"; Cox, *The Wire-Cutting War*, 5.

66 Aten-1928, 78–79, HML&HC. The accounts published in the 1939 article and the 1945 memoir were short, near-verbatim pieces, and perhaps in deference to surviving relatives no names were mentioned. Aten, "Six and One-Half Years in the Ranger Service," Part II, 130. For Aten-1941, the old-time Ranger's story had undergone an alteration: "I was cutting along with them and when we got there, Copeland and me, another man, a friend of mine—we dropped back when we came to the live oak trees. It was all planned. Captain Scott went out and demanded their surrender. Those fellows weren't going to surrender, and jumped behind their horses and opened fire," see p. 87; Havins, *Something About Brown*, 39, differs slightly from Aten: "Lovell died within an hour, while Roberts died in Brownwood, where he had been taken, after having a bullet removed from under his shoulder blade."

67 Strait, "The Baugh Families," 13; *The Saturday Herald* (Decatur, Illinois) November 13, 1886: "At eleven o'clock the cutters were heard coming up the line of fence. They were permitted to pass a few of those in ambush, but on arriving opposite him Captain Scott demanded their surrender, stating that they were rangers. His only answer was a pistol shot. Then the firing became rapid on both sides. The moon

was bright and clear, and they could distinguish one another easily....
Jim Lovell, the man killed, was disguised with a false mustache. He
was an old offender. Amos Roberts, the man captured died. Lovell held
the position of constable in an adjoining precinct...." Not surprisingly,
a different characterization of Lovell may be found from his family's
perspective. See Weedon, ed., *Early Communities of Lake Brownwood*,
1st ed. pp. 9–11: "James B. Lovell, born May 10, 1862 in Brown
County and was murdered on Nov. 9, 1886." For this rendition Joe
Copeland is cast as an entrapper:

Copeland met with the Farmer's Alliance and told them that Morg
Baugh had fenced his cattle off from water and asked for some help
to cut his fence. Charles Johnson, John Matthews, Amos Roberts and
Jim [Lovell] volunteered to help him. Copeland then told the Baughs
and they reported it to the Rangers so along with them and several
hired killers, they were waiting for the boys the night of Nov. 9, 1886.
Copeland led them to the place where he told them he wanted the wire
cut and pretending that he had to hide out for natures [sic] course, he
slipped away and unhitched the horses, slipping their reins over the
saddle horn and giving the signal. Charlie Johnson, becoming suspicious, said "Copeland has been gone too long boys, there is something
wrong." They started for their horses and saw the men raise up from
behind a thicket, shooting as they came up. The four boys ran for their
horses but Jim was shot in the back by Oscar Baugh and died immediately. A Ranger shot a hole in John Matthews hat and vest and killed
his horse just as he reached under him to get his gun [rifle]. Amos
Roberts was shot and carried to Brownwood and placed in jail where
he died five days later. Charlie Johnson fell on a rock while he was getting shot at by a Ranger and played dead until the Ranger had gone,
then he slipped his boots off and ran barefooted over the rocks and
cactus, unnoticed.

68 Spellman, *Captain John H. Rogers, Texas Ranger*, 41; Mike Cox, *Texas
Ranger Tales II*, 139.

69 Ibid.: "In an instant it was over. The Rangers holstered their guns and
looked after the two fallen men. Neither had been able to get off a
shot."

70 Private Aten to AG King, November 26, 1886, TSA: "When opposite
the Rangers Capt. Scott demanded there [sic] surrender which was
answered by a shot from one of the parties cutting the fence. The
shooting then became general...."; Aten-1928, 78–79, HML&HC; Aten,
"Fence-Cutting Days in Texas," 444; Strait, "The Baugh Families," 13:
"As they came up, the captain of the rangers called to them to halt.
Immediately everybody began firing." During a pleasurable March
16, 2010, interview with Brown County rancher Bill McInnis, great-

grandson of Sam McInnis, the following tidbit of family oral history was noted. According to Mr. McInnis it was Lev Baugh who had specifically hand-loaded shotgun shells with an extra measure of gunpowder for the fence cutters. When the shooting started it was Lev's two charges of buckshot that took the fight and life from the cutters. Weedon, *Early Communities of Lake Brownwood*, 1st ed., asserts: "The four boys ran for their horses but Jim [Lovell] was shot in the back by Oscar Baugh and died immediately," see p. 10. Oscar "Osh" Baugh was a younger brother of Lev and Morgan Baugh, see Strait, "The Baugh Family," 1; Ruth Griffin Spence, *The Nice and Nasty in Brown County* also places smoking guns in the Baughs' hands: "Within a short time the fence cutters appeared and began cutting the wire. Ranger Captain Scott called on them to halt. As the cutters ran, the Baugh party fired on them and killed two," see p. 30.

71 Whitehead, "That Bloody Fence-Cutting War," 61; Havins, *Something About Brown*, 39–40; Cox, *The Texas Rangers*, 336–37.

72 Cox, *The Wire-Cutting War*, 7.

73 Havins, *Something About Brown*, 40.

74 Ira Aten to Captain Sieker, June 11, 1887, TRHF&M.

75 Captain William Scott to Captain Sieker, December 12, 1886, TRHF&M.

76 Alexander, *Winchester Warriors*, 183–84; George Schmitt, having served several terms as the sheriff of Comal County (New Braunfels), cleaved unto himself a reputation ripe with controversy and contentiousness. The new lieutenant's bullheadedness, now and then an asset for ferreting out criminals, regrettably was matched by his colossal ego; Robert W. Stephens, *Captain George H. Schmitt: Texas Ranger*, 21: "Schmitt's aggressive nature"; Cox, *The Texas Rangers,* 329: "The ranger's ego matched his strong work ethic"; Jean Dale Sherman in a generalized article about the Texas Rangers for the March 1937 edition of *The Cattleman*, sticks with the idealized portrayal: "As they adventured together, a rare comradeship was fostered among the Rangers which they cherished through life. They never indulged in backbiting and petty jealousies," see p. 58.

77 Captain George Schmitt to Captain Sieker, March 31, 1887, TRHF&M.

78 Captain George Schmitt to Captain Sieker, April 4, 1887, TRHF&M.

79 Ira Aten to Captain Sieker, June 11, 1887, TRHF&M.

80 Monthly Return, Company D, December 1886, TSA: Stephens, *Texas Ranger Sketches*, 125–31.

81 Parsons and Fitterer, *Captain C. B. McKinney*, 97–99; DeLord, *The Ultimate Sacrifice*, 59; Robert W. Stephens, *Walter Durbin: Texas Ranger and Sheriff*. The subject of Stephens' biography, J. Walter Durbin, is generally credited—and rightly so—with killing Sheriff McKinney's murderer

George W. "Bud" Crenshaw in the chaparral country of La Salle County near Twohig (now Arteisa Wells). Walter Durbin, Ranger at the time, accompanied by Ranger Albert Calvin Grimes (brother of the Grimes killed at Round Rock during the Sam Bass episode), describes what took place when he approached an already wounded Crenshaw, who at the time was taking potshots at him with a six-shooter. According to Durbin, "I fired several times as fast as I could work my Winchester." Later the suspect who had wounded Deputy Edwards from ambush, James "Jim" McCoy, turned himself in hoping for a better deal. He missed. Although "Pete" Edwards had survived, and would rightly earn respect as a topnotch Texas lawman, McCoy was hanged in San Antonio on August 23, 1889, see pp. 37–44. Interestingly, a year later Walter Durbin was making an inquiry about the price on Crenshaw's head, see Ranger Private J. W. Durbin to Captain Sieker, January 10, 1888, TSA.

Notes to Chapter 8

1 Monthly Return, Company D, January 1887, TSA.
2 P. C. Baird, Deputy Sheriff Mason County, to AG King, January 4, 1887, TSA; Tise, *Texas County Sheriffs*, 357; AG King to Captain Jones, January 7, 1887. "P. C. Baird, Depty. Shff. of Mason County, desired to effect the arrest of a murderer living in his county & wants the assistance of Pvt. Ira Aten of your company. If Aten is not engaged on any important business, and you can spare him for a short time, you will so inform Baird, and send him (Aten) to Mason County on receipt of notification from Baird as to date when he is wanted. If Aten goes to that point, he will have to go on horseback." See Adjutant General Letter Press Book, July 28, 1886–May 4, 1887, 262, TSA.
3 Monthly Return, Company D, January 1887, TSA.
4 Ibid.
5 Captain Jones to AG King, January 14, 1887, TSA; for further exploration of Bill Mitchell's absorbing story, see Sam Conn, "Hot on the Trail of 'Bill' Mitchell, *Bootheel Magazine*, Winter 2009, 8–11; also see C. L. Sonnichsen's *Outlaw: On the Dodge with Baldy Russell* and *Ten Texas Feuds*; for a capsule treatment refer to Dave Southworth's *Feuds on the Western Frontier*, 79–82.
6 Monthly Return, Company D, February 1887, TSA; Monthly Return, Company D, September 1887, TSA: "Sept. 7. Private [Bazzell Lamar] Outlaw went to Carorters pasture and Brackett in search of Bill Mitchell wanted for murder. Learned that he had left the country. Supposed to be in N. Mexico"; Stephens, *Bullets and Buckshot in Texas,* 34: "It seems likely that his correct names was Bazzell Lamar Outlaw or Bazel Lamar Outlaw."

7   Ibid.; Tise, *Texas County Sheriffs*, 204; for supplemental data regard-
    ing the Ake family, see Rick Miller, *Bloody Bill Longley*, 70–71; David
    Johnson, *The Mason County "Hoo Doo" War, 1874–1902*, citations
    throughout and Dennis McCown, "In Pursuit of the Lost Man,"
    National Association for Outlaw and Lawman History, Inc. Quarterly,
    July–December 2007, 7–13.

8   Monthly Return, Company D, March 1887, TSA; Captain Jones to
    Captain Sieker, May 15, 1887, TSA: "Aten informed me that Genl.
    King had promised to pay his expenses while he was attending Court,
    and that was the reason that I approved it and sent it without com-
    ment. The Sheriff of Uvalde did attach and take him to Brownwood.
    When Aten returns I will have him attend to this matter. He is now
    in Lampasas attending Court"; Havins, *Something About Brown*, sug-
    gests the following named individuals were indicted by the Brown
    County Grand Jury as a result of the November 9, 1886, shoot-out on
    the fence line: A. S. (Ace) Mathews, William Green, Charley Tuck-
    ness, Frank Johnson, Charlie Johnson, Bob Parrock, and Shep (Ship)
    Byrd, see p. 40. That the Johnson brothers were indicted is also a part
    of Johnson oral history, highlighted during pleasant April 6, 2010,
    interviews with descendants by blood or marriage: Vonda Williamson,
    Early, Texas, and Patsy Johnson, Early, Texas. Interestingly, however,
    is the fact that the Johnson brothers were not listed as defendants in
    Rick Miller's comprehensive *Bell County: Crime and Criminals, 1851–
    1902*. In fact, Jeff Johnson was actually subpoenaed as a defense wit-
    ness with a $200 bond guaranteeing his court appearance in cause no.
    3204, *The State of Texas vs. William Green, Ace Mathews and Ship Bird*
    (Byrd), 269.

9   Captain Jones to AG King, January 31, 1887, TSA.

10 Captain Jones to AG King, March 31, 1887, TSA.

11 Aten-1941, 64–65, HML&HC.

12 Monthly Return, Company D, April 1887, TSA.

13 Captain Jones to Captain Sieker, May 2, 1887 TSA: "I have appointed
    Aten 1st Sergt...."

14 Monthly Return, Company D, May 1887. Though it is noted Aten left
    camp for a U.S. District Court appearance at San Antonio, the asser-
    tion that it was in regards to livestock smuggling is only probable
    speculation. Later federal court appearances regarding smuggling case
    are confirmed with citation to primary source material.

15 Jeff Burton, "'A Great Man Hunt'—Correspondence From 'W. B. S.':
    Some Scenes of Outlawry and Gunplay in Texas," *English Westerner's
    Society Brand Book* 18 (1975–76): 11–34; R. Michael Wilson, *Great
    Train Robberies of the Old West*, 64–65: "All the while Cornett, who
    seemed to be in charge, sucked on a candy stick.... and one newspaper

went so far as suggesting he be called 'Captain Dick with the candy stick'"; Parsons and Brice, *Texas Ranger N. O. Reynolds*, 303; Bill S. Price, *Bill Whitely: Outlaw*, 39–41.

16   Richard Dillion, *Wells, Fargo Detective: A Biography of James B. Hume*, 235–36; Stephens, *Bullets and Buckshot in Texas*, 62: "Cornett severely beat the man with his pistol. After emptying the safe, the gang robbed the mail car, then Cornett, Whitley and Powell robbed and manhandled the passengers."

17   Wilson, *Great Train Robberies*, 64.

18   Jeffrey Burton, *Western Story*, European edition, 91 n.17: "The loot was put at some $7,000, a little over $5000 of it from the Wells, Fargo safe. It seems likely that the true amount was about twice that figure."

19   Parsons and Brice, *Texas Ranger N. O. Reynolds*, 303: "El Paso County Sheriff James H. White was a passenger and it was he who identified the leader as 'Captain Dick' Cornett...."

20   Dillon, *Wells, Fargo Detective*, 236.

21   Monthly Return, Company D, June 1887, TSA.

22   Sergeant Aten to Captain Sieker, August 6, 1887, TSA.

23   Sergeant Aten to Captain Sieker, August 7, 1887, TSA.

24   Parsons and Brice, *Texas Ranger N. O. Reynolds*, 307; Wilson, *Great Train Robberies*, 57; DeLord, *The Ultimate Sacrifice*, 60; Dillard, *The Noble John Olive*, 61; Price, *Bill Whitely: Outlaw*, 53.

25   Burton, "A Great Man Hunt," 25, quoting the *St. Louis Globe-Democrat*: "The first crime perpetrated by Barbour and Whitley after the separation into pairs in Burnet County was the assassination of Deputy Sheriff Stanley in Williamson County"; *San Antonio Daily Express*, August 7, 1887: "A dispatch from Sheriff Olive, of Williamson county, states that his deputy Bill Stanley, was ambushed and assassinated last night. John Barber and Bill Whitley are the supposed assassins"; DeLord, *The Ultimate Sacrifice*, 60, 72: "It was thought two men, John Barbour and Will Whitley, who were wanted in several states, killed Stanley because he was searching for them."

26   Harold L. Edwards, *Goodbye Billy the Kid*. After thorough research the author knocks sideways any twentieth or twenty-first century romanticism by comprehensively citing newspaper reports actually contemporaneous to Billy the Kid's death, 79, 101, 119; Alexander, *Lawmen, Outlaws, and S. O. Bs*, vol. 2, 214.

27   Bob Boze Bell, "50 Things You Don't Know About Wyatt Earp," *True West*, July 2003, 26: "There is no official record of Wyatt being legally married to two of his three wives. And two of Wyatt's so-called wives have been accused of being 'on the line' (prostitutes)" and, "Wyatt was a bartender longer than he was a lawman."

28   Sergeant Aten to AG King, August 11, 1887, TSA: "Please find
     enclosed the oath of John R. Hughes"; Monthly Return, Company D,
     August 1887, TSA; Fort Worth *Star-Telegram*, December 27, 1914: "I
     [John R. Hughes] enlisted at Georgetown on Aug. 10, 1887…."; Oath
     of Office, John R. Hughes, August 10, 1887, courtesy Chuck Parsons;
     also, C. L. Douglas, *The Gentlemen in the White Hats: Dramatic Episodes
     in the History of the Texas Rangers,* 148: "[John R. Hughes]….enlisted at
     Georgetown to start a career that would make him the half-veiled hero
     of Zane Grey's Lone Star Ranger."

29   Ibid., "We leave for up about Lampasas Co. to-day. Will write you when
     I deem it necessary."

30   Aten, "Six and One-Half Years in the Ranger Service," Part I, 112:
     "After this incident [Wes Collier shooting] I induced Hughes to join
     the Ranger Service…. From this introduction grew a friendship that
     has steadily ripened as the years passed."

31   Sergeant Aten to Captain Sieker, October 29, 1887, TSA; Monthly
     Return, Company D, October 1887, TSA: "16 [October]—Private
     John Hughes reached camp"; Monthly Return, Company D, Novem-
     ber 1887, TSA: "Capt. Jones and Company reached Rio Grande City
     in Starr County and located camp 3 miles from town…. Out 22 days.
     Marched 342 miles."

32   DeLord, *The Ultimate Sacrifice*, 60.

33   Sergeant Aten's supplemental report to the adjutant general detailing
     duties while on detached service, February 29, 1888, TSA.

34   Sergeant Aten to Captain Sieker, October 29, 1887, TSA.

35   Burton, "A Great Man Hunt," 25, quoting from the *St. Louis Globe-
     Democrat*: "Very soon after this the Texas officers succeeded in
     locating the place of refuge in the [Indian] Territory. One afternoon
     Sheriff Olive, Deputy Sheriff Hoyle, Sheriff Evans, of Fannin County,
     and Rangers Eaton and Bailey left Paris [Texas]. They rode all night
     hard, but a relative of the men, who was guarding them, had given a
     warning. Barbour and Whitley suddenly left their camp at midnight
     and started for the Territory [*sic*, Texas]. Five hours later the Texas
     posse rode up, to discover that the birds had flown. They started back
     to Texas on the trail, and at one place were in sight of the robbers, but
     with the advantage of fresh horses Whitley and Barbour distanced
     the pursuit." No doubt the Texas Ranger mentioned as "Eaton" in this
     newspaper account was a phonetic error, and in point of fact, it should
     have read "Aten." The "Bailey" mentioned in the newspaper article was
     more likely W. C. Bailey, Special Agent for the International & Great
     Northern branch of the Southern Pacific Railroad, rather than a Texas
     Ranger. See *Austin Daily Statesman*, May 25, 1887; Dillard, *The Noble
     John Olive*, 74–75.

36 Sergeant Aten to Captain Sieker, February 28, 1888, TSA.

37 Sergeant Aten to Captain Sieker, January 14, 1888, TSA; Sergeant Aten's February 29, 1888, supplemental report as cited; Sergeant Aten had not been the only Texas Ranger hunting for Whitley and Barber in the Indian Territory. So, too, was John Rogers. See Spellman, *Captain John Rogers, Texas Ranger*, 55.

38 Monthly Return, Company D, February 1888, TSA.

39 Sergeant Aten to Captain Sieker, October 29, 1887, TSA.

40 Captain Jones to AG King, March 15, 1888, TSA: "I have appointed J. W. Durbin Corporal. He is an old Ranger and has been an officer before and is a good man"; typescript memoirs of J. Walter Durbin: "I rec letter Stateing that wee has been transferred to Capt Frank Jones Co and to take every thing and report to him at Realitos Sta as he was on his way up from Rio Grande City with his Co pitched camp six miles north of Realitos in Bob Saviage ranch....," courtesy Robert W. Stephens.

41 Stephens, *Walter Durbin: Texas Ranger and Sheriff*, 70.

42 Ann Jensen, ed., *Texas Ranger's Diary and Scrapbook*, 40.

43 Stephens, *Bullets and Buckshot in Texas*, 33, 46 n. 4.

44 Stephens, *Walter Durbin: Texas Ranger and Sheriff*, 78.

45 Alexander, *Winchester Warriors*, xi.

46 *Arizona Miner*, January 17, 1879; Bob Alexander, *John H. Behan: Sacrificed Sheriff*, 48.

47 Monthly Return, Company D, February 1888, TSA.

48 Stephens, *Bullets and Buckshot*, 208; Burton, "A Great Man Hunt," 23: "One thing that prompts the suspicion that there is a secret chapter back of the killing of Cornett is the fact that, soon after the tragedy, Will Jacobs, who is mentioned in [Edward] Reeves' confession, came in and surrendered. He was wanted for various offenses. It is known that he was in the confidence of the robbers and that he had been in Cornett's company some time before the killing. Then there was a close bond between Allee and Jacobs. Allee was a deputy sheriff as well as a ranchman. In a killing scrape a long time ago, in which Allee and Jacobs were concerned, Allee got off, the burden of the blame being thrown upon Jacobs. The latter, it is believed, has been playing into the hands of the State official, trying to make peace for himself in that way. It is probable that Cornett went to Allee's place through Jacobs' influence, and that the outlaw was entrapped partly for the reward and partly on an assurance of leniency for past offenses."

49 Captain Jones to AG King. June 24, 1888, TSA.

50 Stephens, *Bullets and Buckshot*, 64–69; Wilson, *Greatest Train Robberies*, 67; Parsons and Brice, *Texas Ranger N. O. Reynolds*, 304: "Well-known gunfighter-lawman Alfred Y. Allee now appeared on the scene. On February 12, 1888 Allee caught up with Brack Cornett and

shot him to death in a Frio County pasture"; Jeff Burton, "The Most Surprised Man in Texas," *Frontier Times*, March 1973, handles the killing of Cornett this way: "On the morning of the 12ᵗʰ 'Captain Dick' was approached from behind as he knelt by a fire. Sensing danger, he whirled about, drawing his gun. Quick as he was, he stood no chance. He was shot three times from close range, with instant and fatal effect. The shooting was done by either Allee or Jacobs, or by both of them. Allee's story as he told it in Pearsall a few days later, included no mention of Jacobs...." See p. 51.

51 Ibid., 72; Price, *Bill Whitley: Outlaw*, 61.
52 Monthly Return,. Company D, March 1888, TSA.
53 Adjutant-General's Office Railway Pass, courtesy Sally Walker and Leta Rutter Hawks, granddaughters of Calvin Grant Aten.
54 Monthly Return, Company D, April 1888, TSA.
55 Sergeant Aten to Captain Sieker, April 29, 1888, TSA: "The 25¢ is for my younger bother being sworn in."
56 Stephens, *Texas Ranger Sketches*, 15.
57 Captain Jones to Captain Sieker, March 1, 1888, TSA.
58 Sergeant Aten to Captain Sieker, April 30, 1888, TSA.
59 Richard F. Selcer, *Fort Worth Characters*, 155; Oliver Knight, *Fort Worth: Outpost on the Trinity*, 102: "On the El Paso site later were the Pickwick and Delaware hotels, both known throughout the ranch country...."; Richard Selcer, ed., *Legendary Watering Holes: The Saloons That Made Texas Famous,* 245: "For a time, the White Elephant held bragging rights to being the biggest saloon in the city. Equally important, it was just a few minutes walk from such downtown gathering places as the Pickwick and Mansion Hotels...."
60 Sergeant Aten to Captain Sieker, May 10, 1888, TSA.
61 Sergeant Aten to Captain Sieker, April 17, 1888, TSA.
62 Blackburn, *Wanted: Historic County Jails of Texas*. 106; Gournay, *Texas Boundaries*, 71.
63 Ibid.; Monthly Return Company D, July 1888, TSA; Tise, *Texas County Sheriffs*, 163.
64 Monthly Return, Company D, July 1888, TSA; Aten's travel to Austin is also substantiated by the International and Great Northern Railway Pass issued to "Sergeant Ira Aten, Company D, Frontier Battalion... one 'Ranger' Ticket to.... Austin," authorized by Captain Jones on July 24, 1888, TSA.
65 Monthly Return, Company D, November 1888, TSA.
66 Stephens, *Bullets and Buckshot*, page 117 for King's geographical and physical description; for King's proclivity for popping the cork, see Alexander, *Winchester Warriors*, 218, 225; also, Captain Jones to AG King. September, 4, 1889, TSA: King was "too drunk to be efficient and

it is impossible to keep him sober"; Aten, "Six and One-Half Years in the Ranger Service," Part II, 131: "I went back to the company for Jim King, who had been tried and tested at my side through many hardships and difficulties. King was a fiddler—not a violinist...."; Aten's remark about going back to the company to contact King is interesting in light of the entry in Company D's Monthly Return of August 1888, TSA: "[Aug.] 4. Prvt. King under orders from Genl. King left to join Sergt. Aten in Williamson County." Additionally, that Aten was already in Williamson County is confirmed by International and Great Northern Railway Pass for "Sergt. Ira Aten....to Round Rock," in TSA.

Notes to Chapter 9

1 Gard, *Frontier Justice*, 116; R. A. Davis the former county surveyor of Ellis County, Texas, was in an 1892 profile characterized as "one of the substantial agriculturists of Ellis County." See the Lewis Publishing Company's *Memorial and Biographical History of Ellis County, Texas*, 490–91.

2 Alexander, *Winchester Warriors*, 218; Private Hughes to Captain Sieker. May 15, 1888, TSA; Wyvonne Putman, ed., *Navarro County History*, 196.

3 Private Hughes to Captain Sieker, May 26, 1888, TSA: "he talks freely to me about stealing cattle. He and I stold [*sic*] a stake rope a few days ago and expect to kill a beef as soon as we eat up what he had on hand when I came. Then if he knows who the wire cutters are I think he will tell me."

4 Private Hughes to Captain Sieker, June 13, 1888, TSA.

5 Monthly Return, Company D, June 1888, TSA.

6 Aten, "Fence-Cutting Days in Texas," 444: "He [Governor Ross] gave me instructions to go to Navarro county to arrest the fence cutters, leaving the method of doing so up to me. 'Stop that fence cutting at all costs,' were the only orders he gave"; Judith Ann Benner, *Sul Ross: Soldier, Statesman, Educator*, 170.

7 Ibid.; Aten-1928, 83, HML&HC; Hart Stillwell, "Dinamite Aten and His Big Boom," *True Western Adventures*, October 1959, 63. The misspelling of dynamite in the piece's title is probably a purposeful error, keeping in line with some of Aten's wording. Referring to "Novorro" County, rather than "Navarro" is perhaps an inadvertent typo, although it is repeated throughout. In any event, the article does rely heavily on Aten's actual letters to Captain Sieker regarding the Navarro County fence cutting investigation.

8 Sergeant Aten to Captain Sieker, August 20, 1888, TSA: "I got as far as Mexia...."; interview with Navarro County Sheriff Leslie "Les" Cotten,

November 9, 2009; John L. Davis, *The Texas Rangers: Images and Incidents*, 70: "He [Aten] and Jim King traveled by wagon to their assignment disguised as farm laborers."

9   Ibid.; confusingly, Preece in *Lone Star Lawman* attributes the cutters' arrest to a blabbering barmaid, "Flirting Nell," see p. 162. Though perhaps not relevant it is interesting to note that Alfred Henry Lewis in his string of popular turn-of-the-century novels, the *Wolfville* series, features the heroine "Faro Nell."

10   Ibid.; Wilkins, *The Law Comes to Texas*, 275.

11   Ibid.

12   Ibid.; Webb, *The Texas Rangers: A Century of Frontier Defense* mistakenly quotes from the letter on page 430: "I would rather be at the camp and only get $30 per month than get $50 per month and have to work after fence-cutters." The $50 should read $500. The misprint seems insignificant and was probably a simple typographical error. However, the higher figure more clearly illustrates Aten's utter frustration with having to work this undercover investigation.

13   Ibid.; Webb, *The Texas Rangers: A Century of Frontier Defense* seems to quote Ira Aten's letter to Captain Sieker of August 20, 1888, in full. Unfortunately Aten's remarks about resigning from the Rangers unless promoted has been inadvertently or purposefully excised. See pp. 429–30; the same may be said of Webb's "The Fence-Cutters," 13.

14   Clearly, Aten had a favorable relationship with Sieker, much more so than many other Rangers. That may be impetus for his comfort level in mentioning the desire for a commission; Utley, *Lone Star Justice* highlights that very fact on page 236: "A protégé of Lam Sieker, he [Aten] was full of ambition, ability, and self-confidence." And, "In long letters to his friend and mentor, Lam Sieker, now battalion quartermaster, he [Aten] detailed his adventures, frustrations, and complaints," 237.

15   Cordia Sloan Duke and Joe B. Frantz, *6,000 Miles of Fence: Life on the XIT Ranch of Texas*, 198.

16   Aten, "Six and One-Half Years in the Ranger Service," Part II, 131; Sergeant Aten to Captain Sieker, August 20, 1888, TSA; Sergeant Aten to Captain Sieker, August 31, 1888, TSA.

17   Ibid.; Sergeant Aten to Captain Sieker, August 31, 1888, TSA: "we dident have money enough to get it fixt. Besides the black-smith (as luck would have it) went to Corsicana on a 'spree' & of course we could not have got our wagon wheel fixt if we had wanted to but we dident want to very bad"; Aten, "Fence-Cutting Days in Texas," 445; Gard, "The Fence-Cutters," 11.

18   Sergeant Aten to Captain Sieker, August 31, 1888, TSA.

19 Ibid., "these two parties who gave these three away had been in to a great-deal of it & they seeing they would be caught sooner or later concluded to give a way the balance & get what reward they could & clear them-selves. So they told the Shff. also, Judge Frost...."

20 Ibid.

21 Ibid.; Sergeant Aten to Captain Sieker, September 17, 1888, TSA.

22 Ibid.

23 Ibid.

24 Sergeant Aten to Captain Sieker, September 17, 1888, TSA.

25 Sergeant Aten to Captain Sieker, August 20, 1888, TSA.

26 Sergeant Aten to Captain Sieker, August 31, 1888, TSA.

27 Sergeant Aten to Captain Sieker, September 1, 1888, TSA.

28 Sergeant Aten to Captain Sieker, September 17, 1888, TSA.

29 Burton, "The Most Surprised Man in Texas," 53; Burton, "A Great Man Hunt," 28; J. Marvin Hunter, ed., "A Train Robbery Prevented," *Frontier Times*, May 1926, 44; Price, *Bill Whitley Outlaw*, 92.

30 Ibid.; Dillard, *The Noble John Olive*, quoting the *Williamson County Sun*, 284–86.

31 Sergeant Aten to Captain Sieker, September 17, 1888, TSA; Alexander, *Winchester Warriors*, 219.

32 Sergeant Aten to Captain Sieker, August 31, 1888, TSA.

33 Alexander, *Winchester Warriors*, 219; Aten-1928, 80-81, HML&HC: "We staid around nearly two months. They did not cut any fence while we were there."

34 Sergeant Aten to Captain Sieker, October 8, 1888, TSA.

35 Jerry Thompson, *A Wild and Vivid Land: An Illustrated History of the South Texas Border,* 131; Alexander, *Winchester Warriors*, 221.

36 Captain Jones to Captain Sieker, September 24, 1888, TSA: "The wires have been cut and there is no telegraphic communication with Starr Co. Sebree is in the U.S.—post under protection of the Commander. I am informed that 60 armed Mexicans demanded that Sebree be delivered to them, and had to be threatened with Gatling guns to induce them to leave."

37 *Laredo Times*, September 28, 1888.

38 Telegram, AG King to Captain Jones, September 22, 1888, TSA.

39 Captain Jones to Captain Sieker, August 31, 1888, TSA.

40 Captain Jones to AG King, September 29, 1888, TSA.

41 Captain Jones to AG King, September 30, 1888, TSA.

42 Captain Jones to AG King, October 9, 1888, TSA; Spellman, *Captain J. A. Brooks, Texas Ranger*, 69.

43 Sergeant Aten to Captain Sieker, October 8, 1888, TSA.

44 Monthly Return, Company D. October 1888, TSA.

45 Captain Jones to AG King, October 17, 1888, TSA.

46 James Farber, *Texans with Guns*, 46: "DIABOLICAL IS THE WORD to describe the plan Ira Aten hatched to do away with the fencecutters whose activities he and Jim King had been sent in the summer of '88 to arrest in several counties in the 'Fencecutters' War'"; Sergeant Aten to Captain Sieker, September 17, 1888, TSA: "& went to work (or pretending to work) for the Love ranche about two miles west of Richland & 3 miles of the fence that they have been cutting mostly. The Love ranche is run by two good men & they Know who we are & they are helping us every way possible. They have about 12,000 acres under fence or I mean was under fence before the wire was cut.... They will put it up whenever I say so, but I don't deem it a wise idea for them to put it up yet a while, owning to us just going to work for them"; Sergeant Aten to Captain Sieker, October 8, 1888, TSA: "& I will soon put a quietus on fence-cutting that it will soon enter into history."

47 Aten, "Six and One-Half Years in the Ranger Service," Part II, 131: "I got a scheme in my head...."; Aten-1928, 81, HML&HC: "We got tired of staying there, and I conceived the idea of putting dynamite on the fence they had been cutting."

48 Sergeant Aten to Captain Sieker, September 17, 1888, TSA.

49 Ibid.

50 Sergeant Aten to Captain Sieker, August 31, 1888, TSA.

51 Sergeant Aten to Captain Sieker, October 8, 1888, TSA.

52 Ibid.: "Their [sic] has not been a fence cut since we have been in the co. mostly because there has been so few up where they cut fence at all."

53 Ibid.; Aten-194, 91, HML&HC. Here Aten asserts that he "fixed half a dozen or more of the these [bombs] on the fence that had been cut." Clearly these remarks, made half a century after his Navarro County assignment, are in conflict with his contemporary remarks. It makes for a great story but begs a question. If no cut fences had been rebuilt, how could he place a bomb on "the fence that had been cut" when snipping of the wire was necessary for ignition?

54 Ibid.

55 Sergeant Aten to Captain Sieker, October 15, 1888, TSA; Farber, *Texans with Guns*, 47: "There seems to be no record of bombs being used...."; Putman, *Navarro County History*, 14: "Weeks went by and nothing happened. Months went by, some said the report of the dynamite was a fake but no one really knew and no one wanted to take a chance to find out"; again, for his later interview, Mr. Aten reports that he was ordered to remove and destroy the devices he had planted along the fence lines. The hyperbole is evident: "There was corn stalks around there. So I put them on the corn stalks a little ways and set fire and they exploded. It just aroused the whole county. They thought it

was an earthquake. It caused quite an excitement." See, Aten-1941, 92, HML&HC.

56   Ibid.: "Because I have showed these pasture men how my boom racket can be worked to a perfection & now they know how to work as well as I do...."

57   Walter Prescott Webb, *The Story of the Texas Rangers,* 126: "There is no record his [Ira Aten's] invention was ever used, but for years the rumor persisted that certain pasture fences were dangerous to monkey with"; Utley, *Lone Star Justice,* 237: "No dynamite bomb ever blew up a nipper, but the fear of one produced a marked decline in fence cutting in Navarro County." 237.

58   Monthly Return, Company D, November 1888.

59   Ibid.; Aten, "Six and One-Half Years in the Ranger Service," Part II, 133–34: Though Aten does have a subchapter heading of "The 1888 Election at Roma on the Rio Grande," a review of this section, unlike the other vignettes contained herein, reveals that Aten writes only in the first person by utilizing "we." It seems he may be advantaging an "editorial we" applicable to the Rangers as a whole, rather than highlighting his specific acts. Adding to the possibility that Aten did not make a show at Roma is the following remark in a letter to Captain Sieker: "I left the Co. to attend court in Edwards Co. before they got order to move camp here." See Sergeant Aten to Captain Sieker, December 14, 1888, TSA.

60   Monthly Return, Company D. December 1888, TSA.

61   Utley, *Lone Star Justice,* 237.

62   Sergeant Aten to Captain Sieker, December 14, 1888, TSA; Monthly Return, Company D, December 1888, TSA; Tise, *Texas County Sheriffs,* 363.

Notes to Chapter 10

1   Rick Miller to Author, December 10, 2009; Miller, *Bell County: Crime and Criminals,* 283, 293, 297.

2   Monthly Return, Company D. February 1889, TSA; Captain Jones to AG King, January 31, 1889, TSA.

3   Ibid.; Tise, *Texas County Sheriffs,* 169.

4   Ibid.

5   Monthly Return, Company D. March 1889, TSA; Sergeant Aten to Captain Sieker, March 24, 1889, TSA: "I arrested the whole out-fit on head of Nueces on the 1st of this month upon suspicion of them being horse thieves. Found six shooter on their person, they gave a $400 bond each for that. I could not find anything else against them...."; Aten-1941, 68, HML&HC: "They acknowledged that they done the

shooting up the town, got drunk, but as far as his father and younger brother that they didn't have anything to do with it. 'Just this fellow Landers and me,' he [Dick Duncan] said. So we took these two back to town and they drove the wagon and the old man and younger brother followed. They happened into somebody there and they were going by their right names. Just a misdemeanor bond. It wasn't any serious offense, disturbing the peace. This party went on their bond and released them." The obvious discrepancy in the *San Antonio Daily Express* between these two versions is, at this time, unexplainable.

6   B. D. Lindsey to Captain Jones, March 5, 1889, TSA.
7   Ibid.
8   *San Antonio Daily Express*, September 19, 1889.
9   Captain Jones to AG King, March 6, 1889, TSA; the September 23, 1891, edition of the *Galveston Daily News* as reprinted in *Frontier Times*, March 1946, carries a far different assessment: "Much credit is due to Sheriffs Cooke of Maverick and Nolan of Kinney county for their untiring efforts to bring the guilty parties to justice," see page 94.
10 Chris Weatherby, "From No Account to Plain Mean," *Old West*, Summer 1974, 27; Aten-1941, 59, HML&HC; Aten-1928, 100, HML&HC: "[John] Hughes helped me in this case a great deal.... It was a very noted case."
11 Eugene Cunningham, "Frontier Justice: How Old-Time Rangers Solved a Baffling Texas Murder Mystery," *Startling Detective Adventures*, September 1935, 34–35; J. Marvin Hunter, "The Famous Dick Duncan Murder Case," *Frontier Times*, February 1939, 197.
12 Paul Havens, "Border Boss: The Saga of Captain John R. Hughes, Texas Ranger," *True Detective*, July 1940, 35; Cunningham, "Frontier Justice," 39.
13 Cunningham, "Frontier Justice," 37; Aten-1941, 69, HML&HC. Aten identifies a wagon of Bain manufacture.
14 *San Antonio Daily Express*, September 19, 1891; Jeffrey Burton, *The Deadliest Outlaws: The Ketchum Gang and the Wild Bunch*, 21.
15 Ibid.; *The San Saba News*, March 29, 1889: "Dick and Tap Duncan, who are charged with murder of the Williamson family on the Rio Grande, came in Saturday about noon and surrendered to Sheriff Howard.... there is some testimony tending to connect them with the deed, but it is supposed that they can produce evidence sufficient to rebut any against them, or they would not have so readily given up to the officers"; Sergeant Aten to Captain Sieker, March 29, 1889, TSA: "Sheriff Howard of San Saba co. arrested two of the Duncan boys yesterday morning & turned them over to me here. They are wanted for the murder of those three women & one man that was thrown in the Rio

Grande above Eagle Pass some time since"; also, Report of Sergeant Ira
Aten, TSA: "Sergt Aten left camp on March 22, 1889 to go to San Saba
Co. after the Duncan boys & H. W. Landers wanted for the murder
of the Williamson family in Maverick co. Texas. The Duncans were
arrested by the Shiff. the day Aten arrived there & they were turned
over to Aten at Goldthwaite, by Shiff Howard of San Saba co."; Aten-
1941, 71, HML&HC, Aten's remembrances are somewhat different for
this latter-day interview, but the significance of his investigative contribution is not—and should not—be diminished: "I telegraphed them
to arrest Dink [*sic*] and Top [*sic*] Duncan. When I got there to San Saba
I had them arrested and in jail except for Landers."

16   Aten-1941, 74, 69, HML&HC; Aten-1928, 100, HML&HC: "having
     had illegal relations with one of the daughters...."
17   *San Antonio Daily Express*, September 19, 1891.
18   Cunningham, "Frontier Justice," 37. Cunningham's assertion is some-
     what bolstered by Sergeant Aten to Captain Sieker, March 24, 1889,
     TSA.
19   Aten-1941, 74, HML&HC; Cunningham, "Frontier Justice," 39.
20   *Eagle Pass Guide*, December 7, 1889.
21   Ibid.
22   Ibid.
23   Ibid.
24   Ibid.
25   Cunningham, "Frontier Justice," 58.
26   *Eagle Pass Guide*, December 7, 1889.
27   Aten-1941, 71, HML&HC.
28   Alexander, *Winchester Warriors*, 223. Company D Rangers, by this
     time, knew the supposed identities of the dead bodies, but could not
     sustain it at the level required for the courtroom.
29   Cunningham, "Frontier Justice," 58; Mike Whittington, "Hughes and
     Aten Solve the Williamson Family Murders," *Texas Ranger Dispatch*,
     2003.
30   Sergeant Aten to Captain Sieker, March 24, 1889, TSA.
31   Aten-1841, 72, HML&HC.
32   Sergeant Aten to Captain Sieker, March 24, 1889, TSA.
33   Ibid.
34   *San Antonio Daily Express*, September 19, 1891.
35   Ibid.
36   Aten-1941, 71-72, HML&HC; Weatherby, "From No Account to Plain
     Mean," 27: "Some people suspected that he [Landers] had been killed
     by Duncan to eliminate the only witness to the slaying."
37   Sergeant Aten to Captain Sieker, March 24, 1889, TSA.
38   Aten-1941, 72, HML&HC.

39   Monthly Return, Company D, April 1889, TSA.
40   Sergeant Aten to Captain Sieker, May 23, 1889, TSA.
41   Monthly Return, Company D, May 1889, TSA.
42   Sergeant Aten to Captain Sieker, May 23, 1889, TSA.
43   Monthly Return, Company D, June 1889, TSA.
44   Sergeant Aten to Captain Sieker, May 31, 1889, TSA.
45   *San Antonio Daily Express*, September 19, 1891.
46   Ibid.
47   Ibid.
48   Captain Frank Jones to Captain Sieker, May 21, 1889, TSA; Corporal
     Fusselman to Captain Sieker, May 23, 1889, TSA: "As J. W. Durbin has
     quit I take his place"; Stephens, *Bullets and Buckshot*, 172–81.
49   Alexander, *Winchester Warriors*, 223–24.
50   Captain Jones to Captain Sieker, June 5, 1889, TSA.
51   Corporal Fusselman to AG King, June 5, 1889, TSA; Monthly Return,
     Company D, June 1889, TSA: "Found him again on the 4th where Bes-
     langa was killed after firing 8 shots at Fusselman."
52   Ira Aten to Calvin Grant Aten, April, 20, 1890. Copy of letter courtesy
     Robert W. Stephens.
53   Monthly Return, Company D, June 1889, TSA.
54   Della Tyler Key, *In the Cattle Country: History of Potter County, 1887–
     1966*, 59–62; DeLord, *The Ultimate Sacrifice*, 61; Jim Gober, *Cowboy
     Justice: Tale of a Texas Lawman*, asserts on pages 122–23 that Givens,
     the slain Potter County constable, was a paid gunman hired to murder
     him.

Notes to Chapter 11

1   Gourney, *Texas Boundaries*, 38.
2   C. L. Sonnichsen, *I'll Die Before I'll Run: The Story of the Great Feuds
    of Texas*, 234; Ira Aten, "The Jaybird and Woodpecker War," *Frontier
    Times*, April 1939, 309: "The population was about three negroes to
    one white, which made a very bad situation at election time"; Aten's
    story was reprinted in the 1978 June–July edition of *Frontier Times*
    though the title had been altered to "The Jaybird and Woodpecker
    Feud." The text was unchanged; Rafe W. Hawkins, "Blood Bath In
    Texas," *Real West*, October 1957, 7; Southworth, *Feuds on the Western
    Frontier*, adds: "In the late 1880s the population of Fort Bend County
    was nearly eighty percent Black," see page 101.
3   Sonnichsen, *I'll Die Before I'll Run*, 238; Pauline Yelderman, *The Jay
    Birds of Fort Bend County*, 69: "David Nation was the only white man in
    Richmond who called himself a Republican. The Democrats called him
    a 'Black' Republican."

4   Ibid.; Aten-1841, 106, HML&HC: "It wasn't Republicans and Demo-
     crats there, but just two factions, negroes and white people, negroes
     controlled by white people"; Utley, *Lone Star Justice*, 246: "After the
     war, with 90 percent of the population black, a few carpetbaggers
     joined with local scalawags to mobilize the freedmen and assemble a
     powerful political machine. Ostensibly Democratic, since Republican
     invited statewide contempt, it subjected an outraged white minority
     to county governments heavy with black office holders.... Somehow
     the minority faction came to be known as Jaybirds and their oppo-
     nents as Woodpeckers."

5   Bob Alexander, *Lawmen, Outlaws, and S.O.Bs*, vol. 2, 182.

6   *San Antonio Daily Express*, August 18, 1889.

7   Sonnichsen, *I'll Die Before I'll Run*, 267–68, quoting the *Houston Post*.

8   Southworth, *Feuds on the Western Frontier*, 102: "He was aggressive,
     vivacious and had guts which helped earn him the nickname 'Red Hot'
     Frost."

9   Sonnichsen, *I'll Die Before I'll Run*, 239; not unexpectedly, opinions
     about historical figures are sometimes based on perspective. Yelder-
     man, *The Jay Birds of Fort Bend County*, sees munificent qualities in
     Red Hot Frost: "For years his theme by day, and dream by night was
     how to bring honest, decent government to Fort Bend County.... a
     cool, fearless and aggressive person with a dynamic personality," see
     page 63.

10   Ibid.

11   Alexander, *Lawmen, Outlaws, and S.O.Bs*, vol 2, 183.

12   Ibid.; Yelderman, *The Jay Birds of Fort Bend County*, 72: "The question
     of ridding the county of certain negro leaders was discussed and a
     committee was appointed to draw up a list of 'undesirable' negroes
     who were to be ordered to leave the county"; Clarence R. Wharton,
     History of Fort Bend County, 199.

13   Alexander, *Lawmen, Outlaws, and S.O.Bs*, vol. 2, 178–81; for additional
     genealogical data regarding Tom Smith, see A. J. Sowell's *History of
     Fort Bend County*, 229–33.

14   Ibid.; for more on the life and adventures of Tom C. Smith, see Dee
     Cordry, "The Incredible Story of Tom and Frank Smith," *Oklahombres:
     The Journal of Lawman and Outlaw History of Oklahoma*, Winter 1997;
     also Ron Owens, "Oklahoma's Uncommon Smiths," *Oklahoma State
     Trooper*, Winter 1997; for Smith's participation in the notorious John-
     son County War in Wyoming, refer to Robert K. DeArment's *Alias
     Frank Canton*, and for Smith's violent death see Robert Ernst's *Deadly
     Affrays: The Violent Deaths of the US Marshals*.

15   Sonnichsen, *I'll Die Before I'll Run*, 251.

16   Ibid., 252.

17 *Galveston Daily News*, April 2, 1890: "He [Kyle Terry] told the witness
    about the invitations being sent to the woodpecker ball having been
    redirected to objectionable parties, and that Vol. Gibson was charged
    with having sent out these invitations, which was the origin of the
    animus between them"; Wharton, *History of Fort Bend County*, 209.
18 Captain Jones to Captain Sieker, June 25, 1889, TSA.
19 Telegram, Captain Jones to AG King, June 28, 1889, TSA; Monthly
    Return, Company D, June 1889, TSA.
20 Captain Jones to AG King, July 12, 1889, TSA: "I have been ten days
    in Wharton attending the trial of Terry. I am sure that you understand
    the situation of affairs in this County and it will not be necessary to
    Enter into details."
21 Captain Jones to AG King, July 12, 1889, TSA; DeLord, *Ultimate Sacri-
    fice*, 58, for Terry killing a policeman.
22 Captain Jones to AG King, August 8, 1889, TSA.
23 Aten, "The Jaybird and Woodpecker Feud," 21.
24 There has been and still is a reasonable ground for confusion con-
    cerning the correct identities of the Ranger detachment stationed at
    Richmond. Accurately, Sergeant Aten and Frank Schmid were there.
    Preece, *Lone Star Man* asserts that one of the other Rangers was
    Alex McNabb. In truth, Alex McNabb was at Richmond, but was the
    proprietor of the National Hotel, and possibly a part-time Fort Bend
    County deputy sheriff. During a December 4, 2009, interview with
    Mr. Stephens, *Texas Ranger Sketches*, he acknowledged the confusion
    fostered by the misinformation, further advising that although he had
    personally known Mr. Preece, he later determined that the historical
    merit of Preece's work was, regrettably, in many instances unreliable.
    It was only after publication of *Texas Ranger Sketches* in 1972 that he
    had, after exhaustive research, discovered the untrustworthiness of
    Lone Star Man as historical foundation. Since Preece's work is absent
    source citations, there is a likelihood he picked up the name Alex
    McNabb as being a Ranger from C. L. Douglas' *Famous Texas Feuds*
    which was published in 1936, twenty-four years before *Lone Star Man*.
    Douglas' declaration is, on its face, inaccurate: "One of the Jaybird bul-
    lets, however, did catch Private Jones of the Texas Rangers, who came
    out of the courthouse with Ranger Alex McNabb to carry back the
    sheriff," see p. 171; Pauline Yelderman, *Jaybirds of Fort Bend County*
    and William Warren Sterling, *Trails and Trials of a Texas Ranger*, list
    two of the Rangers detailed to Richmond as the Robinson brothers, as
    does Wharton in *History of Fort Bend County*. At TSA there is primary
    source correspondence from Ranger J. R. "Jim" Robinson to Adjutant
    General King, posted from Richmond, during the appropriate time

frame, August 1889. Aten-1941, clearly identifies one of the Rangers as Seth Robertson. Although Robinson and Robertson are a close fit, the first names seem to suggest they could not have been the same person, although the August 27, 1889, edition of the *Galveston Daily News* does reference a "S. D. Robinson" as being at Richmond. That Ira Aten, in later years, was yet befuddled about the sick Ranger's name is confirmed in Cal Aten to Ira Aten, December 12, 1936: "You remember when you were here, we tried to remember who the sick ranger was at Richmond when the citizen battle commenced that evening. I told you I thought it was Ernest Rogers. Since going over the matter thoroughly in my mind I am almost certain that Rogers was the boy." The Company D Monthly Return for April 1889 indicates Private Rogers was discharged on April 11, several months prior to the August riot. The mystery is cleared by examination of the Muster and Pay Roll for the time period. For the purposes of this narrative, relying on primary sources at hand, the four-man detachment assigned to peace-keeping duties at Richmond during August 1889 were: Sergeant Ira Aten, Frank Schmid, J. R. "Jim" Robinson, and D. S. "Seth" Roberson, see TSA; Aten-1928, 44, HML&HC: "Camped in a house...."

25   Aten, "The Jaybird and Woodpecker Feud," 21: "Toward evening I had a feeling that everything was not just right, and told my men they must be very watchful...."

26   Sonnichsen, *I'll Die Before I'll Run*, 261: "Sheriff Garvey was sitting in front of McGhee's saloon and he called Parker over, probably to tell him that he smelled trouble."

27   Alexander, *Lawmen, Outlaws, and S.O.Bs*, vol. 2, 43

28   Yelderman, *The Jay Birds of Fort Bend County*, 95–96.

29   Aten, "The Woodpecker and Jaybird Feud," 21.

30   Aten-1941, 102–3, HML&HC.

31   Alexander, *Lawmen, Outlaws, and S. O. Bs*, vol. 2, 186; Lorine Brinley, *Fort Bend County Cemetery Inscriptions*, vol. 2, 33.

32   *Kingfisher Free Press*, November 10, 1892.

33   *Galveston Daily News*, August 31, 1889.

34   *San Antonio Daily Express*, August 18, 1889.

35   Sonnichsen, *I'll Die Before I'll Run*, 264.

36   Preece, *Lone Star Man*, 194. Again the reader will have to accept or reject this bit of dialogue as he/she sees fit. It is extracted from a segment of purported conversation between Aten and Smith—according to Preece.

37   Stephens, *Texas Ranger Sketches*, 131. Although wounded during the August 16, 1889, street fight at Richmond, Frank Schmid would survive until June 17, 1893. His death was a direct result of the wound,

see Alexander, *Winchester Warriors*, 227. The correspondence between Schmid and his family concerning his injury and the state's reaction to the incurred medical expenses is not only voluminous, but heart-wrenching, see papers in TSA.

38   *San Antonio Daily Express*, August 18, 1889.

39   Ibid.

40   Ibid.

41   Telegram, Sergeant Aten to AG King, August 17, 1889, TSA.

42   Yelderman, *The Jay Birds of Fort Bend County*, 101; Sonnichsen, *I'll Die Before I'll Run*, 266.

43   *San Antonio Daily Express*, August 18, 1889.

44   *Galveston Daily News*, August 20, 1889.

45   Sonnichsen, *I'll Die Before I'll Run*, 256.

46   *Galveston Daily News*, August 20, 1889.

47   Yelderman, *The Jay Birds of Fort Bend County*, 101; Wharton, *History of Fort Bend County*, 213.

48   Ibid., 157. Admittedly the quotation is drawn from Ira's later nomination as a Jaybird candidate for sheriff, rather than the initial appointment, but nevertheless, either instance portends an agreeable Jaybird/Aten affiliation.

49   *Galveston Daily News*, August 20, 1889.

50   Aten-1941, 103–4, HML&HC.

51   Monthly Return, Company D, August 1889, TSA: "Sergt. Aten Discharged Aug. 20/89"; Tise, *Texas County Sheriffs*, 188.

52   Yelderman, *The Jay Birds of Fort Bend County*, 124. Ira Aten's Fort Bend County bondsmen were Sid Winston, J. H. P. Davis, I. W. Jones, M. B. Dunlavy, A. Meyers, Clem Bassett, H. R. Farmer, J. S. Dyer, W. D. Fields, Yandell Feris, J. D. Dyer, and W. I. McFarlane. See, *Galveston Daily News*, August 21, 1889.

53   Certificate of Discharge from Frontier Forces, State of Texas, for Ira Aten, August 20, 1889, HML&HC; also, *San Antonio Daily Express*, August 21, 1889, 172.

54   *Galveston Daily News*, August 22, 1889; *Weimar Mercury*, August 24, 1889; *Uvalde News*. August [?] 1889.

55   Ibid., August 27, 1889.

56   Ibid., August 21 and 22, 1889; Aten-1941, 42, 104, HML&HC. "Didn't have the education to keep those [Fort Bend County] books." And, "So that was when I wired Coffee and wrote him a letter, told him what I had done [become sheriff], told him to come down, had to have him. So he come and was my chief deputy and attended to the tax collection business for me"; *Williamson County Sun*, August 29, 1889: "Ex-Sheriff John T. Olive received a telegram yesterday from Ira Aten, the new

sheriff of Fort Bend county, asking him to come at once and act as special deputy until after the Richmond feud ceased to exist." Newsclip
courtesy Jim Dillard.

57 Yelderman, *The Jay Birds of Fort Bend County*, 125.

58 Cal Aten to Ira Aten, December 12, 1936, courtesy Robert W.
Stephens.

59 *Galveston Daily News*, August 27, 1889.

60 Ibid.

61 Sterling, *Trails and Trials of a Texas Ranger*. Sterling, often historically
inaccurate, does offer his take on Sergeant Aten's actions. The reader
is tasked with judging the merit and validity of his argument: "Just as
a student of military science makes critiques of famous battles, I have
made, from a Ranger's standpoint, a study of the melee in Richmond,
Texas. In it the Rangers played the unfamiliar role of bystanders. It is
true that Sergeant Aten implored both sides to listen to reason, but no
effort was made to disarm them. The reason for this seeming neglect
is at once apparent. The sheriff was the leader of one party, and he
could arm his side by giving them deputyships. It would have been
suicidal to deprive the others of their weapons. Another factor was
the shortage of manpower among the Rangers. Four men were not
enough [no one riot, one Ranger here] to handle a situation of that
gravity. The adjutant general must have been lulled into false security
by the calm before the storm. There can be no other explanation for
reducing his force in the face of an emergency, when it should have
been increased"; see page 392.

62 Sonnichsen, *I'll Die Before I'll Run*, 269.

63 Sheriff Aten to Captain Sieker, September 3, 1889, TSA. Since Sheriff
Aten called on Texas Rangers for assistance in making the arrests,
names of the detainees are listed in a supplement to the Company D
Monthly Return for August 1889. With no attempt to alter or correct
the spellings of their names as listed in the report, the arrested parties, charged with Murder, were: Vol Gibson, F. I. Booth, Ike McFarland, William Stuart, Calvin Blakely, Jim Gibson, S. E. Pearson, C. W.
Parnell, K. R. Ferris, Ruge Peareson, Will Grace, Sid Peareson, Giff
Gibson, Marion Fields, C. A. Beasely, Ernie McFarland, Sullivan Miles,
Yandell Ferris, Jeff Bryant, Harris Mitchell, Will Andus, Sid Wenston,
and Will McFarlane; see papers in TSA.

64 *Galveston Daily News*, August 27, 1889.

65 Ibid.

66 *San Antonio Daily Express*, August 18, 1889.

67 Captain Jones to AG King, September 4, 1889, TSA.

68 *Galveston Daily News*, August 21, 1889.

Notes to Chapter 12

1   Sheriff Aten to Captain Sieker, September 3, 1889, TSA.

2   Captain Jones to AG King, September 1, 1889, TSA.

3   *Galveston Daily News*, August 22, 1889: "Until the selection is made and appointment accepted Sheriff Aten himself will do the outside work"; for an exacting understanding of the role played by and expected of frontier era sheriffs a trip through the pages of Larry D. Ball's *Desert Lawmen: The High Sheriffs of New Mexico and Arizona, 1846-1912* is indispensable—and pleasurable. Although specifically focused on New Mexico and Arizona during their territorial years, Ball's comprehensive study is applicable to sheriffs throughout the West, Texas included. Attention must also be called to Thad Sitton's *The Texas Sheriff: Lord of the County Line*. Particularly spotlighting the role of sheriffs in Texas for a later timeframe—first half of the twentieth-century—Sitton does admirable work: "Citizens expected their county sheriffs to uphold local customs as well as state laws. He had to help constituents with their personal problems, which often had little or nothing to do with law enforcement. The rural sheriff served as his county's 'Mr. Fixit,' its resident 'good old boy,' and the lord of an intricate rural society," See the dust-jacket.

4   *Galveston Daily News*, October 26, 1889.

5   Ibid., June 11, 1890.

6   Ibid., June 12, 1890; Tise, *Texas County Sheriffs*, 243.

7   Reward Notice for horses stolen in Williamson County. Containing handwritten notations written across face by Sheriff Aten. Envelope addressed to "C. G. Aten, Ranger, Montell, Uvalde co. Tex." November 1889. As previously mentioned this brother was named Calvin Grant. In a series of letters from Ira, he always addresses the envelopes to "C. G. Aten," then begins the salutation, "Dear Bro Grant." Courtesy Robert W. Stephens.

8   Yelderman, *The Jay Birds of Fort Bend County*, 128–35. The book's Appendix V reprints the association's constitution and an alphabetical membership roll. Ira Aten is the seventh name from the top, see page 323.

9   Ibid., 320–21; repeated in part by Sonnichsen's *I'll Die Before I'll Run*, 272.

10 *Galveston Daily News*, November 28, 1889.

11 *Eagle Pass Guide*, December 7, 1889; Cunningham, "Texas Ranger: Frontier Justice," has the trial starting later, but does grant the jury was out but an hour and a half, see page 58; Aten-1941, 73, HML&HC: "I was at the trial...."

12   Ibid.; Weatherby, "From No-Account to Plain Mean," 65. The author
     inadvertently confuses the trial date with the date of the earlier Pre-
     liminary Hearing; Hunter, "The Famous Dick Duncan Murder Case,"
     198: "He was taken to Eagle pass and placed in jail and in December,
     1889, he was placed on trial in the district court there."

13   Yelderman, *The Jay Birds of Fort Bend County*, 138.

14   *Galveston Daily News*, December 26, 1889. The newspaper references
     U.S. Marshal Dickenson, rather than Dickerson; Sonnichsen, *I'll Die
     Before I'll Run*, makes reference to "Deputy Dickson from Galveston.
     Dickson was a former Woodpecker county clerk of Fort Bend County
     and he was there to arrest all the Jaybirds for running Ferguson and
     his colored friends out of the country, interfering with a congressional
     election, and otherwise misbehaving," see pages 272–73; J. J. Dicker-
     son served as the U.S. Marshal for the Eastern District of Texas from
     July 20, 1889 to January 15, 1894. Although the federal Indictments
     were returned to Galveston, which is now in the Southern District of
     Texas, at the time there was no Southern District for Texas, and would
     not be until March 11, 1902. Clarification was made during a March 4,
     2010, interview with David S. Turk, Historian, U.S. Marshals Service,
     Washington, DC. Historical data about the tenure of Dickerson as U.S.
     Marshal is courtesy Bob Ernst, U.S. Marshal specialist, historian, and
     author.

15   *Galveston Daily News*, December 25, 1889: "indicted for murder and
     still under custody are:.... and Ira Aten."

16   Yelderman, *The Jay Birds of Fort Bend County*, 54.

17   *Galveston Daily News*, December 26, 1889; Sheriff Aten to Captain
     Sieker, March 19, 1890, TSA.

18   Ibid., December 25, 1889. "Of the fifty-four citizens brought from
     Richmond Tuesday night by United States Marshal Dickenson...."

19   Ibid., December 28, 1889; not surprisingly, Preece, *Lone Star Man*,
     opts to forgo any mention of the federal charges and arrest of Aten.
     The author's oversight might be reflective of misguided biography
     rather than intentional obfuscation since Aten also neglects to address
     the subject in his memoirs. Primary citations confirm the bringing of
     charges, the arrest, and the ultimate dismissal of accusations.

20   *Galveston Daily News*, December 29, 1889.

21   Sonnichsen, *I'll Die Before I'll Run*, 243.

22   Yelderman, *The Jay Birds of Fort Bend County*, 48; Barr, *Reconstruction
     to Reform: Texas Politics, 1876–1906*, 198: "C. M. Ferguson and another
     Negro who sued in federal court because of their forced eviction...."

23   Ibid., 132: "The suits were settled out of court for $11,000.00 plus
     court cost of $500.00 and attorney's fees of $3,000.00, making a

total of $14,500.00, but the final cost to the Jay Birds was about $40,000.00."

24 *Galveston Daily News*, December 26, 1889.

25 Monthly Return, Company D, September and December 1889, TSA.

26 Stephens, *Bullets and Buckshot in Texas*, 52–53; *Galveston Daily News*, April 20, 1887, June 12, 1887, August 24, 1887, November 18, 1887, April 12, 1888, and April 17, 1888.

27 Ibid., 53; Alexander, *Winchester Warriors*, 227; Paul Havens in his July 1940 series for *True Detective Magazine* graciously, but inaccurately, wants to elevate the status of his biographical profile: "Sergeant Aten was nominally in command of the expedition, but since it was Corporal Hughes's case, he allowed the latter to handle the details." Corporal Hughes was the Ranger in command of the detail. Ira Aten was not a Texas Ranger at the time of the incident, but it was his brother Private Cal Aten who participated in the killing of the Odle brothers. The error of placing Ira Aten at the scene of this killing is common.

28 Captain Jones to Captain Sieker, December 25, 1889, TSA.

29 Captain Jones to Captain Sieker, December 31, 1889, TSA.

30 Private Hughes to AG King, December 25, 1889, TSA; Monthly Return, Company D, December 1889, TSA. Unfortunately, as have several writers, Jay Robert Nash in the *Encyclopedia of Western Lawmen and Outlaws* identifies Sergeant Ira Aten as one of the Texas Rangers involved in killing the Odle brothers, rather than his younger brother Private Calvin Grant Aten, see page 15; likewise, Darren L. Ivey, *The Texas Rangers: A Registry and History* follows suit, listing Ira Aten's involvement in the Christmas Day shooting rather than Cal, see page 221. At the time of this incident Ira Aten was no longer a Texas Ranger, but was Fort Bend County sheriff.

31 Cal Aten to Ira Aten, December 12, 1936, courtesy Robert W. Stephens; Alexander, *Winchester Warriors*, 228. It may not have been an *equitable* contest, understandably. Those folks on the bloody ground were well tuned to the life saving importance of getting in the first lick—fair play or not. Second place in a gunfight is not smart.

32 Stephens, *Bullets and Buckshot in Texas*. 54.

33 Sheriff Ira Aten to C. G. Aten, April 20, 1890, copy courtesy Robert W. Stephens.

34 Handwritten memoir of Calvin Grant Aten, April 1938, copy courtesy Robert W. Stephens.

35 Captain Jones to AG King, January 3, 1890, TSA.

36 Sonnichsen, *I'll Die Before I'll Run*, 276.

37 The shooting of Kyle Terry is detailed in more than one edition of the Galveston newspaper, the most complete being February 1, 1890, but the killing is also adequately and concisely recapped in Son-

nichsen's *I'll Die Before I'll Run* and Yelderman's *The Jay Birds of Fort Bend County*; for a melodramatic contemporary account with several hand-drawn illustrations, see *The National Police Gazette*, February 15, 1890, 7.

38 *Galveston Daily News*, January 23, 1890.

39 Ibid.

40 Ibid.

41 Ibid.

42 Aten, "Six and One-Half Years in the Ranger Service," Part II, 140.

43 Sheriff Aten to Captain Sieker, March 19, 1890, TSA. In an earlier letter to Sieker, it seems that Ira was fully aware that maintaining a neutral posture was advisable. See Sheriff Aten to Captain Sieker, March 3, 1890, TSA: "I shall certainly keep out of their fights & act strictly upon the defensive order when personally assaulted."

44 *Galveston Daily News*, April 1, 1890.

45 Ibid., April 2, 1890.

46 Sonnichsen, *I'll Die Before I'll Run*, 277; Southworth, *Feuds on the Western Frontier*, 107: "Before he could be brought to trial for killing Terry, Volney Gibson died of tuberculosis on April 9,1891"; Wharton, *History of Fort Bend County*, 217.

47 Sheriff Aten to Cal Aten, April 10, 1890.

48 Alexander, *Winchester Warriors*, 236–38; Affidavit and Personnel File [Charles Fusselman] for Texas Peace Officers Killed in the Line of Duty, CLEAT; DeLord, *The Ultimate Sacrifice*, 62; Captain Jones to AG King, April 19, 1890, TSA; Captain Jones to AG King, May 2, 1890, TSA; *San Antonio Daily Express*, April 19, 1890; Private Hughes to Captain Sieker, April 18, 1890, TSA; *El Paso Times*, April 19, 1890; Antonio Croce, "In the Line of Duty," *The Texas Gun Collector*, Fall 1996, 13–17. The tongue-in-cheek designation "Hell Paso" comes from the June 25, 1916, edition of the *El Paso Times*.

49 Sheriff Ira Aten to Cal Aten, April 20, 1889.

50 Captain Jones to AG King, February 22, 1890, TSA; Robert W. Stephens, "A Ranger's Grave: The Murder of Jim King," *National Association for Outlaw and Lawman History, Inc. Quarterly*, October/December 2005.

51 "Descendants of Margaret Angelina Elizabeth Aten," typed genealogical summary, courtesy Betty Aten.

52 *Galveston Daily News*, June 5, 1890.

53 Aten-1941, 105, HML&HC: "They gave me a month in August, 1890, to go to the Panhandle and locate my home." Based on the letter cited in the following endnote it appears the leave of absence was granted in June rather than August.

54 Sheriff Ira Aten to Cal Aten, June 28, 1890.

55 Aten, "Six and One-Half Years in the Ranger Service," Part II, 140.

56 Aten-1941, 104, HML&HC.
57 Sterling, *Trials and Trails of a Texas Ranger*. 393.
58 Sergeant Aten to Captain Sieker, September 17, 1888, TSA.

Notes to Chapter 13

1   Gourney, *Texas Boundaries*, 95.
2   Frederick Rathjen, *The Texas Panhandle Frontier*, 238 n. 6; J. W. Wil-
    liams, *The Big Ranch Country*, 71 n. 7.
3   Blackburn, *Wanted: Historic County Jails of Texas*, 65: "The population
    of Castro County in 1890 was nine."
4   J. Wright Mooar, "The Frontier Experiences of J. Wright Mooar,"
    West Texas Historical Association Yearbook, June 1928, 89–92; for an
    insightful look at the social life of frontier towns catering to the wants
    and needs of buffalo hunters the reader is referred to Jan Devereaux's
    Pistols, Petticoats, and Poker: The Real Lottie Deno, No Lies or Alibis. An
    informative look and biographic profile of numerous buffalo hunt-
    ers may be found in the comprehensive work of Miles Gilbert, Leo
    Remiger, and Sharon Cunningham's two-volume *Encyclopedia of Buf-
    falo Hunters and Skinners*.
5   A succinct study of the commercial trade in buffalo bones may be
    found in Ralph A. Smith's "The West Texas Bone Business," *West Texas
    Historical Association Year Book*, 1979; also, Vernon Schmid, "Hides and
    Bones," *Roundup*, December 2006.
6   Castro County Historical Commission, *Castro County, 1891–1981*, vol.
    1, 18: "According to the Abstract Book of all original Texas Land Titles
    in Castro County, there were forty-five men who owned land in Castro
    County before J. W. Carter bought his seventy-two sections. None of
    these men ever lived here however.... According to the Abstract Book,
    in 1877, the first land patented in Castro County was John Alexander,
    June 6, 1877...."
7   Awbrey and Dooley, *Why Stop?* 146.
8   Preece, *Lone Star Man*, 209–10. The author, finding it necessary to
    fabricate dialogue and circumstance, weaves a romantic tale regarding
    Ira Aten and A. G. Boyce, and a conversation about marriage. Ira Aen's
    own remarks deflate this stab at created romanticism. The very first
    sentence in the 1928 interview with J. Evetts Haley is: "A. G. Boyce
    was a cousin of my wife, but I never met him until after I became
    sheriff of Castro County [1893]"; Aten-1928, 1, HML&HC; Aten-1941,
    127, HML&HC: "I wasn't acquainted with him."
9   Sergeant Aten to Captain Sieker, September 17, 1888, TSA.
10 Aten-1941, 107, HML&HC.

11   Castro County Historical Commission, *Castro County, Texas, 1891-
      1981*, vol. 1, 25.

12   Descriptive List, Ira Aten, Company B, Frontier Battalion, signed by
      AG King, November 19, 1890, TSA; Donaly E. Brice, TSA, to author,
      January 26, 2010: "I also checked the muster rolls for Company B
      to determine how long Ira Aten was carried on the rolls as a special
      Ranger without pay. It appears that he was on the rolls through Febru-
      ary 28, 1895. He did not appear on the muster roll for March 1 to
      May 31, 1895. However, he was on the one dated December 1, 1894,
      through February 28, 1895."

13   Aten-1928, 3, HML&HC. "My sweetheart had told me that she would
      never marry me until I quit carrying a six-shooter."

14   Chesley, *Adventuring With the Old-Timers*, 86: "I took her [Imogen's]
      brother, John Boyce, with me, and his father started John on a little
      ranch there [Castro County] at the side of me."

15   Aten-1941, 109, HML&HC. Ira spells Epps' first name "Louis," while
      Deed Records use "Lewis."

16   Ibid.; for insight regarding this subject, see Terry G. Jordan, *Trails to
      Texas: Southern Roots of Western Cattle Ranching*, 143: "Blacks accom-
      panied the Anglo rancher migration to West Texas, where sixty-eight
      of them worked as cowboys by 1880. While these blacks made up
      only 4 percent of the cowboy work force, a far lower proportion than
      claimed by some historians, their presence in West Texas is undeni-
      able. Some worked for the huge XIT Ranch on the Texas High Plains.
      Eventually, a few blacks even became ranch owners in West Texas, and
      Negro cowhands continued to find employment on ranches there into
      the present century"; Haley, *Passionate Nation*, page 379, takes the
      more traditional view, increasing the percentage of minority cowboys:
      "It was a system that functioned on diligent labor and mutual respect,
      and a system that even made it possible for African-Americans to
      move up the economic ladder. Perhaps a third of all cowboys on the
      range were black or Hispanic, operating in a setting where success
      depended more on skill than on ethnic background, and the vast new
      cattle country lacked the heavy baggage of slavery and Reconstruc-
      tion"; while contributions of Hispanic and African-American cowboys
      should not be undervalued, absent a quantifiable study but based
      solely on the plethora of contemporary photographs it does not
      appear that the minority cowboy workforce reached the mark of 30
      percent in the Texas Panhandle.

17   Ibid., 107, "When I went to Castro County I think it was less than a
      hundred voters."

18   Aten-1928, 7. HML&HC.

19 Ibid.

20 Stephens, *Texas Ranger Sketches*, 16–18.

21 Monthly Return, Company D, August 1890, TSA; Ranger C. G. Aten's Certificate of Pay for the quarter ending August 31, 1890, TSA: "and is this day honorably discharged"; although no quantifiable correlation may be attached, it is interesting to note that less than a month prior to Cal Aten's discharge one of his fellow West Texas Company D Rangers was killed in the line of duty at Shafter, Presidio County. See Alexander, *Winchester Warriors*, 239; DeLord, *The Ultimate Sacrifice*, 62; Affidavit and Personnel File (John F. Garvis) for Texas Peace Officers Killed in the Line of Duty, CLEAT.

22 Descriptive List, Ira Aten, Company B, Texas Rangers, May 5, 1891, TSA; Harold J. Weiss, Jr., *Yours to Command: The Life and Legend of Texas Ranger Captain Bill McDonald*, 57–58: "Important cogs in the operation of Company B in 1891.... A Special Ranger of note listed on the muster rolls and assigned to the company by the adjutant general was Ira Aten, famed ex-Ranger sergeant from previous gubernatorial administrations."

23 Special Ranger Ira Aten to AG Mabry, May 31, 1891, TSA: "Four stolen horses captured from thieves. The thieves quit the horses near the line of New Mexico & escaped. Was out 5 days, marched 140 miles. I am afraid their [sic] will be a great deal of horse stealing near & at Amarillo & horses run over in New Mexico. It is very hard to get horses out of New Mexico when they have been stolen here & sold over there. I will guard this co. & act when my duty prompt[s] me"; Weiss, *Yours to Command*, 62–63.

24 Letterhead, Roberts and Aten, R. A. Roberts and Ira Aten, Agents, May 31, 1891, TSA.

25 Castro County Historical Commission, *Castro County, Texas, 1891–1981*, vol. 1, 23.

26 *Granbury News*, September 24, 1891.

27 *El Paso Daily Times*, September 19, 1891; J. Marvin Hunter, "The Famous Dick Duncan Murder Case," *Frontier Times*, February 1939, 198; J. Marvin Hunter, ed., "Dick Duncan's Doom," *Frontier Times*, March 1946, 92–95.

28 *San Antonio Daily Express*, September 19, 1891; *Galveston Daily News*, September 23, 1891, as carried with supplemental remarks in the March 1946 edition of *Frontier Times*, 92–95.

29 Aten-1941, 73, HML&HC. In this instance Ira Aten is chronologically confused, thinking the hanging of Dick Duncan had occurred during 1890 while he was sheriff of Fort Bend County, rather than 1891when he was holding no paid law enforcement commission.

30 Aten-1928, 7, HML&HC.

31   Castro County Historical Commission, *Castro County, Texas, 1891–1981*, vol. 2, 87; Texas State Historical Association, *The New Handbook of Texas*, vol. 2, 650.

32   Aten-1928, 8, HML&HC.

33   Ibid.; the drama between Aten and the McClelland brothers is covered to some extent in Aten's "Six and One-Half Years in the Ranger Service," Part II, 141–42. However, it should be pointed out that rather than recap the story in his own words—apparently not wanting to be a braggadocio—Aten (or Hunter) simply published an account carried in the Amarillo newspaper, followed by a 1936 letter written by Judge L. Gough to Robert H. Allen, El Centro, California.

34   Ibid.; typically, Preece in *Lone Star Man* anoints Aten with a halo, ascribing altruistic motives to Ira's actions, an averment unsupported by facts: "With funds realized from the sale of some steers, he bought a tract of ground and had it mapped as a town site he christened Castro City. Ira offered lots to settlers at much lower prices and on longer time payments than could be had from the McClellands in Dimmitt. At the same time, he announced that Castro City would compete with Dimmitt for the county seat when the election was called," see page 212.

35   Ibid.: "They gave lots to the opposing faction to compromise"; an assertion of trading town lots for cowboy votes in the Texas Panhandle is also made in Willie Newbury Lewis' *Between Sun and Sod*, 207. This horse-tradin' for town lots in the newly forming Amarillo (Potter County) is confirmed by Gober, *Cowboy Justice*, 121: "The colonel had given Holland and Clabe Merchant an interest in his town site as a compromise to unite the Abilene bunch before the election in 1887"; Aten reaffirms that he was given town lots not to support Castro City as Castro County seat: "Old Parson Bandy was trying to make Dimmitt. Before the election a compromise came up and Hillory Bedford gave all of us that was boosting Castro City so many town lots in Dimmitt. I got eighteen town lots in the City of Dimmitt. That was the kind of hold up we put on them." See Aten-1941, 108, HML&HC.

36   Ibid., 12: "Carter had favored Castro City."

37   Frederick Nolan, *Tascosa: Its Life and Gaudy Times*, 93: "Attached to Oldham County for legal purposes were nine other unorganized counties: Castro, Dallam, Deaf Smith, Hartley, Moore, Potter, Randall, Sherman, and Swisher"; Castro County Historical Commission, *Castro County, Texas, 1891–1981*, vol. 1, 27; Gourney, *Texas Boundaries*, increases the number of counties attached to Oldham County for judicial matters: "The judicial district created in Tascosa in 1881 served sixteen nearby unorganized counties," see pages 103 and 211.

38   Aten-1928, 7, HML&HC. Of his feeling for L. Gough, Ira remarked: "I liked him when I first saw him."

39   *Austin Tribune*, February 4, 1940.

40   Aten-1928, 9, HML&HC; Aten-1941, 110, HML&HC: "That was what caused the 'rucous' between the McClelland boys and me."

41   Ibid.; *San Antonio Daily Express*, December 29, 1991. "The McLelland [*sic*] brothers called Ira Aten a liar at a public meeting."; Harold Preece, "I Rode With the Texas Rangers: Lawman Till I Die," Part III, *Zane Grey Magazine*, August 1953. With flair Preece spices the melodrama, writing why Aten did not shoot Andrew McClelland at the town hall meeting: "There was a moment of tense silence. Women were fidgeting nervously. Suddenly a loud wail sounded from a little girl who'd seen her daddy die in a gun duel. That tot decided my course. 'Neighbors,' I said, 'I did more fighting than I want to talk about in the Texas Rangers. But no Ranger ever started a fracas where women and children were present'" see p. 83.

42   Ibid., 10. Admittedly the document does not contain the phrase "son of a bitch," however the inference is clear by the adoption of underlined blank spaces: "Shoot, you s___ b___ (and holding my hands out in front of me) I'll catch the bullet!" Ira's philosophy for a gunfight was well fixed: "But if you are going to kill a man, that is the way you want him; you want him armed," see p. 68. Enthrallingly, and perhaps lending believability to Aten's claim that he would "catch the bullet" is the statement of Big Ed Connell to J. Evetts Haley, October 31, 1927, wherein he retold the story of the Aten/McClelland shooting: "Ira never told anybody that I know of but me, but he said that he had a steel breastplate on," see p. 8, HML&HC. Also see, Aten-1941, 111, HML&HC: "The six-shooter was in my [Ira Aten's] pants. The Winchester was in the wagon in case I needed it."

43   Ibid., 10–12; Ira Aten fails to mention the McClelland shooting in his memoirs. However, in serialized publication for the February 1945 *Frontier Times*, the event is covered by an inclusion as it "appeared in the Amarillo newspaper on November 28, 1991," see page 141; here Aten (or J. Marvin Huntrer) is innocently mistaken about dates. Thankfully, and almost unbelievably, the "legal shuck" for this case exists: The Indictment for Castro County Case Number 1, *The State of Texas vs. Ira Aten* reads "that Ira Aten late of the County of Castro, on the 24th day of December in the year of our Lord one thousand eight hundred and ninety-one, with force and arms, in the County of Castro and State of Texas, did then and there with malice afore thought in and upon Andrew McClellan did make an assaualt with the intent then and there to murder the said Andrew McClellan." Courtesy Carlene Long, Deputy County Clerk, Castro County, Dimmitt, Texas. Somewhat adding to the historic muddle about dates is the wording of the Official Texas Historical Marker on the Castro County Court-

house lawn, which was dedicated on July 4, 1983, but places the Aten/McClelland gunfight on December 23, 1891. See photograph in text. Also, Dedication Program of an Offical Texas Historical Marker commemorating "The Shoot-Out on Jones Street." Program courtesy Clara Vick, Castro County Historical Museum. According to the Indictment the shooting had taken place on December 24, 1891 and could not have been covered in a preceding November newspaper edition. It is, however, obvious that the piece quoted in *Frontier Times* was an extraction from a contemporary newspaper; also, Awbrey and Dooley, *Why Stop?* 146; Castro County Historical Commission, *Castro County, Texas, 1891–1981,* vol. 1, 140; Mark Boardman, "Irate Ira Nails The McClellands!" *True West*, July 2009, 52–53; interestingly, for his serialized reminiscence, Ira Aten, "Six and One-Half Years in the Ranger Service," Part III, March 1945, again offers first-hand commentary from a gunfight participant's viewpoint: "The old Rangers boys all know I was never a 'two gun man,' as one was all I could handle in time of trouble. In fact, I never saw but one two-gun man in all my experiences, and that was on the streets of Dimmit [*sic*], when Andrew McClelland came stepping high up the street with a six-shooter in each hand, telling everyone he met that he was going to kill Aten," see page 160. Furthermore, in this serialized account Aten does not shy away from the fact he was arrested and tried for the December 1891 shooting; Ira Aten to Imogen Aten, November 7, 1936, PPHM.

44   Castro County Historical Commission, *Castro County, Texas, 1891–1981,* vol. 1, 29; Clearly the witnesses are lauding Ira Aten's coolness during the gunfight, and not resorting to six-gun theatrics such as shooting too quick or fanning the Colt's hammer; another witness, Jim Flores, commented: "Aten was shooting like shooting squirrels out of a tree." See Aten, 1941, 114, HML&HC. For a most insightful examination of practical gun handling, and whether or not fellows actually fanned their revolver's hammers, see Stan Nelson's "Fanning the Hammer," in the March 2001 edition of the *Minnesota Weapons Collectors Association News.*

45   R. J. Frye and C. F. Vincent to J. Evetts Haley, June 26, 1927, 5, HML&HC; that Ira Aten was "a scrapper" and capable of acting alone is supported by primary sources. On the other hand a few much more recognizable modern-era names have been exaggerated. See historians Lynn R. Bailey and Don Chaput, *Cochise County Stalwarts: A Who's Who of the Territorial Years,* vol. 1, 114: "And, irony of irony, Wyatt Earp, the most well-known shootist or gunfighter in America's past, was never in a man-on-man gunfight or duel. In fact, it cannot be demonstrated historically that Wyatt Earp ever killed a man. It is true that because

of his presence (the famous shootout; the Tucson rail yard, etc.) certain dead bodies were found, but how they were killed and by whom has never been established with certainty. This is indeed a lamentable record for America's premier 'gunfighter'."

46 *Weekly Amarillo News* [?], December 28, 1891: "Aten waived examination and gave bond to await the action of the grand jury"; after a Grand Jury returned an Indictment in Casto County Criminal Case No. 1, a Capias Warrant for Ira Aten's arrest issued, and he was formally arrested again: see, Sheriff's Return: "Came to hand the 5th day of April 1892, and executed on the 5th day of April 1892, by arresting Ira Aten the defendant named in this Capias and forthwith taking him before the court from which said capais was issued then in session where he entered into recognizance for his appearance." Signed, "C. I. Bedford, Sheriff, Castro County."; Mistakenly the *Weimar Mercury*, January 9, 1892, had reported that the McClelland brothers had been killed by Ira Aten in self-defense. The newspaper went on to praise Ira: "Mr. Aten has the reputation here of being a quiet, but brave and fearless man."

47 Aten, "Six and Half Years in the Ranger Service," Part II, 141.

48 *Austin Daily Statesman*, February 4, 1892; Ira Aten to Imogen Aten, November 7, 1936, PPHM.

49 Aten, "Six and One-Half Years in the Ranger Service," Part III, 157.

50 B. P. Abbott to J. Evetts Haley, June 24, 1927, HML&HC: "The sheriff, Ira Aten, lived about two and a half miles out of town. He had a small ranch," see page 2 ; Ira Aten to Imogen Aten, October 31, 1936: "of the old 'dugout' to which I brought you after our marriage....," PPHM.

51 Aten-1928, 9, HML&HC. Whether justified or not, it is clear Aten and Jim Carter were at odds. During the argument that preceded the Aten/McClelland gunfight. "John Boyce was there that night.... he sat right behind them [the McClleland brothers and Jim Carter], and he said, 'I got my knife and if old Jim Carter went to draw his six-shooter I would have cut his throat." See Aten 1941, 111, HML&HC.

52 Bill Neal, *Getting Away With Murder on the Texas Frontier: Notorious Killings and Celebrated Trials*, 88 and 227; James D. Hamlin, *The Flamboyant Judge: The Story of Amarillo and the Development of the Great Ranches of the Texas Panhandle*, 12.

53 Thomas F. Turner, "Prairie Dog Lawyers," *Panhandle-Plains Historical Review* 2 (1929): 116.

54 Ibid.

55 Neal, *Getting Away With Murder*, 88.

56 Aten-1928, 13, HML&HC; *Weekly Amarillo News* [?], December 28, 1891. "We have known Mr. Aten for a number of years and have never known him to be anything but a very quiet and peaceable citizen, who

always made friends in any community in which he lived." In another newclip [unidentified] the editor writes: "Ira Aten, a man of pleasant address and an obliging nature, but one who has often braved the worst in his frontier life," courtesy HML&HC; Certification of W. B. Beach, Clerk of the District Court of Castro County in Castro County Criminal Case No. 1, *The State of Texas vs. Ira Aten*: "the venue of said cause having been this day [April 5,1892] changed to swisher county [*sic*], Texas by order of the District Court" Courtesy Castro County District Clerk.

57 Castro County Historical Commission, *Castro County, Texas, 1891–1981*, vol. 1, 32.

58 Blackburn, *Wanted: Historic County Jails of Texas*, 65.

59 Alexander, *Fearless Dave Allison*, 27 n.43: "On the cattle ranges, around the campfires and cafés, and at today's livestock sale-barns, away from ladies' hearing, someone guilty of purposefully altering a brand or stealing cattle is purely—and rather simply labeled—a 'Goddamn cow-thief' or a 'son-of-a-bitchin' cow thief.' Even today, a 'Goddamn cow-thief' is not politely referred to generically as a 'rustler'"; Clarke in *A Century of the Cow Business*, confirms: "From that day to this, Association members still so described the cow thief, refraining from calling him a dignified name like 'rustler,' 'mavericker,' etc. They leave those names to fiction writers," see page 15.

60 Castro County Historical Commission, *Castro County, Texas, 1891–1981*, vol. 1, 24.

61 Stephens, *Texas Ranger Sketches*, 18. During a December 28, 2009, interview Mr. Stephens acknowledged that it has been alleged that Eddie Aten shot a man during a saloon dispute over a poker game, prior to enlisting with the Texas Rangers. Mr. Stephens says that thus far he has seen no primary evidence to raise this past a level of the anecdotal. Until backed up by a factual basis—which may happen—this story will have to rest on the heels of but wobbly speculation. There is, however, high probability that this alleged gunplay in the Panhandle has been inadvertently confused with a very real saloon shoot-out involving Ranger Eddie Aten more than a year later and in far West Texas. The El Paso County shooting is solidly supported by primary source material. That episode will be addressed in this text when chronologically appropriate. Adding to the folkloric confusion and indicative of how undocumented oral history is sometimes garbled is a letter from Ira D. Aten (Ira's son) to Shirley Aten Roberts (Cal Aten's granddaughter) on January 26, 1983. Ira D. Aten's comments about his uncle Eddie Aten are not laudatory: "Eddie Aten was, the youngest of the Aten boys was in the Rangers, but not of his free will. He was a no-good and would do anything to get by without working. When my father [Austin Ira] was

a Ranger he rode into El Paso late one night, and as was his custom, he went around to all the saloons to talk to the bartenders who would tell him what 'baddies' were in town. He went in one saloon just as his brother, Eddie, who was gambling at cards, pulled his gun and killed one of the cardplayers. He immediately arrested Eddie and took him to jail. My father's message to him was that he could spend ten years in the State Penitentiary or four years in the Texas Rangers under Captain Jones. He gave him until the next morning to make his choice.... When he got back to see Eddie late the next morning, he didn't have to ask him what his choice was. Eddie immediately said he would be glad to serve four years under Captain Jones...." Copy of letter courtesy Sally Walker and Shirley Aten Roberts. The letter's author also informed the recipient that her grandfather Cal "was never in the Rangers." The chronological inconsistencies and factual deficiencies of this document are more than readily apparent.

62   Dillard, *The Noble John Olive*, 292–307; DeLord, *The Ultimate Sacrifice*, 64; Stephens, *Bullets and Buckshot*. The author has chapters on both James B. Gunn (pages 283–84) and John T. Olive (pages 316–24).

63   DeLord, *The Ultimate Sacrifice*, 63.

64   Ira Aten, Special Ranger, Dimmitt, Castro County, Texas, to AG Mabry, Austin, Texas, October 31, 1892, TSA.

65   Tise, *Texas County Sheriffs*, 94.

66   Aten-1928, 6, HML&HC; Tise, *Texas County Sheriffs*, 94.

67   Aten-1941, 107, HML&HC.

68   Aten-1928, 7, HML&HC.

69   Ibid., 13; *Austin Tribune*, February 4, 1940. Judge Gough said: "In his career he saw only one gun fight and that was when a two-gun man [Andrew McClelland] pulled a gun on a one-gun man [Ira Aten], the former getting the worst of the fight."

70   Ibid., "Judge Gough was my main witness"; Ira Aten to Imogen Aten, November 7, 1936, PPHM; Aten, "Six and One-Half Years in the Ranger Service," Part III, 157; Castro County Historical Commission, *Castro County, Texas, 1891–1981*, vol. 1, 30. According to this account: "and Aten was released from custody when it was learned that the McClelland brothers had left the country without signing a complain [*sic*] against him." True, the McClelland brothers had left for a more favorable clime, and they may not have actually signed any Complaints, but such would not have prohibited the state from bringing charges, although missing their testimony the prosecution would be and was disadvantaged.

71   Castro County Historical Commission, *Castro County, Texas, 1891–1981*, vol. 1, 30. "Two days later the Atens' first child was born"; and

Vol. 2, "Delayed Birth Certificates," 107: "Aten, Marion Hughes, 12-22-92. M."

Notes to Chapter 14

1 Watts, *A Dictionary of the Old West*, 277; Duncan Emrich, *The Cowboy's Own Brand Book*, 36.

2 Castro County Historical Commission, *Castro County, Texas, 1891–1981*, vol. 1, 24; Aten-1928, 7, HML&HC. For an insightful piece about the grasshopper plague overwhelming Texas ranchers and farmers, see Jim Pfluger's "The Glittering Cloud: Rocky Mountain Locusts Invade the Great Plains," *Ranch Record*, Fall 2008, 26–27.

3 Tise, *Texas County Sheriffs*, 94; Duke and Frantz, *6,000 Miles of Fence*, 40, assert Sheriff Perry Cox was turned out for overly imbibing; Castro County Historical Commission, *Castro County, Texas, 1891–1981*, vol. 1, 24, 34: "When the sheriff [Perry Cox] could not get others to sign his bond, he was disqualified for the office. The Commissioner's Court was called together to appoint a new sheriff to fill the vacancy. Only one name was mentioned, that of Ira Aten. He accepted the office for the remainder of that term"; Ira Aten says a Castro County commissioner approached him and advised, "We are going to get rid of Perry Cox. They are stealing us out and we are going to get rid of him someway," see Aten-1941, 15, HML&HC.

4 Chesley, *Adventuring With the Old-Timers*, 87.

5 Aten-1928, 3, HML&HC; Ira Aten to Imogen Aten, October 31, 1936, PPHM: "It was there [Dimmitt] that I almost broke your heart when I accepted the appointment as sheriff of Castro county while you were on a visit to your old home in Austin in the spring of 1893."

6 Aten, "Six and One-Half Years in the Ranger Service," Part III, 157.

7 Ibid.

8 Blackburn, *Wanted: Historic County Jails of Texas*, 65: "The courthouse, completed in December 1892, was struck by lightning in August 1906 and burned to the ground. The court records show no suggestion of any jail until the second courthouse was built in 1908. That facility was less than secure. Sometimes the sheriff would lock up a prisoner only to encounter him on the street a few hours later. If unobserved, the captive would usually return to eat his meals or spend the night"; that Imogen Aten helped her husband discharge the duties of office is really not debatable, since at the time most wives of county sheriffs did. In Aten's "Six and One-Half Years in the Ranger Service," Part III, Ira confirmed: "She [Imogen] was a wonderful aid to me while I was sheriff, even taking her turn in helping me guard the prisoners," see

page 157. That she buckled on six-shooters is drawn straight from Preece, *Lone Star Man,* 220.

9   Corporal Carl Kirchner to AG Mabry, July 2, 1893, TSA; George W. Baylor to AG Mabry, July 9, 1893, TSA; Alexander, *Winchester Warriors,* 264.

10 Ibid.; Stephens, *Texas Ranger Sketches,* 18–19; Ira Aten, "Texas Honors a Ranger Captain," *Frontier Times,* May 1939, 327–28; Donald M. Yena, "Texas Authority in Metal: Badges, History and Related Artifacts," *The Texas Gun Collector,* Spring 2003, 5; Candice DuCoin, *Lawmen on the Texas Frontier: Rangers and Sheriffs,* 127–29.

11 W. C. Jameson, "Incident at Pirate Island," *True West,* November 1988, 44. The author takes a more critical and analytical look at the incident.

12 Aten-1928, 5-6, HML&HC.

13 Aten, "Six and One-Half Years in the Ranger Service," Part III, 158.

14 Ibid.; Aten-1928, 4, HML&HC.

15 Ibid.

16 Ibid., 160.

17 Aten-1928, 4, HML&HC; Ira is in error—probably a typo—in placing the Cordels in Castro County as early as 1881. See, Castro County Historical Commission, *Castro County, Texas, 1891–1981,* vol. 1, 24: "Two brothers, Fred and Oscar Cordel filed a claim northeast of Dimmitt about 1891."

18 Ibid.: "You could go to their [Cordel's] ranch any time and always see a quarter of beef hanging up, but you could see no hides."

19 Ibid.

20 Aten, "Six and One-Half Years in the Ranger Service," Part III, 158.

21 Ibid.; additional information on these extraordinary and notable Texas ranches may be found in Bill O'Neal's *Historic Ranches of the Old West*; J. Evetts Haley's *The XIT Ranch of Texas* and *Charles Goodnight: Cowman and Plainsman*; and David J. Murrah's *C. C. Slaughter: Rancher, Banker, Baptist.*

22 Aten-1928, 1, HML&HC.

23 Aten, "Six and One-Half Years in the Ranger Service," Part III, 158; Aten-1941, 16, HML&HC: "I drove to Tulia and got Frank Scott, sheriff, and Bob Bishop the JA foreman, and we took the trail ...."

24 The term "loose herding," as used by Ira Aten, although not common outside cowmen and cowboy circles, is not inaccurate. Watts, *Dictionary of the Old West* says on page 201: "To loose herd was to allow a herd of animals to spread out but not to scatter at will, usually so that the animals might graze"; Aten's explanation is basically the same.

25 Ibid.; mistakenly, Ira identified Thatcher as Thacker, an understandable lapse; M. Huffman to J. Evetts Haley, November 30, 1927, 48,

HML&HC; George H. Shirk, *Oklahoma Place Names*, 44: "Cheyenne, County seat of Roger Mills County. Post Office established April 11, 1892."

26 Aten-1928, 5, HML&HC. For the reader in want of overly melodramatic dialogue associated with these arrests, Preece's *Lone Star Man* will fit the bill. See pages 221–23.

27 Aten, "Six and One-Half Years in the Ranger Service," Part III, 158.

28 Ibid.

29 Ibid., 159.

30 Ibid.; Duke and Frantz, *6,000 Miles of Fence*, 107: "Ira Aten's taste of rustling is more or less typical. A former Texas Ranger, he built a reputation for tracking stolen cattle while sheriff of Castro County, once returning more than three hundred head, plus the thieves, from the Washita River in Indian Territory."

31 Ibid., 160.

32 Aten-1928, 6, HML&HC.

33 Aten, "Six and One-Half Years in the Ranger Service," Part III, 158; Indictments: Cause No. 96, *The State of Texas vs. William Burkett*, Theft of Cattle, and Cause No. 99, *The State of Texas vs. Howard Thatcher*, Theft of Cattle. Courtesy Armstrong County (Claude) District Clerk Connie Spiller and Deputy Clerk Terresa Collins.

34 Castro County Historical Commission, *Castro County, Texas, 1891–1981*, vol. 1, 25.

35 Ibid.

36 Stephens, *Texas Ranger Sketches*, 36; Ed Connell to J. Evetts Haley, October 31, 1927, 1, HML&HC.

37 Captain Hughes to AG Mabry, December 9, 1893, TSA.

38 Captain Hughes to AG Mabry, December 1, 1893, TSA.

39 Ibid.

40 Alexander, *Winchester Warriors*, 271; Monthly Return, Company D, December 1893, TSA.

41 Captain Hughes to AG Mabry, December 1 and 9, 1893, TSA.

42 Captain Hughes to AG Mabry, December 31, 1893, TSA; Monthly Return, Company D, December 1893, TSA.

43 Birthdays for the issue of Austin Ira and Imogen Boyce Aten are courtesy Betty Aten, Frank L. Aten's granddaughter and Gary Boyce Radder, Ira Aten's grandson.

44 Phone interview with Mr. Bobby Santiesteban, Research Specialist, Texas General Land Office (TGLO), Austin, Texas, January 12, 2010; Proof of Settlement Under Homestead Act, Castro County, Oldham Land District, Lewis Epps, September 11, 1890; Land Deed transfer from Lewis Epps to Frank L. Aten, June 13, 1891; Land Deed transfer from Frank L. Aten to Ira Aten, April 29, 1892; and Proof

of Settlement Under Homestead Act, Castro County, Oldham Land District, Lewis Epps survey, January 15, 1894, courtesy TGLO.

45   Leta Glyn Rutter Hawks (Cal Aten's granddaughter), Commerce City, Colorado, to author, September 2009.

46   Monthly Return, Company D, May 1894, TSA; Alexander, *Winchester Warriors*, 277–78; Captain Hughes to AG Mabry, July 14, 16, 17 and 19, 1894; Captain Brooks to AG Mabry, July 14 and 15, 1894; Monthly Return, Company D, July 1894, TSA: "[July] 14: Corpl. Aten and three men started to Temple on account of strike on rail road. Retuned on 27th. While out traveled by rail road 2278 miles."

47   J. E. Moore to J. Evetts Haley, July 6, 1927, 3, HML&HC.

48   Aten-1941, 37, HML&HC: "They accused Rube Boyce, a cousin of my wife, and all of robbing that stage. The whole four times, and they were indicted in the federal court and put in the jail at Austin. They told it on him that he robbed the stage and would go across the divide over on the Llano. It was all open country then and nobody lived in it. They accused him and indicted him in a number old cases, Rube Boyce, and he laid in jail there at Austin, and while in jail there—in those days they gave a permit for the wives or family to bring them in something extra to eat. His wife brought him in a basket of food one day, and it had a false bottom in it, and in that bottom she had a six-shooter. The jailer looked at it and didn't see any false bottom. When the jailer come to let his wife out, Rube had this six-shooter and held off the jailer and put him in jail. His wife had a nice horse tied outside and old Rube slipped down the steps and jumped on the horse and was gone. The first man that ever broke out of the brand new jail at Austin at that time. They said it couldn't be gotten out of. The old one they could all the time." Alexander, *Winchester Warriors*, 147–48; O. C. Fisher, *It Occurred in Kimble*, 218–20; Robert S. Weedle, "The Pegleg Stage Robbers," *Southwest Heritage*, March 1969, 5.

49   Ibid., 39.

50   Hunter, *The Trail Drivers of Texas*, 672–73; Aten-1928, 1, HML&HC: "A. G. Boyce was a cousin of my wife, but I never met him until after I became sheriff of Castro County"; Chesley, *Adventuring With the Old-Timers*, 87: "So Colonel Boyce came down to see me. I wasn't acquainted with him at the time"; Awbrey and Dooley, *Why Stop?*, 64: "The last land engagement of the Civil War was fought near this site on May 12–13, 1865, thirty-four days after Robert E. Lee surrendered at Appomattox."

51   O'Neal, *Historic Ranches*, 27–28; M. Huffman to J. Evetts Haley, November 30, 1927, 11–12, HML&HC; Paul I. Wellman, *The Trampling Herd: The Story of the Cattle Range in America*, 282.

52   Haley, *The XIT Ranch of Texas*, 75: "As a cowman in Indian Territory he [Campbell] became noted for his parsimony, traditionally antagonistic to the code of the cow camp. But inversely propionate to his penuriousness on his own ranch was his extravagance on the XIT."

53   Ibid., 102.

54   Ibid., 100; M. Huffman to J. Evetts Haley, November 30, 1927, 11, HML&HC: "A. L. Matlock a lawyer from Fort Worth, came out and was general manager about the time Boyce came in. He was to look into the matter and see if he could find where the money went"; O'Neal, *Historic Ranches*, 30: "Graft, shoddy managerial practices, and outright theft flourished, while the huge ranch became a known hangout for horse and cattle thieves"; Texas State Historical Association, *The New Handbook of Texas*, vol. 6, 1101–2.

55   Lewis Nordyke, "The Ranch That Changed the West," *Readers Digest*, September 1945, 109. This is a reprint of Nordyke's article as it first appeared in the December 1944 edition of *The American Mercury*.

56   Ibid., 110. Quoting a letter from A. L. Matlock to George F. Westover, October 9, 1887; Bessie Patterson, ed., *Deaf Smith County: The Land and Its People, 1876–1981*, 9: "'Escarbada' means 'scrapings'—by scraping small pits in the sand water could be found"; Gary L. Lindsey, "Weather Watchers," *Roundup*, Spring 2006, 35: "The Escarbadas building was originally erected in 1886 on Tierra Blanca Draw, one mile east of the New Mexico state line in Deaf Smith County, or about 35 miles west of Hereford"; XIT records courtesy PPHM reference the Escarbada sans the "s"; February 9, 2010, interview with Terry Humble.

57   Handwritten remembrances, "The Life of J. W. Holston," 25: "We Rangers had to carry 120 Rounds of ammunition on ever[y] Scout we went on. So a Winchester Belt and Six-shooter Belt and the two Guns did not hold the required rounds of ammunition. So for pass time more than anything else I made three little rowes [*sic*] of shell loops on my Pistol scabbard that made my outfit hold the exact amount of rounds we were required to carry on a Scout. I was the only one in my Company thus reged [*sic*] out." Copy of manuscript courtesy Amy Parker. J. W. Holston's service as a private in the Frontier Battalion is confirmed by TSA Certificates of Pay and Enlistment Roll. For an excellent discussion of typical Texas Ranger gun-carrying leather, see Stan Nelson, "Some Thoughts on Gun Leather," *Minnesota Weapons Collectors Association News* 22, no. 1 (January 2008): 12–13.

58   Haley, *The XIT Ranch of Texas*, 102.

59   O'Neal, *Historic Ranches*, 27; Vernon Schmid, "Wire for the West," *Roundup*, February 2010, 16; Lawrence M. Woods, *British Gentlemen*

in the Wild West: The Era of the Intensely English Cowboy, 186: "The XIT itself held absolute sway over parts of ten counties in Texas, and its western boundary fence ran nearly two hundred miles with scarcely a jog to offend the eye. This empire—for so it was—was the fief of a board of directors, and they ruled as surely within their boundaries (and sometimes beyond) as did many sheriffs of the day."

60   Doug Perkins and Nancy Ward, *Brave Men and Cold Steel: A History of Range Detectives and Their Peacemakers*, 61: "In the early years, the [XIT] brand was carried by as many as 150,000 Longhorn cattle"; for an article written by Mrs. T. V. Reeves for the May 1927 edition of *The Cattlemen*, and also carried in the June issue of *Frontier Times* (before publication of Haley's *The XIT Ranch of Texas*) the author tallies the XIT's fencing materials: "Fencing alone was a stupendous task; 240 carloads of wire, 101,200 posts and a carload of staples were freighted from Fort Dodge, Kansas, a distance varying from 250 to 270 miles. This fence, even in the old days of low prices, cost $171,000," see page 5.

61   Haley, *The XIT Ranch of Texas*, 105; Duke and Frantz, *6,000 Miles of Fence*, 6. A calculation tabulating at 6,000 miles of fence is based on building a four-wire fence, fifteen hundred miles in length. 4 x 1500=6,000; the Escarbada Division was cross-fenced. See, Lew Haile to Boone McClure, March 11, 1959, PPHM; J. E. Moore, "Early Work on the XIT Ranch," *Frontier Times*, November 1939, 76: "When Boyce came on the ranch as general manager he fired a good many undesirables, and in that way he got the name of being pretty hard-boiled."

62   J. E. Moore to J. Evetts Haley, 3, HML&HC; Lewis Nordyke, *Cattle Empire, the Fabulous Story of the 3,000,000 Acre XIT*, 235; Haley, *The XIT Ranch of Texas*, 106: "Topography conspired with the rustlers of eastern New Mexico to give the cowboys of the Escarbada Division much trouble"; Worth Jenning interview as contained in R. L. Duke, XIT Interviewsn 2–3, HML&HC: "In the early nineties the Rustlers had been making quite a lot of trouble on this [Escarbada] division"; Haley, 110–11, for description of Cook, later a Deaf Smith Co. sheriff; Tise, *Texas Sheriffs*, 152.

Notes to Chapter 15

1   Aten-1928, 1, HML&HC; Aten, "Six and One-Half Years in the Ranger Service," Part III, 161; Chesley, *Adventuring With the Old-Timers*, 87: "My wife bitterly opposed my going over there. Said, 'I feel like you are going to your doom.' [She] Was opposed, though he [A. G. Boyce] was her second cousin. She almost hated him afterwards, but she kind of got over it."

2   J. E. Moore to J. Evetts Haley, July 6, 1927, HML&HC; Worth Jen-
    nings interview in the HML&HC: "On March 1st 1895, I began work
    for the XIT. Mr. Ira Aten was the Boss—and a fine, square shooting
    fellow."

3   Tise, *Texas County Sheriffs*, 94. The author enumerates "James E.
    Boyce" rather than "John E. Boyce" for Ira's replacement as Castro
    County Sheriff; Chesley, *Adventuring With the Old-Timers*, 87: "My
    brother-in-law, John Boyce was my deputy. When I [Ira Aten] resigned
    he was appointed sheriff"; John Ely Boyce would stand reelection
    in 1896 and 1898, serving as Castro County Sheriff until November
    1900.

4   Fred Tarpley, *1001 Texas Place Names*, 100–1; In Patterson, *Deaf Smith
    County*, p. 110, Texas Ranger Ed Connell's daughter, Eddie, wrote:
    "Mother often said the hardest part of pioneer life was being so far
    from a doctor. She had to send a note to the doctor at Amarillo by a
    cowboy on horseback, who would return a day later with medicine,
    diagnosis and instructions"; a synopsis of the 1883 Cowboy Strike is
    found in Robert E. Zeigler's "The Cowboy Strike," *Ranch Record*, Winter
    2007, 13. Plausibly the figure of eighty miles from Amarillo is depen-
    dent on where one starts in Deaf Smith County, and is certainly not
    unreasonable for a trip originating at Escarabada headquarters near
    the New Mexico territorial line.

5   Gourney, *Texas Boundaries*, 98; Awbrey and Dooley, *Why Stop?* 224–25;
    Tise, *Texas County Sheriffs*, 152; Blackburn, *Wanted: Historic County
    Jails of Texas*, 96–97; G. B. Combs to Lois L. Allen, June 5 and 23,
    1937, PPHM: "This part of the ranching country [Escarbada Division]
    kept a freighter on the road most of the time. He came in, unloaded,
    and went back after more supplies."

6   Aten-1928, 1, HML&HC; Aten-1941, 127, HML&HC: "Jim [McLaren]
    was one of these slack fellows, and thieves took charge of the ranch....
    So slack the ranch was about to get away from him...."

7   William Timmons, *Twilight on the Range: Recollection of a Latterday
    Cowboy*, 42–43; B. P. Abbott to J. Evetts Haley, June 24, 1927, 14,
    HML&HC: "Jim McLaren was foreman on the Escarbada before Ira
    Aten"; William H.Forbis, *The Cowboys*, 67; Nordyke, *Cattle Empire*, 207.

8   Ira Aten to AG Mabry, February 24, 1895, TSA; Aten-1928, 103,
    HML&HC; Weiss, *Yours to Command*, 331 n.106: "Mabry also ordered
    that Aten, Arrington, and three other Rangers be dropped from the
    rolls of Company B for failure to turn in monthly reports." Appar-
    ently—from the chronology—the AG made the request for Ira to
    surrender his Descriptive List straight to Aten, and then told Captain
    McDonald to drop him from the Company B roster. Mention that
    Ira's salary was $75 per month is gleaned from several sources, and is

confirmed by XIT payroll accounts housed at PPHM. As examples, two
are cited specifically: one for February 27, 1899, and one for January
31, 1901.

9   Aten-1928, 36, HML&HC: "I brought Wood Saunders up from El Paso
right after I took charge of the ranch and put him at Trujillo camp
to look out for thieves on the west side. He was an ex-Ranger"; and
"Across from Tombstone, outside the Escarbada pasture, there was a
strip of country in which there some little men which we called 'the
strip.' They gave us a great deal of trouble, and I put Ed Connell over
there," 34 and 35; Ed Connell to J. Evetts Haley, October 31, 1927, 5,
HML&HC: "Aten had his windows at the Escarbada painted green. I
was still a Ranger then and keeping a camp for the Syndicate Ranch."
C. L. Douglas, *Cattle Kings of Texas*, 305. Chapter 21 is titled "Protection Men"; Eddie Connell Trussell (Big Ed Connell's daughter) wrote
that her mother said that the Tombstone Camp "was about as cheer-
ful as its name." See, Patterson, *Deaf Smith County*, 110; also, Eddie
Connell Trussell, "Fiddler on the Phone," *Frontier Times*, April- May
1974, p. 39: "Papa had been with the XIT on two different tenures;
1895–1896 as a protection man...."; Lillie Mae Hunter, *The Moving Finger*, 36: "When Ira had finished his term as sheriff, he was hired by the
Syndicate as a sort of unofficial law officer to help reduce rustling on
their great domain"; Robert K. DeArment explores the adventures of
"protection men" on the Texas cattle ranges in an article for *Old West*,
Spring 1991, "The Protection Man," a nonfiction tale taking place in
the Panhandle; DeArment expands on the subject material in *Deadly
Dozen: Twelve Forgotten Gunfighters of the Old West*, 99–114; also see
Matt Dodge, "Shootout in Standifer Thicket," *Oldtimers Old West*,
December 1978; for a book-length look, see Bill O'Neal's *The Bloody
Legacy of Pink Higgins*.

10   Ed Connell to J. Evetts Haley, August 22, 1927. HML&HC. That
wholesale cattle stealing was underway in the region during this
timeframe—not just on the XIT—is clearly revealed by William Curry
Holden in *The Espuela Land and Cattle Company: A Study of a Foreign-
Owned Ranch in Texas*, 212: "Beginning in 1896, the amount of stealing steadily increased"; W. J. "Scotch Bill" Elliott, *The Spurs*, 121: "The
courts of Dickens and adjoining counties were soon overflowing with
cases of cattle theft. By 1899 it became necessary for the Manager of
the Spurs to employ men whose only business was to ride the range
and suppress those cattle thieves."

11   Ed Connell to J. Evetts Haley, October 31, 1927, HML&HC; Ira Aten to
Captain W. J. McDonald, January 2, 1896, TSA:

      Owing to the lawlessness in this [Deaf Smith] & Parmer Cos., I
write to see if you could place one of your best men in this county to

assist capturing & ferreting out the many crimes. This & Parmer Co. lays along the line of New Mexico & is open to the many criminals beyond our border who come in & out at will. Cattle & horse stealing are the principle crimes although setting the grass a fire is frequent & large bodies of grass is often burned. I am sorry to mention that our Shff is not as vigilant as he ought to be & the stockmen has but little protection from him. This County is very thinly settled & needs a Ranger or two to keep the criminals from New Mexico from running rough shod over the honest citizens & doing as they please. I would not make this request if I did not believe it was necessary & that good would result. I ranged for 8 years in Co. "D" & have an idea what affect the present [sic] of a ranger in a county will have among criminals. At your service any time.

12 Aten-1928, 31, HML&HC. For further reading about livestock thievery and lawlessness across the XIT's line in New Mexico Territory, refer to David Remley's *Bell Ranch: Cattle Ranching in the Southwest, 1824–1947*, particularly 141–43.

13 Ibid., 30; Ira Aten to Imogen Aten, November 5, 1936, PPHM.

14 Ibid., 31. "My wife [Imogen] would go to the door and be in the light so they could see it was a woman and find out what was wanted. Ed Connell's wife used to go to the door at Tombstone."

15 Ibid., 19, 20, 103. During the trail-driving season Frank Fuller was a noted boss drover. Aten characterized him and C. R. Smith as "the best cowmen I ever had"; Nordyke, *Cattle Empire*, tells a similar story about Allen "W. A." Stagg, cowboy and future sheriff of Oldham County, see p. 187; O'Neal, *Historic Ranches*, 35, 55; J. H. Weems to Mary H. Gaetz, May 5, 1941, PPHM: "Some of the boys on the ranch didn't do anything else only 'wolf.' Different ranches paid $5.00 a scalp for the big ones. Frank Fuller and Charlie Orr were two who didn't do anything for years but 'wolf.' Made big money. Sometimes get into a den and get a dozen young ones. They'd run them down on horses too"; J. Frank Dobie in *The Longhorns* examples one tactic employed by wolfers: "One way to shoot wolves was to stake out the head of a slaughtered beef, and then with two dry hides, which would stay in any kind of propped position, make, a little off to one side, a tent-shaped blind for concealing a man with a gun. The wolves would come to eat on the beef head"; see page 234.

16 Ibid., 22; Robert F. Pace and Donald S. Frazier, *Frontier Texas: History of a Borderland*, 238.

17 Ibid., 3–37; H. K. Baughn to J. Evetts Haley, June 25, 1927, 6, HML&HC; A. Pierce McDonald to J. Evetts Haley, June 25, 1927, 55, HML&HC: "I began work on the Escarbada.... Ira Aten was foreman there.... We tallied over 32,000 head of cattle on that division that

fall.... The spring work on that division began from May 1 to 10 and would finish up in November or December. The wagon ran steadily"; C. R. Smith to J. Evetts Haley, August 11, 1927, 87, HML&HC: "I began work on the Escarbada Division.... Ira Aten was boss.... They worked twenty-five men during the summer and about fifteen during the winter. The first year I was there we branded 10,000 calves...."

18   Ira Aten to Imogen Aten, November 5, 1936, PPHM; Ira Aten, "Crossing High Water in a Wagon," *Frontier Times*, May 1941, 367: "My wife and four children went along with us in our big covered hack, especially built for her and the children to follow the cow outfit around over the ranch when she got lonesome at ranch headquarters."

19   Aten-1928, 3–37, HML&HC; for an account of a rattlesnake killing a Panhandle cowboy and confirmation that diamondbacks were not foreign to the section, see Willie Newbury Lewis, *Tapadero: The Making of a Cowboy,* 103: "The plains are not the habitat of the diamondback, but my husband did run across two of them."

20   Aten-1928, 26, HML&HC.

21   XIT Trujillo and Tombstone Camp Diaries, quotation from Tombstone Diary, courtesy of HML&HC.

22   Haley, *The XIT Ranch of Texas*, 112; Douglas, *Cattle Kings of Texas*, 328.

23   Aten-1928, 105, HML&HC.

24   Ibid.; that Ira Aten ruled the XIT with an iron hand is widely accepted. Nordyke, *Cattle Empire*, 111: "Aten put the 'fear of God' into fence cutters"; during the 1928 interview Aten advised Haley: "When I left the ranch, I told John Armstrong that the only way to handle those men [thieves] was through fear...," 102; Also, Aten-1941, 41: "I saw right then the only way to control those fellows was through fear—make them believe you would fight, whether you would or not—rumple up on them"; Ira's warnings were not hogwash. His replacement, Armstrong, was killed.

25   Ibid.; although he might have intended a slightly different connotation, J. Evetts Haley, on p. 125 of *The XIT Ranch of Texas*, hits square the nail of reality: "the XIT was an institution of law. It did for the western tier of Panhandle counties what county organization had failed to do."

26   Ed Connell to J. Evetts Haley, October 31, 1927, 12, HML&HC; Worth Jennings' interview: "Aten could spot a criminal as far as he could see him," see page 3 in HML&HC; Tise, *Texas County Sheriffs*, 152.

27   Ibid., 5; Ivan Cates, *The XIT Ranch: A Texas Legacy*, 38: "Ira Aten used the greatest precaution when traveling...."; Aten-1928, 104, HML&HC: "I expected to be killed at any time after I went there [Escarbada]."

28   Aten-1928, 14, HML&HC.

29 Haley, *The XIT Ranch of Texas*. The complete set of "General Rules of the XIT Ranch," may be found in an appendix, 241–45. Claims that the Escarbada cowboys carried six-shooters are numerous both in primary and secondary accounts, a fact likely kept hidden from Chicago ownership: "Agin John V. Farwell did not know all about this arming of the Escarbada." See Nordyke, *Cattle Empire*, 235; Aten-1928, 102: "This stretch of fence next to Endee [New Mexico] was the only one on the ranch that they rode everyday. Every man that rode it carried a Winchester and six-shooter, and everybody knew it."

30 Nordyke, "The Ranch That Changed the West," 108.

31 Ibid.

32 Lewis, *Tapadero*, 100. Another group that had little use for the XIT were employees of the Santa Fe Railroad because "workers often had to dismount their trains to chase cattle from the XIT Ranch off the tracks to be able to get through town, the area was identified as *Bull Town*. The name was dignified as *Bovina* [Parmer County] when the post office was established, but the name retained the reference to the troublesome cattle." See Tarpley, *1001 Texas Place Names*, 31.

33 Anderson Witherspoon to Frank Jones, July 2, 1937, PPHM.

34 Nordyke, "The Ranch That Changed the West," 109. An on-scene player, Jack Culley, amplifies the negativity many Panhandle folks felt about the XIT: "Nor did it injure a man's character seriously to kill an XIT beef." See *Cattle, Horses and Men*, 243; Nordyke, *Cattle Empire*: "Thus the XIT was surrounded by people who detested it." And, "Probably the 'anti-hospitality' law did more to arouse bitterness than anything else." See pages 209 and 212.

35 Stephens, *Texas Ranger Sketches*, 16; interviews with Cal Aten's granddaughters, Shirley Aten Roberts, Sally Walker, and Leta Hawks; unidentified newsclip, April 4, 1939: Cal Aten "moved to Deaf Smith County and worked as a cowboy on the famous XIT for several years," courtesy TRHF&M; XIT pay records archived at PPHM clearly reveal wages drawn by Cal Aten. Two examples would be a February 27, 1899, check for $25 and an October 15, 1900, check for $25.

36 Monthly Return, Company D, July 1895, TSA.

37 Shroyer, *Williamson County, Texas*, 57. The children of Frank and Josie were Viola, Ivan Forest, Lois, Wilson Cunningham, Clarence Bell, and Oren McCormick.

38 Aten-1928, 105, HML&HC; Aten's assertion that he carried a constable's commission is supported by a listing of Deaf Smith County Constables, Ira's for Precinct 3. See Patterson, *History of Deaf Smith County*, 86; Certificate of Election, Ira Aten, Constable, Precinct 3, Deaf Smith County, Texas. October 14, 1901. Signed by John D. Sayers, Governor of Texas, courtesy Gary Boyce Radder.

39 Ibid., 106.

40 Ed Connell to J. Evetts Haley, October 31, 1927, 12, HML&HC.

41 Ibid., 9–12; Tarpley, *1001 Texas Place Names*, 157.

42 Haley, *The XIT Ranch of Texas*, 112; Aten-1928, 30, HML&HC. The civil lawsuit will be mentioned in the text when chronologically appropriate; Worth Jennings interview: "So he [A. G. Boyce] selected Mr. Aten as foreman, who in turn selected Ed Connell and Wood Saunders and boy! There was a trio of real man hunters...." see p. 3, housed in the HML&HC.

43 Aten-1928, 27, HML&HC.

44 Betty Aten and Gary Boyce Radder interviews and genealogical data based on their research.

45 For interesting commentary about "Son-of-a-Bitch Stew" refer to Ramon F. Adams, *Come an' Get It: The Story of the Old Cowboy Cook*, 91–97; see also Forbis, *The Cowboys*, regarding a similar recipe for "Sonofabitch Stew," 87. Nineteenth-century cowboys frequently referred to their saddles as "caques" or "hulls"; see Thomas H. Rynning, *Gun Notches: A Saga of Frontier Lawman Captain Thomas H. Rynning*, 144; Aten, "Six and One-Half Years in the Ranger Service," Part III, 164: "Each man had two bad bronc horses in his mount, and after dinner [lunch] was the time to ride them. Some six or eight men would ride their broncs all at once—a regular six-ring circus—and such pitching and bucking you never saw before"; Aten-1928, 65, HML&HC: "I prohibited them smoking cigarettes any where but at a windmill. They never always observed this, but it made them be more careful"; Jim Pfluger,"Wild Fire on the Plains," *Ranch Record*, Spring 2009, 22: "After that fire, all XIT employees were ordered to only smoke near windmill tanks where all the grass had been trampled down to the bare ground and where water was available."

46 Transfer of Title [Deed], from Allen Bell to Ira Aten, specifically described property, Williamson County, Texas, executed September 20, 1897; Castro County Historical Association, Castro County, Texas, 1891–1981, 132. In this instance "Bell" is identified as Barclay T., rather than his brother Allen. The legal document examined is styled Allen G. Bell to Ira Aten.

47 Promissory Note from Frank L. Aten to Ira Aten, October 27, 1897.

48 Aten-1928, 27–28, HML&HC.

49 Lewis, *Tapadero*, 100: "and on the west by the three million acres of the XIT, the most unpopular outfit in the Panhandle"; Patterson, *History of Deaf Smith County*, 9: "These men helped enforce Aten's strong-hand tactics with rustlers."

50 Haley, *The XIT Ranch of Texas*, 243.

51   Duke and Frantz, *6,000 Miles of Fence*, 45.

52   Ibid., 51.

53   Ira Aten, "Early Day Fires in the Panhandle," *Frontier Times*, October 1939; Aten, "Six and One-Half Years in the Ranger Service," Part III. Curiously, in this piece Ira Aten references two different years for the same event, taking the XIT job as Division Manager: first, "In the fall of 1894, about two months after I took charge of the XIT Ranch, the Texas Panhandle was the scene of the most disastrous prairie fire I ever witnessed," 161; second, "When I took charge of the XIT Ranch in January of 1895, all of the plains cattle had been moved back in the Canadian breaks. It became my duty to see that there were plenty of fire guards plowed during the following summer, when the rains made the ground soft enough to plow," 162. The gaff is unintentional and understandable. The second quotation is correct regarding the timeline of his resignation as Castro County Sheriff and the new job as a XIT Division Manager.

54   Duke and Frantz, *6,000 Miles of Fence*, 54; Robert Julyan, *The Place Names of New Mexico*, 124; T. M. Pearce, *New Mexico Place Names: A Geographical Dictionary*, 54.

55   Ibid., 56.

56   Ibid.

57   Ed Connell to J. Evetts Haley, October 31, 1927, 4–5, HML&HC.

58   Duke and Frantz, *6,000 Miles of Fence*, 40; Aten, "Six and One-Half Years in the Ranger Service," Part III, 165; Patterson, *History of Deaf Smith County*, 87. Ira Aten is enumerated as a multi-term Deaf Smith County Commissioner in Precinct 3; Pauline Durrett Robertson and R. L. Robertson, *Cowman's Country: Fifty Frontier Ranches in the Texas Panhandle, 1876–1887*, 159; Aten-1941, 115, HML&HC: "While I was foreman of the XIT's I was also a county commissioner of that [Deaf Smith] county"; Certificate of Election, Ira Aten, County Commissioner, Precinct 3, Deaf Smith County, Texas. November 12, 1896, signed by J. P. Connell, County Judge, courtesy Gary Boyce Radder.

59   Patterson, *Deaf Smith County*, 16, 22, 580; Ira Aten to Imogen Aten, November 7, 1936, PPHM: "You will recall the ranch headquarters were 35 miles west of here near the New Mexico-Texas state line and where you lived for 6 years prior to moving to Hereford in 1901 after the railroad was built...." ; U.S. Federal Census, 1900, Justice Precinct 3, Deaf Smith County, Texas.

60   Alexander, *Winchester Warriors*, 287–89; Leo N. Miletich, *Dan Stuart's Fistic Carnival*. The author quotes Stuart's reaction to the Texas Legislature passing a law prohibiting prizefighting on p. 59: "I will still proceed under the law as it is and hunt other fields [find somewhere

outside Texas]. You see I am now, and have been, law-abiding. Yes, sir, the contest will not come off in Texas."

61   Weiss, *Yours to Command*, 118: "I [John Hughes] have not tried to conceal the fact that I would prevent the fight from taking place in Texas but have always expressed myself that I did not think they would try it on Texas soil."

62   Monthly Return, Company D, February 1896, TSA; Weiss, *Yours to Command*, 114: "[Eddie] Aten trailed different trains with ring equipment and carpenters from El Paso to Langtry, Texas and reported these movements to Captain Hughes"; Miletich, *Dan Stuart's Fistic Carnival*. Interestingly the author gives an account of Eddie Aten's forcefulness on p. 171: "In the dead of night, two Rangers watched a flatcar of lumber being hitched to a westbound train and climbed on the engine. The engineer took one look at Ranger Ed Aten and brusquely declared, 'You're not going to ride on this engine. If you try it, I'll knock you off with the shovel.' The Ranger was in no mood to debate according to *Robert's Rules of Order*. Aten pressed the muzzle of his .45 into the engineer's stomach and told him to pull out. The lumber went as far as Strauss, New Mexico, then came back, picked up some carpenters, and continued east. Aten stayed with it"; Also see C. L. Sonnichsen's *The Story of Roy Bean: Law West of the Pecos*, 186: "He was the scaredest [*sic*] engineer in Texas when Aten eased the muzzle of a .45 up against his stomach and told him what to do next."

63   Weiss, *Yours to Command*, 118: "Bringing the other Ranger companies to the city [El Paso] was an overkill that should have been avoided."

64   Patterson, *History of Deaf Smith County*, 9.

65   Aten, "Six and One-Half Years in the Ranger Service," Part III, 165.

66   Aten family genealogical research as cited.

67   Haley, *Passionate Nation*, 381; Robertson, *Cowman's Country*, 159: "the XIT operated without profit for its lifespan of 27 years"; Nordyke, *Cattle Empire*, 246: "Thus the XIT went on the block"; interview with John T. "Doc" Baker, grandson of George Washington and Caroline Brumley, March 18, 2010, Dallas, Texas.

68   Julyan, *The Place Names of New Mexico*, 280; Pearce, *New Mexico Place Names*, 127–28; George B. Anderson, *History of New Mexico: Its Resources and People*, vol. 2, 882: "He [Sheriff Street] had considerable trouble with the rustler element when the county was first organized...."; for more on the life of James Alexander Street, the controversy, as well as highlighting his tenure with the New Mexico Territorial Mounted Police and, later, a distinguished career as a Special Agent with the Federal Bureau of Investigation, refer to the exhaustively researched work of Chuck Hornung, in particular, *Fuller-*

ton's Rangers: A History of the New Mexico Territorial Mounted Police and Jewel Street Pickrell's sketch in *Quay County, 1903–1985*, 687.

69   Patterson, *Deaf Smith County*, 110.

70   Chesley, *Adventuring With the Old-Timers*, 88.

71   Ibid.; Ira Aten to Joe Fraizer, October 12, 1904, courtesy Nicky Olson, Director, XIT Museum, Dalhart, Texas; Aten, "Crossing High Water in a Wagon," 368: "The fall of 1904 my wife became very sick and the doctor said I would have to take her to a lower altitude and warmer climate"; Aten-1941, 150, HML&HC.

72   Aten-1928, 114, HML&HC.

73   Ibid.

Notes to Chapter 16

1   Wayne Gard, *Cattle Brands of Texas*, 27: "The XIT brand, designed by John Blocker about 1885, was used on what once was the largest fenced ranch in the world."

2   Chesley, *Adventuring With the Old-Timers*, 88; U.S. Federal Census, 1910, El Centro, Imperial County, California.

3   Aten,"Six and One-Half Years in the Ranger Service," Part III, 165.

4   Aten family genealogical research as cited; Aten, "Crossing High Water in a Wagon," 368: "Another baby girl was born to us. We called her our 'Golden West Baby'."

5   Ira Aten to Brothers and Sisters, February 1, 1942. Reprinted in *Frontier Times*, April 1942, 265–69.

6   Ira Aten to Imogen Aten, December 6, 1936, PPHM: "Ira D [Dunlap] met me at Niland [California] and we went down to our cattle ranch, two miles west of Calipatria. This ranch is 190 feet below sea level and is a 1,700 acre ranch consisting of irrigated farms nearly all in alfalfa. Every member of our family owns some land within its confines. Ira D owns the cattle and operates the ranch. This is absolutely a feeder ranch and no cattle are raised on it. Every fall a supply of four to five thousand best grade steers are brought in from Utah, Arizona, New Mexico and Texas for the season's feeding"; Ira Aten to Brothers and Sisters, [?] 1943, courtesy UT-CMA and Chuck Parsons.

7   Robert J. Burdett, ed., *American Biography and Genealogy: California Edition*, 945.

8   Letterhead, Imperial Irrigation District. El Centro, California; *Imperial Valley Weekly*, August 13, 1953.

9   Aten, "Six and One-Half Years in the Ranger Service," Part III, 165; fascinatingly for the student of outlaw/lawman history is the fact that one of the most notorious outlaws of the fading Old West era, William

Ellsworth "Elzy" Lay, worked as an irrigations system manager for
the Imperial Valley Irrigation District. See Harvey Lay Murdock (Elzy
Lay's grandson), *The Educated Outlaw: The Story of Elzy Lay of the Wild
Bunch*, 77–78; Alexander, *Lawmen, Outlaws, and S. O. Bs*, vol. 2, 121.

10 Hamlin, *The Flamboyant Judge*, 94–98; Bill Neal, *Sex, Murder, and the
Unwritten Law: Courting Judicial Mayhem, Texas Style*, 167–69; Texas
State Historical Association, *The New Handbook of Texas*, vol. 1, 681.
Here the date of Al Boyce Sr.'s death is given as November 13, 1912;
that Texas still maintained an aura of feud mentality may be evidenced in H. Glazbrook, Manager, the Prairie Cattle Company to E. B.
Elliston, September 20, 1912: "I saw accounts of the Boyce killing in
the papers, and I am inclined to believe this will not be the end of it,"
courtesy, Nicky Olson, Director/Curator, XIT Museum, Dalhart, Texas.

11 Ibid., 96 n. 4; Aten-1928, HML&HC: "and if he had, we were going to
kill him." During a press interview for the January 16, 1936, edition
of the *Imperial Valley Weekly* retired Texas Ranger Captain John R.
Hughes characterized Ira Aten's low-key deportment during tight
spots: "No, he [Aten] didn't talk much, and he didn't bluster, but
when the going was rough he knew how to handle himself. He was a
Ranger."

12 Ibid.; Texas State Historical Association, *The New Handbook of Texas*,
vol. 1, 682.

13 Stephens, *Texas Ranger Sketches*, 19–20.

14 Ibid.

15 *Marks and Brands of Oldham County*, Book 1, 205. Phonetically speak-
ing the brand 8N sounds similar to "Aten." On October 10, 1904, Ira
Aten registered the 8N and 8N brands in Oldham County (Vega),
Texas. On November 10, 1906, the 8N brand was transferred to C. G.
(Cal) Aten, and on August 7, 1912, Cal Aten registered the 8N brand
in his own name. Brand Book inspection courtesy Becky Groneman,
County/District Clerk, Oldham County, Vega, Texas; Ira Aten in a
November 13, 1936, letter to Imogen describes Cal's agricultural
operation at Lelia Lake, Donley County. "He has a nice place here—on
a beautiful high hill with a large house on it and a large barn in the
rear. He has more nice alfalfa than any place I have seen since I left El
Paso. The land is sub-irrigated here, along the creek things grow nicely
without much rain," letter in PPHM; Margaret Walker, ed., *Oldham
County, 1881–1981*, 58, 60, and 195.

16 Charles H. Harris III and Louis R. Sadler, *The Texas Rangers and the
Mexican Revolution: The Bloodiest Decade, 1910–1920*, 509. Interesting
for any aficionado of nineteenth-century Texas Ranger history would
be an extract from Ira Aten to Imogen Aten, November 25, 1936, in
PPHM: "It rained a little last night. Still cloudy and warm. Austin [Cal's

son] called for me and we went down to the old Ranger camp [Camp Leona, Uvalde County]. My brother [Calvin] Grant joined the Ranger service in 1888, about a year before I quit the service. He was camped at this camp several years and became attached to it. Thirty years after he quit the Ranger service he bought the pasture the old Ranger camp was in and has made a good ranch out of it for his boys. The sentiment of letting anyone else have the old camp was too strong for him. The boys have cleaned out the brush and the old camp looks as natural as life, Fifty years ago. The old live oaks and pecan trees are standing as sentinels over the past. The scar on the old tree I nailed the feed box on and tied my horse to for nearly four years is still there."

17 Ibid., 396–97; Enlistment, Oath of Service, and Description Ranger Force, C. G. Aten, June 1, 1918. TSA; Descriptive List, C. G. Aten, June 1, 1918, TSA; *Clarendon News*, April 6, 1939; Charles H. Harris III, Frances E. Harris, and Louis R. Sadler, *Texas Ranger Biographies: Those Who Served, 1910–1921*, 11.

18 Shroyer, *Williamson County, Texas*, 57–58.

19 Stephen Zimmer, "Vermejo Park: A History of a New Mexico Ranch," *Ranch Record*, Winter 2009, 16: "and the ranch was turned over to Ira Aten Jr. who leased it solely to run cattle." The author's negligble mistake is understandable: There was no Ira Aten, Jr. The Vermejo Park Ranch was leased to Ira Dunlap Aten, Austin Ira Aten's young-est son; see also Ira Aten to Sister and Brothers, April 20, 1939: "He [Cal Aten] was to meet me and Captain Hughes at Ira D.'s New Mexico cattle ranch at Vermejo Park in June. I was looking forward with much pleasure to seeing him there," courtesy Sally Walker and Shirley Aten Roberts.

20 J. Marvin Hunter, ed., "Captain Ira Aten's Unique Letter," *Frontier Times*, April 1942, 268; telephone interview with Betty Aten, Febru-ary 1, 2010; Ira Aten's letter to Brothers and Sister, [?] 1943. Courtesy Betty Aten.

21 Aten-1928, HML&HC.

22 Hamlin, *The Flamboyant Judge*, 235, and n. 1.

23 Adams, *Six-Guns and Saddle Leather*, 269: "Owing to a threatened law-suit, which forced it off the market, the first edition has become quite rare. In 1953 it was reprinted with some changes and omissions...."

24 Aten, "Six and One-Half Years in the Ranger Service," Part III, 161; Ira Aten to Imogen Aten, November 5, 1936, PPHM: "South of here [Tucumcari, NM], ten miles, is Rancho Mesa Rodando where the Spikes gang was killed in 1901. You will remember the Spikes family in Lubbock County sued the XIT ranch company for a million dollars in 1929 for the story I gave [J. Evetts] Haley of that killing and it was printed in the XIT ranch historical book. That case was tried in 1932

and the jury in the case vindicated my story and refused to give the Spikes family a cent of damages"; Ira Aten, by his own account, was not personally involved when the Spikes boys were slain: "There were six or eight thieves and all were transients except this married man and his brother, who were killed about a month later. Their name was Spikes. Dick was the married one and Pat the single one. Dick was killed by the party and Pat married Dick's widow later. They sent us word at the time, but we did not have time to get there before they had killed them," see Aten-1928, 34, HML&HC. Perhaps Ira's remarks about the "Spikes gang" should have been somewhat tempered in light of an absence of felony convictions. Why a civil trial jury failed to award monetary damages would best be explained by them: The jury may have "vindicated" Aten's account—or, on the other hand, reached their legally binding conclusion for a myriad of reasons. For an alternative look at the killing of the Spikes boys, see John (Dub) Bedingfield's "The Spikes-Gholson Feud," which appeared in the December 1985 edition of *Real West* 18, 32–35; also, Nellie Witt Spikes and Temple Ann Ellis, *A History of Crosby County, Texas*, 413–14: "John and Dick met their death at the hands of some unknown murderers who lay behind a bluff and shot them from their horses, as they came riding in home from removing a drift fence." And, for that particular episode as well as an adroitly written and researched piece regarding lawlessness in northeastern New Mexico Territory—across the line from the XIT—refer to Karen Holliday Tanner and John D. Tanner, Jr. in "Henry Hawkins and the Mesa Hawks Gang," *Wild West History Association Journal*, June 2010.

25   Hamlin, *The Flamboyant Judge*, 256. The civil lawsuit is covered in detail, Chapter 12, "Libel Suit, In-laws and Outlaws," 233–56; It seems later in life Ira Aten somewhat toned down his views about the Spikes boys: "The Spikes was so far away from there, at Tucumcari, that they didn't depredate on the XIT ranch. If the cattle got in there they would eat them. All would. A person didn't need to be an outright thief to eat a stray cow. They will kill stray cows around, especially from the big ranches like the XIT.... If our cattle went over there they ate them," see Aten-1941, 140, HML&HC.

26   *The* [El Centro] *Morning Post*, August 7, 1953; *Imperial Valley Press*, August 23, 1984; J. Marvin Hunter, ed., "Pioneered In California," *Frontier Times*, April 1939, 314.

27   Unidentified newsclip, October 11, 1944, courtesy Betty Aten: "He described a trial in El Centro police court in the early days when he sensed that a man was going to shoot him while he was testifying in a liquor case. 'Take him out,' Aten shouted to Mobley Meadows, then sheriff of Imperial county. Meadows dragged the man outside and

searched him. He had a pistol in each pocket. 'I was glad it ended that way,' Aten told his audience, 'because if he had started to draw those pistols I would have had to shoot him' "; that Ira Aten still maintained law enforcement authority is additionally extrapolated from Hunter, ed., "Pioneered in California," *Frontier Times*, April 1939, 314: "was second constable in Imperial township."

28   Ira Aten to Imogen Aten, November 20, 1936, PPHM. Predictably Ira Aten abhorred unnecessary violence and shied away from speciously inflating his biographic balloon or overestimating his own importance. Sometimes other Old West personalities were not near so circumspect. As but one example, note the remarks of well-regarded Arizona historian and writer Lynn R. Bailey in *Henry Clay Hooker and the Sierra Bonita*, who characterized Wyatt Earp as "the West's greatest windbag," see page 172; Wyatt Earp's less than stellar reputation was well known throughout the contemporary Old West: "Wyatt Earp: Arrested for hose stealing, prostitution and stealing school funds." See Bob Boze Bell, "When the Legend Becomes Fact," *True West*, May 2010, 6. Unlike Wyatt Earp, who never garnered public esteem through the electoral process, nineteenth-century Panhandle Texas sheriff Jim Gober, perhaps himself a tad controversial, nevertheless voiced his opinion of the overrated Earp: "Maybe Wyatt Earp would do, for he had the reputation of shooting men when they were either unarmed, or had their hands high up in the air." See Gober, *Cowboy Justice*, 171.

29   Aten-1941, 32, HML&HC. The fact that Ira reviewed Webb is made clear in a September 13, 1941, letter Ira Aten wrote Western writer J. C. "Jeff" Dykes, now in UT-CAH: "Walter Prescott Webb got his data from the Adjutant Gen't office, for his book, 'The Texas Rangers.' I have no copies of my stories not even the original...."

30   Jay Hyams, *The Life and Times of the Western Movie*, 52. Although not conclusive, an entry in John Reynolds Hughes' personal journal is interesting. The notation for January 25, 1930: "Went to Picture show—The Lone Star Ranger—El Centro." The inference is reasonable. While visiting with Ira Aten in California, the two went to the "picture show." Diary entry courtesy Chuck Parsons.

31   Ibid., 44. "When the Depression took hold, westerns fell out of favor as audiences sought more light-hearted entertainment, saved money by tuning in their radios, and showed their preference for another— far more contemporary—type of film: the gangster film."

32   A synopsis of the history for *Frontier Times* magazine may be found in James A. Browning's and Janice B. McCraw's, *A Complete Guide to Hunter's Frontier Times*. Ira Aten's contributions are listed on page eight.

33   This particular photograph is perhaps the most frequently published image of Ira Aten. Interesting, indeed, is the February 20, 2010,

correspondence to author from noted Texas Ranger historian Robert W. Stephens:

> In regard to Ira Aten, Walter Durbin's daughter-in-law gave me Durbin's collection of photos of his Ranger friends. Among these was his copy of the well known and frequently published photo of Ira Aten mounted. A notation on the back in Durbin's handwriting states that Aten was wearing Durbin's six-shooter and was mounted on Durbin's horse. Also shown is Durbin's Winchester in the saddle scabbard. I have never revealed this information before.

34   Well-regarded Old West photo collector John McWillimas, Three Rivers, California, confirmed during an informative telephone conversation that he now owned the photograph, and the inscription on its reverse aligns correctly with Mr. Stephens' letter to the author. The fact that both Hughes and Aten were well-known Texas Rangers is indisputable. Though it was in the format of a novel, the ever prolific Western writer Zane Grey particularly through a series of interviews with John Hughes and other Company D Rangers, based his hit *Lone Star Ranger* on their accounts of the wild and woolly Old West. This is explored more fully in Mike Cox's *Texas Ranger Tales: Stories That Need Telling*, 120–46. Chesley, *Adventuring With the Old-Timers*, 81.

35   Ibid.

36   Ibid., 82, 89 n. 11: "Aten refers to the famous libel suit over J. Evetts Haley's *The XIT Ranch of Texas and the Early Days of the Llano Estacado.*"

37   Ibid.

38   Aten-1941, HML&HC.

39   Chesley, *Adventuring With the Old-Timers*, 80–90.

40   J. Marvin Hunter, ed., "Captain Ira Aten's Unique Letter," *Frontier Times*, April 1942. Another letter using the same general format, thought to have been written during the last quarter of 1943, courtesy Shirley Aten Roberts; another copy courtesy UT-CAH and Chuck Parsons.

41   Adams, *Six-Guns and Saddle Leather*, 29.

42   Ira Aten to Brothers and Sisters, [?] 1943. "Here I am, a star border with Mrs. Aten and the girls and having the time of my life with our 3 ½ year old grandson and only grandson [grandchild]"; Lona Shawver, *Chuck Wagon Windies and True Stories*, 76. "He [Ira Aten] farms and ranches in the Imperial Valley, near El Centro, and his wife and daughters live in Burlingame.... Recently when they were trying to persuade Captain Aten to stay with them all the time, he said: 'I tell them that when I get old, I will come live with them all the time, but I am not going to acknowledge that I am old yet.' He spends the summers at Burlingame and the winters at El Centro, looking after the farms and ranches. He was eighty-five on September 3, 1947."

43   Unidentified newsclip, October 11, 1944.

44   Martin, *Border Boss*, Introduction by Mike Cox, 13. An assertion that Ira Aten and John Hughes maintained contact during their twilight years is generally accepted, a fact that is bolstered by primary source correspondence between the two, as in: Aten to Hughes, December 7, 1942; Aten to Hughes, May, 6, 1945; Aten to Hughes, May 18, 1945; and Aten to Hughes, May 12, 1946, all courtesy TRHF&M. References to face to face visits may also be found in the series of 1936 letters from Ira Aten to his wife, cited extensively throughout this text, courtesy PPHM. Mention of Hughes making a trip to California to visit with Ira Aten may be found in the October 20, 1947, edition of the *Imperial Valley Farmer*.

45   *Imperial Valley Press*, August 23, 1984.

46   *Imperial Valley Weekly*, August 13, 1953; *The Morning Post* [El Centro], August 7, 1953; *Imperial Valley Press*, August 12, 1953; Imperial Valley *District News*, September 1953 edition; J. Marvin Hunter, ed., "Captain Ira Aten Dies In California," *Frontier Times*, October–December 1953, 453–54; *San Mato Times*, August 6, 1953; *Dallas Morning News*, December 12, 1953, byline Wayne Gard, "Old Texas Ranger Rides Final Trail." James A. Browning, *Violence Was No Stranger: A Guide to the Grave Sites of Famous Westerners*, 7: "He [Ira Aten] died in Burlingame, California, and is buried in the Aten family plot, Block 7, Lot 2, in Evergreen Cemetery two miles east of El Centro, California. There is a marker. He is buried beside his wife, Imogene B. Aten (May 21, 1867–March 3, 1957)...."

47   Ira Aten (actually Harold Preece, though Aten has the byline), "I Fought These Masked Rustlers," *Real West*, May 1963, 20–22, 46–47.

48   Ira Aten to J. C. Dykes, September 13, 1941, UT-CAH.

49   Preece, *Lone Star Man*, 13.

50   Ira Aten to Brothers and Sisters, [?] 1943.

Bibliography

Non-published research sources—manuscripts, typescripts, theses, dissertations, tape recordings, official documents, courthouse records, tax rolls, petitions, correspondence, prison records, licensing records, census records, interviews, etc.—are thoroughly cited in chapter endnotes.

The primary source underpinnings for this volume are official records of the Frontier Battalion as found in the Adjutant General Files, and the Texas Ranger Correspondence Files, housed at the Texas State Archives and Library Commission, Austin, Texas. Additionally indispensable were the Vertical Files and Photographic Archives as maintained at the Research Center, Texas Ranger Hall of Fame and Museum, Waco, Texas. Also of more than significant value were the series of interviews maintained at the Nita Stewart Haley Memorial Library and History Center, Midland, Texas, and interviews, letters, and XIT Ranch records from the Research Center, Panhandle-Plains Historical Museum, Canyon, Texas.

Books:

Adams, Ramon F. *Six-Guns and Saddle Leather: A Bibliography of Books and Pamphlets on Western Outlaws and Gunmen*. Mineola, NY: Dover Publications, 1998.

———. *Come an' Get It: The Story of the Old Cowboy Cook*. Norman: University of Oklahoma Press, 1972.

Alexander, Bob. *Winchester Warriors: Texas Rangers of Company D, 1874–1901*. Denton: University of North Texas Press, 2009.

———. *Fearless Dave Allison: Border Lawman*. Silver City, NM: High-Lonesome Books, 2003.

———. *Lawmen, Outlaws, & S. O. Bs.* Vol. 2. Silver City, NM: High-Lonesome Books, 2007.

———. *John H. Behan: Sacrificed Sheriff*. Silver City, NM: High-Lonesome Books, 2002.

Anderson, George B. *History of New Mexico: Its Resources and People*. Vol. 2. Los Angles: Pacific States Publishing Company, 1907.

Andreas, Lyter & Co. *Atlas Map of Knox County Illinois*. Davenport, IA: Self published, 1870.

Aten, Ira. *Six and One-Half Years in the Ranger Service: The Memoirs of Ira Aten, Sergeant Company D, Texas Rangers*. Bandera, TX: Frontier Times, 1945.

Awbrey, Betty Dooley, and Claude Dooley. *Why Stop? A Guide to Texas Historical Roadside Markers*. Houston: Lone Star Books, 1978.

Bailey, Lynn R. *Henry Clay Hooker and the Sierra Bonita*. Tucson, AZ: Westernlore Press, 1998.

_____, with Don Chaput. *Cochise County Stalwarts: A Who's Who of the Territorial Years*. 2 vols. Tucson: Westernlore Press, 2000.

Ball, Larry D. *Desert Lawmen: The High Sheriffs of New Mexico and Arizona, 1846–1912*. Albuquerque: University of New Mexico Press, 1992.

Barr, Alwyn. *Reconstruction to Reform: Texas Politics, 1876–1906*. Austin: University of Texas Press, 1971.

Benner, Judith Ann. *Sul Ross: Soldier, Statesman, Educator*. College Station: Texas A&M Press, 1983.

Blackburn, Ed, Jr. *Wanted: Historic County Jails of Texas*. College Station: Texas A&M University Press, 2006.

Brinley, Lorine. *Fort Bend County Cemetery Inscriptions*. Vol. 2. Houston: Self published, 1985.

Brown, John Henry. *Indian Wars and Pioneers of Texas*. Austin, TX: State House Press, 1988.

Browning, James A. *Violence Was No Stranger: A Guide to the Grave Sites of Famous Westerners*. Stillwater, OK: Barbed Wire Press, 1993.

———, with Janice B. McCravy. *A Complete Guide to Hunter's Frontier Times*. Austin, TX: Eakin Press, 2000.

Bruce, Leona. *Bannister Was There*. Fort Worth, TX: Branch-Smith, 1968.

Burdette, Robert J., ed. *American Biography and Genealogy, California Edition*. Chicago: Lewis Publishing, Nd.

Burton, Jeffrey. *Western Story*. European edition. England: Palomino Books, 2008.

———. *The Deadliest Outlaws: The Ketchum Gang and the Wild Bunch*. Denton: University of North Texas Press, 2009.

Carlson, Paul H. *Texas Woollybacks: The Range Sheep and Goat Industry*. College Station: Texas A&M University Press, 1982.

Casey, Robert J. *The Texas Border and Some Borderliners*. New York: Bobbs-Merrill Company, 1950.

Castleman, Harvey N. *Sam Bass, the Train Robber: The Life of Texas' Most Popular Bandit*. Girad, KS: Haldeman-Julius Publications, 1944.

Castro County Historical Commission. *Castro County, Texas, 1881–1981*. 2 vols. Dallas, TX: Taylor Publishing Company, 1991.

Cates, Ivan. *The XIT Ranch: A Texas Legacy*. Channing, TX. Hafabanana Press. 2008.

Chapman, Charles C. *History of Knox County, Illinois*. Chicago: Blakely, Brown & Marsh, 1878.

Chesley, Hervey E. *Trails Traveled, Tales Told: Adventuring With the Old-Timers*. Midland, TX: Nita Stewart Haley Memorial Library, 1979.

Clarke, Mary Whatley. *A Century of the Cow Business—The First Hundred Years of the Texas and Southwestern Cattle Raisers Association*. Fort Worth, TX: Np, 1976.

Collins, Michael L. *Texas Devils: Rangers and Regulars on the Lower Rio Grande, 1846–1861*. Norman: University of Oklahoma Press, 2008.

Coolidge, Dane. *Fighting Men of the West*. New York: E. P. Dutton & Co., 1932.

Cox, Barbara J. *Baugh's of Brown County, Texas, 1803–1993*. Gaithersburg, MD: Self published, 1996.

———. *The Wire-Cutting War of Brown County, Texas, 1883–1888*. Gaithersburg, MD: Self published, 1991.

Cox, Mike. *The Texas Rangers: Wearing the Cinco Peso, 1821–1900*. New York: Forge Books, 2008.

———. *Texas Ranger Tales: Stories That Need Telling*. Plano, TX: Republic of Texas Press, 1997.

———. *Texas Ranger Tales II*. Plano, TX: Republic of Texas Press, 1999.

Culley, John H. (Jack). *Cattle Horses & Men of the Western Range*. Tucson: University of Arizona Press. 1984.

Davis, John L., *The Texas Rangers: Images and Incidents*. San Antonio, TX: Institute of Texan Cultures, 1991.

DeArment, Robert K. *Alias Frank Canton*. Norman: University of Oklahoma Press, 1996.

———. *Deadly Dozen: Twelve Forgotten Gunfighters of the Old West*. Norman: University of Oklahoma Press, 2003.

DeLord, Ronald G., ed. *The Ultimate Sacrifice: Trials and Triumphs of the Texas Peace Officer*. Austin, TX: Police Officers Memorial Fund, 2000.

Devereaux, Jan. *Pistols, Petticoats, and Poker: The Real Lottie Deno, No Lies or Alibis*. Silver City, NM: High-Lonesome Books, 2009.

Dillard, Jim. *The Noble John Olive: The Life and Death of Williamson County Sheriff John T. Olive*. Georgetown, TX: Self published, 2004.

Dillon, Richard. *Wells, Fargo Detective: A Biography of James B. Hume*. Reno: University of Nevada Press, 1986.

Dobie, J. Frank. *The Longhorns*. New York: Bramhall House, 1961.

Douglas, C. L. *Cattle Kings of Texas*. Austin, TX: State House Press, 1989.

———. *Famous Texas Feuds*. Austin, TX: State House Press, 1988.

———. *The Gentlemen in the White Hats: Dramatic Episodes in the History of the Texas Rangers*. Dallas, TX: South-West Press, 1934.

DuCoin, Candice. *Lawmen on the Texas Frontier: Rangers and Sheriffs*. Round Rock, TX: Riata Books, 2007.

Duke, Cordia Sloan, with Joe B. Frantz. *6,000 Miles of Fence: Life on the XIT Ranch of Texas*. Austin: University of Texas Press, 1975.

Edwards, Harold L. *Goodbye Billy the Kid*. College Station, TX: Creative Publishing, 1995.

Elliott, W. J. "Scotch Bill." *The Spurs*. 1939. Buffalo Gap, TX: State House Press, 2010.

Emrich, Duncan. *The Cowboy's Own Brand Book*. New York: Dover Publications, 1954.

Ernst, Robert. *Deadly Affrays: The Violent Deaths of the US Marshals*. NP: Scarlet Mask, 2008.

Farber, James. *Texans With Guns*. San Antonio, TX: The Naylor Company, 1950.

Farrow, Marion Humphreys. *Troublesome Times in Texas*. San Antonio, TX: The Naylor Company, 1960.

Featherston, Edward Baxter. Ed. Vera Featherston Back. *A Pioneer Speaks*. Dallas, TX: Cecil Baugh Co., N.d.

Fisher, O. C. *It Occurred in Kimble*. San Angelo, TX: Talley Press, 1954.

Forbis, William H. *The Cowboys*. New York: Time-Life Books, 1973.

Gammel, Hans Peter. *The Laws of Texas, 1822–1897*. 10 Vols. Austin, TX: Gammel Books, 1898.

Gatto, Steve. *The Real Wyatt Earp: A Documentary Biography*. Silver City, NM: High-Lonesome Books, 2000.

Gard, Wayne. *Cattle Brands of Texas*. Dallas, TX: First National Bank of Dallas, n. d.
———. *Frontier Justice*. Norman: University of Oklahoma Press, 1949.
Gilbert, Miles, with Leo Remiger and Sharon Cunningham. *Encyclopedia of Buffalo Hunters and Skinners*. 2 vols. Union City, TN: Pioneer Press, 2003 and 2006.
Gillett, James B. *Six Years with the Texas Rangers, 1875–1881*. New Haven, CT: Yale University Press, 1925.
Gober, Jim. Ed. James R. Gober and B. Byron Price. *Cowboy Justice: Tale of a Texas Lawman*. Lubbock: Texas Tech University Press, 1997.
Gournay, Luke. *Texas Boundaries: Evolution of the State's Counties*. College Station: Texas A&M University Press, 1995.
Graybill, Andrew R. *Policing the Great Plains: Rangers, Mounties and the North American Frontier, 1875–1910*. Lincoln: University of Nebraska Press, 2007.
Grisham, Noel. *Tame the Restless Wind: The Life and Legend of Sam Bass*. Austin, TX: San Felipe Press, 1968.
Haley, J. Evetts. *The XIT Ranch of Texas, and the Early Days on the Llano Estacado*. Norman: University of Oklahoma Press, 1967.
———. *Charles Goodnight: Cowman and Plainsman*. Norman: University of Oklahoma Press, 1977.
Haley, James L. *Passionate Nation: The Epic History of Texas*. New York: Free Press, 2006.
Hanna, Tryoce Stambaugh, ed. *Deaf Smith County: The Land and Its People, 1876–1981*. Hereford, TX: Deaf Smith County Historical Society, 1982.
Hamlin, James D. *The Flamboyant Judge: The Story of Amarillo and the Development of the Great Ranches of the Texas Panhandle*. Canyon, TX: Palo Duro Press, 1972.
Hardin, John Wesley. *The Life of John Wesley Hardin: As Written By Himself*. Norman: University of Oklahoma Press, 1977.
Harris, Charles H. III, with Louis R. Sadler. *The Texas Rangers and the Mexican Revolution: The Bloodiest Decade, 1910–1920*. Albuquerque: University of New Mexico Press, 2004.
———. with Frances E. Harris and Louis R. Sadler. *Texas Ranger Biographies: Those Who Served, 1910–1921*. Albuquerque: University of New Mexico Press, 2009.
Havins, T. R. *Something About Brown: A History of Brown County, Texas*. Brownwood, TX: Banner Printing Co., 1958.
Henry, Will. *The Texas Rangers*. New York: Random House, 1957.
Hewett, Janet. *The Roster of Union Soldiers, 1861–1865*. Wilmington, NC: Broadfoot Publishing Company, 1999.
———. *Supplement to the Official Records of the Union and Confederate Armies. Part II—Record of Events*. Wilmington, NC: Broadfoot Publishing, 1995.
Holden, William Curry. *The Espuela Land and Cattle Company: A Study of a Foreign-Owned Ranch in Texas*. Austin, TX: Texas State Historical Association, 1970.
Horan, James D. *The Outlaws: Accounts by Eyewitnesses and the Outlaws Themselves*. New York: Gramercy Books, 1995.
Hornung, Chuck. *Fullerton's Rangers: A History of the New Mexico Territorial Police*. Jefferson, NC: McFarland and Company, 2005.
Hunter, J. Marvin, ed. *The Trail Drivers of Texas*. Austin: University of Texas Press, 1986.
Hunter, Lillie Mae. *The Moving Finger*. Borger, TX: Plains Printing Company, 1956.

Hyams, Jay. *The Life and Times of the Western Movie*. New York: Gallery Books, 1983.

Ivey, Darren L. *The Texas Rangers: A Registry and History*. Jefferson, NC: McFarland and Company, 2010.

Jensen, Ann, ed. *Texas Ranger's Diary and Scrapbook*. Dallas, TX: The Kaleidograph Press, 1936.

Johnson, David. *The Mason County "Hoo Doo" War, 1874–1902*. Denton: University of North Texas Press. 2006.

Jordan, Terry G., *Trails to Texas: Southern Roots of Western Cattle Ranching*. Lincoln: University of Nebraska Press, 1981.

Julyan, Robert. *The Place Names of New Mexico*. Albuquerque: University of New Mexico Press, 1998.

Key, Della Tyler. *The Cattle Country: History of Potter County, 1887–1966*. Quanah, TX: Nortex Publishing, 1972.

Kilgore, D. E. *A Ranger Legacy: 150 Years of Service to Texas*. Austin, TX: Madrona Press, 1973.

Knight, Oliver. *Fort Worth: Outpost on the Trinity*. Norman: University of Oklahoma Press, 1953.

Kraisinger, Gary, and Margaret Kraisinger. *The Western: The Greatest Texas Cattle Trail, 1874–1886*. Newton, KS: Mennonite Press, 2004.

Lamb, Alan J. *An Aten Genealogy*. Santa Fe, NM: Alan J. Lamb Publications. 1997.

Lee, Katie. *Ten Thousand Goddam Cattle: A History of the American Cowboy in Song, Story, and Verse*. Flagstaff, AZ: Northland Press, 1976.

Lewis Publishing Company. *Memorial and Biographical History of Ellis County, Texas*. Chicago, IL: The Lewis Publishing Company, 1892.

Lewis, Willie Newbury. *Tapadero: The Makings of a Cowboy*. Austin: University of Texas Press, 1972.

_____ *Between Sun and Sod*. Clarendon, TX: Clarendon Press, 1938.

McCallum, Henry D. and Frances T. McCallaum. *The Wire That Fenced the West*. Norman: University of Oklahoma Press, 1965.

Marohn, Richard C. *The Last Gunfighter: John Wesley Hardin*. College Station, TX: Creative Publishing, 1995.

Martin, Charles. *A Sketch of Sam Bass, the Bandit*. Norman: University of Oklahoma Press, 1997.

Martin, Jack. *Border Boss: Captain John R. Hughes—Texas Ranger*. Austin, TX: State House Press, 1990.

Mauldin, Patti, ed. *The Genealogy and History of Brown County Sheriffs*. Brownwood, TX: The Brown County Historical Society, 2008.

Metz, Leon Claire. *The Encyclopedia of Lawmen, Outlaws, and Gunfighters*. New York: Checkmark Books, 2003.

———. *John Wesley Hardin: Dark Angel of Texas*. El Paso, TX: Mangan Books, 1996.

———. *The Shooters*. El Paso, TX: Mangan Books, 1976.

Miletich, Leo N. *Dan Stuart's Fistic Carnival*. College Station: Texas A&M University Press, 1994.

Miller, Rick. *Sam Bass & Gang*. Austin, TX: State House Press. 1999.

———. *Bounty Hunter*. College Station. TX: Creative Publishing. 1988.

———, ed., *Bell County: Crime and Criminals, 1851–1902*. Harker Heights, TX: Self published, 2005.

———. *Bloody Bill Longley*. Wolfe City, TX: Henington Publishing Company, 1996.

Moore, Stephen L. *Savage Frontier: Rangers, Riflemen, and Indian Wars in Texas*. 4 vols. Denton: University of North Texas Press, 2002–2010.

Morris, John Miller. *A Private in the Texas Rangers: A. T. Miller of Company B Frontier Battalion*. College Station: Texas A&M University Press. 2001.

Murdock, Harvey Lay. *The Educated Outlaw: The Story of Elzy Lay of the Wild Bunch*. Bloomington, IN: AuthorHouse, 2009.

Murrah, David J. *C. C. Slaughter: Rancher, Banker, Baptist*. Austin: University of Texas Press, 1981.

Nash, Jay Robert. *Encyclopedia of Western Lawmen and Outlaws*. New York: Da Capo Press, 1994.

Neal, Bill. *Sex, Murder and the Unwritten Law: Courting Judicial Mayhem, Texas Style*. Lubbock: Texas Tech University Press, 2009.

———. *Getting Away With Murder on the Texas Frontier: Notorious Killings and Celebrated Trials*. Lubbock: Texas Tech University Press, 2006.

Nolan, Frederick. *Tascosa: Its Life and Gaudy Times*. Lubbock: Texas Tech University Press, 2007.

———. *The Wild West: History, Myth & The Making of America*. Edison, NJ: Chartwell Books, 2000.

Nordyke, Lewis. *John Wesley Hardin: Texas Gunman*. Edison, NJ: Castle Books, 1957.

———. *Cattle Empire: The Fabulous Story of the 3,000,000 Acre XIT*. New York: William Morrow, 1949.

Norris, John A., ed. *Life and Adventures of Sam Bass: The Notorious Union Pacific and Texas Train Robber*. Dallas, TX: Dallas Commercial Steam Print, 1878. (Ramon Adams believes the author to be a newsman named Morrison.)

Norvell, Estelle Mae, ed. *Students' History of Williamson County*. Np. Nd.

O'Neal, Bill. *Historic Ranches of the Old West*. Austin, TX: Eakin Press, 1997.

———. *Encyclopedia of Western Gun-Fighters*. Norman: University of Oklahoma. 1979.

———. *Cattlemen vs. Sheepherders*. Austin, TX: Eakin Press, 1989.

———. *The Bloody Legacy of Pink Higgins*. Austin, TX: Eakin Press, 1999.

Pace, Robert F. with Donald S. Frazier. *Frontier Texas: History of a Borderland to 1880*. Abilene, TX: State House Press, McMurry University, 2004.

Parsons, Chuck, with Donaly E. Brice. *Texas Ranger N. O. Reynolds: The Intrepid*. Honolulu: Talei Publishing, 2005.

———. *John B. Armstrong. Texas Ranger and Pioneer Ranchman*. College Station: Texas A&M University Press, 2007.

———, and Gary P. Fitterer. *Captain C. B. McKinney: The Law in South Texas*. Wolfe City, TX: Hennington Publishing Co., 1993.

Patterson, Bessie. *A History of Deaf Smith County: Featuring Pioneer Families*. Hereford, TX: Pioneer Publishers, 1964.

Pearce, T. M., ed. *New Mexico Place Names: A Geographical Dictionary*. Albuquerque: University of New Mexico Press, 1965.

Penniger, Robert. Translated from German by C. L. Wisseman. *Fredericksburg, Texas... The First Fifty Years*. Fredericksburg, TX: Self published, 1896.

Perkins, Doug, with Nancy Ward. *Brave Men and Cold Steel: A History of Range Detectives and Their Peacemakers*. Fort Worth, TX: Texas & Southwestern Cattle Raisers Foundation, 1984.

Perry, C. R., Ed. Kenneth Kesselus. *Memoir of Capt'n C. R. Perry of Johnson City, Texas: A Texas Veteran*. Austin, TX: Jenkins Publishing Company, 1990.

Pickrell, Jewel Street, cont. *Quay County, 1903–1985*. Lubbock, TX: Craftsman Printers, Quay County Book Committee, 1985.

Preece, Harold. *Lone Star Man: Ira Aten, Last of the Old Texas Rangers*. New York: Hastings House, 1960.

Price, Bill S. *Bill Whitley: Outlaw*. Austin, TX: Nortex Press, 1995.

Putman, Wyvonne. *Navarro County History*. Vol. 1. Quanah, TX: Nortex Press, 1975.

Rathjen, Frederick W. *The Texas Panhandle Frontier*. Austin: University of Texas Press, 1973.

Raymond, Dora Neill. *Captain Lee Hall of Texas*. Norman: University of Oklahoma Press, 1982.

Remley, David. *Bell Ranch: Cattle Ranching in the Southwest, 1824–1947*. Las Cruces, NM: Yucca Tree Press, 2000.

Reynolds, John N. *A Kansas Hell: Life in the Kansas Penitentiary*. Atchison, KS: The Bee Publishing Company, 1889.

Robertson, Pauline Durrett, and R. L. Robertson. *Cowman's Country: Fifty Frontier Ranches in the Texas Panhandle, 1876–1887*. Amarillo, TX: Paramount Publishing Co., 1981.

Robinson, Charles M. III, *The Men Who Wear the Star: The Story of the Texas Rangers*. New York: Random House, 2000.

Romer, F. *Makers of History: A Story of the Development of the History of Our Country and the Part Played in it by the COLT*. Hartford. CT: Colt's Patent Fire Arms Manufacturing Company, 1926.

Rosa, Joseph G., with Robin May. *Gun Law: A Story of Violence in the Old West*. Chicago: Contemporary Books, 1977.

Rynning, Thomas H. *Gun Notches—A Saga of Frontier Lawman Captain Thomas H. Rynning as Told to Al Cohn and Joe Chisholm*. San Diego, CA: Frontier Heritage Press, 1971.

Sam Bass Café. *True Story of Sam Bass, The Outlaw*. Round Rock, TX: Sam Bass Café, 1950.

Sauer, Alice Braeutigam, cont. *Pioneers in God's Hills: A History of Fredericksburg and Gillespie County, People and Events*. Fredericksburg, TX: Gillespie County Historical Society, 1974.

Scarbrough, Clara Stearns. *Land of Good Water: A Williamson County, Texas, History*. Georgetown, TX: Williamson County Sun Publishers, 1973.

Selcer, Richard F. *Fort Worth Characters*. Denton: University of North Texas Press, 2009.

———, ed. *Legendary Watering Holes: The Saloons That Made Texas Famous*. College Station: Texas A&M University Press, 2004.

Shawver, Lona. *Chuck Wagon Windies and True Stories*. San Antonio, TX: The Naylor Company, 1950.

Shillingberg, William B. *Tombstone, A. T.—A History of Early Mining, Milling, and Mayhem*. Spokane, WA: Arthur H. Clark Company, 1999.

———. *Dodge City: The Early Years, 1872–1886*. Norman: Arthur H. Clark and Company, 2009.

Shirk, George H. *Oklahoma Place Names*. Norman: University of Oklahoma Press, 1965.

Sitton, Thad. *The Texas Sheriff: Lord of the County Line*. Norman: University of Oklahoma Press, 2000.

Smith, Tevis Clyde. *Frontier's Generation: The Pioneer History of Brown County with Sidelights on the Surrounding Territory*. Brownwood, TX: Self published, 1931.

———. *From the Memories of Men*. Brownwood, TX: Moore Printing Company. 1980.

Spellman, Paul N., *Captain John H. Rogers, Texas Ranger*. Denton: University of North Texas Press, 2003.

———*Captain J. A. Brooks, Texas Ranger*. Denton: University of North Texas Press, 2007.

Spence, Ruth Griffin. *The Nice and Nasty in Brown County*. Brownwood, TX: Banner Printing Co., 1988.

Spikes, Nellie Witt, and Temple Ann Ellis. *A History of Crosby County, Texas*. San Antonio, TX: Naylor Co., 1952.

Stephens, Robert W., *Texas Ranger Sketches*. Dallas, TX: Self published, 1972.

———. *Walter Durbin: Texas Ranger and Sheriff*. Dallas, TX: Self published, 1970.

———. *Bullets and Buckshot in Texas*. Dallas, TX: Self published, 2002.

———. *Captain George H. Schmitt: Texas Ranger*. Dallas, TX: Self published, 2006.

———. *Texas Ranger Indian War Pensions*. Dallas, TX: Self published, 1975.

Sterling, William Warren. *Trails and Trials of a Texas Ranger*. Norman: University of Oklahoma Press, 1959.

Sonnichsen, C. L. *I'll Die Before I'll Run: The Story of the Great Feuds of Texas*. Lincoln: University of Nebraska Press, 1964.

———. *Outlaw: On the Dodge with Baldy Russell*. Athens, OH: Swallow Press, 1965.

———. *The Story of Roy Bean: Law West of the Pecos*. New York: Devin-Adair Company, 1958.

Southworth, Dave. *Feuds on the Western Frontier*. Np: Wild Horse Publishing, 1999.

Sowell, A. J., *History of Fort Bend County*. Houston, TX: W. H. Coyle & Co., 1904.

Tarpley, Fred. *1001 Texas Place Names*. Austin: University of Texas Press, 1980.

Texas State Historical Association. *The Handbook of Texas*. 6 vols. Austin, TX: Texas State Historical Association, 1996.

Thompson, Jerry. *A Wild and Vivid Land: An Illustrated History of the South Texas Border*. Austin, TX: Texas State Historical Association, 1997.

Thompson, Karen R., with Jane H. Digesualdo. *Historical Round Rock, Texas*. Austin, TX: Eakin Press, 1985.

Thrapp, Dan L. *Encyclopedia of Frontier Biography*. 3 vols. Lincoln: University of Nebraska Press, 1988.

Timmons, William. *Twilight on the Range: Recollections of a Latterday Cowboy*. Austin: University of Texas Press, 1974.

Tise, Sammy. *Texas County Sheriffs*. Hallettsville, TX: Tise Genealogical Research, 1989.

Trimble, Marshall. *Arizona: A Panoramic History of a Frontier State*. New York: Doubleday & Co., 1977.

Utley, Robert M. *Lone Star Justice: The First Century of the Texas Rangers*. New York: Oxford University Press, 2002.

Walker, Margaret, ed. *Oldham County, 1881–1981*. Vega, TX: Oldham County Historical Commission, 1981.

Wallace, Ernest, with David M. Vigness, and George B. Ward, eds. *Documents of Texas History*. Austin, TX: State House Press, 1994.

Walter, John F. *Seventy-Seventh Illinois Infantry*. NP: Self published. 1997.

Watts, Peter. *A Dictionary of the Old West*. New York: Promontory Press, 1977.

Webb, Walter Prescott. *The Texas Rangers: A Century of Frontier Defense*. Austin: University of Texas Press, 1965.

———. *The Great Frontier*. Boston, MA: Houghton Mifflin, 1952.

———. *The Story of the Texas Rangers*. Austin: Boulder House Book from Encino Press, 1971.

Weedon, Pattie Lee Cross, ed. *Early Communities of Lake Brownwood: A History of the First Families Who Settled in the Northern Part of Brown County Between the Pecan Bayou and the Jim Ned Creek*. Brownwood, TX: Self published. Two editions. First no date. Second 1980.

Weiss, Jr., Harold J. *Yours to Command: The Life and Legend of Texas Ranger Captain Bill McDonald*. Denton: University of North Texas Press, 2009.

Wellman, Paul L. *The Trampling Herd: The Story of the Cattle Range in America*. Garden City, NY: Doubleday & Company, 1939.

Wharton, Clarence R. *History of Fort Bend County*. San Antonio, TX: Naylor Company, 1939.

White, James C. *The Promised Land: A History of Brown County, Texas*. Brownwood, TX: Brownwood Banner, 1941.

Wilkins, Frederick. *The Law Comes to Texas: The Texas Rangers, 1870–1901*. Austin, TX. State House Press, 1999.

Williams, J. W. *The Big Ranch Country*. Austin, TX: Nortex Press, 1971.

Wilson, R. Michael. *Great Train Robberies of the Old West*. Helena, MT: Twodot-Globe Pequot, 2007.

Woods, Lawrence M. *British Gentlemen in the Wild West: The Era of the Intensely English Cowboy*. New York: The Free Press, 1989.

Wooten, Dudley G., ed. *A Comprehensive History of Texas, 1685 to 1897*. Dallas, TX: William Scharff, 1898.

Yeldrman, Pauline. *The Jay Birds of Fort Bend County*. Waco, TX: Texian Press. 1979.

Periodicals:

Ainsworth, E. M. "Old Austin and Round Rock Road to Fort Concho." *Frontier Times*. July 1929.

Aten, Ira. "Fence Cutting Days in Texas." *Frontier Times*. July 1939.

———. (as told to Harold Preece) "I Fought These Masked Rustlers." *Real West*. May 1963.

———. "The Jaybird and Woodpecker War." *Frontier Times*. April 1939.
———. "The Jaybird and Woodpecker Feud." *Frontier Times*. June–July 1978.
  [reprint of above article]
———. "Early Day Prairie Fires in the Panhandle." *Frontier Times*. October 1939.
———. "Swimming Cattle Across the Canadian." *Frontier Times*. April 1941.
———."Crossing High Water in a Wagon." *Frontier Times*. May 1941.
———. "Six and One-Half Years in the Ranger Service." Four parts. *Frontier Times*.
  January–April. 1945.
Baker, John T. "Las Escarbadas." *Ranch Record*. Winter 2007.
Bedingfield, John (Dub). "The Spikes-Gholson Feud." *Real West*. December 1985.
Bell, Bob Boze. "I Should Have Killed Them All." *Cowboy Chronicle*. May 2008.
———. "Fifty Things You Don't Know About Wyatt Earp." *True West*. July 2003.
———. "When the Legend Becomes Fact." *True West*. May 2010.
Boardman, Mark. "Ira Aten Nails the McClellands." *True West*. July 2009.
Burton, Jeff. "A Great Man Hunt—Correspondence from W. B. S.: Some Scenes of
  Outlawry and Gunplay in Texas." *English-Westerners Brand Book*. 1975–76.
———. "The Most Surprised Man in Texas." *Frontier Times*. March 1973.
Cogswell, John. "Installation of Barb Wire in Texas." *Frontier Times*. July 1939.
Conn, Sam. "Hot on the Trail of 'Bill' Mitchell." *Bootheel Magazine*. Winter 2009.
Cordry, Dee. "The Incredible Story of Tom and Frank Smith." *Oklahombres: The Jour-
  nal of Lawman and Outlaw History of Oklahoma*. Winter 1997.
Croce, Antonio. "In the Line of Duty." *The Texas Gun Collector*. Fall 1996.
Cunningham, Eugene. "Frontier Justice: How Old-Time Rangers Solved a Baffling
  Murder Mystery." *Startling Detective Adventures*. September 1935.
Day, James M. "El Paso's Texas Rangers." *Password*. Winter 1979.
DeArment, Robert K. "The Protection Man." *Old West*. Spring 1991.
Dobie, J. Frank. "Fifty Years of Battling for Interests of Range Cattlemen. *The
  Cattleman*. March 1927.
Dodge, Matt. "Shootout in Standifer Thicket." *Oldtimers Old West*. December 1978.
Fox, Richard K., ed. "Tough Times in Texas." *The National Police Gazette*. February
  15, 1890.
Gard, Wayne. "The Fence-Cutters." *The Southwestern Historical Quarterly*. July 1947.
Hatley, Allen G. "Ira Aten, Last of the 'Old Texas Rangers'." *Western Outlaw-Law-
  man History Association Journal*. Winter 2005.
Havens, Paul. "The Saga of Captain John R. Hughes, Texas Ranger." *True Detective*.
  Four-part series. June–September 1940.
Hawkins, Rafe W. "Blood Bath in Texas." *Real West*. October 1957.
Hewitt, J. E. "The Battle of Mansfield, LA." *Confederate Veteran Magazine*. January
  1925–December 1925.
Holt, R. D. "Introduction of Barb Wire Into Texas and the Fence Cutting War." *West
  Texas Historical Association Yearbook*. June 1930.
Hunter, J. Marvin. "Morg Baugh of Brownwood." *Frontier Times*. September 1946.
———, ed. "The Famous Dick Duncan Murder Case." *Frontier Times*. February
  1939.
———, ed. "Captain Ira Aten's Unique Letter." *Frontier Times*. April 1942.
———, ed. "A Train Robbery Prevented." *Frontier Times*. May 1926.
———, ed. "Pioneered In California." *Frontier Times*. April 1939.

————, ed. "Dick Duncan's Doom." *Frontier Times*. March 1946.

————, ed. "Sheriff's Experience With Fence Cutters." *Frontier Times*. July 1930.

Jameson, W. C. "Incident at Pirate Island." *True West*. November 1988.

Jay, Roger. "The Peoria Bummer—Wyatt Earp's Lost Year." *Wild West*. August 2003.

Jobes, Harold D. "Fence Cutting and a Ranger Shoot-out at Green Lake." *Wild West History Association Journal*. October 2009.

Kelley, Dayton. "Ranger Hall of Fame." *FBI Law Enforcement Bulletin*. May 1976.

Lee, C. E. "The Fence-Cutters War In Texas." *Frontier Times*. July 1931.

Lindsey, Gary L. "Weather Watchers." *Roundup*. Spring 2006.

McCown, Dennis. "In Pursuit of the Lost Man." *National Association of Outlaw and Lawman History Quarterly*. July–December 2007.

Mays, George Carlton. "Wyatt Earp: Climax at the O. K. Corral." *Famous Lawmen of the Old West*. Fall 1965.

Mooar, J. Wright. "Frontier Experiences of J. Wright Mooar." *West Texas Historical Association Year Book*. 1928.

Moore, J. Ealy, "Early Work on the XIT Ranch." *Frontier Times*. November 1939.

Morando, B. "Ira Aten: Texas Ranger." *Famous Lawmen of the West*. Special Edition of *Real West*. Fall. 1965.

Nelson, Stan "American Double Action Pocket Revolvers, 1875–1900." *Minnesota Weapons Collectors Association News*. January 2009.

————. "Some Thoughts on Gun Leather." *Minnesota Weapons Collectors Association News*. January 2008.

————. "Fanning the Hammer." *Minnesota Weapons Collectors Association News*. March 2001.

Nordyke, Lewis. "The Ranch That Changed the West." *Readers Digest*. September 1945.

Owens, Ron. "Oklahoma's Uncommon Smiths." *Oklahoma State Trooper*. Winter 1997.

Parsons, Chuck. "The Jesse Evans Gang and the Death of Texas Ranger George R. Bingham." *Journal of Big Bend Studies 20*. 2008.

————. "An Incident in West Texas: The Jesse Evans Gang and the Death of Texas Ranger George R. Bingham." *Western Outlaw-Lawman History Association Journal*. Winter 2006.

Pfluger, Jim. "Wild Fire on the Plains." *Ranch Record*. Spring 2009.

————. "The Glittering Cloud: Rocky Mountain Locusts Invade the Great Plains." *Ranch Record*. Fall 2008.

Preece, Harold. "I Rode With the Texas Rangers: Hell on the Border." *Zane Grey's Western Magazine*. May 1953.

————."I Rode With the Texas Rangers: War on the Salt Grass." *Zane Grey's Western Magazine*. June 1953.

————. "I Rode With the Texas Rangers: Lawman Till I Die. *Zane Grey's Western Magazine*. August 1953.

T. V. Reeves [Mrs.]. "The Transformation of the XIT Ranch." *Frontier Times*. June 1927.

Schmid, Vernon, "Hides and Bones." *Roundup*. December 2006.

———— "Wire for the West." *Roundup*. February 2010.

Schreier, Philip. "Walker's Walkers: The Colt Walker Revolvers of Captain Samuel H. Walker, Texas Ranger." *Man at Arms*. No. 3. 1998.

Shannon, Ted. "Ira Aten and the Disappearing Killer." *The West*. February 1965.

Sherman, Jean Dale. "A Century With the Texas Rangers." *The Cattleman*. March 1937.

Spangberger, Phil. "Colt's Rivals." *True West*. June 2005.

Smith, Ralph. "The West Texas Bone Business." *West Texas Historical Association Yearbook*. 1979.

Stanley, Samuel. "The Fence-Cutters War." *Real West*. August 1985.

Stephens, Robert W. "A Ranger's Grave: The Murder of Jim King." *National Outlaw and Lawman History Association Quarterly*. October–December 2005.

Stewart, William. "Days of Free Range in Texas." *Frontier Times*. September 1947.

Stillwell, Hart. "Dinamite Aten and His Big Boom." *True Western Adventures*. October 1959.

Tanner, Karen Holliday and John D. Tanner, Jr. "Henry Hawkins and the Mesa Hawks Gang." *Wild West History Association Journal*. June 2010.

Traylor, Maude Wallis. "Two Famous Sons of a Famous Father." *Frontier Times*. November 1933.

Trussell, Eddie. "Fiddler on the Phone." *Frontier Times*. May 1974.

Turner, Thomas F. "Prairie Dog Lawyers." *Panhandle-Plains Historical Review* 2. 1929.

Weatherby, Chris. "From No Account to Plain Mean." *Old West*. Summer 1974.

Webb, Walter Prescott. "The Fence-Cutters." *True West*. May–June 1963.

Weddle, Robert S. "The Pegleg Stage Robberies." *Southwest Heritage*. March 1969.

Weiss, Jr., Harold J. "Organized Constabularies: The Texas Rangers and the Early State Police Movement in the American Southwest." *Journal of the West*. January 1995.

Whitehead, Ruth. "That Bloody Fence Cutting War." *The West*. December 1969.

Whittington, Mike. "Hughes and Aten Solve the Williamson Family Murders." *Texas Ranger Dispatch*. 2003.

Willcox, Seb S. "The Laredo City Election and Riot of 1886." *The Southwestern Historical Quarterly*. July 1941.

Yena, Donald M. "Texas Authority in Metal: Badges, History and Related Artifacts." *The Texas Gun Collector*. Spring 2003.

Young, Roy B. "Wyatt Earp, Outlaw of the Cherokee Nation." *Wild West History Association Journal*. June 2010.

Zeigler, Robert E. "The Cowboy Strike." *Ranch Record*. Winter 2007.

Zimmer, Stephen. "Vermejo Park: A History of a New Mexico Ranch." *Ranch Record*. Winter 2009.

Newspapers:

New York Times

Round Rock Leader

Daily Index Appeal

San Antonio Daily Express

Galveston Daily News

Imperial Valley Weekly Press

Dallas Daily Herald

Corpus Christi Caller

El Paso Times
Fort Worth Daily Gazette
St. Louis Globe-Democrat
Laredo Times
Kingfisher Free Press
Uvalde News
Austin Tribune
Austin Daily Statesman
Burnet Bulletin
San Antonio Daily Light
Houston Post
Clarendon News
Imperial Valley District News
The San Saba News

Liberty Hill Ledger
Fort Worth Star-Telegram
Arizona Miner
Eagle Pass Guide
Weimar Mercury
Granbury News
Weekly Amarillo News
El Centro Morning Post
San Mateo Times
El Paso Herald
New York Herald
Williamson County Sun
Imperial Valley Farmer

Index

A

B

D

E

Steiber, ------ 171
Stewart, Britt–170
Stewart, Frank–170
Stiles, S. E.–50
Street, James Alexander–308
Stroope, John L.–220
Stroope, Lizzie–220
Stuart, Dan–305, 306
Sutton County, Texas–47
Sweeten, John–170
Swisher County, Texas–264

T

Tannehill, Lyle–311
Taylor, Felix–64, 83
Terry, J. Kyle–194, 195,197, 212, 214, 223, 227
Terry, Will–220
Texas Rangers–evolution 26–28
Thatcher, Howard–264, 266, 267
Thomas, Appleton–102
Thompson, Johnny–86
Thornton, Bill–79
Thorpe, ----- (doctor)–99
Thruamn brothers–93
Tiernan, Patrick–224
Timmons, William–282, 283
Timon, Hugh–32
Tom Green County, Texas–91
Travis County, Texas–93–94. 102
Treadwell, Billy–119
Tucker, Campbell–183
Tucker, T. F.–261
Tumlinson, Joe–57, 66, 79
Turner, Bill–183
Turner, J. E.–240
Turner, Kenneth–244
Turner, Rosalla Ann–240

U

Underwood, Fred–86
Uvalde County, Texas–34, 39, 55, 68, 71, 90–91, 126, 182, 188

V

Van Ripper, William–156
Vandale, Earl–326
Vaughn, Edward Samuel–125
Vincent, C. F.–247
Votaw, William–60, 68, 81

W

Wade, William T. "Witt"–197, 198, 203, 210
Walter, John–54, 129
Warden, James–1
Ware, Bill–102
Ware, Richard Clayton–4
Ware, Robert W.–328
Wayne, John–322
Weakley, Joseph–110
Webb County, Texas–63, 77, 81, 85–86, 88, 90
Webb, Walter Prescott–322
Wells, George–94–95
West, C. S.–148
West, Duval–156
West, Hezekiah P. "Ki"–150, 163, *picture* 159
Weston, J. M.–200
Wharton County, Texas–194
Wheat, Ira L.–92, 170, 220, 222
White, ------286
White, Emmett–33, 249
White, Shad–179
Whitley, Cordelia–133, 134
Whitley, William Henry–132 -135, 137–141, 155, 156
Wilcox, A. M.–86
Wildrich, George–204
Williamson County, Texas–1, 6, 18, 19, 23, 25, 29, 44, 50, 92–100, 135,
    136, 137, 145, 147, 150, 192, 252, 253, 270, 318
Williamson, Benjamin–176, 178, 180
Williamson, Beulah–176
Williamson, Mrs. ------174, 176
Williamson, Robert M. "Three Legged Willie"–1
Wilmore, T. M.–91
Wilson, Adrian–92
Wilson, Green–250, 254